CLINTON IN HAITI

Clinton in Haiti: The 1994 U.S. Invasion of Haiti

Dr. Philippe R. Girard

palgrave
macmillan

CLINTON IN HAITI
© Dr. Philippe R. Girard, 2004.

First published in 2004 by
PALGRAVE MACMILLAN™
175 Fifth Avenue, New York, N.Y. 10010 and
Houndmills, Basingstoke, Hampshire, England RG21 6XS
Companies and representatives throughout the world.

PALGRAVE MACMILLAN is the global academic imprint of the Palgrave Macmillan division of St. Martin's Press, LLC and of Palgrave Macmillan Ltd. Macmillan® is a registered trademark in the United States, United Kingdom and other countries. Palgrave is a registered trademark in the European Union and other countries.

ISBN 1–4039–6716–4 (hc)

Library of Congress Cataloging-in-Publication Data

Girard, Philippe R.
    Clinton in Haiti : the 1994 U.S. invasion of Haiti / Philippe R. Girard.
        p. cm.
    Includes bibliographical references and index.
    ISBN 1–4039–6716–4 (hc)
        1. Haiti—History—American intervention, 1994–1995. 2. Clinton, Bill, 1946–
    3. United States—Foreign relations—1993–2001. 4. United States—Military policy. I. Title.

F1928.2.G57 2004
327.7307294'09'049—dc22   2004049760

A catalogue record for this book is available from the British Library.

Design by Newgen Imaging Systems (P) Ltd., Chennai, India.

First edition: December 2004

10 9 8 7 6 5 4 3 2 1

Printed in the United States of America.

Contents

Acknowledgments

I conducted most of the research for this book when studying at the Contemporary History Institute at Ohio University, whose facilities proved invaluable. Research for this book was funded in part by a Contemporary History Institute Fellowship, a John and Elizabeth Baker Peace Fellowship, and a John Houk Memorial Research Grant.

I would like to thank Dr. Michael Grow, Dr. Alonzo Hamby, Dr. Harold Molineu, and Dr. Chester Pach for their insightful comments during and after the completion of the manuscript. I also would like to express my gratitude to the various people interviewed for this book, who graciously spent much of their time answering my questions.

There is only one thing more pleasant than going on research trips to exotic islands: having a beloved Penelope to come back to. I was lucky enough to have not one, but three beautiful women waiting for me: my wife Preble and my daughters Cécile and Hélène.

List of Abbreviations and Foreign Terms

AFP	*Agence France-Presse*
ANDP	*Alliance Nationale pour la Démocratie et le Progrès*
AP	*Associated Press*
APEC	Asia Pacific Economic Cooperation
Attaché	paramilitary unit
Blan	white man, or foreigner (slightly derogatory)
BLTS	*Bureau de Lutte contre le Trafic de Stupéfiants*
CARICOM	CARIbbean COMmunity
CAS	Committee on Armed Services
CFA	House Committee on Foreign Affairs (until 1994)
CFR	Committee on Foreign Relations (U.S. Senate)
Chef seksyon, or chef de section	section chief (Haitian Army)
CIA	Central Intelligence Agency
CIR	House Committee on International Relations (after 1995)
CNVJ	*Commission Nationale de Vérité et de Justice* (National Truth and Justice Commission)
CNN	Cable News Network
Corvée	forced labor, during the first U.S. occupation of Haiti
CR	*Congressional Record*
DC	Washington (District of Columbia)
DEA	Drug Enforcement Agency
Dechoukaj	uprooting, or manhunt
FAdH	*Forces Armées d'Haïti* (Haitian Army)
FARA	Foreign Agents Registration Act, or archives of the Foreign Agents Registration Unit of the Department of Justice.
FBI	Federal Bureau of Investigation
FBIS	Federal Broadcast Information Service Daily Report
FNCD	*Front National pour le Changement et la Démocratie*

FOIA	Freedom of Information Act
FR	*Federal Register*
FRAPH	*Front Révolutionnaire pour l'Avancement et le Progrès Haïtiens*, then *Front Révolutionnaire Armé pour le Progrès d'Haïti* (paramilitary group)
GATT	General Agreement on Tariffs and Trade
Gendarme	rural policeman
GDP	Gross Domestic Product
GOH	Government of Haiti
HDI	Human Development Index
HIPC	Heavily Indebted Poor Countries
HNP	Haitian National Police (also PNH)
Houngan	Voodoo priest
HR	House of Representatives
IDB	Inter-American Development Bank
IMF	International Monetary Fund
INS	Immigration and Naturalization Service (now known as Bureau of Citizenship and Immigration Services)
IPSF	Interim Public Security Force
JCS	Joint Chiefs of Staff
JTF	Joint Task Force
Kombit	communal farming
Lafanmi Lavalas	Lavalas Family political party
Lafanmi selavi	family is life
Lavalas	flood
Loa	Voodoo spirit
Lumpen	underclass
Makout or Macoute	Duvalierist militia
Mambo	Voodoo priestess
Marassa	twin
Mission civilisatrice	duty to civilize
MICIVIH	Mission CIVIle en Haïti
MINUHA	*Mission des Nations Unies en Haïti* (also UNMIH)
MNF	Multinational Force
MREs	Meals Ready to Eat, or Morally Repugnant Elites
Mulâtre	person of mixed European and African descent (mulatto)
NAFTA	North American Free Trade Association
Neg	Nigger (no pejorative connotation in Creole)
NGO	Non Governmental Organization
NSA	National Security Adviser, or National Security Archives
NSC	National Security Council
NY	New York
NYT	*New York Times*

OAS	Organization of American States
OPIC	Overseas Private Investment Corporation
OPL	*Organisation Politique Lavalas, then Organisation du Peuple en Lutte*
PAP	Port-au-Prince
PBS	Public Broadcasting Service
PNH	*Police Nationale d'Haïti* (also HNP)
ROEs	Rules Of Engagement
ROTC	Reserve Officer Training Corps
RS	Registration Statement
SEAL (Navy)	SEa-Air-Land
Souket lawouze	collectors of the dew (low-level rural policemen)
SS	Supplemental Statement
SWHA	Subcommittee on Western Hemispheric Affairs
Tap-tap	small public bus
UNSC	United Nations Security Council
UNMIH	United Mission in Haiti (also MINUHA)
USACOM	United States Atlantic Command
USAID	United States Agency for International Development
USDOS Disp.	United States Department of States Dispatch
USGPO	United States Government Printing Office
USG	United States Government
USS	United States Senate
Telediol	rumor mill
Vévé	Voodoo sign
WP	*Washington Post*
WSJ	*Wall Street Journal*
Zenglendo	bandit

CHAPTER ONE

INTRODUCTION

A Late-Summer Night's Speech

Night had fallen on Washington, DC. The intense struggle for power that characterized the city abated as the day came to an end. Members of the political and economic elite—most of them Whites—had gone home, but the homeless—most of them Blacks, as was the vast majority of the city's population—were looking for a bench to spend the night on. This was no time to stay out. Criminality was rampant, guns abounded, and the pot-holed streets, broken meters, and dilapidated neighborhoods indicated that the city was broke and that municipal power had failed. Nevertheless, this was the capital of an intensely patriotic people with a proud military record, and, in the glimmering white presidential palace, not far from the monuments dedicated to the heroes of the war of independence, on 15 September 1994, the president prepared to inform his fellow citizens in a national television address that the country was about to go to war. As was his habit, William J. Clinton probably finished his speech at the last minute, changing sentences as he went through the text. As was their habit, operators of the teleprompter probably grumbled that they would never be ready, while political advisers wondered whether their boss would deliver a speech he had had no time to prepare.[1] As usual, the president was perfect. While grave and presidential, he managed to reach everyone's heart by appealing to the nation's idealistic instincts.

> My fellow Americans: Tonight I want to speak with you about why the United States is leading the international effort to restore democratic government to Haiti.
>
> [Dictator of Haiti Raoul] Cédras and his armed thugs have conducted a reign of terror—executing children, raping women, and killing priests. . . . Recent news reports have documented the slaying of Haitian orphans by the nation's deadly police thugs. . . . International observers uncovered a terrifying pattern of soldiers and policemen raping the wives and daughters of suspected political dissidents—young girls, 13 years old, 16 years old. People were slain and mutilated, with body parts left as warnings to terrify others. Children were forced to watch as their mothers' faces were slashed with machetes. . . . May God bless the people of the United States and the cause of freedom.[2]

The speech was the climax to three years of U.S. diplomatic efforts aimed at bringing back to power Jean-Bertrand Aristide, who had been elected president of

Haiti in 1990 and overthrown less than a year later in a military coup. As Clinton spoke, two aircraft carriers, the USS *America* and the USS *Eisenhower*, were on their way to Haiti. Accompanied by a flotilla of supporting vessels, they carried 100 helicopters that would ferry special operations forces and the 10th Mountain Division to their assigned targets.[3] A special force was ready to capture junta leader Raoul Cédras.[4] Soldiers were pre-positioned in "Gitmo," the U.S. base in Guantánamo, Cuba. At Pope Air Force Base near Fort Bragg, NC, thousands of paratroopers from the 82nd Airborne Division were finalizing preparations for the largest airborne attack since World War II. The American eagle was ready to strike its prey.

Night had also fallen on Port-au-Prince, Haiti. The intense struggle for power that characterized the city abated as the day came to an end. Members of the political and economic elite—many of them light-skinned *mulâtres* (mulattoes)—had gone home, but beggars—most of them Blacks, as was the vast majority of the city's population—were looking for a sidewalk to spend the night on. This was no time to stay out. Criminality was rampant, guns abounded, and the pot-holed streets, open sewers, and dilapidated neighborhoods indicated that the city was broke and that municipal power had failed. Nevertheless, this was the capital of an intensely patriotic people with a proud, if distant, military record, and, near the glimmering white presidential palace, not far from the monuments dedicated to the heroes of the war of independence, on 15 September 1994, Raoul Cédras, head of the military junta that ruled Haiti, was also preparing for war. As he watched Clinton's speech, Dan Rather of CBS *News* asked him if he was willing to step down. "Absolutely false. We're probably going to endure an invasion. We're going to defend ourselves until death."[5] The Haitian rooster was ready for the fight.

Haitians started bracing themselves for a U.S. invasion in late July 1994, when the United Nations Security Council authorized the United States to use all necessary means, including force, to overthrow the Cédras regime. In front of foreign journalists, army officers trained a supplemental militia in the use of World War I-vintage guns; some militiamen even had to train with wooden sticks. As there was always the possibility that an armed citizenry might turn against the ruling clique, militiamen had to give back their weapons after training, which made this fighting force effective from 7 a.m. to 3 p.m. only (the U.S. planned to attack at night, with real guns).[6] Enlisted personnel lacked modern weapons, training, and morale as well, but equally ill-equipped Haitian guerrillas, helped by tropical diseases and Voodoo powers, had defeated large French, English, and Spanish expeditionary forces during their war for independence.[7]

By 1994, the United States had found cures against most tropical diseases, but Voodoo remained an unknown force. The junta-nominated president, Emile Jonassaint, was a *houngan* (Voodoo priest) and threatened to unleash spells and HIV-infected syringes on unsuspecting GIs. Poison powders, powerful *loas* (spirits), and Ogou, the God of war, would do the rest. "We will fight and face the invader. Zombies in the first line and us behind them," announced Jonassaint, who also told intimates that Haiti was "the last remnant of the lost continent of Atlantis, and that the Whites want to invade to steal the magical philosopher's stone."[8] Others talked of "poison powders and plants that make skin peel off" and of an "army of 60,000 invisible zombies."[9] The confrontation stepped up on 8 September, when two *houngans* and four *mambos* (female priests) drew magical signs called *vévés* on the sidewalk near the U.S. Embassy.[10] The tactic seemed to pay off. In the eyes of many Haitians, a wave of natural calamities, including a Mississippi flood, hurricane Andrew, and a Los Angeles earthquake, were clear signs that the Gods were angry at America. When a Cessna 150 crashed two floors below Clinton's empty White House bedroom on 12 September, many Haitians surmised that Clinton was destined to share the sad fates of Woodrow Wilson, Warren Harding, and Herbert Hoover, who had overseen the first U.S. occupation of Haiti in 1915–1934.[11]

The face-off between the 82nd Airborne and an army of invisible zombies would have been an interesting match-up but, as it turned out, it never took place.

The Carter Mission

For all the war talk, many in the administration, including Clinton, had been agonizing over the invasion for months.[12] As late as 11 September, Secretary of State Warren Christopher was still offering the junta amnesty if they would agree to step down and leave Haiti.[13] With polls clearly showing that Americans were unwilling to die for Haiti, any way to minimize casualties, even at the cost of striking a deal with people Clinton had just described as murderers, rapists, and thugs, was welcome.

Clinton returned to diplomacy—one last time. Former President Jimmy Carter, who had been in contact with Haitian President Aristide since 1990 and with junta leader Cédras since the summer of 1994, urged Clinton repeatedly to give peace one last chance.[14] Swayed by Carter's argument that an invasion would result in many casualties on both sides, Clinton put together a team headed by Carter, former chairman of the Joint Chiefs of Staff Colin Powell, and Chairman of the Senate Armed Forces Committee Sam Nunn. Their mission was to go to Port-au-Prince, to meet Cédras, and to convince him to leave of his own accord. This was a risky proposition for Clinton. He bypassed the standard diplomatic hierarchy.[15] He would be criticized if he conceded anything to dictators. He could also come across as less experienced than Carter and Powell.[16] To prevent Carter from negotiating on his own, Clinton also sent Pentagon, White House, and State Department officials, including State Department special negotiator to Haiti Michael Kozak and National Security Council Director of Inter-American Affairs Larry Rossin, refused to grant any further concessions to the junta, and kept in constant contact with the Carter team.[17]

Carter, Nunn, and Powell left early on 17 September arriving in Port-au-Prince shortly after noon.[18] Each member of the team had his role to play in a bad cop/good cop scenario. Carter was the peacemaker, convinced that the dictators had been misunderstood and that they would leave if offered amnesty and self-respect—Carter even invited Cédras to speak to his Sunday school in Plains, GA. Nunn was there to prove that Congress and the American people stood behind their president. Powell, a veteran of Vietnam and the Gulf War, was a reminder that an invasion was imminent.[19] The three men faced a Haitian negotiating team led by Cédras himself.

Lt. Gen. Raoul Cédras' personality remains a mystery to this day. During the Duvalier dictatorships, which his father and brother served as top officials,

Cédras graduated from the Haitian Military Academy, instructed the elite Leopards unit, and trained—ironically enough—in the United States. He climbed the hierarchy quickly, reaching, at the age of 43, the rank of Lieutenant General, the highest in the Haitian Army.[20] Married, with three children, polite and likable, he helped ensure that the 1990 presidential elections unfolded peacefully. A close adviser described him as a stuttering, "very, very shy" man.[21] Yet, in September of 1991, Cédras became the leader of the military junta that overthrew Aristide, while claiming he had not planned the coup himself. Days after the coup in which soldiers gunned down dozens of Aristide supporters, he declared that there was no coup d'état, and that "I have never ordered the soldiers to shoot at the people and I never will."[22] He claimed he had no power but ruled the country for the next three years, while the regime committed human rights abuses that he said he did not condone. The Carter team did not know whether his stated refusal to compromise Haitian sovereignty was yet another lie, but they could assure him and his wife that they would live the country alive and rich.

Lt. Col. Philippe Biamby, the second most influential member of the junta and the Haitian Army's Chief of Staff, was unlikely to be swayed by monetary promises. Young, single, he lived between his mother's home and the army barracks. A few days shy of his forty-second birthday, he also was the son of a top Duvalierist official and a 1973 graduate of the Haitian Military Academy with training experience in the United States. Armed with a reputation for toughness (he allegedly shot himself in the stomach at age 11 to experience what it felt like), he was beloved by his men and feared by the population, often ordering the former to persecute the latter. After a failed coup attempt in 1989, he spent six months in a New York immigration jail, during which he nurtured a deep enmity for the United States. Like Cédras, he boasted that he would prefer to die than allow U.S. troops in Haiti. Unlike Cédras, he probably meant it.

Lt. Col. Michel-Joseph François, 37 in 1994, was the third, most secretive member of the triumvirate. Another son of a Duvalierist official, he graduated in 1981 from the Haitian Military Academy, where he studied under Cédras, then received training in Fort Benning, GA. and Lackland Air Force Base, Tex. His men crushed popular resistance during the 1991 coup. He denied being anything but a soldier, but he wore a police uniform, worked in the police headquarters, and supervised the repression in the capital (adding to the confusion, from its creation in 1916 until its dissolution in 1995, the Haitian armed forces served both as the country's army and as its main police force). He also enriched himself very quickly, presumably through the drug trade, which he also denied. Having announced that he was willing to leave before Carter even got to Haiti, he was unlikely to derail the negotiations, which he boycotted.

The first meeting between the U.S. envoys and the Haiti's military rulers took place in the army headquarters. Hanging prominently on the walls were pictures of six U.S. officers from the 1915–1934 U.S. occupation of Haiti ("we never forget our history," Cédras told Powell[23]). A loaded M-16 leaned against the wall. Cédras refused to surrender. After a meeting with Haitian parliamentarians and a dinner with prominent business leaders, another round of negotiations ended inconclusively at 2 a.m.

At the suggestion of former prime minister Marc Bazin, the U.S. team met Cédras and his influential wife Yannick at their home early on Sunday morning; Carter publicly praised her for helping convince her husband to step down. She "was impressive, powerful, and forceful," Carter said. "And attractive. She was slim and very attractive."[24] After meeting with President Jonassaint, an 81-year-old former jurist, Voodoo priest, and parliamentarian, talks resumed inside military headquarters. The team was supposed to leave by noon, lest they get caught in the fighting, and Carter begged Clinton for more time. The invasion remained set for midnight, twelve hours away.

Minutes ticked by. In the White House Oval Office, Clinton was on the phone monitoring the talks while working on the *New York Times'* crosswords (doing several things at once was his normal mode of operation). National Security Adviser Anthony Lake and U.S. Special Envoy to Haiti William Gray III were so nervous they broke a tooth and a crown, respectively.[25] In Port-au-Prince, negotiators kept an eye on CNN, including a "drop-dead blonde" at a fashion show that particularly drew the attention of Carter and his aides.[26] When the first planes took off from Pope Air Force Base in North Carolina at 6:47 p.m., Clinton begged Carter—unsuccessfully—to leave Haiti within the next half-hour.[27] Powell decided it was time for the "bad cop" to enter the scene.

> I leaned across the table. 'Let me make sure you understand what you're facing,' I said. I began ticking off my fingers: two aircraft carriers, two and a half infantry divisions, twenty thousand troops, helicopter gunships, tanks, artillery. I kept it up, watching the Haitians' spirits sink under the weight of the power I was describing.[28]

National Security Council (NSC) staff members were keeping contact with Washington in a nearby office that usually belonged to a mysterious Canadian adviser to Cédras, Lynn Garrison. Frustrated not to be a part of the negotiations, Garrison tried to listen through the door, then remembered that there was a small balcony overlooking his office. He climbed there and eavesdropped as messages poured in from Washington. One of them in particular drew his attention: the 82nd Airborne had taken off from Pope Air Force Base. Garrison told Biamby, who burst into the negotiating room declaring that negotiations were off and that it was time to fight—Powell recalls being impressed by Haiti's intelligence capabilities.[29]

Cédras drew different conclusions. Realizing that Powell's threat was real, he negotiated the last outstanding points and took the team back to the presidential palace. President Jonassaint signed the agreement so that Cédras would not be on the record as the man who invited the Americans in. The Carter–Jonassaint agreement, signed by an American president no longer in office and a Haitian president the United States did not officially recognize, offered political amnesty in exchange for a promise that President Aristide would be allowed to return to Haiti on 15 October. Remarkably adept at negotiating with a weak hand, Cédras also managed to obtain before his departure a month later, U.S. payments and services worth $1 million.[30] Considering that he was an outgunned, ousted dictator hated by many of his own people, Cédras' ability to wrest concessions from his American opponent must rank as one of the greatest diplomatic feats of all times, putting him on a par with

Ti-Malice, the popular trickster of Haitian folklore who always outsmarts the ponderous Uncle Bouki.

By the time the accords were signed, planes loaded with U.S. paratroopers were already in the air on their way to Haiti; others were about to leave Guantánamo. Morale was high, war paint was on, and the soldiers looked forward to seeing combat in a Caribbean island. Suddenly, the order came to turn around; the operation was off. After getting confirmation, the planes turned around and flew home. The military *coitus interruptus* left the men incredulous and angry. They would not get the coveted gold star proving they had dropped in a combat zone.[31]

Under the accords, the invasion still took place, albeit in a permissive environment. On September 19, three thousand troops landed in Port-au-Prince, preparing the ground for a 22,000-troop occupation army. Sgt. Damon Arnett barely had time to step out of his helicopter before he was interviewed live on CNN. "Emotions were running high," he said. "Going over the shoreline, we didn't see much but a city that we're unfamiliar with. Then, when we landed over here, I saw a bunch of press, which was good. I assumed, if the press was here, then the enemy probably wasn't."[32] Arnett's assumption was correct. Because of the last-minute cancellation, the first few days, however hectic and disorganized, saw no U.S. casualties. One question remained, however: why had Clinton decided to invade Haiti in the first place?

Looking for Motives

During his first two years in office Clinton had focused on the economic home front. Clinton, a member of the Vietnam generation, withdrew from Somalia and refused to intervene in Bosnia and Rwanda. Presidential Decision Directive 25, signed a few months before the Haiti invasion, set a series of stringent requirements before U.S. troops could be engaged in peacekeeping operations and asked for a reduction of U.S. contributions to the United Nations. The document called for greater Department of Defense involvement in preparing peacekeeping operations, which, knowing the military's aversion to peacekeeping, was likely to severely limit U.S. interventionism.[33] Three years later, PDD 56 outlined a complex process of interagency planning before any intervention could be undertaken, and concluded that "given the [presumably low] level of U.S. interests at stake in most of these situations," there was no reason to maintain troops in the field for a lengthy amount of time.[34]

Everything militated against an intervention in Haiti itself. The U.S. crusading impulse had suffered a heavy blow less than a year before when 18 Rangers were ambushed and killed in Mogadishu. Haiti's sad history and the failure of a previous U.S. occupation (1915–1934) did not bode well for the invasion's success. Most congressmen were opposed to an intervention in Haiti, as were most leading newspapers and Americans. Latin Americans complained of a resurgent U.S. imperialism in the region. Haiti was the poorest nation in the Western Hemisphere, and U.S. economic interests in the island were extremely limited. There was no powerful European enemy seeking to gain a foothold in the island. The Cédras regime was too busy harassing its own people to pose a threat to anyone else. After decades of deforestation and land erosion, Haiti had become the poor, barren, overpopulated western third of a northern Caribbean island, well on its way to becoming a desert, yet without the oil. Why would an already embattled President risk his political career and U.S. lives to bring an anti-American president back to an island many Americans would not even be able to locate on a map? So unclear were the motives of Operation Uphold Democracy that witty soldiers, recycling a joke dating back to Operation Just Cause in Panama five years earlier, nicknamed it Operation Just Because.

On the other hand, the Haitian situation had proved a constant sore for the Clinton administration. After he was ousted by Cédras in September 1991, Aristide moved to Washington, D.C., where, with the help of liberals sympathetic to his cause, he maintained pressure on the U.S. government. Having called for the restoration of democracy in Haiti during his 1992 campaign, Clinton hardened the economic embargo former President George H.W. Bush had imposed after the coup and urged the military junta to accept a negotiated solution. In July 1993, his administration seemingly scored a major foreign policy victory when Cédras signed the Governors' Island accords, in which the Haitian general promised to let Aristide return to Haiti as president on 30 October. Yet, two weeks before the transition was to take place, Cédras' henchmen refused to let U.S. and Canadian peacekeepers aboard the USS *Harlan County* dock in Port-au-Prince, thereby preventing Aristide's return and humiliating the Clinton administration in full view of television crews. By the time Clinton announced to the American people on 15 September 1994, that a military intervention in Haiti was necessary, Aristide had been living in exile for almost three years, and the Clinton administration had been trying, unsuccessfully, to facilitate his return for over 18 months.

In the absence of declassified documents, one must approach the question of U.S. motives with caution, avoiding the Charybdis of official justifications and the Scylla of improvable conspiracy theories. The following chapters examine six possible reasons why the United States invaded Haiti. One hypothesis is that the Clinton administration may have tried to derive economic benefits from an occupation. Second, Clinton may have responded to idealistic aspirations, namely, the restoration of democracy and the end of human rights abuses. Third, Clinton may have decided to restore his country's credibility, battered by a series of foreign-policy failures and Clinton's incapacity to impose his will on a small island located in the U.S. sphere of influence. Fourth, he may have wanted to stem the flow of drugs and refugees coming from Haiti. Fifth, he may have hoped that looking strong abroad would help him on the domestic political front. Sixth, he may have been swayed by a lobbying campaign orchestrated by Haitian president-in-exile Jean-Bertrand Aristide.

Once the issue of causation—Clinton's policy motives—has been clarified, the analytical scope of this study turns to the issue of consequences: what did the occupation force achieve in Haiti, and what impact did it have on that country? The initial task U.S. soldiers faced was how to handle the first, uneasy weeks of the invasion, when they ruled the island jointly with the Haitian Army they were initially supposed to eradicate. The second objective, starting with Aristide's return on 15 October 1994, was peacekeeping. U.S. troops had to put an end to the Haitian armed forces' oppression of the Haitian people, to prevent Haitians from seeking revenge against their former oppressors, and to create an independent police force capable of taking over these tasks when U.S. troops departed. The last, longer-term mission, which started when the United Nations took over on 31 March 1995, was nation-building. Haiti's economy and political system had to be rebuilt, virtually from scratch, in order to create the prosperous, peaceful, law-abiding democracy Clinton had called on his fellow citizens to install in his 15 September speech. This ambitious undertaking, if successful, would have marked a new beginning in Haiti's 500 year history.

Chapter Two

Haiti Before the U.S. Intervention

For all its corrupt cruelty, the military junta that ruled Haiti from 1991 to 1994 was merely the latest in a long list of despotic regimes. After Haiti earned its independence in a glorious, if particularly bloody, war, it went from being the richest to the poorest country in the Western Hemisphere, while its ruling elite produced a long dynasty of dictators, each of them seemingly trying to outdo his predecessors' greed and cynicism. With only brief respites of hope, Haiti's tragic history, described in works with titles such as *Written in Blood* and *Best Nightmare on Earth*, is the story of a downward spiral from hell to worse, from harsh colonial rule to further violence, poverty, and tyranny.[1]

Violence

Christopher Columbus encountered Haiti, which he named Hispaniola, during his first voyage in 1492.[2] With the timber salvaged from the wreck of one of his ships, 40 seamen built Fort *Navidad*, Spain's first colony in the New World, on Haiti's northern coast. When Columbus returned, a year later, the fort was in ruins and the Spaniards nowhere to be found. The local natives, Tainos, had slain and probably eaten them. Violence, then and later, was to become central to Haiti's history. Within 40 years, the number of Indians on the island had dropped from an estimated population of half a million to a mere 600 survivors. So severe was the toll taken by smallpox and hard labor that within 10 years the Spaniards were importing African slaves to make up for a dwindling supply of indigenous labor.

In 1625, Frenchmen settled in La Tortue (Tortuga), a small island north of Hispaniola, which quickly became a legendary sanctuary for the pirates of the Caribbean. From there, they attacked convoys of Spanish galleons loaded with the wealth of the New World. In the treaty of Ryswick (1697), Spain rid itself of the burden altogether and ceded the western part of Hispaniola, by then a backwater area of the Spanish Empire, to the French. They renamed it St. Domingue.

Gold was sparse, but St. Domingue's climate, land, and African labor made it the richest colony in the Caribbean, with highly profitable plantations that flourished in one of the New World's most brutal slave systems. African life was so cheap that keeping the slaves alive was not a pressing requirement. In four to seven years, they produced enough to pay for the initial investment. The planters fed them poorly, often requiring that they produce their own food after work. Cruel treatments were the norm. Slaves were burned in boiling cane, branded, buried alive, burnt at the stake, smeared with molasses so that ants could eat them, mutilated, and raped. Violence had by then engulfed the island entirely.

Amazingly, this era marked the apex of Haiti's economic development. Covered with sugarcane, coffee trees, mango trees, banana trees, bougainvillea, indigo, and cotton, the "Pearl of the Antilles," as France's golden goose was known in the eighteenth century, produced half of Europe's consumption of tropical produce and two-thirds of France's overseas trade. It is difficult today to imagine what St. Domingue must have been like. The island's luxuriant forests, the planters' elaborate lifestyle, and the wealth they commanded have long since disappeared. Because of land erosion, Haiti's rich soil is now gone with the rain, and the country must import sugar.

After the Jamaican-born slave and Voodoo priest Dutty Boukman launched Haiti's war for independence in 1791, violence intensified. Rebel slaves impaled white babies on pikes, raped and cut to pieces their mothers, and literally sawed their fathers in two after having tied them between planks. The planters responded in kind, killing every runaway slave they captured, and breaking their leaders' limbs on the wheel. Under the leadership of Boukman, Toussaint L'Ouverture, and Jean-Jacques Dessalines, Haiti's revolutionaries successfully beat back invasions by France, England, and Spain, the three most powerful imperial powers of the time. Even Napoléon's best troops melted away, defeated by guerrilla warfare, forbidding terrain, malaria, and yellow fever. When Haiti finally proclaimed its independence on 1 January 1804, the country was in ruins. The first census, taken 20 years later, estimated the population at 350,000, half of what it had been before the war started. St. Domingue changed its name once more, to Haiti—"mountainous island," in the Tainos' native language. In 1825, France recognized the independence of its former colony in exchange for a 150 million francs indemnity, 60 million of which Haiti never paid.

Reverse Development

Freed from its colonial shackles, Haiti could have developed tremendously. It did not. Agricultural wealth, the island's most important asset, declined to the extent that, two centuries later, the country that once was a major exporter of foodstuffs must rely on international charity to feed its population. So low have expectations fallen that in 1991, when Jean-Bertrand Aristide first became president, he defined his goal as being able to give each Haitian a mere one meal per day.[3]

How could Haiti have sunk so low? Scholars inside and outside of Haiti have been quick to blame the impact of colonial rule.[4] The cost of the war for independence, compounded by the payments to France, bankrupted the young state, as did the money spent on costly fortifications to prevent a possible European invasion. Haiti was cut off from its natural markets, most notably the United States, where southern slaveholders regarded any contact with the rebellious island as subversive (the United States finally recognized Haiti in 1862). Yet, the United States, which gained its independence barely 21 years before Haiti did, also had to face the legacy of colonialism and slavery, as well as a war against its former mother country in 1812. Once destitute compared with Haiti, the United States now has a per capita income 100 times higher than its southern neighbor's, proving that two centuries of independence are enough to erase the colonial legacy. Haiti, the Western Hemisphere's second oldest independent country, is also the hemisphere's poorest, as well as, when it could still afford it, one of its most noted imperialists. L'Ouverture invaded its Dominican neighbor in 1801, Dessalines in 1805, Faustin Soulouque in 1849 (twice) and 1855; Haiti also occupied the Dominican Republic from 1829 to 1844.

During the debate over the exact phrasing of Haiti's declaration of independence, Louis Boisrond-Tonnerre famously argued, "we should have the skin of a *blan* [white man] for parchment, his skull for inkwell, his blood for ink and a bayonet for pen!"[5] This quip was more than mere poetic license. Four months later, in April 1804, black revolutionary leader Dessalines ordered that all Whites in the country be put to death. Only a few non-Frenchmen, doctors, and priests were spared. The massacre destroyed all of Haiti's skilled class, forced the country into decades of international isolation, and ruined its economic prospects. Thereafter, Haiti's mulatto elite often monopolized power, but its education and wealth were used mostly for political plots and conspicuous consumption, while occasional black dictators proved equally inept and corrupt. In a controversial work, a former employee of the U.S. Agency for International Development (USAID) went so far as to say, "there is something going on in the minds of the Haitians that impedes progress and facilitates the perpetuation of a stagnant, exploitative, repressive system."[6]

Disagreement over the economic organization of the new state increased its political and geographical fragmentation. In the northern regions, Henry Christophe forced former slaves to remain on plantations under a refurbished feudal system called *fermage*, while, in the south, Alexandre Pétion and Jean-Pierre Boyer distributed small plots to independent farmers. Since Haiti's wealth stemmed mostly from export crops produced in large plantations, the north grew richer while the south decayed, but the political appeal of yeomanry was too great. After Christophe's death in 1820, Boyer reunited the island under his rule. Viscerally opposed to plantation work, the majority of former slaves became small independent farmers, each of them cultivating a tiny plot of land that was further divided between the farmer's heirs after his death. Small, low-productivity subsistence farming on submarginal plots has remained the dominant form of agriculture down to the present day. Indeed, farming, which for lack of capital is now heavily reliant on human labor and the hoe, is less advanced technically than it was in colonial days, when oxen and irrigation were the rule.

Poverty became self-perpetuating. Producing at a subsistence level, Haitians could not accumulate the capital that would have allowed them to enlarge their holdings, to invest in more efficient farming techniques, and to provide their offspring with a decent education. In desperate need of any source of income and energy, Haitians turned to cutting their island's magnificent forests, made charcoal, and sold it as cooking fuel. Deforestation, in a country characterized by steep terrain and violent rainstorms, meant rapid soil erosion, further diminishing the supply of arable land for farming. Deprived of valuable topsoil, farmers further resorted to woodcutting.

Today, forest cover has dwindled to less than 3.9 percent of Haiti's territory.[7] Attempts at reforestation have failed.

A highly competitive political environment also meant that only the most ruthless leaders reached national office. Once in power, enriching oneself quickly became the main goal, as no assurance could be made that the incumbent's presidency would not be violently cut short. Corruption and instability turned away any potential investor.

The Land of the Unfree

The war for independence was much more complex than a simple struggle between white planters and black slaves. Englishmen and Spaniards fought both Whites and Blacks, while the French were divided between revolutionary abolitionists and planters hoping to reestablish the old regime. Some Blacks fought for foreign allies, or for the new French Republic, or for the extermination of the white race, or against rival Blacks. The *mulâtres* (mulattos) supported, and betrayed, both sides. Fading St. Domingue was a political mess, and nascent Haiti retained the pattern. In the 72 years from 1843 to 1915, Haiti experienced 102 revolts, civil wars, and revolutions. Only 5 of Haiti's 34 founding fathers who signed the 1804 declaration of independence died of natural causes.[8] More often than not, Haiti's rulers were creatively cruel, colorfully corrupt, and met an untimely end when they did not manage to go into exile fast enough. From Henri Christophe, who killed himself (allegedly with a silver bullet) in 1820, to Jean-Baptiste Riché (overdose of aphrodisiacs, 1847), Sylvain Saenave (executed, 1869), Cincinnatus Leconte (blown up, 1912) and Tancrede Auguste (poisoned, 1913), Haiti's political history rivaled the most imaginative novels. From 1867 to 1915, no fewer then 15 presidents ruled the island, including 6 in 1911–1915 alone. In 1915, when a crowd literally dismembered the last of those Haitians call the "*présidents éphémères*" (ephemeral presidents), J. Vibrun Guillaume Sam, U.S. President Woodrow Wilson decided that it was time to bring stability to Haiti. The U.S. occupation lasted from 1915 to 1934.[9]

Stability would prevent foreign powers, particularly Germany, from taking a foothold in the Caribbean, and it benefited U.S. companies greatly, but a humanitarian impulse was also at play as the U.S. occupation force built hospitals, roads, and barracks, and reorganized the country's finances, while Haiti paid back its external debt. This desire to do good was fueled by a sense of superiority that bordered on outright racism. Secretary of State William J. Bryan always found Haitians amusing ("Dear me, think of it! Niggers speaking French!" he told *Banque d'Haïti's* John Allen in 1912), while a U.S. official confided to Franklin D. Roosevelt that, while eating with the Haitian minister of agriculture in 1917, he "couldn't help saying to [him]self that that man would have brought $1,500 at auction in New Orleans in 1860 for stud purposes."[10] For Haitians, the occupation was the humiliating proof that their country had failed. *Noirisme*, a political current emphasizing nationalism and racial pride, appeared. Revolts multiplied, most famously under the leadership of Charlemagne Peralte (executed by U.S. forces in 1919), and Americans put them down mercilessly before leaving in 1934. The usual period of instability followed, culminating in five separate governments in 1956–1957 alone.

In 1957, black country doctor François Duvalier won the national elections and became Haiti's newest dictator.[11] "Elected" president-for-life in 1964, Papa Doc Duvalier governed the country until his death in 1971, when his son Jean-Claude or Bébé Doc took over. The United States, hovering between anti-Communism and human rights concerns, generally supported the regime. Duvalier gathered much popular support for his *noiriste* agenda, but his rule also marked a peak in political terror and the utter ruin of a nation already in shambles. Though a doctor himself, Duvalier enjoyed watching prisoners being tortured through a hole pierced in a wall of his apartments. Madame Max, the vicious leader of the *Tonton Macoutes* (Duvalier's private police), designed inventive sexual tortures for Fort Dimanche prisoners.

Economic incompetence was Baby Doc's area of expertise. With little taste or training for his position, he tried to overcome his educational shortcomings by studying hard—falling asleep, or so he said, every night with his books (taking naps during classes was indeed a central element of his learning style). Along with motor-cycles, Haitian women were Baby Doc's passion, and one of them, Michèle Bennett, whom he married in 1982, accelerated his eventual downfall. Her appetite for money dwarfed the petty embezzlement schemes that had characterized the regime up to that point. Paid $100,000 a month in a country in which the average peasant rarely earned more than $200 a year, Michèle still felt the need for extra kickbacks to finance her million-dollar shopping sprees to New York, Miami, and Paris. This display of indecent wealth, in the midst of a country mired in misery, undermined Baby Doc's popularity.

Meanwhile, the country's economy spiraled downward. Starting in May 1982, all of Haiti's pigs were slaughtered to prevent an epidemic of African swine fever from spreading to the U.S. mainland (to this day, Haitians point to this episode as a proof of a giant U.S. conspiracy to destroy Haiti). AIDS scared away potential tourists. Foreign aid, representing 70 percent of the state's budget, diminished because of corruption and human rights abuses. During a March 1983 state visit, Pope John Paul II declared in a famous speech, "things have got to change here."[12] Strikes multi-plied, as did plots. U.S. Secretary of State George Shultz delivered the final blow when he announced on 3 February 1986 that the Reagan administration would like to see a democratic government in Haiti.[13] On 7 February after allegedly cursing the presidential bed with the blood of two unbaptized male babies sacrificed for the occasion, the Duvaliers and their suite fled on an American C-141 to Guantánamo Bay, then to the French Riviera. As space on the plane was limited, the Duvaliers abandoned part of their entourage, including Michèle's grandparents, to make some room for the jewels, furs, and artwork they were bringing along with them.

In March 1987, a new constitution (Haiti's twenty-fourth) was ratified by popular referendum, creating a semi-presidential system similar to that of France, but the 1986–1990 period was a period of Duvalierism without Duvalier rather than of true democracy.[14] The November 1987 general elections, cancelled after election-day violence sanctioned by the army killed 22 voters, were followed by a period of renewed political instability. Of the six governments in power from 1988 to 1991—Conseil National de Gouvernement (7 February 1986–7 February 1988), Leslie Manigat (7 February 1988–20 June 1988), Henry Namphy

(21 June 1988–17 September 1988), Prosper Avril (17 September 1988–10 March 1990), Hérard Abraham (10–13 March 1990), and Ertha Pascal Trouillot (13 March 1990–7 February 1991)—only Manigat was elected, this in an overtly rigged election. Under pressure from the international community, relatively honest presidential elections were finally held on 16 December 1990. They saw the victory of a young renegade priest named Jean-Bertrand Aristide.

Jean-Bertrand Aristide

Aristide was born on 15 July 1953 to a family of peasants of moderate means outside Port-Salut, in southwestern Haiti.[15] After his father died when Aristide was three months old, Aristide's mother took him and his elder sister to Port-au-Prince. According to Aristide, the Salesian priests who educated him "considered [him] to be a brilliant student."[16] Shortly after he was ordained a priest on 3 July 1982, he was sent to study in Israel, Greece, and Canada, where he picked up five foreign languages, a Master's degree in psychology, and a Ph.D. in theology.

But politics, not theology, proved to be Aristide's calling. He came back in 1985 as priest of the St. Jean Bosco parish in a slum area of the capital and made a name for himself by preaching against Duvalier and his henchmen, the *Tonton Macoutes*. Bright, well educated, courageous, a master of Creole, the French-African dialect used by most poor Haitians, sharing the poverty of his compatriots, fighting the church and army many Haitians feared, still outside the corrupting rink of power, Aristide combined the features of a Haitian intellectual with those of a populist leader. His physical frailty increased his appeal. President Sténio Vincent (known as "Papa Vincent") and François Duvalier ("Papa Doc") had been fatherly figures. Aristide ("Titid"), like Jean-Claude Duvalier ("Bébé Doc"), was a child to be nurtured, loved, and protected. Aristide's political success lay more in articulating his message in words his fellow Haitians could relate to than in his ability to create a brand new ideology. Anti-Americanism, an insistence on the socialist aspects of the gospels, and a criticism of the country's elite were fairly typical of the theology of liberation that Aristide supported.[17]

Aristide's rise to fame also took place as his country's economic fortunes reached a low ebb. With a per capita GDP of $375 in 1990, Haitians had a life expectancy at birth of 53 years. Twenty-eight percent of children under the age of five were malnourished. The illiteracy rate reached 60 percent. Forty-six percent of Haitians had access to clean water.[18] Haiti was the poorest country in the Western Hemisphere, on a par with sub-Saharan Africa.

Aristide's sermons earned him the hatred of the conservative leadership of the Haitian church, most notably the Papal nuncio, Paolo Romero. The Salesians expelled Aristide from the order on 18 December 1988 (Aristide renounced priest-hood in October 1994). He also became the target of several assassination attempts (the number—up to seven—and exact circumstances vary according to witnesses). The most famous attempt occurred on 11 September 1988, when *Macoutes* attacked his church while he was preaching mass. Armed with machetes and guns, they killed 13 parishioners before setting the church on fire. Seventy-seven were wounded as well, including a pregnant woman (in later days, *Macoutes* invaded the general hospital to finish her off, but doctors hid her). Aristide miraculously escaped. To this day, his most dedicated enemies claim he engineered the attack to draw criticisms on Duvalierists, and that he had some flesh from the victims mixed with the wax of candles for special ceremonies.[19]

Aristide's ability to escape all these assassination attempts must have made Haitians think that, like the great Voodoo chiefs of Haiti's past, such as Henri Christophe and François Duvalier, normal bullets bounced off his chest harmlessly, and that he could disappear at will. The power of secret numbers was on his side. The Duvaliers relied on the magical power of 22, the day on which Papa Doc was elected (22 September 1957) and inaugurated (22 October 1957), and his son took over the country (22 April 1971) and married his wife (22 April 1980).[20] Aristide trusted the power of 7, the day on which Duvalier left Haiti (7 February 1986), a coup against Aristide failed (7 January 1991), and he was twice inaugurated (7 February 1991, 7 February 2001). He was overthrown seven months into his first presidency, only to come back after 1,111 days in exile, another ominous number. Many, including Aristide himself, saw him as an envoy from God. Explaining his decision to preach despite threats made against him, he later wrote: "So I said: I will come to the place called Calvary. If this was to be my last day, as it seemed, then I would carry my cross."[21] When he was suspended from the Salesian order in 1988, he reassured his supporters by reminding them that Jesus had no established church of his own. Two years later, he presented his presidential bid as "a fight between God and the Devil."[22] "The Devil" was also the nickname of one of Aristide's main political opponents, Emmanuel Constant.

The 1990 Presidential Campaign and its Aftermath

Popular interest in the December 1990 presidential elections was originally low, reflecting the bad taste the 1987 elections had left in the mouths of frightened voters.[23] Any hope that the election would proceed peacefully diminished when Roger Lafontant, Duvalier's former Interior Minister, returned from the Dominican Republic in July 1990 to run for president. Aristide, who had long dismissed the electoral process as meaningless, declared his candidacy at the last minute. His official goal was to "stop the *Macoutes*," but one may surmise that political ambition also played a role.[24] Aristide admits enjoying being a leader as a child and maneuvering not to be sent to rural parishes when he was a priest.[25] The electoral commission rejected Lafontant and two other former Duvalierists' candidacies on technical grounds, but Aristide stayed in the race.

The U.S. Embassy favored Marc Bazin, a pro-American official from the International Monetary Fund (IMF) representing the centrist *Alliance Nationale pour la Démocratie et le Progrès* (ANDP), but to anyone else it was clear that the momentum of the election had changed with the arrival of the popular priest. Voter registration alone doubled in the days following his candidacy. The political coalition *Front National pour le Changement et la Démocratie* (FNCD) quickly elbowed aside Victor Benoît, the winner of an internal primary, and chose Aristide as its candidate. Aside from its anti-*Macoutes* message, Aristide's platform was thin. The first part of his program, *La chance qui passe* ("today is the day"), was only published days before the election, while the second part, *La chance à prendre* ("seize it"), appeared after the election. Both, written in French, were inaccessible to the illiterate, Creole-speaking majority of the voters. The symbols of Aristide's campaign, *lavalas* (the river of mud that follows violent storms, cleaning everything in its path) and *ko kalité* (the beloved Haitian rooster, used in cockfights and Voodoo ceremonies), had much more evocative power among the masses.

Aside from a 5 December grenade attack on Panaméricaine Street, there were no major disruptions of the election until the balloting itself. On 16 December 1990, millions of voters went to the polls under the supervision of a legion of international observers that included Jimmy Carter. Many polling places did not open until noon. Bulletins were not always there, voting booths nonexistent, the ballot boxes made of cardboard. When darkness interrupted counting, many election officials took the ballot boxes home with them. Within 24 hours, the electoral commission announced that Aristide had won 70 percent of the vote, despite the fact that only 1 percent of the ballots had been counted by then. The official results, published on 23 December, gave Aristide 67.48 percent of the vote. Forty percent of the ballots had been counted. Everyone agreed that Aristide had been the popular choice, but the vote was no cleaner than the 1957 election that brought Duvalier to power.

Before Aristide could be sworn in, however, on the night of Sunday, 6 January 1991, Roger Lafontant announced on TV that he had taken over the presidential palace and was henceforth Haiti's newest president. Hérard Abraham, commander in chief of the army, refused to support the coup and forced Lafontant to surrender. Lynch mobs followed along with three days of *dechoukaj* ("uprooting") during which they beat the Papal Nuncio, sacked Lafontant's party's headquarters, and killed 125 people suspected of being former *Macoutes*. Some of the victims were eviscerated, others emasculated or dismembered. A few instances of cannibalism were also reported.[26] So profound was the hatred for the old order that *Le Nouvelliste* (Haiti's *New York Times*) lavished praise on the mob's use of *Père Lebrun*, or "necklacing," a torture imported from South Africa consisting in attaching a tire filled with gasoline around someone's neck before setting it on fire.[27]

> Made-to-order tires [to burn opponents to death] were distributed to some people suspected of being closely or remotely connected to Lafontant. Machetes red with the blood of men were floating in the air like flags. . . . The night of January 7 was blessed with promises, one could already see the new dawn, gardens against hunger, hospitals for health, schools for children, songs for hope.[28]

The First Aristide Presidency (7 February to 30 September 1991)

Even though few foreign heads of state attended the inauguration, many Haitians hoped for a new dawn when Aristide and his prime minister, close friend René Préval, were inaugurated on 7 February 1991. Alas, the new president accumulated political *faux-pas*. In his inaugural speech, he announced that all but one of the army's senior officers were fired (the one survivor, Hérard Abraham, was sacked in July). The Catholic Church, already an enemy of liberation theology, was furious over the January attack against the papal nuncio. Aristide's reliance on the urban and rural poor, which rich Haitians refer to pejoratively as "*le lumpen*," made him few friends among the elite, as did his decision to fire many public servants to replace them with his supporters. The United States, while supportive of the democratic transition, was cautious, and the Dominican Republic, which expelled 25,000 Haitian cane cutters in July-August 1991, was openly hostile.[29] Aristide's electoral coalition swept the Parliament, but it was a political conglomerate with little ideological unity, already jockeying for the spoils of power, and he had no organized party of his own. A direct appeal to the people was his only weapon, and its frequent use led to troubling incidents.

On 4 April 1991, former president Ertha Pascal-Trouillot was sent to the national penitentiary, then put under house arrest under accusations of graft and complicity in the 6 January coup (she was finally released after intense international pressure).[30] On 29 July, the trial against Lafontant and 21 other coup plotters began in Port-au-Prince. It ended the following day, after a 24-hour nonstop session. The pre-trial inquiry had lasted a mere 15 days. Five legal interns were provided to the accused on the day of the trial, as all professional lawyers had declined the case for fear of being killed. Little formal defense was necessary anyway, as the president of the tribunal had announced before the trial even began that "the accused will be found guilty."[31] The accused were indeed found guilty and received sentences ranging from 10 years to forced labor for life, despite a Haitian law specifying that the maximum sentence for such a crime was only 15 years.[32] Most disquieting was the 3 August speech in which Aristide congratulated the tire-wielding crowd that had threatened the jury. "If the demonstrators grouped in front of the tribunal of Port-au-Prince on July 29 had not brandished the threat of *Père Lebrun* [burning someone to death], Roger Lafontant and his accomplices would not have been sentenced to life in prison."[33]

Aristide also lost his support in the parliament. He refused to accept any member of the FNCD, the electoral coalition that had supported his presidential campaign, in his government, even though this party now controlled both chambers. When the parliament discussed a vote of no-confidence against Prime Minister René Préval on 13 August, a pro-Aristide crowd coalesced around the building, holding tires. At least one deputy was molested and the session was suspended (many deputies were afraid to come back, and the Parliament did not meet the following day for lack of a quorum). Préval refused to even appear in the chamber.

A famous 27 September 1991 speech, in which Aristide made a thinly veiled apology for burning *Macoutes*, increased tensions.[34] Two days later, when Sylvio Claude, an opponent of Aristide, delivered a speech criticizing the president, several hundred Aristide supporters, including Aristide deputy Jean-Claude Jean-Baptiste, forced him to drink gasoline, necklaced him with tires, and burnt him.[35]

The army, still reeling from Aristide's firing of all its senior officers, found other reasons to hate Aristide. He created a special security force, raising the specter of a new *Macoute* army similar to the one that had marginalized the Haitian Army under Duvalier. He promoted junior officers loyal to him. He refused to make permanent Raoul Cédras' 2 August appointment as interim commander in chief. As former oppressors of the people, Haitian soldiers complained of being prime targets for necklacers.[36] If we are to believe Cédras, Aristide had "warned me [Cédras] that the crowds could do to me what they had done to others."[37]

What exactly happened on 27 to 29 September 1991 remains controversial. According to Cédras, the army rank-and-file was increasingly concerned about Aristide's speeches and the necklacing incidents. Cédras begged Aristide on the phone to ask the mobs to stop their grisly actions, "but he said no, that the people in the streets knew what they had to do."[38] Cédras later explained, "Aristide poured fear onto the scales, one grain at a time until even the dogs stayed off our streets at night. . . . People were being necklaced for any real or imagined fault. Finally, the last grain of sand overbalanced the scales and Aristide was on his way to Venezuela."[39] When the Frère barracks revolted under the leadership of police chief Michel Francois, Cédras agreed to head a grassroots revolt that he claimed he had done all he could to avoid. In his 1 October speech to the nation, he claimed the army coup had just averted a new Duvalier-style dictatorship.[40]

Aristide's version emphasized the deviousness of the man he had chosen as commander in chief, saying that on 28 and 29 September Cédras assured him on the phone that the rumors of a coup were unfounded. When his house was encircled by shooting soldiers, Aristide used French Ambassador Jean-Raphaël Dufour's armored car to reach the presidential palace on the morning of the thirtieth. Immediately arrested, Aristide was taken to the army headquarters on the other side of the street. "Cédras was there, in a happy mood, calm and smiling, and announced that from now on he was the president. He looked very proud of himself."[41] One of Aristide's supporters was shot, eight others beaten before his eyes, and the soldiers started debating whether or not to kill him (according to Cédras' adviser, Aristide lost his nerve, cried, vomited, and defecated).[42] After the intervention of the U.S., French, and Venezuelan ambassadors, Cédras, probably fearing an international backlash, allowed Aristide to leave for Venezuela.

The exact role played by the United States is even more controversial. That the U.S. Embassy was aware of coup rumors seems probable. As early as 23 September, U.S. Ambassador Alvin Adams warned Préval that the army was unhappy.[43] That Ambassador Adams engineered the coup is considered a fact in Haiti, but there is no evidence to confirm this belief.[44] One person who cannot be blamed for the coup was Lafontant, who was murdered in his cell on 29 September. Theories to explain his death range from a last-minute Aristide cleanup to a French secret service operation.[45]

The Cédras Junta

During the days immediately following the coup, soldiers and *attachés* (paramilitary units) roamed the slum areas deemed favorable to Aristide, reportedly killing one hundred civilians.[46] Blanket repression continued in weeks to come, then focused on enemies of the regime. As under Aristide and Duvalier, the regime claimed that the human rights abuses were committed by vigilantes it did not control. In an effort to show that civilians, not the army, were in charge, Joseph Nérette became president, followed by Emile Jonassaint, while Jean-Jacques Honorat assumed the prime ministership, followed by René Théodore, Marc Bazin, and Robert Malval. But it was clear that the three *hommes forts* in Haiti were Commander in Chief Raoul Cédras, who justified the coup in a televised speech, Port-au-Prince Police Chief Michel François, who masterminded the coup and the ensuing repression, and Army Chief of Staff Philippe Biamby.[47]

On 3 October, in response to the coup, the Organization of American States (OAS) suspended economic relations with Haiti. The following day, President Bush froze Haiti's accounts in the United States (executive order 12775), then imposed a trade embargo on 28 October (executive order 12779). The junta nevertheless refused to abandon power, and the Bush administration limited itself to ineffectual protests.[48]

With Clinton's inauguration in January 1993, the balance tilted in Aristide's favor. In February 1993, the United Nations sent a force of human rights observers to Haiti (MICIVIH, after its French acronym) to help the OAS observers already present. The United Nations Security Council then adopted Resolution 841 on 16 June to impose a worldwide oil and arms embargo and to freeze Haitian leaders' assets. Forced to negotiate, Cédras and Aristide signed on 3 July 1993 an agreement in Governors Island (NY), under which the junta, in exchange for an amnesty, promised to let Aristide return on October 30 as President.[49] The United Nations lifted sanctions on 27 August. Then, on 23 September, it created a police and construction force of 1,267 to deploy to Haiti in October (UNSC Resolution 867). Aristide also chose a new prime minister, mulatto businessman Robert Malval, who left for Haiti and put together an interim government.

The UN resolution, which expressed concern "about the escalation of politically motivated violence in Haiti," also showed the limitations of the Governors' Island accords.[50] Both sides had negotiated under pressure, rather than because of a genuine commitment to a peaceful solution. Aristide and Cédras even refused to meet face to face, and U.S. and UN–OAS special envoys Lawrence Pezzullo and Dante Caputo had to shuttle back and forth between delegations. During the summer, electricity to the U.S. Embassy in Port-au-Prince was cut off, while ever more numerous corpses were dumped at dawn in front of UN observers' hotels. On 11 September 1993, armed men took Aristide's friend Antoine Izméry out of the Church of the Sacré Coeur where he was attending mass and shot him pointblank in front of three UN observers and a journalist.[51]

One month later, on 11 October 1993, members of the FRAPH, a political and paramilitary organization close to the regime, prevented U.S. and Canadian servicemen aboard the USS *Harlan County* from landing in Port-au-Prince, where they were set to facilitate Aristide's scheduled return. The ship turned tail. Guy Malary, minister of justice under Aristide, died on the fourteenth when assassins linked to the army sprayed his car with bullets. The Security Council resumed sanctions and evacuated remaining members of the MICIVIH (a few dozen UN and OAS observers came back in January and May 1994 before being expelled on 18 July 1994). October 30, the date set for Aristide's return under the Governors' Island accords, came and went. Aristide rejected one last February 1994 attempt at a negotiated resolution. With the failure of negotiations, and as the embargo showed no sign of weakening the junta's resolve, the crisis could very well have died down inconclusively. A widely quoted study showed that the number of children dying in Haiti had jumped from 3,000 to 4,000 children a month because of the embargo.[52]

In late March 1994, Clinton initiated a month-long review of his Haitian policy that concluded that a tougher stance was necessary. William Gray III replaced Lawrence Pezzullo, accused of being too mild, as U.S. special envoy to Haiti. On 2 May, Clinton refused for the first time to rule out the use of U.S. force. The Security Council banned all nonscheduled flights and denied visas to all members of the junta and their families. Any nonhumanitarian trade with Haiti was forbidden. A ban on all U.S. commercial flights and fund transfers to Haiti of more than $50 a month per family took effect a month later. UNSC Resolution 940 (31 July) authorized "member states to form a multinational force under unified command and control and, in this framework, to use all necessary means to facilitate the departure from Haiti of the military leadership."[53]

The U.S. military machine had been fine-tuning contingency plans since the *Harlan County* incident in October 1993. In May 1994, it practiced the invasion of a Caribbean island during maneuvers codenamed *Agile Provider*, then started amassing troops in Cuba, North Carolina, and aboard a flotilla of vessels off the coast of Haiti. Despite its reluctance to fight on Aristide's behalf, the U.S. Army was now ready to respond to the president's call to arms. After hesitating for the better part of the year, Clinton finally made up his mind "in late August or the first days of September."[54] Detailed plans for an invasion appeared in the press. The days of indecision ended on 15 September, when Clinton announced on national television that "Cédras and his armed thugs" had to go.[55] Diplomacy had come to an end.

One question still remained unclear, however: how had the Clinton administration's support for Aristide become a determination to bring him back to power by any means necessary?

CHAPTER THREE
ECONOMIC INTERESTS

Americans, many of whom migrated to the United States to better their economic future, are often accused of being materialists for whom the accumulation of wealth is the most important aspect of daily life. It does not take a giant leap of faith to conclude that the U.S. government is as concerned with financial gain as its citizens are. Time and again, scholars, particularly in Latin America, have described American presidents as obedient tools of powerful multinationals, ready to send in the Marines whenever courageous nationalist leaders threaten corporate profits. U.S. policy in Latin America, according to that view, is simple: it is green, rectangular, and comes in $1, 5, 10, 20, 50, and 100 denominations. Protecting the financial well being of one's constituents' is arguably a laudable objective, but the pursuit of economic goals is usually denounced as a manifestation of imperialism. Are America's tremendous economic success and Latin America's underdevelopment not sufficient proof that Uncle Sam has sucked away the wealth of his hapless neighbors? In the Haitian case, assembly factories working for U.S. contractors would be the most likely economic culprits, which would make the 1994 intervention the first Wal Mart War.[1]

Economic imperialism may be a theoretically attractive explanation for U.S. policy in Latin America, but, as facts go, it simply does not work in the Haitian case. To be sure, the murderous, embargo-ridden military junta ruling Haiti contradicted the Clinton administration's vision of the world as a small, happy village united by a common passion for entrepreneurship, free trade, and high-speed internet access, but economic considerations did not drive the administration's Haitian policy. Aristide was an unlikely candidate for economic exploitation, Haiti's economic value was negligible, and there is no evidence that U.S. companies lobbied for intervention.

The Clinton Administration Promoted Free Trade and Capitalism Worldwide

Rabid anti-Communists might have been reluctant to see a former antiwar protester who had visited the Soviet Union in 1970 occupy the White House, but they did not need to be afraid: Clinton was a New Democrat, that is, an old-style, conservative one. Spreading free market democracy was one of the few constant elements in Clinton's foreign policy. NAFTA, the December 1994 Summit of the Americas (advocating a hemispheric free trade zone by 2005), the November 1995 APEC meeting (advocating a similar goal for the Pacific rim), the GATT Uruguay Round (signed on April 1994), permanent normal trade relations with China, the Mexican and Asian financial crises, and trade disputes with Japan, Europe, and China dominated his presidency. "It's the economy, stupid" got Clinton elected, and sustained national prosperity allowed him to remain popular in the face of personal scandals.

The end of the Cold War left capitalism as the only available economic model and turned international battlegrounds to the economic arena. The United States, slowly recovering from a recession, was shocked to realize that former defeated countries prospered, or, to use Paul Tsongas' 1992 sound bite, that "the Cold War was over, Japan won." Clinton's 1992 campaign pamphlet aimed at *Putting People First* and accordingly relegated foreign policy to small print, but the would-be president found the issue of free and fair trade central enough to feature it prominently in his introductory chapter on strategies for change, the only foreign policy issue to receive such treatment. The chapter on national security similarly opened with two sections on economic renewal, concluding that "economic strength is a central element of our national security policy."[2] In February 1993, 30 years after John F. Kennedy's celebrated address, Clinton delivered a speech at American University in Washington, DC. Clinton's main message was economic: to preserve its power, the United States had to strengthen its economy, and to do so it needed to trade.[3]

Two weeks later, U.S. trade representative Mickey Kantor emphasized the same point in testimony before the Senate Finance Committee. "Past administrations have often neglected U.S. economic and trading interests because of foreign policy and defense concerns. The days when we could afford to do so are long past. In the post–Cold War world, our national security depends on our economic strength. . . . When all is said and done, opening foreign markets is our main objective."[4] With similar bluntness, Secretary of State Warren Christopher announced at his nomination hearing, "we will not be bashful about linking our high diplomatic goals with our economic goals."[5]

Other administration nominees were equally unlikely to advocate a dictatorship of the proletariat. Secretary of the Treasury Lloyd Bentsen was a 71-year-old Senator from Texas. His deputy, Robert C. Altman, was a New York investment banker. Director of the Office of Management and Budget Leon E. Panetta, a former member of House Budget Committee, advocated fiscal responsibility and chose Alice Rivlin, a deficit hawk from the congressional Budget Office, as his deputy. Cochairman of Goldman Sachs Robert E. Rubin and Laura d'Andrea Tyson headed the National Economic Council, a Clintonian creation. Commerce Secretary Ronald H. Brown, before dying in a 1996 plane crash, actively promoted U.S.-made goods.

It can be difficult to separate economics and idealism, for the two have been traditional U.S. foreign policy goals since nineteenth-century struggles for the rights of neutrals to trade and Woodrow Wilson's 1917 Fourteen Points in which he mixed open markets and worldwide democracy in the same ideological pudding. For many American presidents, freedom ought to rule everywhere, in the political sphere *and* the economic arena. The confusion between the two was most obvious in National Security Adviser Anthony Lake's September 1994 *New York Times* op-ed piece on behalf of the intervention. Democratic idealism, he argued, "serves our interests.

Democracies create free markets that offer economic opportunity, and they make for reliable trading partners."[6]

Nevertheless, however frequently economic interests were invoked in other areas, they rarely made their way into the Haiti debate itself. Deputy Secretary of State Strobe Talbott's February 1995 comment "our intervention in Haiti made sense for reasons of American self-interest. That includes our economic self-interest" was highly unusual.[7] Aristide and Haiti's dubious ability to increase U.S. companies' earnings could explain this lack of enthusiasm.

Aristide's Leftist, Anti-American Views

Cédras was typical of corrupt Latin American strongmen with whom U.S. business-men have found it easy to do business. Aristide was the archetypical nationalistic, anti-American, left-leaning leader whom U.S. businessmen have regarded as anath-ema. Dumping the former for the latter did not make much business sense. An advo-cate of the theology of liberation preached by Father Gustavo Gutierrez, Aristide opposed capitalism and the country that exemplified it. He considered Argentine revolutionary Ernesto "Che" Guevara a model and hoped that one day the poor would "knock the table of privilege over and take what rightfully belongs to them."[8] During his first presidency, Aristide launched verbal attacks against the *Front des Malfaiteurs Hypocrites* (front of hypocritical racketeers, a pun on the Créole acronym for IMF) and asked Parliament to raise the minimum wage from $3 to 4.80 a day, against the wishes of the USAID. During his exile in Caracas, Aristide listed his enemies as "the four As:" *argent* (money), the army, ecclesiastical authorities, and America.[9] He described the Vatican and the United States' opposition to his ideas as "the alliance of the two imperialisms: political and religious."[10] He then blamed foreign powers for Haiti's economic woes.

> Europe owes us a debt. In fewer than fifteen years, Spain extracted fifteen thousand tons of gold here, after having exterminated the Indians. As for France, we would never finish if we tried to recite all that it took from us. . . . The colonial powers, including the United States, must make amends for the wrong inflicted on the colony or protec-torate in those days. The debt experts, when they speak of our liabilities, need to add up the second column of their own accountability.[11]

The money necessary to fund his social programs could only come from local bourgeois and international lenders, so Aristide found himself obliged to tone down his rhetoric in an effort to secure funding. His 1991 Labor Day speech, avoiding the stridency of its Soviet-era counterparts, had "some sweet talk for the bourgeois. . . . We must reach a policy of alliance. Alliance between the bourgeois capital and the revolutionary capital of the popular flood." Aristide further distin-guished between patriotic bourgeois willing to reinvest their wealth locally and the *patripoches* (traitors).[12] He slashed public spending (including his salary) and fired 8,000 public employees. These neoliberal measures helped him to obtain increased international funding for his projects, from $200 million (1990–1991) to $380 million (1991–1992), but this sudden conversion to the virtues of interna-tional capitalism was recent and probably superficial.[13] Haiti's economic destitution further diminished Aristide's attractiveness.

Haiti's Poverty

On 31 December 1987, the barge *Khian Sea*, filled with 15,000 tons of Pennsylvania and New Jersey waste that it had unsuccessfully tried to get rid of during the previous 18 months, docked in Gonaïves, Haiti. It asked for permission to unload the ship's contents, paid for it, received it, and had enough time to dump 4,000 tons of its toxic load directly onto the beach before local public outcry and an international campaign led by Greenpeace forced the barge to leave.[14] Young prostitutes marketing their innocence to 1970s sex tourists; Duvalier literally selling cane cutters to his Dominican neighbor; a country so destitute its very environment and inhabitants are up for sale at a steep discount: this is the human reality hiding behind the dry statistical evidence of Haiti's misery. By the time the United States intervened, in 1994, Haiti's per capita GDP reached $260, 30 percent below its level prior to the 1991 coup.[15]

In this context, Haiti had little to no economic value for the United States. During the ten years preceding the invasion, U.S. exports to Haiti averaged three to five hundred million dollars a year, then dropped to 205 million dollars in 1994 because of the embargo, then rose to $500 to 600 million a year after 1994, barely $200 million more than before the coup. By comparison, exports to Jamaica topped a billion dollars; those to the Dominican Republic totaled $2.8 billion; exports to Mexico reached almost $51 billion. All these exports were a drop in the sea of total U.S. exports for that year ($633 billion), themselves a fraction of the U.S. gross domestic product ($7,054 billion). The entire GDP of Haiti, slightly above $2 billion, amounted roughly to that of an American town of 70,000 people. Hard-boiled U.S. officials conspiring with multinationals to overthrow Cédras would probably have spent some time looking at their own statistics, and these would have convinced them that Haiti was not worth invading (appendix). Direct U.S. investments in Haiti totaled a mere $29 million in 1992, most of it in light manufacturing.[16]

Haiti's destitution kept labor costs low, which, along with its proximity to the U.S. mainland, could have targeted the island as a potential host for assembly factories and the apparel industry. But the aftermath of the invasion, which was anything but an economic windfall for the factory-assembly sector, proved otherwise. In 1996, the U.S. exported $76 million of various manufactured articles to Haiti and imported $114 million worth of similar goods (appendix I). Even if one assumes that all this trade concerned the assembly sector, and that the difference in value represented the U.S. profit, the 1996 benefit of the U.S. invasion came to a grand total of $38 million, not enough to pay for three of the $13 million Blackhawk helicopters used in the invasion. After the invasion, the United States pledged $696 million in foreign aid to Haiti and the international community offered over $3.4 billion for 1994–1997, amounts that dwarfed any profit foreign companies could have derived from an invasion.[17] Technically speaking, as an exporter of agricultural products and an importer of manufactured products, the United States was in a dependency relationship with Haiti. Judging by the ballooning trade with China and Mexico during the 1990s, U.S. companies considered these two countries to be more attractive sources of cheap labor.

As a humanitarian gesture, U.S. food exports to Haiti continued unabated despite the embargo, so there was little pressure from this sector to intervene militarily.

Manufactured articles, representing 80 percent of Haitian exports to the United States, were initially excluded from the embargo as well.[18] But even when the Clinton administration included them in the embargo,[19] and when Haitian assembly factories began to close down, the clothing industry remained apathetic.

The Clothing Industry Lobby did not Support U.S. Policy in Haiti

An analysis of campaign contributions to presidential and congressional candidates during the 1990s shows that the clothing industry gave less money during the two years that preceded the 1994 intervention than during any campaign cycle save 1989–1990. Bill Clinton and other Democratic presidential candidates received less money than their Republican adversaries. Rep. Robert Torricelli (D-NJ) aside, congressional leaders who opposed the intervention often received more money than its supporters did. Aristide-basher Sen. Jesse Helms (R-NC) jumped from thirty-eight to fifth most important Senate recipient between 1992 and 1996 (appendix II)

Because it was often Haitian-owned and -operated, it was difficult for the assembly sector to engineer sympathy for its plight in Washington. Typically, in Haiti as in other countries, U.S. retailers relied on local factories that hired a few hundred employees, oversaw production, and shipped the finished product. These small companies, which suffered most from the continuing embargo, had little political clout in Washington, DC; names like Allied Assemblers, Charles Handal and Co., Coles Manufacturing, Fresam Manufacturing, Monel Industries, and Quality Garments never made the Fortune 500 list. Their U.S. clients, including household names such as K-Mart, Wal Mart, and the Walt Disney Co., could easily import their products from elsewhere.

When they did testify in Congress, lobbyists from the clothing industry made public their concern that the Clinton administration was *not* following the policy they advocated. As political instability took a toll on their ability to operate their business, they recommended that it be minimized. Recognizing the *de facto* regime would thus have been their first choice. Restoring Aristide to power was the next best thing, but only as long as it could be done quickly and painlessly. On the other hand, a policy of diplomatic isolation and gradually increasing economic sanctions, followed, after years of uncertainty, by an invasion, was the worst possible alternative. Slow-paced, painful, and indecisive, it would most likely ruin the country and its business class. This is what Andrew Postal, the president of Judy Bond, Inc., a corporation that manufactured women's blouses in Haiti, and chairman of the Haiti task force for Caribbean-Latin American Action (C-LAA), a nonprofit organization designed to promote the private sector in the Western Hemisphere, explained to the House Subcommittee on Western Hemisphere Affairs in July 1993. This "slow half-baked embargo. . . . was terribly poor public policy. . . . We met with the State Department at the time of its inception. We told them it was going to fail."[20] During a July 1992 visit to Haiti, a C-LAA delegation similarly explained that businessmen wanted "a favorable climate to be reestablished," no matter under which government.[21] Had they been in charge of U.S. policy in Haiti, invading immediately, or, better yet, putting an end to economic sanctions, would have been their policy of choice.

Despite the Clinton administration's general comments on the need to pursue both economic and foreign policy goals, the link between these two objectives appeared tenuous in the Haitian case. From a business perspective, there was no logical rationale justifying maintaining an embargo for years and then sending a large, costly invading party to place a left-wing populist in the presidential palace of a nation mired in misery. The Clinton administration would most likely not have disputed this conclusion. In its public rhetoric, it depicted the 1994 invasion of Haiti as, first and foremost, a disinterested, idealistic crusade on behalf of democracy.

CHAPTER FOUR
RESTORING DEMOCRACY

Unlike many older states, the United States has always been a Republic—its very Declaration of Independence doubled as a statement of democratic faith. Its inhabitants, many of whom left their motherland to seek greater economic, religious, and political freedom in the United States, celebrated their adopted nation as a city upon a hill, a new Jerusalem, and, as the Statue of Liberty allegorizes, a beacon of freedom. So dominant is the republican–democratic ideal that the two current main parties were named after it, while alternative forms of government, such as monarchy, fascism, and communism, were dismissed as anti-American.

Heading a nation with deep democratic roots, most U.S. political leaders have advocated a foreign policy characterized by its messianic activism on behalf of freedom and democracy. Presidents urged their fellow Americans to "make the world safe for democracy" (Woodrow Wilson), to defend the "Four Freedoms" (Franklin D. Roosevelt), to defeat the "Evil Empire" (Ronald Reagan), and, after the end of the Cold War, to create a "New World Order" inspired by the global victory of democracy (George H. W. Bush).[1]

This idealistic, pro-democratic stance also marked U.S. foreign policy in Latin America. The Monroe Doctrine (1823) warned European autocracies not to expand their colonial empires in Latin America, which James Monroe earmarked as a safe haven for democracy. The need to preserve the Western Hemisphere against Nazism and Communism similarly led U.S. presidents to present their Latin American policy during the Roosevelt presidency and during the Cold War as a crusade to defend democracy. Because many nominally democratic governments targeted individual opponents for repression, the goal became, during James E. Carter's presidency, to promote human rights. After democratic regimes took over in most of Latin America during the 1980s, the OAS' Santiago declaration (June 1991) expressed the organization's commitment to preserving democracy in the Americas.

U.S. foreign policymakers' constant rhetorical celebration of democracy has left scholars divided. Some, taking official statements at face value, have concluded that there has been a genuine U.S. desire to see democracy flourish in Latin America.[2] Others have agreed that ideological morality shaped American perceptions of the United States' worldwide role, but that its emphasis on the superiority of the U.S. model of liberal democracy frequently had chauvinistic and racist overtones.[3] Others have simply dismissed the self-proclaimed U.S. duty to promote democracy in the

Western Hemisphere, expressed in such declarations as the Monroe Doctrine, as a convenient pretext to extend U.S. political and economic hegemony over Latin America.[4]

It is difficult to gauge the influence of the United States' democratizing impulse on the 1994 U.S. intervention in Haiti. The Clinton administration repeatedly made clear its attachment to the democratic ideal, both worldwide and in Haiti proper, where human rights violations were numerous enough to prompt serious concerns.[5] And yet, the administration's avoidance of democratic procedures when they proved impractical, as well as Aristide's less-than-perfect record as Haiti's first "democratic" president, suggest that democracy was, at best, one factor among others, and, at worst, a mere rhetorical device used to "sell" the invasion to domestic and international audiences.

The Clinton Administration's Rhetorical Commitment to Democracy

Clinton's personal background may explain his idealism and his commitment to democracy. As a young man, he played the role of the peacemaker between his mother Virginia and his alcoholic stepfather Roger Clinton Sr. (the effort proved successful: after divorcing, the two married again). He showed his compassionate side when he helped the Red Cross bring food supplies to black neighborhoods plagued by riots in the wake of Martin Luther King, Jr.'s assassination.[6] Portraying himself as a common American from Hope, Arkansas, he claimed to feel everyone's pain. Town-hall meetings, which were Clinton's favorite medium during his first year in office, sent a clear message: he took his cues directly from the people. Citizens could e-mail questions to their president@Whitehouse.gov.

Many cabinet members, including National Secretary Adviser Anthony Lake, his deputy (and future NSA) Sandy Berger, Secretary of State Warren Christopher, and Ambassador to the United Nations (and future secretary of state) Madeleine Albright, were holdovers from the Carter administration, during which the promotion of democracy and human rights had been heralded as cornerstones of U.S. foreign policy. Lake had criticized America's abandonment of its ideals in Vietnam, while Albright, a native of Czechoslovakia, was unlikely to advocate a Munich-style surrender to dictatorships (she coined the expression "assertive multilateralism").

Clinton made clear his personal bias in favor of democratic activism in official statements. On inauguration day, 1993, William Jefferson Clinton left Monticello for Washington, following the road Thomas Jefferson, a fellow southerner, Democrat, namesake, and president, followed in 1801.[7] In his inaugural address, Clinton announced that "today, a generation raised in the shadows of the Cold War assumes new responsibilities in a world warmed by the sunshine of freedom. . . . Our hopes, our hearts and our hands are with those on every continent who are building democracy and freedom. Their cause is America's cause."[8] "To support the global march toward democracy," Clinton announced on June 4, is "one of the cornerstones of our foreign policy."[9] In September 1993, in response to criticisms that the Clinton administration had no clear foreign policy vision, Christopher, Lake, Albright, and Clinton delivered four well-publicized speeches in favor of what Lake called "pragmatic idealism." The United States, they said, had a vested interest in seeing democracy triumph. Democracies, in Clinton's own words, "rarely wage war on one another. They make more reliable partners in trade, in diplomacy, and in the stewardship of our global environment."[10]

Undersecretary of State for Political Affairs Peter Tarnoff was the only top official uncomfortable with an activist idealism. Talking off the record to journalists in May 1993, he confided that the United States had neither the will nor the means to intervene everywhere on behalf of democracy. In its effort to limit the political impact of the comments, the State Department privately chastised Tarnoff, emphatically denied that his views were representative of official U.S. foreign policy, and even refused to reveal his name, referring to Tarnoff by the alias "Brand X."[11]

Official U.S. commitment to Haitian democracy was equally strong. As early as 1986, the Reagan administration had hoped "to set Haiti on a path towards true democracy" in the wake of Duvalier's departure, while a year later the French, U.S., and Canadian Ambassadors to Haiti reaffirmed their support for democracy in a joint meeting.[12] The Bush administration, even though it refused to intervene militarily, unequivocally stated that the 1991 coup was unacceptable.[13] Allusions to democracy also strewed OAS official and private comments on Haiti.[14]

In his September 1994 address to the nation, four days prior to the intervention, Clinton explained to the American people that the need to restore democracy was the single most important explanation for his decision to invade Haiti. First, Clinton asserted, this was a clear-cut case in which a democratically elected leader had been overthrown in a military coup. Second, oppressive rule in Haiti encouraged Haitians to flee to the United States. Third, democracy's progress over the previous decade had left Haiti as one of only two dictatorships in the Western Hemisphere (the other was Cuba). Fourth, democratic governments were more reliable economic and political partners.

> Just four years ago, the Haitian people held the first free and fair elections since their independence. . . . But eight months later, Haitian dreams of democracy became a nightmare of bloodshed. . . . No American should be surprised that the recent tide of migrants seeking refuge on our shores comes from Haiti and Cuba. After all, they are the only nations left in the Western Hemisphere where democratic government is denied; the only countries where dictators have managed to hold back the wave of democracy that has swept our entire region, and that our government has so actively promoted and supported for years. . . . History has taught us that preserving democracy in our own hemisphere strengthens America's security and prosperity. . . . May God bless the people of the United States and the cause of freedom.[15]

Before and after the intervention, Clinton and other administration officials repeated in similar fashion that their attachment to democracy required that Aristide be restored to power.[16] To further clarify the military intervention's primary goal, the Clinton administration named it "Operation Restore Democracy" and heralded Aristide's physical return to Haiti as the litmus test of the operation's success. In light of the political situation prevailing in Haiti, which Clinton described in graphic detail during his 15 September 1994 speech, the administration's rhetoric seemed amply justified.

Haiti's Appalling Human Rights Situation

By overthrowing Aristide, the junta rejected the Haitian people's democratic will expressed during the December 1990 elections that brought Aristide to power. It spent the following three years persecuting political opponents, thus proving that it was as dedicated to violating individual Haitians' human rights as it had been to stamping out the Haitian people's democratic aspirations.[17] During the days following the September 1991 coup, the junta made a concerted effort to hide the magnitude of the repression. To eliminate witnesses, soldiers finished off the wounded in hospitals and dumped bodies in mass graves at Ti Tanyen, 10 miles north of the capital. They threatened, or killed, those who asked for the corpses of their deceased relatives. They also killed radio journalist Jacques Gary Simeon. Repression became more overt in later years, as the junta convinced itself that it would remain in power, and proved fatal to such prominent Aristide friends as Antoine Izméry (11 September 1993), Guy Malary (13 October 1993), and Jean-Marie Vincent (28 August 1994).

As likely Aristide supporters, inhabitants of poor areas, students, and the young bore the brunt of the repression. The two bloodiest massacres took place in the traditionally restless town of Gonaïves (22 April 1994) and the giant slum Cité Soleil (27 December 1993). Political opponents could expect short prison terms (often no more than a week), almost always associated with torture. Their ankles and wrists attached to a pole, victims endured severe beatings (*djak*). Guards also liked smacking both ears violently, a painful and deafness-inducing torture (*kalot marassa*).[18] Depending on the idiosyncrasies of the local strongman, variations included hitting genital parts, forcing people to drink blood and sewage, and preventing prisoners from going to the bathroom under penalty of eating their feces. Most infamous were "Saddam Hussein" (prison guard Mondelus Norelus), who in August 1994 obliged one prisoner to eat his own ear, then engraved his initials in his flesh, and Josel Charles, a soldier who liked to be called Capitaine Z (last letter of the alphabet, after which there is nothing left).[19]

The repression, even though it lacked the gory sophistication of the Papa Doc era, used political rape on an unprecedented scale. Rape usually took place in the house of the victim, or even in the middle of the street, in front of the family. It was not uncommon for all women of the family (ranging from 10 to 80 years old) to be raped, or for a son to be forced to rape his mother.[20] Banditry often merged with political repression. Paramilitary forces, such as *attachés zenglendos*, and members of the *Front Révolutionnaire pour l'Avancement et le Progrès Haïtiens* (FRAPH), paid themselves by sacking the victim's house and exacting a ransom from prisoners as the price for freedom.

Aristide claims that the repression killed between three thousand and five thousand Haitians. The Haitian National Truth and Justice Commission (*Commission Nationale de Vérité et de Justice*) only documented 576 murders and 335 disappearances, but for lack of means the count was incomplete outside the capital.[21] Because of the difficulty of accessing remote areas, the junta's efforts to hide bodies, and the limitations of Haiti's judicial system, the exact number will probably never be known, but there is little doubt that, from 1991 to 1994, the junta ranked as one of the most politically oppressive regimes in the world. What is more difficult to ascertain, on the other hand, is the impact Haiti's human rights crisis had on the Clinton administration's daily policy decisions.

The Clinton Administration's Policy was not Always Consistent with its Stated Commitment to Democracy

When democratic idealism conflicted with other substantive goals, the Clinton administration generally decided to push idealism aside, thus suggesting that democracy and human rights were only two, secondary elements of its agenda. It was willing to accept Chinese human rights abuses for the sake of commerce. In Russia, it offered only a mild rebuke to the attack on the Parliament (1993) and the wars in Chechnya (1994–1996, 1999–) in order to safeguard Russia as a pro-Western, responsible nuclear power. Given the large number of nondemocratic countries in the world, some of them U.S. allies, one is left wondering why the administration found itself defending Haitian democracy while it overlooked Saudi, Egyptian, and Chinese autocracy.

In Haiti, the Clinton administration was willing to abandon its ideals in order to convince the military junta to step down peacefully. The Governors' Island accords (July 1993), UN Security Council Resolution 940 (July 1994), and the Carter–Jonassaint agreement (September 1994) all promised the junta a general amnesty for the political crimes they had committed while in office. The United States also acquiesced in Joaquin Balaguer's fraudulent 16 May 1994 electoral victory in the Dominican Republic in exchange for the promise that the Dominican government would enforce the embargo against Haiti more effectively. After the invasion, the U.S. government offered a comfortable life in exile to any of the "MREs" (morally repugnant elite) who would willingly leave Haiti, repeating an offer it had already made a few months before.[22] It then refused to extradite former supporters of the junta such as Emmanuel Constant, even though they were responsible for numerous political murders in 1991–1994 (see chapter ten), while court-martialing a U.S. soldier who overzealously investigated human rights violations in Haitian prisons [see chapter nine].

So eager was Clinton to restore democracy in Haiti that he side-stepped democracy in the United States, refusing to ask for congressional approval of the intervention, even though the Mitchell–Nunn Amendment to the Defense Appropriation Act for 1994 specifically prohibited the use of any military funds for a military intervention in Haiti without explicit congressional approval. Clinton bypassed the ban, and, with troops already in Haiti, congressmen had to limit themselves to ineffectual protests.[23]

Because the administration's public statements about political crimes committed in Haiti suddenly became more numerous and pointed as the intervention approached, one must ponder whether this well-publicized horror was sincere or merely part of a last-minute attempt to strengthen public support and awareness. Until February 1994, Haiti's human rights situation was described in a few pages of the annual State Department human rights report.[24] An April 1994 cable originating in the U.S. Embassy in Haiti even downplayed the importance of human rights, asserting that "the Haitian left manipulates and fabricates human rights abuses as a propaganda tool."[25] Then, from April 1994 onwards, a flurry of special emergency interim reports—no less than three in six months—attacked the junta with much greater stridency. The last one was released during the State Department's daily briefing, a mere six days before the invasion.[26]

Idealism is so popular with the American people that one can always suspect policymakers, who also happen to be politicians, of using democracy as a fig leaf hiding their real motives. According to Clinton's political adviser Dick Morris, Clinton, while not a prisoner of the polls, "used polling instead to discover what arguments would be most persuasive in getting popular support for a [foreign policy] decision."[27] Since Clinton's private polls showed that idealism would help convince the American people that the invasion was necessary, taking his high-minded speeches at face value is questionable.[28] Clinton's political advisers, who expected Americans to respond enthusiastically to democratic ideals, recommended that he couch the official rationale for the invasion in idealistic terms (chapter seven).

The administration's determination to advance the Western Hemisphere's trend towards democracy[29] was equally dubious. Theoretically, the Summit of the Americas, set for December 1994, could have constituted a deadline by which Aristide had to be restored to power so that Fidel Castro could be singled out as the lone autocrat in Latin America. In fact, Richard E. Feinberg, who was in charge of Latin American affairs in the Clinton administration's National Security Council and oversaw the U.S. participation in the Summit of the Americas, remembers that the summit was "not decisive. It was nice that Aristide was restored before the summit, but it was not decisive."[30]

The very name of the intervention invited incredulity. Administration critics asserted that restoring Haitian democracy would inevitably be a complex task, as there had never been much of it to begin with. There were frequent comments to the effect that the United States had occupied the island for 19 years in 1915–1934 without making any significant inroad into creating a stable political system. Congressman Eni F. H. Faleomavaega, the delegate from the American Samoa, was blunt: "Seven million people live in Haiti; approximately 90 percent are in sheer poverty, and I was wondering if—in most realistic terms, if we could ever build a true democracy in that island country where they have never seriously given that kind of political maturity in providing for that."[31] Sen. Lauch Faircloth (R-NC) agreed: "you can teach a kangaroo to do the limbo about as quick as you are going to be able to establish democracy in Haiti, because in 150 to 200 years they have not had it."[32]

Administration members publicly avoided such politically incorrect judgments on the maturity of the Haitian polity. On the other hand, they openly admitted that Aristide, while elected in a relatively democratic election, had not always ruled in a democratic manner, which makes it unclear why they made his restoration the main goal of Operation Restore Democracy. Clinton admitted in November 1993, "Aristide may not be like you and me . . . but two-thirds of the Haitians voted for him."[33] Lake viewed Aristide as "a democrat, but one who plays by the winner-takes-all rule of Haiti's political culture."[34] Indeed, Aristide's poor democratic record as president seriously undermined Clinton's claim that the 1994 intervention was motivated by a desire to restore democracy in Haiti.

Aristide's Human Rights Record During his First Presidency

During his years in exile (1991–1994), U.S. opinion of Aristide was extremely polarized. His most dedicated supporters saw the Haitian priest as a Gandhi- or Mandela-like figure who had brought democracy to his people. Enemies such as Sen. Jesse Helms (R-NC) saw him as a "psychopath" who rejoiced in mob rule and grisly murders.[35] Taking the middle road, the *New York Times* hoped that Aristide had gone from being a new "Robespierre" to a new "Gandhi" during his exile in the United States.[36] While many criticisms were excessive, Aristide's record was mixed at best. He was elected in a relatively democratic, though by no means perfect, election. Once in power, he routinely disregarded democratic parliamentary practices and incited his supporters to commit human rights abuses.

Contrary to oft-repeated press reports, Aristide was not the first democratically elected president of Haiti. Parliament had elected presidents during the 1930s and 1940s (French presidents of the Third and Fourth Republics were elected in similar fashion; so are U.S. presidents when the electoral college is divided). The 1957 presidential election that brought Papa Doc to power saw widespread fraud, but the nationalist country doctor was popular at the time.[37] The truly novel democratic change was Aristide's reliance on the masses. Refusing to deliver pompous speeches in the French language, as was the norm in Haitian politics, he was a master of the Creole dialect spoken by the hundreds of thousands of Port-au-Prince slum dwellers who had heretofore been excluded from the political system (today, even rich mulattoes make an effort to address the people in Creole).[38]

The line between popular democracy and mob rule, however, was often thin. During the 1986 post-Duvalier massacre of *Macoutes*, Aristide confessed that he "stood and marveled at the justice of the people. . . . they were doing God's work."[39] Because of the dangers associated with being an opposition activist during the Duvalier years, Aristide developed a rhetorical style based on allegory, double meaning, and jokes—the listener understood what was meant, but Aristide could always claim he had not said anything.[40] The use of Creole for inflammatory attacks, and of French for innocuous statements aimed at an international audience, further increased the ambivalence of Aristide's speeches. After he was overthrown, debates in the United States focused on whether he had encouraged his followers to use *Père Lebrun* or necklacing (burning someone to death).[41]

In defense of Aristide's democratic record, one must point out that human rights violations were much less numerous during his presidency than under previous regimes, and that his supporters, not he, committed them.[42] When faced with armed opposition, as during the Lafontant coup, mobs were the only weapon of self-defense in Aristide's arsenal. Given the limitations of the judicial system, lynching was the only efficient mode of retribution, and, after thirty years of Duvalierism and five years of military regimes, there was much to be avenged. In the words of Aristide's leftist friend Patrick Elie, "his speeches were those of a revolutionary leader who had no weapons except the people. The Haitian masses did not complain; on the contrary, they criticized him for being too timid."[43]

Aristide also claimed his speeches had been taken out of context, but the complete transcripts of the major speeches he delivered during his first presidency

(February-September 1991) left little room for doubt. Shortly before his inauguration, when many supporters of the failed Lafontant coup were hacked to pieces or burnt in the streets, Aristide's public comments failed to condemn the violence. In a radio speech in Creole, he noted,

> you are at the same time happy and sad, happy because Roger Lafontant and other terrorists like him are in jail, and sad, because he and his accomplices are not in your hands. I understand your desire to catch the powerful *Macoutes* today so that they do not destroy you tomorrow. This is legitimate. . . . there must be a disciplined brigade above, an attentive brigade below, and *Macoutes* must be caught in the middle.[44]

On 4 August, 1991, after Lafontant and his accomplices were condemned to hard labor for life, in a show trial during which a crowd surrounded the tribunal and threatened to kill the judges if the sentence was not harsh enough, Aristide addressed a youth rally at Croix-des-Bouquets.

> Was there Père Lebrun inside the courthouse? [audience yells no] Was there Père Lebrun in front of the courthouse? [audience yells yes] Did the people use Père Lebrun? [audience yells no] Did the people forget it? [audience yells no] Do not say that I said it [laughter] [passage indistinct].
>
> In front of the courthouse, for 24 hours, Père Lebrun became [word indistinct]. The Justice Ministry inside the courthouse had the law in its hands, the people had their cushion outside. The people had their little matches in their hands. They had gas nearby. Did they use it? [audience yells no] That means that the people respect [audience yells the Constitution] Does the Constitution tell the people to forget little Père Lebrun? [audience yells no]. [Several sentences indistinct] The people are the law, meaning what they do is constitutional. The law respects the Constitution.
>
> When the people heard: life in prison, the people forgot their little gas and little Père Lebrun. Was Père Lebrun used on that day? [audience yells no] If it had not gone well, would the people have used Père Lebrun? [audience yells yes] Therefore, when through education one learns how to write Père Lebrun and learns how to think Père Lebrun, one does not use it when it is unnecessary.[45]

On 27 September 1991, when Aristide came back from attending a session of the UN General Assembly in New York, he heard persistent rumors that a coup was in preparation. He sent away diplomats who had come to welcome him at the airport, gathered a crowd in the slum of Cité Soleil, and walked to the National Palace where he delivered a forceful speech in Creole. The crowd covered most of the Champ de Mars in downtown Port-au-Prince; many brandished tires. "This was the scariest thing I have ever seen," remembers a foreign journalist who saw the speech.[46] Footage of the scene shows an uneasy Cédras standing a few meters behind his president. The use of Creole and the absence of foreign observers suggested that the harangue would be bellicose. Aristide first warned the bourgeois of the risk they ran for refusing to invest their wealth locally.

> If you do not do so, I feel sorry for you. Really, I do. [laughter from crowd] It will not be my fault because this money you have is not really yours. You acquired it through criminal activity. . . . Today, seven months after 7 February, on a day ending in seven,

I give you one last chance. I ask you to take this chance, because you will not have two or three more chances, only one. Otherwise, it will not be good for you. [applause]. . . . If I speak to you this way, it does not mean that I am unaware of my power to unleash public vindication, in the name of justice, against all thieves, in an attempt to recover from them what is not theirs. A word to the wise is enough.

A few minutes later came the widely quoted passage that would haunt Aristide during his exile.

However if I catch a thief, a robber, a swindler, or an embezzler, if I catch a fake Lavalas, if I catch a fake . . . if you catch someone who does not deserve to be where he is, do not fail to give him what he deserves. [crowd cheers] Do not fail to give him what he deserves! Do not fail to give him what he deserves! Do not fail to give him what he deserves! [ba yo sa yo merite]

Your tool is in your hands. Your instrument is in your hands. Your Constitution is in your hands. Do not fail to give him what he deserves. [loud cheers from crowd] That device is in your hands. Your trowel is in your hands. The bugle is in your hands. The Constitution is your hands. Do not fail to give him what he deserves.

Article 291 of the Constitution, which is symbolized by the center of my head where there is no more hair [he was referring to Lafontant, who was bald], provides that *Macoutes* are excluded from the political game. *Macoutes* are excluded from the political game. *Macoutes* are excluded from the political game. Do not fail to give them what they deserve. Do not fail to give them what they deserve. You spent three sleepless nights in front of the National Penitentiary. If one escapes, do not fail to give him what he deserves. [loud cheers]

You are watching all *Macoute* activities throughout the country. We are watching and praying. We are watching and praying. If we catch one, do not fail to give him what he deserves. What a nice tool! What a nice instrument! [loud cheers] What a nice device! [crowd cheers] It is a pretty one. It is elegant, attractive, splendorous, graceful, and dazzling. It smells good. Wherever you go, you feel like smelling it. [crowd cheers] It is provided for by the Constitution, which bans *Macoutes* from the political scene. Whatever happens to them is their problem. . . . Words will thus cease to be just words and will instead be translated into action.[47]

Two days later, a crowd necklaced Aristide opponent Sylvio Claude in les Cayes, and the Haitian Army, claiming that Aristide targeted its members for necklacing, overthrew Aristide.

The centrality of democratic messianism in both the U.S. foreign policy tradition and in the official rhetoric used to justify the 1994 intervention in Haiti makes it easy to portray the intervention as a democratic crusade. Nevertheless, the Clinton administration's tendency to abandon democracy when it conflicted with other goals, its awareness that making idealistic statements was the easiest way to convince the American people of the need for a U.S. intervention, and its support for a statesman who, while elected by a majority of Haitians, had encouraged human rights abuses against his enemies while in office all hint that the administration's commitment to democracy alone was not sufficient to prompt a military intervention. Other factors were at play, one of which was the realization that the U.S. government's helplessness in Haiti undermined its credibility worldwide.

CHAPTER FIVE
U.S. CREDIBILITY

Paradoxically, while a culturally self-centered American people has historically paid little attention to the rest of the world, its foreign-policy elite spent much of the Cold War worrying about what foreigners thought of the United States. More specifically, Cold War U.S. foreign policymakers expended considerable energy in working to persuade foreign leaders that the United States' international power was "credible." Unlike economic and strategic interests, the concept of U.S. international credibility exists only in the eye of the beholder, making it difficult to define or quantify. "A blend of resolve, reliability, believability, and decisiveness," credibility means that foreign governments believes that the United States will act with "firmness, determination, and dependability."[1]

Even though credibility is a psychological phenomenon whose objectives are perceptions (prestige, trustworthiness) rather than tangible assets (sea lanes, iron ore, cannons), its preservation ranks high in U.S. policymakers' agendas, for they are convinced that deteriorating international credibility would jeopardize U.S. security. By persuading potential foes that aggression on their part will elicit a strong U.S. response, international credibility acts as an instrument of deterrence. By reassuring allies that the United States will stand by them in times of crisis, it is a guarantee of loyalty and alliance maintenance. Or so several generations of U.S. foreign policymakers have believed. Maintaining credibility, according to this view, requires constant firmness and assertiveness abroad. To act otherwise runs the risk of being perceived as weak by enemies and allies alike. "Consequently," historian Robert McMahon writes,

> U.S. leaders must be extraordinarily careful that their statements and actions always send the proper signal. If a signal of irresolution is conveyed or an image of weakness projected, even in an area of peripheral strategic and economic value, American credibility could be severely damaged, possibly leading either allies or adversaries to take actions detrimental to the United States in vital areas.[2]

The prominent role that credibility concerns played in U.S. foreign policy during and after the Cold War stemmed in part from the failures of appeasement at Munich in 1938. According to the "lessons" learned in the 1930s, yielding to an enemy, far from securing peace, merely encouraged new, bolder aggressions. Accordingly, because the United States after World War II was a superpower at the center of an extensive international alliance system, its power, and its willingness to project its power, were under constant scrutiny by its allies, particularly in Europe—allies, who, it was feared, might reach accommodation with the Soviet Union if the United States was perceived to be losing momentum in the Cold War balance of power.

Proving that the United States was committed to defending allies threatened by communist penetration was one of the main justifications for entering the Vietnam War. If the United States withdrew from the region entirely, Lyndon B. Johnson said in July 1965 as he pondered whether to increase U.S. military involvement in South Vietnam, "wouldn't all these countries say that Uncle Sam was a paper tiger?"[3] Richard Nixon voiced similar concerns in April 1970 when he announced his intention to invade Cambodia. "If, when the chips are down, the world's most powerful nation, the United States of America, acts like a pitiful, helpless giant," Nixon told Americans, "the forces of totalitarianism and anarchy will threaten free nations and free institutions throughout the world. It is not our power but our will and character that is being tested."[4] The U.S. defeat in Vietnam both undermined and reinforced the credibility credo. It proved that demonstrating U.S. assertiveness worldwide could be costly and ultimately unsuccessful, but it also imperiled the carefully built perception that the United States was willing, and able, to help its allies, thus inciting enemies to apply renewed pressure. Diplomatic setbacks during the Carter presidency, particularly in Iran, Afghanistan, and Nicaragua, gave added credence to these fears.

Latin America was a place where U.S. presidents could hope to restore their country's battered credibility. In Latin America, the preponderance of U.S. power and the absence of key strategic interests meant that the chief rationale for U.S.—that is interventions—was to demonstrate the credibility of U.S. power to observers elsewhere. Any reluctance or passivity on the part of the United States to project its power in defense of its interests in its own sphere of influence could call into question America's ability to impose its will elsewhere. According to University of North Carolina political scientist Lars Schoultz, U.S. policy in Central America in the early 1980s was based on precisely such notions.

> Central America was accepted as a symbol. Because it was a place of almost no intrinsic importance, the. . . . objective was to demonstrate to the world that the United States was once again serious about containment. . . . Central America was a logical, even convenient, place to force a test of wills. . . . It was a place where the United States could win. And . . . once Washington had publicly awarded Central America its central symbolic role in U.S. security policy, then there was no turning back. Rhetorical commitment served to create a vital interest, an interest in not having to back down and suffer a loss of credibility.[5]

Clinton took over as president of the United States two years after the fall of the Soviet Union had dramatically changed the contours of the international system. Nevertheless, maintaining U.S. credibility remained as important as ever to U.S. leaders. In order for the United States to secure its position as the leader of the post–Cold War international system, Clinton had to convince potential foes, even if they were small and strategically insignificant, that his administration remained prepared to deploy its armed forces, even if they had been partially demobilized, to defend his vision of a new world order dedicated to U.S.-style free-market democracy. Looking strong, resolute, and assertive in projecting U.S. power internationally would convince recalcitrant, uncooperative foreign states to embrace U.S. democratic and economic values. To remain passive in the face of the rising number of small-scale "low-intensity" conflicts that broke out in the Cold War's aftermath would only encourage would-be mischief-makers to ignore U.S. admonitions and to turn the world into chaos.

Convincing other world leaders that he meant what he said proved difficult for Clinton. Candidate Clinton had outlined an ambitious foreign policy agenda, but President Clinton set out to accomplish it in cautious, inconsistent, and at times incoherent, fashion. This policy resulted in a bloody debacle in Somalia and continued humiliation in Haiti, the poorest nation in the U.S. "backyard," putting in question the U.S. willingness and ability to project its power, and forcing Clinton to intervene in Haiti, in his own words, "to uphold the reliability of the commitments we make and the commitments others make to us."[6]

Clinton's Foreign Policy (1993–1994): Ambitious Goals, Wavering Policies, Limited Achievements

When he assumed responsibility for U.S. foreign policy in 1993, Clinton hoped to make the U.S. victory in the Cold War complete. Building on the prevailing belief that the U.S.-led "New World Order" pursued by George Bush marked the "end of history" (Francis Fukuyama), as well as on his 1992 campaign promises to help Haitians, Bosnians, and Somalis, his administration tried to spread peace, to increase trade, to expand democracy's grasp, and to maintain the U.S. status as the world's superpower.[7] Clinton was nevertheless aware that he had been elected on an America-first platform and that good stewardship of the economy, not foreign activism, would earn him reelection. The Vietnam precedent and the Pentagon's reluctance to undertake peacekeeping missions also urged caution, which translated into the careful wording of Presidential Decision Directive 25 (3 May 1994), setting 18 "rigorous standards of review" before U.S. troops could participate in a peacekeeping mission.[8] Clinton was facing the traditional dilemma of U.S. foreign policy: Americans expect their leaders to fight for a more democratic world, but, fearing foreign entanglement with equal passion, they refuse to endorse long, costly wars abroad.[9] This ambivalence shaped a disappointing first year in office, during which grandiose calls for world peace were followed by weak-kneed, shifting policies and a heavy reliance on allies and the UN, raising genuine doubts concerning Clinton's and America's courage, interest in world affairs, and ability to lead.

The famous Rabin–Arafat White House handshake (13 September 1993) and the ratification of NAFTA (8 December 1993) were Clinton's sole foreign policy triumphs during his first 18 months in office. An air attack against Iraq (June 1993) provided a short boost in the polls, but Saddam Hussein remained in power, and regular, ineffective bouts of bombing remained the norm for the remainder of Clinton's stay in office. Clinton remained virtually silent in the face of the Tutsi genocide in Rwanda (April-July 1994).[10] The multiplication of local conflicts worldwide, whose handling the United States delegated to the United Nations, confirmed that there would be no *Pax Americana* under Clinton. By 1994, the United Nations was involved in 20 separate peacekeeping operations, 15 of which had begun since 1989.[11]

Clinton's use of the United Nations as a surrogate State Department fed Republican accusations that the Clinton administration had forsaken U.S. world leadership. In 1995, Senate minority leader Bob Dole (R-KS) introduced the Peace Powers Act, which would have deducted U.S. military costs from the peacekeeping dues the United States owed the United Nations. In the House of Representatives, Rep. Lee Hamilton (D-IN) introduced the National Security Revitalization Act with the avowed goal of keeping Americans out of UN peacekeeping operations. The anti-United Nations campaign culminated in the 1996 presidential campaign, when Dole promised that, if he were elected, the president, not "Bootrus-Bootrus" (as he called UN Secretary General Boutros Boutros-Ghali), would make the decision about sending U.S. troops in harm's way.[12] Clinton felt obliged to respond that "the reason we have supported [UN peacekeeping] missions is not, as some critics in the United States have charged, to subcontract American foreign policy but to strengthen our security, to protect our interests, and to share among nations the costs and effort of pursuing peace."[13] To steal the thunder from Dole's attack, and to blame the Somalia fiasco on some multinational scapegoat, Clinton conducted a campaign to deny Boutros-Ghali a second term as secretary general, while his Ambassador to the United Nations accused UN peacekeeping operations of being characterized by "a kind of programmed amateurism."[14]

Whether subservient to the United Nations or not, Clinton's foreign policy was particularly muddled and ineffective in Bosnia. In a typical April 1993 statement, Clinton explained that his policy was that "the U.S. should always seek an opportunity to stand up against—at least speak out against—inhumanity."[15] After Yugoslavia broke up in 1991 and Bosnia became a battleground for Serb, Muslim, and Croatian forces, the Clinton administration, anxious not to be drawn into the conflict, encouraged U.S. allies to provide a European answer to this European conflict. On the other hand, as the war went on, the United States' status as world superpower made it difficult to stand by passively as a well-publicized war raged in the heart of Europe. In May 1993, Secretary of State Warren Christopher went to Europe to propose his administration's preferred alternative, "lift and strike" (lift the UN embargo on weapon exports to Bosnia, strike Serbian targets from the air). In a blow to the U.S. capacity to lead, European leaders spurned the proposal, and the war, along with U.S. inactivity, resumed for two more years. The U.S. media's extensive coverage of the war, Europeans' rejection of U.S. leadership, and continued fighting made Bosnia a symbol of a U.S. foreign policy that seemingly did not dare to assume its responsibilities abroad, and that failed to impose its views when it did. Aware of the credibility implications, Christopher felt "the need to vindicate U.S. leadership," while Clinton confided that "this policy is doing enormous damage to the United States and to our standing in the world. We look weak. . . . We have a war by CNN. Our position is unsustainable, it's killing the U.S. position of strength in the world."[16]

Editorialists' assessments of Clinton's foreign policy were acerbic.[17] They accused Clinton of rapidly building a record of failures and of squandering his country's credibility by not carrying his threats out. According to *U.S. News and World Report*, "Bill Clinton has retreated from nearly every line that he has drawn in the sand, from Mogadishu to Port-au-Prince to Beijing. He squandered the authority of his office on fruitless pleas to tiny Singapore not to cane a convicted American vandal."[18] "President Clinton was impressive when he talked about domestic issues in his [1994] State of the Union address," observed the *New York Times*.

> How different it was when he turned to foreign affairs. . . . To call his comments shallow would be a compliment. In their blithe optimism they seemed strangely— scarily—disconnected from reality. Does he know that European unity is frail and fraying, that Europe and the United States have no credibility as guarantors of security after our failure to stop Serbian aggression?[19]

U.S. policy in Somalia, while more active, was equally shifting, ineffective, and poorly regarded. In 1992, with president-elect Clinton's approval, Bush ordered U.S. troops to the horn of Africa to provide food supplies to hungry Somalis. The mission was originally limited to humanitarian assistance, and both Bush and Clinton planned to extricate U.S. troops within months.[20] But after the death of 24 Pakistani UN peacekeepers in June 1993, the United Nations, with U.S. military assistance, pledged to capture Somali warlord Muhammad Farrah Aidid. Disaster struck on 3 October 1993, when 18 U.S. Rangers died in an ambush as they tried to arrest Aidid. Adding insult to injury, footage of a dead Ranger's naked body dragged through the streets of Mogadishu appeared repeatedly on U.S. television. Clinton vowed revenge, but Aidid remained at large and U.S. troops withdrew within six months. A desire to limit the credibility cost of the Somalia fiasco was evident when Clinton, in a 7 October address to the nation, explained that he would wait until 31 March 1994 before ordering the troops home. "If we were to leave today. . . . Our own credibility with friends and allies would be severely damaged. . . . All around the world, aggressors, thugs and terrorists will conclude that the best way to get us to change our policies is to kill our people. It would be open season on Americans."[21] The speech proved prescient. Four days later, Haitians associated with the junta declared open season on Americans in Port-au-Prince.

The *Harlan County* Humiliation (11 October 1993)

According to the July 1993 Governors' Island accords, Aristide was to return to Haiti on 30 October, preceded by a 1,267-strong international UN force whose mission was to train the Haitian Army. As described by U.S. General John J. Sheehan, the democratization of the Haitian armed forces would proceed by osmosis. "On every one of these construction projects with the Seabees and the Marines and the Canadians, a Haitian soldier or group of soldiers is going to work with them because, very frankly, the best teachers of democracy we have in this nation are the young lance corporals and corporals who can teach some of these Haitians what they need to know."[22] The presence of foreign soldiers on Haitian soil, it was also hoped, would facilitate the political transition from Cédras to Aristide.

The human rights situation deteriorated markedly over the summer and Cédras showed increasing signs that he would use any excuse not to abide by the letter of the agreement. The USS *Harlan County*, carrying 225 U.S. and Canadian soldiers set to join the first elements of the UN force already in Haiti, nevertheless departed for Port-au-Prince, with the USS *Fairfax County* set to follow her on 16 October. Hundreds of miles away, on a Sunday morning news program, U.S. Defense Secretary Les Aspin was facing the difficult task of guaranteeing the U.S. soldiers' safety in the wake of the Somalia carnage.

[ABC *News* journalist George] WILL: Can you tell me, is it the case, as I've read reports, that they [U.S. members of the UN force *en route* to Haiti] are armed only with side arms?

Sec. Les ASPIN: They are armed with the- they are armed in a way that will be able- they will be able to protect their own lives and their own safety. They are not armed sufficiently in order to do a peacekeeping job.

[ABC *News* journalist Samuel] DONALDSON: Do they have armor?

Mr. WILL: What are-

Mr. DONALDSON: Do they have armor?

Sec. ASPIN: No, no, no. They're not doing a peacekeeping job-

Mr. DONALDSON: But they may be attacked.

Sec. ASPIN: No. No, look, look, we got to understand what we're talking about here.

Mr. DONALDSON: How can you be certain they're not going to be attacked, Mr. Secretary?

Sec. ASPIN: Sam, the point is they have the capability to protect themselves for their own safety. They have the M-1- the M-16 rifles.[23]

The comment was a small-scale diplomatic disaster. As the UN force's sole mission was to train the Haitian Army, the Governors' Island accord only authorized members of the force to carry small side arms, not powerful M-16s. The plan Aristide submitted to UN Secretary General Boutros-Ghali for the professionaliza-tion of Haiti's army similarly called for foreign advisers armed with "handguns intended for their personal protection," and Aristide's Premier Robert Malval had assured the junta that any heavier weapons would constitute a violation of the Governors' Island accords.[24] When, a day after Aspin's *faux pas*, a wire from the French news agency AFP reported that the *Harlan County* would remain in Haitian waters after landing troops, Cédras opposed the deployment of troops, claiming that the force's military-grade equipment was not in keeping with its limited mission, and that his country's sovereignty was imperiled.[25]

On 11 October the *Harlan County* skirted the glistening beaches of the Ile de la Gonâve, approached the less pristine waters of the Port-au-Prince harbor, and found that an old Cuban tanker already occupied the berth where its troops were supposed to land. The situation was even worse on the dock, where U.S. Embassy attaché Vicky Hudleston hoped to welcome the troops. As uniformed Haitian police stood by, members of the *Front Révolutionnaire pour l'Avancement et le Progrès* Haïtiens, a right-wing paramilitary party associated with the junta (the acronym FRAPH meant "to hit"), surrounded her car, wielded machetes, chanted "remember Somalia," and molested Embassy spokesman Stanley Shrager.[26] TV crews were there to film this scene, as well as the *Harlan County* as it waited all day at sea for orders. On 12 October, the ship's captain, concerned that he might be fired upon, set sail for Cuba. The Pentagon refused to send the *Harlan County* back unless its troops were better armed, which was incompatible with the nature of the mission, and the White House, against UN wishes, aborted the mission altogether.[27]

The *Harlan County*'s retreat unleashed a torrent of criticism. Chairman of the Senate Armed Forces Committee Sam Nunn (D-GA) feared that backing down in the face of danger seriously undermined the credibility of U.S. foreign policy. "We are down here and, by golly, we are going to train you whether you want it or not, and we are going to kick your top man out. But there is one caveat. If you shoot one of us, we are going home. That is weird. . . . To those who do not want us, all you have got to do is shoot one of us, and we are out of here."[28] Sen. Tom Harkin (D-IA) concurred. "The mightiest nation on Earth, one that just beat Saddam Hussein, being faced down by a rag-tag element of no more than 100 drug traffickers, smugglers, and murderers, and we turned around and tucked our tail and ran. . . . If we cannot support duly elected democratic governments 800 miles from our shores, again what kind of message will we send to potential coup leaders?"[29] Boutros-Ghali was equally concerned by the damage this "humiliation" had done to "the prestige of the United Nations, held up to ridicule by the incoherence of American policy."[30]

Most Embassy cable traffic remains classified, but one may surmise what the State Department's reaction was upon reading excerpts of foreign press articles selected by the U.S. Information Service. In a few months' time, the USIS agency in Bonn, Germany reported that the U.S. had been "led by the nose" (*Frankfurter Allgemeine and Rheinische Post*, October 1993), was an "apprentice" (*Frankfurter Rundschau*, January 1994) characterized by its "helplessness" (*Frankfurter Allgemeine*, October 1993), and led by a president able to make only "empty threats" (*Stuttgarter Zeitung*, November 1993).[31]

In the White House, administration officials debated what the proper response should be. Clinton was so outraged that he could not find a single word in the English language that would properly describe the humiliation. In a letter to Congress, he later characterized the *Harlan County* incident as "aggapent," a word not found in any dictionary (it may have referred to "agape," a state of wonder and amazement).[32] Whether the Haitian Army received police training or not was of little importance. But the incident took place within days of the Mogadishu disaster; it pitted a ragtag band of ill-armed protesters against hundreds of U.S. soldiers and seamen, with the protesters emerging as clear winners; it was televised; it signaled to military officers all over Latin America that overthrowing democratic governments would not result in a U.S. response; and it substantiated critics' claims that the Clinton administration kept setting out to save the world, then backed down for fear of U.S. casualties.

The *Harlan County* incident proved that credibility concerns were a diplomatic reality, not just an intellectual pastime. Cédras had watched on television as U.S. congressmen, fearing a second Mogadishu, voiced their opposition to the Haiti deployment, and concluded that it would take little pressure to make the U.S. forces go home. Credibility mattered. Should the U.S. look weak on one side of the world, other nations might test its resolve thousands of miles away. There was a real risk that, emboldened by the Somali and Haitian precedents, enemies of the United States would multiply such incidents, confident that killing a few U.S. servicemen, far from inviting military retaliation, would result in a quick withdrawal. With U.S. troops stationed everywhere from Colombia to Saudi Arabia, South Korea, Italy, Turkey, Panama, and Honduras, amidst sometimes hostile populations, tolerating defiance could quickly result in a diplomatic and military catastrophe.

Preserving America's credibility required that a few dozen protesters' provocation not be left unpunished. Days after the *Harlan County* incident, Assistant Secretary of State for Inter-American Affairs Alexander Fletcher Watson told Congress that "demonstrating U.S. resolve in a region with strong historical, cultural, economic, and political ties to the U.S." would help "enhance U.S. influence and credibility internationally."[33] But the memory of the Somalia intervention was still fresh in everyone's mind. On 14 October, according to interviews with participants, the White House was veering toward intervention at the instigation of Gore, Lake and Christopher. The Pentagon, which had not been enthralled with the *Harlan County*'s mission to begin with, protested.

> [Secretary of Defense Les] Aspin argued, "Be careful. Look at the last time we invaded Haiti." After the [14 October White House] meeting, Aspin called [conservative adviser David] Gergen, who was in New York, and said, "Jesus Christ, we're about to go to war with Haiti." Gergen replied, "You're kidding." "No," Aspin said. "Get your ass down here." [Gergen came back in time for an 8 o'clock White House meeting on the morning of the 15th.] But by then emotions had cooled. It was decided to seek the reimposition of UN economic sanctions. . . . Also, six ships would be sent to patrol Haiti to enforce the sanctions—and make the United States look stronger.[34]

Lake defended the administration's position by saying that "you don't do an invasion in 24 hours," but he also spoke of a "terrible humiliation."[35] He and other NSC members discussed the options and concluded that, in the long term, an invasion was the only solution. Richard Feinberg, Senior Director of the NSC's Office of Inter-American Affairs from 1993 to 1996, was attending a White House meeting when news of the *Harlan County* incident broke out.

> People were still shell-shocked from Somalia, and the military was dead against the use of force, so there was no invasion then. But the incident was critical. It resulted in tremendous political criticism and contributed to the decision to intervene a year later.[36]

"I'm never going to wimp out like I did in Haiti again," Clinton later confided to his entourage.[37]

"The Devil"

Intelligence failures made the *Harlan County* incident even more humiliating for the Clinton administration. Despite many clear warning indicators, the CIA had failed to predict the hostility that greeted the ship in Port-au-Prince. The tightening political repression over the summer culminated on 11 September with the murder of Antoine Izméry, so overt it could only be construed as a provocation. Interviewed a few weeks before his death, Izméry himself predicted that Aristide's return "is not going to happen."[38] FRAPH members demonstrated against the deployment of U.S. troops throughout September, and on 3 October their leader, Emmanuel Constant, announced at a televised press conference that he would oppose the landing. Chief of Police Michel Francois did likewise.[39] In a 1992 internal memo discussing the Protocol of Washington, a precursor of the Governors' Island accord, an adviser wrote to Cédras that "even if the Protocol mentions the return to power of President Aristide, the concrete enforcement of this clause is utopic and will be hard to enforce."[40]

Despite the minimal military opposition that the Haitian demonstrators were capable of mobilizing against the *Harlan County*'s forces (Constant's plan was to run away as soon as the troops landed), the CIA informed the White House that troops waiting in the *Harlan County* for orders would be at risk if they set foot in Port-au-Prince. U.S. special envoy to Haiti Lawrence Pezzullo, based on information he received from his own informants, insisted that there was no danger, but the CIA prevailed. According to Pezzullo, "Cédras said on several occasions to our people 'I couldn't believe that you pulled the ship out on the basis of that demonstration.'"[41] The U.S. military's own intelligence sources described the situation in Port-au-Prince as "semi-permissive" (passive resistance was possible, but it would present no physical danger to U.S. forces).[42]

It took another few months for Clinton to realize that his intelligence had not only failed, but had actually betrayed him. Constant, who engineered the 11 October humiliation, was at the time paid $700 a month as a CIA informer.[43] As such, he had informed his U.S. employers *ahead of time* that his organization was planning to demonstrate against the *Harlan County*, but that FRAPH members had no intention of fighting and would pose no threat whatsoever (FRAPH was an anti-Aristide, but pro-American party). CIA operatives thus warned Washington of a threat they knew did not exist, presumably in order to scare Clinton administration policymakers and thereby forestall the return of an Aristide they did not like. Constant told his story two years later in a CBS interview.

Ed Bradley: Did the CIA station chief [John Kambourian] say to you, "I think this is a bad idea. Don't . . ."

Constant: No-

Bradley: call this demonstration?

Constant: Absolutely not. He never told me anything like that.

Bradley: Was there any concern—did anyone express concern about a threat to American lives?

Constant: No. I guaranteed him that the demonstration was simply a media frenzy that I wanted to create. That has nothing to do—no life was threatened. . . .

Bradley: After you scuttled the president's plan to restore Aristide to power, does the CIA start to distance itself from you?

Constant: No, absolutely not. That's when I picked up more power, more political clout.[44]

Constant, a.k.a "Toto," a.k.a "Gamal," was the son of François Duvalier's Army Chief of Staff Gérard Emmanuel Constant.[45] "Toto," born in 1956, lived in the

United States during the 1980s, first as a student, then as a representative of the Duvalier regime in Washington, DC. He returned to Haiti as a teacher at the Haitian National Intelligence Service. Constant's involvement with U.S. intelligence started around Christmas 1991, when, codenamed "Gamal" (after Egypt's Gamal Abdul Nasser), he became a CIA informer. This, the CIA later declared, did not constitute an endorsement of Constant's politics, but was merely a way to collect information on human rights abuses—the CIA similarly hired many promising young men, including Manuel Noriega of Panama.[46]

Constant indeed did know much about human rights abuses. He committed many of them himself, earning yet another nickname: "the Devil." In August 1993, he founded the *Front Révolutionnaire pour l'Avancement et le Progrès Haïtiens* (then *Front Révolutionnaire Armé pour le Progrès d'Haïti*). His goal was to protest the July 1993 Governors' Island accords, the economic embargo, and foreign intervention.[47] Like Duvalier's *Volontaires pour la Sécurité Nationale* (or *Macoutes*), FRAPH pretended to be a political party and a youth organization, but the initiation rites entailed nothing the typical GOP or YMCA chapter would require. New members had to watch as beatings were performed, then were asked to join in.[48] FRAPH, which eventually claimed 200,000 to 400,000 members with 297 local bureaus, was most infamous for the 27 December 1993 fire in Cité Soleil. Retaliating for the murder of two of its members, FRAPH members surrounded the notoriously pro-Aristide slum, set it on fire, shot those trying to flee, and prevented firemen from accessing the site. Depending on accounts, 4 to 36 people died; 5,000 lost their homes.[49] Constant denied insistent rumors that he was responsible for the fire in these terms: "If it had been me, there would be no more Cité Soleil."[50] A U.S. journalist in Haiti remembers Constant as "a drunk, a cocaine addict, who just loved violence. The day the *Harlan County* tried to dock, Toto was on the dock with a chrome-plated .45, just shooting at people."[51]

The CIA was aware of Constant's murderous activities. An October 1993 agency report entitled "Haiti's Far Right: Taking the Offensive" suggested that Constant, then on the CIA's payroll, had taken part in the assassination of Justice Minister Guy Malary.[52] In November 1993 and April 1994, Constant's name appeared on the list of "blocked Haitians" deemed so close to the regime that one needed to ask the Office of Foreign Assets Control for permission to conduct business with them; money owed them had to be deposited in a blocked account in New York.[53] CIA payments to Constant were thus made in direct violation of U.S. laws.

During Carnival 1994, Constant boasted on CBS that he wanted to become Haiti's president. Investigating his case, Clinton learned that he was on the CIA payroll and complained accordingly. The CIA thus put him "on ice" and payments came to an end (contacts resumed six months later when the United States invaded Haiti). In the meantime, Clinton's ability to impose his will on his own administration and on the coup leaders remained in doubt.

The Economic Embargo's Ineffectiveness Allowed the Junta to Remain in Power

Supporters of the junta publicly humiliated the Clinton administration during the *Harlan County* incident, but the very survival of the junta, from September 1991 to September 1994, was in and of itself a blow to U.S. credibility. Cédras' No refusal to step down was a constant reminder that the United States could not even control the destiny of a poor, powerless island located in a traditional U.S. sphere of influence. The Clinton administration's unsuccessful attempt to force the junta to step down voluntarily proved that the cornerstone of its policy, an economic embargo against Haiti, was a complete failure.

Days after the 1991 coup that ousted Aristide, the United States and the OAS instituted an economic embargo. Initially limited to oil and weapons, the embargo, at Aristide's urging and with UN backing, eventually included everything but a few food products, medicine, and cooking fuel. Even purchases of medical products, which were not technically humanitarian in nature because they were not gifts, had a hard time circumventing the embargo. The goal, according to an internal *Lavalas* document dating from the fall of 1992, was to weaken the rich importers who supported the junta. "We must propose a firm blockade of financial and commercial relations of the handful of economic agents who supported the coup."[54] Despite its record of ineffectiveness in previous foreign policy crises ranging from Italy's invasion of Ethiopia in 1935–1936 to Fidel Castro's takeover of Cuba in 1959, an embargo was a popular policy because it endangered no U.S. lives. From Iraq to Bosnia and Haiti, embargoes multiplied during the 1990s.

That the embargo hurt was never in question. Haiti's industrial production is almost nil, its agricultural yield is insufficient, and the island relies on imports for survival. A November 1993 Harvard University study, extrapolating from a case study in Maissade, revealed that 4,000 Haitian children were dying each month of malnutrition and disease, compared to a pre-embargo rate of 3,000. These 1,000 additional monthly deaths dwarfed the number of victims of the political repression, thus putting the legitimacy of the embargo in question and causing a significant uproar in the United States.[55]

The political effectiveness of the embargo, on the other hand, was dubious. In the age of surgical strikes, the embargo was the economic equivalent of carpet-bombing. The poor it was supposed to help suffered the most, while the junta enriched itself through contraband. Those of sufficient means could buy what they desired, a fact the U.S. Embassy, which bought contraband gasoline for its cars and electricity generators, knew all too well. An adviser to Cédras observed, "when things tightened, General Cédras remained untouched, the rich simply paid a little more for what they desired."[56] The United States waited until June 1993 to freeze the financial assets of supporters of the junta. Following the July 1993 Governors Island accords, the freeze was lifted from 27 August to 18 October 1993, which gave members of the junta enough time to repatriate assets out of the United States.[57]

The embargo also stimulated a mass exodus of boat people from Haiti, and, in the long run, ran the risk of ruining the reputation of Aristide, who was living a comfortable life in exile while asking for tighter sanctions against his own people. By early 1994, the failure of the embargo had become clear to members of Congress such as Chairman of the House Subcommittee on Foreign Affairs Robert G. Torricelli (D-NJ) who doubted that a regime willing to torture its political opponents would pay attention to its citizens' empty stomachs. "By definition, these military leaders do not care about the potential victims either of the coup or of the embargo."[58] By prolonging a situation in which the junta successfully continued to defy the United States, the embargo's obvious ineffectualness powerfully reinforced a growing perception of U.S. weakness in Haiti, leaving military force as the Clinton administration's only remaining option.

The Use of Force Became the Only Way to Restore Credibility

With the obvious failure of negotiations and economic sanctions by 1994, the National Security Council reevaluated the administration's policy options. Larry Rossin, a NSC staff member specializing on Haiti, told Lake in early March that negotiations would never work. Lake, after a series of conversations with Aristide and Deputy Secretary of State Strobe Talbott that month, came to the same conclusion. In early April, as Lake and Clinton's political adviser George Stephanopoulos were on their way to Cleveland for the inauguration of Jacobs Field, both agreed that a credible threat of force was necessary to secure Aristide's return. They defended their case at two White House meetings on 15 April and 7 May 1994. The military, most notably Chairman of the Joint Chiefs of Staff John M. Shalikashvili, voiced objections, and Clinton remained committed to sanctions only.[59]

Even though Clinton continued to agonize over the decision throughout the summer, it was clear that this internal debate had an impact on him. In late April 1994, after a formal White House interview, Clinton admitted to reporters that he was seriously reviewing his Haiti policy. With a candor uncommon in Washington, he confided, "we ought to change our policy. It hasn't worked. . . . We need to change our policy."[60] On 2 May, for the first time, Clinton refused to rule out the possible use of force. That same month, the U.S. Atlantic Command organized "Agile Provider," a joint maneuver involving 44,000 troops practicing the invasion of a "fictional" Caribbean island. Paratroopers multiplied exercises throughout July and August and the press started reporting that an invasion was in the plans. General John J. Sheehan, who was overseeing planning for the invasion, went to Haiti several times and told Cédras that "I have two sets of uniforms, my dress uniform and my combat one. You can make the choice which one I'm wearing the next time we meet."[61] The message to Cédras was clear: do what you are told, or you will be facing the full wrath of the U.S. armed forces.

The Haitian military was not impressed. While this saber rattling went on, demonstrators defied U.S. authorities in front of U.S. cameras, chanted slogans, and painted Voodoo signs on crosswalks to ward off an invasion. It was not until the very eve of the invasion, when Biamby received reports that planes were taking off from Fort Bragg, that the junta actually took the threat seriously. Newspaper articles mentioning that the junta intended to defend itself with hastily trained volunteers armed with wooden sticks and Voodoo spells, by playing into U.S. views of Haiti as a backward country, made it even harder for the administration to explain its inability to chase the junta out of power.

By September 1994, Clinton had been promising for more than two years that democracy would be restored to Haiti. Negotiations, economic sanctions, and threats had all failed, as had other attempts to bring peace to Bosnia and to end hunger in Somalia. The Clinton administration now had to live up to its word or lose its credibility. In his 15 September speech to the nation, Clinton talked of the need "to uphold the reliability of the commitments we make and the commitments others make to us. . . . the United States also has a strong interest in not letting dictators—especially in our own region—break their word to the United States and the United Nations."[62]

The media concurred. *Time Magazine* ran the banner "this time we mean business."[63] "Mr. Clinton," pointed out the *New York Times*, "left himself few options except to invade." Twelve days later, it wondered "whether the President's underlying motive was the preservation of his own credibility after threatening military action so often."[64] In the words of Chairman of the House Foreign Affairs Committee Lee Hamilton (D-IN), "do we mean what we say? If we don't mean what we say, our credibility suffers."[65]

"Haiti," Lake declared on 12 September, "will send a message far beyond our region—to all those who seriously threaten our interests."[66] This was an ironic moment for Lake. In 1970, when Richard Nixon secretly invaded Cambodia, saying that the United States could not afford to look like a "pitiful, helpless giant," Lake resigned from the NSC in protest. Twenty-four years later, he found himself advocating an invasion for the very same purpose.

By 1994, Haiti had become the symbol of Clinton's unsuccessful foreign policy record: overly cautious in its refusal to risk U.S. lives, ineffectual in its use of the embargo, occasionally shameful as during the *Harlan County* incident, his policy jeopardized the credibility of U.S. foreign policy in Latin America and elsewhere. Clinton upped the ante by threatening to use force, then, reluctantly, used force when the junta remained undeterred.

CHAPTER SIX

NATIONAL SECURITY

New Security Priorities

Clinton, the first post–Cold War president, came to office at a time when the Soviet Union was but the shadow of itself, the United States was the world's sole super-power, and inimical countries were too few and too weak to constitute a major threat to U.S. national security. Few presidents had inherited such a favorable environment, and Haiti was unlikely to upset this new imbalance of power.

Haiti's only strategic asset was its proximity to the United States and to the Windward Passage, which controls one of the main sea lanes to the Panama Canal, but Cédras' also air force and navy were too small to present any threat to U.S. shipping. The junta was a dagger pointed at the heart of its own people. Cédras did not threaten U.S. citizens in Haiti, and a Grenada-style invasion to "save" them would only have put them at greater risk.[1] In a post–Cold War world, there was no potential patron to change Haiti's strategic importance from nil to minor. The great political contortions to which Clinton submitted himself during the invasion to limit the number of U.S. casualties confirmed that the stakes were low. In earlier moments, when key U.S. interests had been imperiled, as during the Civil War and World War II, Americans had been willing to die by the hundreds of thousands. Just as French and British soldiers debated whether one should die for Danzig in 1939, Americans wondered whether it was wise to die for Aristide. Rather than Operation Restore Democracy, the 1994 intervention could have been labeled "Mission: Negligible."[2]

In February 1992, the Pentagon, the White House, and the National Security Council collaborated on a draft of the Defense Planning Guidance, a key policy paper presenting U.S. strategy for 1994–1999. Its main goal was "to prevent any hostile power from dominating a region whose resources would, under consolidated control, be sufficient to generate global power." Based on a realistic appraisal of America's interests reminiscent of George F. Kennan's 1946 Long Telegram, it gave Latin America a secondary role. Western Europe, Russia, the Middle East, and East Asia, not Latin America, formed the list of the vitally important regions that could not be allowed to fall into hostile hands.

On the other hand, Haiti could have fallen within the secondary goals delineated in subsequent paragraphs. "Sources of regional conflict and instability" were to be eliminated in order to facilitate "the spread of democratic forms of government and open economic systems." Narcotics trafficking was specifically mentioned as one of those "wrongs."[3] Bureaucratic politics also encouraged this shift away from traditional strategic concerns. New threats to U.S. internal security, such as immigration and drugs, justified the national security apparatus' continued existence as it emerged from the Cold War. In 1991, President Bush launched National Security Review 29, a review of the intelligence community's role in the post–Cold War world. The resulting fact sheet identified narcotics, along with terrorism, nuclear proliferation, economic intelligence, and technology transfer as the new security issues that assumed greater importance in the wake of the Soviet Union's demise.[4] Congress created its own commission, which reached similar conclusions, as did planners at the Office of Naval Intelligence and the U.S. Atlantic Command.[5]

Haiti, however minimal its importance on the world stage, thus presented two potential risks: (1) drug smuggling, and (2) instability close to U.S. borders, which could bring in a flood of immigrants. Despite the U.S. war on drugs and the juntas' connections with drug traffickers, drugs remained a side issue in 1991–1994. The administration, on the other hand, was very sensitive to immigration pressures, largely because its refugee policy could have adverse political repercussions.

Drugs

With the exception of British, French, and U.S. attempts to lower Chinese barriers against the opium trade in the 1830s, drugs did not become central to U.S. foreign policy until domestic drug use rose drastically during the Nixon administration, particularly among Vietnam War draftees. The "war on drugs" received renewed impetus under the leadership of First Lady Nancy Reagan. National Security Decision Directive 221 (8 April 1986) presented narcotics trafficking as a national threat.[6] The Anti-Drug Abuse Act of 1988 and the National Defense Authorization Act for 1989 asked the intelligence community and the Department of Defense to take part in the war. In 1992, the commander of the U.S. Southern Command described drug interdiction as his most important mission.[7]

In Peru and Colombia, traffickers funded rebel movements with the enormous profits generated by the drug trade, thus destabilizing existing governments. They also undermined the rule of law, prompting Bushs' Deputy Assistant Secretary of State for International Narcotics Matters, William Olson, to argue that traffickers attack "the very institutions that are necessary for democratic government."[8] The corollary, in the words of Clintons' Assistant Secretary for International Narcotics Matters, Robert S. Gelbard, was that spreading democracy was an effective anti-drug strategy, as democratic governments "do not succumb to the corrosive influence of narco-corruption and intimidation."[9] Drugs were also blamed for every domestic social evil, including crime, broken families, and AIDS. Fighting drugs was the kind of popular issue that every presidential candidate found essential to emphasize.

George H.W. Bush, named head of the anti-drug South Florida Task Force in 1982, pledged once he became president to escalate the war on drugs, invading Panama in 1989 with the avowed goal of capturing drug trafficker Manuel Noriega. The invasion, aside from making Bush appear strong and resolute, silenced critics who blamed him for hiring drug warlords during his tenure as CIA director.[10]

Bill Clinton had a more personal relation to addictive substances. Even though Clinton asserted that no smoke ever reached his lungs, both he and Al Gore had tried marijuana. His half-brother Roger Clinton Jr. peddled cocaine and served a year in prison for that offense.[11] His half-sister Dianne Dwire Welch was arrested in 1986 as she attempted to sell 50 pounds of marijuana and was sentenced to 45 years in prison (she was freed after 6 years). Paradoxically, Clinton's lack of credibility on the drug issue may have forced him to be even more active in order to make a new reputation for himself. On 9 February 1994, Clinton announced his "new" drug control strategy, which, as previous ones, emphasized prevention and punishment at home and eradication abroad. Clinton could count on Attorney General Janet Reno's help. As assistant state attorney of Dade County, Florida (1979–1987), then state attorney (1987–1993), she recommended increased federal involvement to reduce the number of crimes connected to drug trafficking.[12]

The Drug Situation in Haiti, Though Disquieting, did not Prompt Concerns

Haiti, a headquarters for pirates during the buccaneer era, is located halfway between Colombia and Florida, making it an ideal transit area where planes and boats can stop and refuel before hopping to Florida. Michèle Duvalier and her family allegedly dabbled in cocaine trafficking. Her brother Franz was arrested in San Juan in March 1982 for planning to smuggle drugs and was sentenced to four years in prison.[13] Stewardesses on her father's airline, Haiti Air, smuggled cocaine.[14] Following Duvalier's fall, the Haitian Army became deeply involved in the drug traffic, as Prosper Avril, army officer and dictator (1988–1990), now admits.[15] In 1989, the U.S. Senate, frustrated by Haitian authorities' refusal to extradite Colonel Jean-Claude Paul, commander of the Dessalines Barracks and middleman, concluded that "there is little hope that serious inroads can be made into the Colombian narcotics trafficking through Haiti until legitimate democratization efforts are undertaken."[16]

During his presidency, Aristide prosecuted drug dealers, accusing Duvalierists of securing through the drug trade funds that were later used to undermine him politically.[17] Once in exile, he repeatedly tried to portray the junta members as drug-dealing thugs, accusing them in a UN speech of making a $200 million profit off the $1.2 billion worth of drugs transiting through Haiti each year.[18] Patrick Elie, a friend of Aristide, remembers telling the CIA station chief in Port-au-Prince, as well as officials in Washington, that junta member Michel François was a drug trafficker.[19]

In April 1994, Sen. John F. Kerry (D-MA) organized a Senate subcommittee hearing starring Gabriel Taboada as the main witness. Taboada, a favorite of federal courts for his willingness to finger former associates (including Noriega), was a former Colombian car and cocaine dealer associated with the Medellin Cartel. Comparing Haiti to a "bridge" between Colombia and Florida, Taboada claimed that in 1984 he met Michel François, a future member of the triumvirate that overthrew Aristide, in Pablo Escobar's office in Medellin.[20]

Strangely, the administration did not pursue the Haitian drug issue. Annual reports of the House Select Committee on Narcotics Abuse and Control rarely mentioned Haiti until 1995. The 1993 International Narcotics Control Strategy

Report on Haiti, released in April 1994 as the administration was reexamining its Haiti policy, admitted having "no evidence directly linking senior GOH [Government of Haiti] officials to drug trafficking, though rumors and (unsubstantiated) allegations abound. . . . The *de facto* government maintains the same anti-drug policies and bureaucratic mechanisms as the Aristide government."[21] A month later, when he was asked whether there was a drug problem in Haiti, all State Department Spokesman Michael McCurry could remember was that he had a ready-made answer for this question, but could not find it nor recall what it said. "As a question of drug trafficking, it was not as urgent as other cases that we looked at in the region. . . . We'll fish it out and get it to you."[22] He never did. Paradoxically, the 1991 International Narcotics Control Strategy Report on the Aristide presidency was harsher.

> While it has not been GOH policy to encourage or facilitate the production or distribution of illicit narcotic or psychotropic drugs or other controlled substances, we have frequently received reports of the involvement of government and military personnel in narcotics trafficking. There were even media allegations during the brief Aristide regime of the President's link to a notorious Haitian drug trafficker.[23]

The Clinton administration's refusal to attack the junta as a haven for drug traffickers was most puzzling. An in-depth investigation would probably have uncovered that several high-ranking Haitian Army officers had been, or still were, implicated in drug trafficking, thus providing a popular rationale for invading Haiti, but Clinton failed to make the connection in public. It was only three years *after* the invasion that Michel François was indicted in Miami for helping to smuggle 33 metric tons of Colombian cocaine and heroin from 1987 to 1994.[24] Immigration, on the other hand, did not go unnoticed. Continued political repression in Haiti, along with the country's worsening economic situation, encouraged Haitians to flee to the United States, where the political problems their arrival provoked contributed to Clinton's decision to invade Haiti.

Haitian Immigration

The people of Haiti have long been what a 1991 World Bank document described as Haiti's "one abundant resource."[25] French settlers, Henri Christophe, and the Marines during the first U.S. occupation, imposed slavery, *fermage*, and the *corvée* (forced labor). When Dominican strongman Rafael Trujillo massacred an estimated 25,000 Haitian immigrants in 1937, Haitian President Sténio Vincent agreed to settle the matter for $30 a head (the price of a good pig). Vincent later lowered the indemnity to $535,000 cash, which he and his friends divided among themselves.[26] The Duvalier regime streamlined this cynical trade, exacting a fee for every Haitian laborer sent to the Dominican Republic. Still today, poor farmers frequently sell some of their children to wealthier Port-au-Prince families, where these household slaves are known as *restaveks*. During the 1970s, sexual tourism flourished, while Luckner Cambronne, one of Papa Doc's associates and the head of Hemocaribian, sold Haitian blood, plasma, and cadavers to U.S. hospitals and medical schools, which earned him the nickname of "vampire of the Caribbean."[27]

Because of the AIDS epidemic, however, not even the Haitians' own bodies are deemed valuable anymore, so emigration has become the only potential source of income. The Duvalier dictatorships triggered the first large waves of Haitian immigration to the United States. Until the late 1970s, the educated middle class, fleeing political repression, formed a large part of the Diaspora. As the economic situation deteriorated in the 1970s, the poor felt the urge to leave as well. In a famous incident, 116 Haitians fled their country by boat in September 1980. The boat barely managed to make it to the deserted Bahamian island of Cayo Lobos where those still alive survived off sea shells, rain drops, and roots of scrub. One refugee swam away, was rescued by a fishing boat, and sent back to Haiti, where Haitians learned about their compatriots' plight. After the Duvalier government refused to rescue them, the Bahamians captured the 102 desperate Haitian survivors, clinging to every rock in order not to leave, and sent them back home.[28] Many such boat people drowned in the dangerous sea crossing, and the few that made it to the United States were often sent back under a 1981 U.S.–Haitian agreement allowing the Coast Guard to stop and return economic refugees found in international waters off Haiti (Proclamation 4865 and Executive Order 12324, 29 September 1981).[29] Despite the risks, the Haitian community in the United States is now a million strong.

Immigration pressures increased after the 1991 coup. An estimated 50,000 to 150,000 Haitians tried to leave the country for the Dominican Republic, the Bahamas, France, Canada, and the United States. An additional 300,000 Haitians were in internal exile.[30] Aristide emphasized that his return would solve the problem. "Before I became president, we know how many Haitians were leaving the country fleeing repression. Once I became president, we know how the Haitians were staying in Haiti."[31]

The U.S. reaction to immigration was shaped by its historical experience. This nation of immigrants, whose first colony in the northeast was founded by a boatload of 102 refugees as hungry, seasick, and desperate as the Cayo Lobos Haitians were, has traditionally welcomed new arrivals, while complaining that they depress wages, particularly during uncertain economic times such as the early 1990s, and that they upset the ethnic make-up of the nation. Haitians suffered from the racial prejudices that the Irish, the Italians, and the Jews once suffered from. They were seen as poor, illiterate, Creole-speaking, AIDS-ridden, Voodoo-worshipping Blacks with none of the anti-Communist affiliation that helped Vietnamese, Cuban, and Eastern European immigrants gain acceptance.

After the 1991 coup, Bush tried to prevent boat people from reaching the U.S. mainland, where they could have benefited from legal assistance. Refugees were instead screened in Guantánamo, Cuba. As this still allowed too many Haitians in, Bush instituted in-country processing in February 1992. Haitians had to apply for political asylum at the U.S. Embassy in Port-au-Prince, a particularly dangerous move considering the political situation in 1991–1994.[32] In direct violation of international law, refugees caught on the high seas were returned to Haiti whether they qualified for political asylum or not (Executive Order 12807, 24 May 1992).

"No part of the American story," Clinton and Gore wrote in a 1992 campaign pamphlet, "is more important to preserve than our rich and proud tradition of responding to the yearnings in all people for personal freedom, political rights, and economic opportunity."[33] Yet, once elected, the Clinton administration launched a general crackdown on illegal immigration. "The simple fact" Clinton announced in July 1993, is "that we must not—and will not—surrender our borders to those who wish to exploit our history of compassion and justice."[34] Clinton reinforced border patrols along the Mexican border, which was lined with thousands of miles of fences.

Clinton's Haitian refugee policy was equally contradictory. After promising to put an end to the forced repatriation of Haitian refugees during the 1992 campaign, Clinton claimed once elected that people had only understood "half the message" and announced that the United States would keep sending Haitians back to their country.[35] Robert Pastor, who, along with future National Security Adviser Anthony Lake, drafted the 1992 campaign statement criticizing Bush's immigration policy, was meeting with Aristide when Clinton called to announce that the forced repatriation of Haitian refugees would continue as before. To convince Aristide to endorse his decision, Clinton reportedly promised that he would eventually restore Aristide to power.[36] On inauguration day, one boat left Haiti, was promptly seized by the U.S. Coast Guard, and its 163 passengers sent back to Haiti.[37]

The fear of a Haitian exodus shaped U.S. policies in Haiti. In an effort to limit the economic incentive to leave Haiti, the economic embargo excluded basic food staples and cooking oil. Revealingly, the U.S.-sponsored July 1993 accord between Cédras and Aristide was signed on Governors Island, a Coast Guard base of operations in New York City. Lower courts denounced the forced repatriation of Haitian refugees as contrary to § 243 (h) of the Immigration and Nationality Act and article 33 of the United Nations Refugee Convention, but the Supreme Court upheld the administration's right to automatically turn away refugees seized at sea.[38] Admiral Paul D. Miller, who helped plan the 1994 invasion, saw "nine million Haitians off our shores—and they *all* want to be your neighbors."[39] Transcripts of a closed October 1993 congressional hearing show that the fear of immigration was as potent with the legislative branch of government as it was with the military and the executive and judicial branches.

> Senator Carl Levin (D-Mi): The only way to stem [immigration] is if somehow or other there is a democratic government in Haiti. . . . We can return them a lot more easily without facing the claims of asylum.
>
> Undersecretary of Defense Walter B. Slocombe: That is absolutely our most direct and concrete interest. . . .
>
> Senator John W. Warner (R-VA.): Walt, why are we not up front? [Immigration] is the only argumentation that I can use back in my State, I guarantee you. . . .
>
> Levin: For God's sake, put the practical and the pragmatic first. The public can understand. We had a flow of refugees, and they are still trying to get here, even though fewer. The court orders us even to take them if they have AIDS, in some cases. And people can understand. We have to stop this flow and be able to return them.[40]

A Racist Policy?

It would be unjust to accuse Clinton administration officials of being racist. Clinton spent the first years of his life in an African American district, grew up in a poor single-parent household, played the saxophone, loved to gorge on soul food, and had so much in common with many black Americans that Toni Morrison once described him as the first black president (Clinton relished the comparison).[41] Warren Christopher defended African Americans during his career as lawyer and politician.[42] Nonetheless, one cannot help but compare the Haitians' fate with that of lighter-skinned Cuban boat people. The former were sent back without even the benefit of a hearing, while the latter were welcomed as anti-Communist heroes (Cubans also benefited from the strength of the Cuban–American lobby). Haitians suffered from similar discrimination in France, Canada, and neighboring Caribbean countries.

Testimonies from translators working in Guantánamo show that there was a conscious effort to limit the number of Haitians entering the country, however justified their claim for political asylum might be. One such translator complained that interviews of applicants were short and biased. "The adjudicators would say 'you are the ones giving Haiti a bad reputation—cut out that political crap.'" Refugees suffered from bad treatment, including food deprivation. U.S. military personnel reportedly told one Haitian: "the dog in my house is better than you are."[43] Cultural differences also undermined the process. INS officers and U.S. soldiers routinely asked Haitians if they were involved in politics. This was essential in trying to determine whether they could claim political asylum, but Haitians came from a country where it was dangerous to reveal one's political preferences, especially to uniformed personnel.[44]

Whether the junta's rule was repressive or not became the central issue. If it was not, Haitians were economic, not political, refugees and could be sent back. If it was, the low approval rate reflected a racist, illegal bias against Haitians. This placed the administration in a strange position. On the one hand, it denounced the Cédras regime as autocratic and worked to reinstate Aristide as democratic president of Haiti. On the other hand, it minimized the extent of the repression to give less credence to asylum claims and purported that Haitians only suffered from economic woes—which the U.S.-sponsored embargo made much worse.

The dilemma fed a stream of administration assessments of the political situation in Haiti that directly contradicted the official accusation that the junta was a savage dictatorship. In 1992, a team from the Immigration and Naturalization Service visited Haiti to investigate the fate of refugees it had forcibly sent back. "The monitoring efforts of repatriates have not produced a single victim of abuse of any kind," the report concluded. "The team was repeatedly told [by army officials] that neither the military nor the police is the least bit interested in the returning citizens and they had nothing to fear."[45] A 1993 State Department report argued that there were widespread human rights violations, but that the junta did not target refugees. "Repatriated Haitian boat people do face, of course, the same harsh conditions and lawlessness facing Haitians in general."[46] A 1994 cable from the U.S. embassy in Port-au-Prince attributed abuses to the "high level of structural, or endemic, violence in Haiti" and saw economic conditions as the primary cause of emigration.[47] Blanket repression of slums, where Aristide supporters lived, made it difficult for candidates to prove that they were individually targeted.

Immigration advocates denounced such assessments. The American Immigration Lawyers Association, based on its own inspection tour, saw Aristide's ousting, not economic conditions, as the main reason why Haitians left the country.[48] Ira Kurzban, legal counsel for the Haitian Refugee Center in Miami, argued that there was a real threat of danger for refugees who were sent back, as did William O'Neill of the Lawyers Committee for Human Rights.[49] The junta's puppet-president, Emile Jonassaint, announced in July 1994 that refugees trying to flee Haiti would face punishment under a 1980 decree banning clandestine emigration.[50]

Arguing that the junta persecuted everyone but those who fled was a position difficult to sustain for the administration. As months passed, the congressional Black Caucus, whose support was essential for the success of Clinton's legislative agenda, became more vocal in its denunciation of the U.S. immigration policy. Rep. Charles Rangel (D-NY) complained that Haitians were not treated "with the same caliber of humane treatment as we treat European and other refugees," then made his criticism more blunt: "Now, what makes Haiti so different? Is it the color?"[51] Sen. Tom Harkin (D-IA) concurred. "Now, I do not want to accuse anyone of racism or anything else . . . but what if 5,000 Cubans got in a boat and came to Miami? Would we pick them up and send them back to Cuba? Absolutely not."[52] In November 1993, Rep. Carrie P. Meek (D-FL) introduced H.R. 3663 to put an end to the forced repatriation of Haitian refugees, and, on 12 April, TransAfrica's Randall Robinson, joined temporarily by director Jonathan Demme and actor Danny Glover, started a well-publicized hunger strike to protest the repatriation of refugees.[53]

Aristide was equally vocal. On 6 April 1994, he announced his intention to withdraw Haiti from the 1981 treaty allowing the United States to apprehend Haitian boat people, then attacked U.S. policy as "a racist policy."[54] The treaty specified that it would cease to take effect six months after a party denounced it. Aristide's move thus put pressure on Clinton to solve the Haitian crisis before early October 1994.[55] The issue of Haitian immigration was beginning to gain the public's eye.

Shifting Policies on Immigration

The first sign of a shift in U.S. immigration policy occurred in June 1993, when a Brooklyn judge ordered a Guantánamo camp for AIDS victims closed and its occupants sent to the United States. The administration did not appeal the decision. In December, Assistant Secretary of State for Human Rights John Shattuck said that the immigration policy needed review, which prompted a strongly worded State Department denial.

Nine days into Randall Robinson's hunger strike, four hundred Haitian refugees were let into the United States. After negotiating with Robinson, the administration announced on 8 May that refugees would be processed in Haiti, at sea, or in detention centers outside the United States. Rates of acceptance rose, as did the number of Haitians taking to the sea, putting pressure on the administration at the very moment Cuban *líder máximo* Fidel Castro unleashed his own stream of refugees. Reversing himself one last time, Clinton announced on 5 July that all Haitian boat people would be repatriated, even if they were victims of political oppression. Over the summer of 1994, Panama agreed to host 10,000 Haitian refugees on a Panamanian island, but negotiations foundered when U.S. officials proposed to use a U.S. military base in Panama instead; other countries, when contacted by the U.S. government, declined to let Haitians in.[56]

Clinton's constant waffling on immigration issues reflected the dilemma he faced. Allowing eight million Haitians to enter the United States was tantamount to political suicide. Refusing to grant political asylum to boat people fleeing a dictatorship targeted him for criticisms that his policy was racist and illegal. He was under heavy pressure to allow Haitians in, only to move back when the more lenient policy sent thousands of Haitians to the shores of Florida. Only the restoration of Aristide, which would make it easier to prove that asylum-seekers were economic refugees, could cut the Gordian knot. "Thousands of Haitians have already fled toward the United States," explained Clinton in his 15 September 1994 speech. "As long as Cédras rules, Haitians will continue to seek sanctuary in our nation. . . . Three hundred thousand more Haitians, 5 percent of their entire population, live in hiding in their own country. If we don't act, they could be the next wave of refugees at our door."[57]

Immigration was Mostly a Political, not Security, Concern

From a purely strategic point of view, there was no immigration problem, as the Coast Guard cutters surrounding Haiti were very effective in preventing Haitians from leaving their country. In 1994, the United States admitted only 664 Haitian refugees. The estimated increase in the illegal Haitian population in the United States from 1992 to 1996 was 17,000, a mere fraction of the 1.6 million increase in the overall illegal population during the same time period. Had he decided to invade one country to stop immigration, Clinton would have been better off sending a Pershing-type expeditionary force across the Rio Grande. In 1994 alone, legal immigration from Mexico topped 110,000. In addition, an estimated 2.7 million illegal Mexicans immigrants lived in the United States in 1996. By that standard, Canada, with 97,000 illegal immigrants in 1996, was another good candidate for a U.S. invasion [appendix III].

One could also have questioned whether an invasion would relieve immigration pressures. The administration assumed that the refugee problem was political, not economic, and that illegal immigration would stop should Aristide be restored to power. The large flow of immigrants from countries more democratic than Cédras' No Haiti, such as Mexico and Jamaica, suggested otherwise. Haitians, who would have been better off crossing the land border to the Dominican Republic had they been only motivated by an urge for greater freedom, were in search of economic opportunities Aristide could not offer.

The political dimension of a refugee crisis, on the other hand, was something Clinton was keenly aware of from his experience as Governor of Arkansas. In 1980, when 125,000 Cubans fled their homeland during the Mariel boatlift, 18,000 of them were sent to Arkansas. On 26 May, and again on the 31 May, hundreds of Cuban refugees escaped from Fort Chaffee (federal troops guarding the Cubans did nothing to stop them, but the state police managed to round them up). Despite a solemn promise to the contrary, the Carter administration sent additional refugees from Wisconsin, Pennsylvania, and Florida to Fort Chaffee in August. Clinton's reaction, as reported by a travel aide, was straightforward:

> You're fucking me! How could you do this to me? I busted my ass for Carter. You guys are gonna get me beat. I've done everything I could for you guys. This is ridiculous! Carter's too chickenshit about it to tell me directly![58]

In the Democratic gubernatorial primary, held one day after the first Cuban riot, turkey farmer and political laughing stock Monroe Schwarzlose earned 31 percent of the vote. On Election Day, both Clinton and Carter lost their seats. Clinton blamed his defeat, the second of only two defeats in his political career, on the Mariel boatlift.[59] In the summer of 1994, most administration officials attending Whitewater hearings seemed to have forgotten everything about their past, but as former staffers in the Carter White House and the Clinton Governor's Mansion, they kept in mind that their boss had lost an election in part because of Caribbean boat people.

The administration's refugee policy was not politically sustainable over the long run. It received criticism from international organizations that pointed out its illegality. The Black Caucus denounced it as racist. Still, polls showed that 73 percent of Americans thought that Haitians picked up by the Coast Guard should be sent back to their country.[60] Constantly shifting between his pledges that he would accept political refugees and his decisions to the contrary, Clinton looked indecisive. "The use of force," says Richard Feinberg, the Latin American specialist in the National Security Council, was "the only way to get out of a box. Clinton was trapped. Politically, he could not send the immigrants back, and he could not accept them either."[61] To debate the weight of such political factors requires us to leave the shores of sunny Florida and to direct our search to the foggy bottoms of the Potomac River.

CHAPTER SEVEN
DOMESTIC POLITICS

A U.S. president's use of foreign policy to achieve gains in the domestic political arena is generally regarded as reprehensible in the United States, where Sen. Arthur Vandenberg's dictum that "politics stop at the water's edge" has long been regarded as a fundamental underpinning of the U.S. political system. Using taxpayers' money as pork, gerrymandering districts, and drafting laws to help wealthy campaign contributors are patterns of behavior acceptable in the District of Columbia. But manipulating U.S. foreign policy, launching wars, and risking soldiers' lives to further a president's political interests are considered inappropriate behavior for occupants of the White House.

Critics often accused Clinton, whom they saw as a poll-driven politician's politician lacking core principles, of committing that very offense. In their view, the invasion of Haiti was a way to direct attention away from domestic scandals. In similar fashion, they later noticed that Clinton launched missile attacks against Afghanistan and the Sudan on 20 August 1998, three days after apologizing on national television for misleading the public about his relationship with Monica Lewinsky, and against Baghdad on 16 December 1998, three days before the House voted on articles of impeachment. That year, audiences thronged to see *Wag the Dog*, a movie portraying a president's decision to invade Albania in order to revive sagging polls (one year later, Clinton intervened in Kosovo).

Clinton was indeed a political genius who managed to survive through eight years of scandals and conservative ascendancy, and who, assisted by a plethora of political advisers, polled with abandon. But reducing the 1994 intervention to a mere gimmick dictated by polls would be a gross oversimplification of the truth. Such polls showed that Haiti was low on most Americans' agendas. Congressmen and the press were equally uninterested in Haiti.

Domestic political influences played a more indirect, two-pronged role.[1] When he entered the White House, Clinton had two major goals. The first was creating a public health care system, a feat so great—even Franklin D. Roosevelt, Harry S. Truman, and Lyndon B. Johnson fell short of it—that it would surely constitute the cornerstone of his legislative legacy. Second, Clinton hoped to become the first Democratic president since Roosevelt to complete two full terms. By 1994, both goals seemed compromised. The votes needed to pass his health care plan in Congress were in short supply. In addition, accusations that Clinton was an unfaithful, waffling president unable to follow a forceful course in Somalia, Bosnia, and Haiti had made major dents in his approval ratings, threatening his chances for reelection to a second term in 1996.

Invading Haiti could help solve both problems. First, small but active political lobbies such as the congressional Black Caucus and Representatives from New York, New Jersey, and Florida—states whose votes were crucial in Congress—urged Clinton to fulfill his 1992 campaign promise that he would treat Haitian refugees fairly and try to restore Aristide to power. Second, presidential advisers thought that intervening abroad would answer widespread concerns that Clinton lacked presidential character and that an invasion of Haiti was likely to be easy, short, and successful.

Many Americans were Quietly Opposed to an Intervention

President Clinton was elected on an America-first platform. Uninspired by Bush's attempts to create a new world order and concerned by an economic recession, the American people chose a president who pledged to serve their, not other peoples', interests. Accordingly, public interest in Haitian democracy was low. In August 1994, one month before the U.S. intervened, no more than *one* percent of Americans ranked Haiti as the most important problem facing their country, behind crime (30 percent), health care (21 percent), and the economy (13 percent). In previous polls, interest in Haiti was too low to be recorded. A few days after the invasion, only 20 percent of Americans had a favorable impression of Aristide.[2]

TV coverage of U.S. foreign affairs, which first burst into the national scene during the Vietnam War, became paramount during the age of the 24-hour news cycle. Round-the-clock TV coverage of starving Somalis and of a dead U.S. Ranger dragged through the streets of Mogadishu played a key role in getting the United States in, and then out, of Somalia. A January 2000 interagency report on the effectiveness of U.S. humanitarian policies in the 1990s started with the following summary:

> Because of intensified media coverage and accelerated communications directly from inside crisis zones, the harsh realities of mass suffering are now transmitted swiftly into multiple channels—and America's living rooms. As seen during Haiti, Mitch, Kosovo and the Turkish and Taiwanese earthquakes, these visual images can stimulate intense domestic pressure to do more, better, and more quickly.[3]

But coverage of the Haitian crisis did not dominate the news until the invasion itself. Images of dead Haitians washing on the shores of Florida competed with the Rwandan genocide, the war in Bosnia, the American withdrawal from Somalia, the deaths of Richard M. Nixon and Jackie Kennedy, the O.J. Simpson trial, the Paula Jones lawsuit, the Whitewater scandal, the baseball strike, the Lillehammer Winter Olympics, and the 1994 midterm elections.

Nor was the press calling for an invasion. After the *Harlan County* debacle, *Time* wondered aloud: "Is Haiti Worth It?" and answered in the negative.[4] *U.S. News and World Report* waited until May 1994 to publish its first story on Haiti.[5] Haiti did not make the cover of *Newsweek* until 19 September 1994, when a banner in the top-right corner asked "Haiti: is this invasion necessary?" The *National Review* labeled Aristide a "Marxist President," not a flattering epithet in this conservative weekly, and concluded that Haiti was not ready for democracy anyway.[6] Progressive magazines were more sympathetic, but hesitated to advocate U.S. intervention in the Caribbean.[7]

Chairman of the Senate Foreign Relations Committee Jesse Helms described Haiti's President as "a psychopath."[8] Other Capitol Republicans agreed.[9] A majority of congressmen, though less outspoken, had mixed views of Aristide and thought that Haiti was not worth invading. Yet, precisely because Haiti did not matter to them, they paid little attention to the crisis as it unfolded. Because of a two-week summer recess lasting until 12 September 1994, Congress remained largely silent as the Haiti crisis reached its climax. Since Clinton was himself enjoying a 13-day vacation in Martha's Vineyard, Congress deluded itself into thinking that Haiti was not a pressing issue. Then, ten days before the invasion, the administration advocated an invasion with renewed stridency. The ten-day military countdown to the invasion, launched on 10 September, was shortened by a day around 15 September. The first troops were thus scheduled to land on Sunday night, one day before congressmen could express formal opposition.[10]

When it suddenly became clear that an invasion was under way, many congressmen at last made their reservations about an intervention public. Democrats, afraid that an unpopular intervention would harm the party and their reelection prospects, called the White House to express concern.[11] The Senate Committee on Armed Services, filled with members from the South and the Midwest (traditional bedrocks of isolationism and conservatism), hastily scheduled its first hearing on Haiti on 28 September. Republican Representatives, most of whom had never spoken about Haiti before, came out to oppose H.J. Res. 416, which provided after-the-fact support for the invasion.[12] But this sudden flurry of activity, coming after months of silent indifference, took place as U.S. troops were already on their way to Haiti, and was thus much less influential than the views expressed repeatedly over the previous two years by some of Clinton's most essential allies, particularly representatives from Florida and the New York area and members of the Black Caucus.

Political Lobbies Supporting Aristide were Few but Vocal

Aristide started his 1990 presidential campaign in the United States, where he also raised a good share of the funds needed for his presidential bid. The loyalty and political weight of the Haitian Diaspora, which he called Haiti's "Tenth Department," remained unquestioned during his years of exile.[13] Haitian Americans had stepped into the political arena for the first time in April 1990, when more than 50,000 of them marched in New York to protest a ruling from the Food and Drug Administration preventing them from donating blood (the FDA rescinded its order). Two weeks after the 1991 coup that ousted him, over 60,000 Haitians demonstrated in support of Aristide in lower Manhattan. Mass demonstrations, also in New York, followed on 26 April and 30 September 1992. The July 1993 negotiations took place on Governors' Island, not in Manhattan, for fear that Aristide's supporters might disrupt the talks.[14] As most Haitian Americans lived in New York, Boston, and Miami, congressmen representing these districts, particularly if they belonged to the congressional Black Caucus, paid great attention to Haitian issues.

These congressmen constituted a large portion of Clinton's slim congressional majority. With only 259 Democrats in the House of Representatives (out of 435 Representatives) and 57 Democrats in the Senate (out of 100 Senators), Clinton could not pass his legislative agenda, including the health-care plan that he hoped would secure his role in history, if representatives from Haitian American districts and members of the Black Caucus abandoned him.[15] Health care first burst into the political landscape in November 1991, when Democratic candidate Harris Wofford won a surprising Senatorial victory by running on health care issues.[16] With ballooning health-care costs, expected to top $1 trillion by 1994 (or 15 percent of the U.S. GDP, the most of any industrialized country), Americans faced rapidly rising insurance premiums, or, for the uninsured, the threat of personal bankruptcy in case of a medical emergency.[17] "I've had more people talk to me about their health care problems, I guess, than anything else," declared Clinton during the second presidential debate of the 1992 campaign. "It's a big human problem and a devastating economic problem for America. And I'm going to send a plan to do this within the first hundred days of my Presidency."[18]

Within five days of being inaugurated, Clinton picked his own wife to head his health-care reform panel; the following fall, he introduced a 1,342-page behemoth bill in Congress. Neither the House nor the Senate ever voted on a health-care bill, which makes it difficult to estimate how many votes were needed for such a bill to pass, but as early as September 1993, with a barrage of "Harry and Louise" advertisements sponsored by the Health Insurance Association of America and the dogged opposition of the Republican leadership, it was clear that securing every vote in Clinton's thin majority was a necessity. A pro-Aristide Haiti policy, which New Yorkers, Floridians, and the congressional Black Caucus insisted on, could help achieve that goal.

The "New York–Florida" lobby was most influential in the House Committee on Foreign Affairs, where 15 out of 45 members came from New Jersey, New York, and Florida.[19] Rep. Robert J. Torricelli (D-NJ) chaired the subcommittee on the Western Hemisphere, in which half of the members came from New Jersey and Florida.[20] Other Floridians, though not officially members, attended subcommittee hearings, including Rep. John L. Mica, a Florida Republican who stopped by to complain that "yesterday we had two Haitian children and adults wash up on the shores of our state."[21] So regionally unbalanced were hearings on Haiti that one New Jersey representative noted "let me answer my good friend from New Jersey, we are New Jerseyans here and Floridians it seems, it is interesting."[22] The committee and its subcommittee held no fewer than 15 hearings in the 15 months prior to the invasion.[23] Rep. Joseph P. Kennedy III (D-MA) was another influential supporter of Aristide.

Floridians, who hosted a large Haitian community and manned the frontline in the immigration and drug wars, had a strong vested interest in seeing Aristide returned to power in Haiti.[24] In a letter to the Florida legislature presenting his report *The Unfair Burden: Immigration's Impact on Florida* (1994), Democratic Governor Lawton Chiles complained about the "staggering costs that Florida citizens must pay as a direct result of federal immigration policy." He announced that he would lobby Washington officials and sue the federal government for the cost of taking care of illegal immigrants, which he estimated at $2.5 billion in 1993. Haitians represented 17 percent of the undocumented alien population in Florida.[25] Attorney General Janet Reno, herself a Floridian, needed little background information to handle this legal challenge. In the 103rd Congress, Florida's already large political clout increased as the size of its congressional delegation, reflecting the state's rapidly growing population, increased from 19 to 23.[26]

The balance of power in the Senate was less skewed toward pro-Aristide forces. Aristide could count on Christopher J. Dodd (D-CN), a former Peace Corps volunteer in the Dominican Republic. As Chairman of the Senate Foreign Relations Committee's Subcommittee on Western Hemisphere and Peace Corps Affairs, Dodd was able to front-load hearings with pro-Aristide witnesses.[27] But Jesse Helms proved an equally dedicated adversary.

Members of the congressional Black Caucus were probably Aristide's most helpful political allies. Clinton could ill afford to ignore the Black Caucus' concerns. African American voters proved essential in Clinton's gubernatorial and presidential victories. In the 103rd Congress, the Black Caucus' membership rose from 26 to 40, the largest increase since Reconstruction.[28] Clinton thus cultivated African Americans' friendship, attended every single congressional Black Caucus dinner, the first U.S. president to do so, and regularly invited African American leaders to the White House to discuss a variety of issues, including Haiti (the day before Clinton announced his intention to invade Haiti, he called NAACP president Kweisi Mfume to ask for his advice).[29] He appointed an African American, William Gray III, as U.S. special envoy to Haiti, and asked another, Colin Powell, to join the Carter team sent to Port-au-Prince to negotiate Aristide's return. "African-Americans were impressed with that uncanny, unparalleled access many of our people had to the president," remembers Rev. Jesse Jackson.[30]

The Black Caucus' rationale for pressuring the administration on Haitian issues had much to do with their political, racial, and personal bonds with the Haitian government-in-exile. Some Representatives, such as Major R. Owens, the chair of the Caucus' Haiti task force and the Representative of New York's 11th district, had large Haitian American constituencies. Many black congressmen felt that, as fellow Blacks and former slaves, Haitians and African Americans had much in common (contrary to Aristide, Cédras was a light-skinned *mulâtre*). In the words of Rep. John Conyers (D-MI), "there are a lot of African-Americans that consider that except for where that boat landed coming from Africa, they might be Haitians themselves."[31] The Aristide camp cultivated personal relationships with members of the Black Caucus.[32] Christophe Wargny, who accompanied Aristide in exile, noted that Aristide

> lost no occasion to express his friendship, to make himself heard, to mention this instinctive communion that linked him, to his people, to American Blacks, to remind that he was, in Washington, the exiled friend.[33]

In their dealings with the administration, members of the Black Caucus advocated policies very similar to those Aristide was calling for himself. They complained that, contrary to Clinton's 1992 campaign promises, the U.S. Coast Guard turned most Haitians away, often without even the benefit of a hearing. They also insisted that Aristide be restored to power, which, when it became clear that a stricter economic embargo would not be sufficient, meant a U.S. military intervention. The Black Caucus's Haiti task force adopted its first resolution asking for an invasion of Haiti on 20 October 1993; some members were already calling for an intervention a year earlier.[34]

Given the American public's general lack of interest in Haitian affairs, convincing the administration to embrace the Black Caucus' cause required an active lobbying campaign on its part. A bare nine days after his inauguration, Clinton received his first letter in favor of Aristide, signed by 44 congressmen, many of them members of the Black Caucus, who reminded him that they were "representatives of key constituencies."[35] Members of the Black Caucus spoke on Aristide's behalf in Congress, appeared on television, and organized fundraisers; they also attended the January 1994 Miami Conference, which Aristide and his supporters organized to publicize their request that the junta be ousted, if necessary by an intervention. On 21 April 1994, six Democratic members of Congress were arrested after staging a short sit-in in front of the White House to protest the repatriation of Haitian asylum-seekers.[36] The demonstration took place as TransAfrica's Executive Director Randall Robinson pursued a 27-day hunger strike for the same reason.[37]

A few days later, Clinton confided to reporters that Robinson was right and that he needed to change his refugee policy.[38] The relaxation of immigration restrictions proved temporary, but the Black Caucus nevertheless scored an important point. Clinton asked U.S. special envoy to Haiti Lawrence Pezzullo, an Italian American unwilling to use force, to step down and replaced him with William Gray III, the president of the United Negro Fund, who advocated a harder line against the junta. The dinner Clinton held in honor of the Black Caucus two days before the invasion was a mere coincidence, but it was also a good reminder of the role the Caucus played in pushing Clinton to intervene. According to Rep. Major Owens (D-NY), Haiti would have been a secondary priority for the Clinton administration

if we had not pressed. I think that in the final analysis, the fact that [Clinton] wanted a positive relationship with us made him look at the situation very seriously, and made him move in a forceful way, more rapidly than he intended to.[39]

The political equation was difficult for Clinton. He had to respond to the demands of a small, but dedicated minority, whose votes he needed to advance his legislative agenda, while keeping in mind that there was a silent majority unwilling to invade Haiti. He had to reconcile liberal interventionists wanting the United States to be the world's policeman and the old isolationist stock that would be outraged if body bags came home. He had to deal with an unprecedented situation in which liberals clamored for an intervention in the Caribbean while conservatives, the CIA, and the Pentagon complained that this would put an autocrat in power. "What would they have me do?" Clinton confided in private. "What the f . . . would they have me do?"[40] To make matters worse, the Haitian crisis unfolded as Clinton faced so many setbacks and scandals domestically that he looked indecisive, weak, or even incompetent.

Clinton Faced a Difficult Domestic Political Situation

Clinton's presidency was in a tailspin before it even started.[41] Having promised to draft a cabinet that "looked like America," Clinton had to keep a delicate balance between liberals and centrists, Whites and Blacks, Carter veterans and young campaign workers, and men and women. Many of the 6,000 presidential appointments were thus not announced until the last minute, or even into the administration, so that few of them had their staffs and agendas ready for the first Hundred Days. Presenting himself as an outsider who would change the ways of Washington, Clinton hired few experienced aides. After twelve years out of the White House, the Democratic bench to pick from was limited, and Clinton was equally reluctant to diminish an already slim congressional majority by hiring experienced congressmen. Of his entire initial White House staff, only political adviser George Stephanopoulos and Legislative Director Howard Paster had extensive Washington experience.

Having finally chosen appointees, Clinton then had to face resignations. "Nanny problems" (illegal immigrants hired for menial tasks) forced Zoe Baird to withdraw her candidacy as potential attorney general. Even Associate White House Counsel William Kennedy, whose job was to screen potential nominees for "nanny problems," had to resign when the press discovered that he had one of his own.[42]

Once he finally started working, Clinton faced one problem after another, from gays in the military to Waco and a costly haircut in Los Angeles. The budget passed (with tax hikes), NAFTA was ratified, the Brady Bill voted, and the Middle East peace accords signed, but only the latter was popular with voters. October 1993 saw two major foreign policy fiascos, in Mogadishu, where 18 U.S. Rangers were killed, and in Port-au-Prince, where the *Harlan County* turned around after encountering light resistance. In December, Arkansas troopers revealed that they had helped Clinton find sexual partners when he was Governor of Arkansas. The *New York Times* and the *Washington Post* revived the Whitewater scandal. Edward Fiske was named independent counsel in January 1994 (Kenneth Starr replaced him in August). In February, Paula Jones accused Clinton of sexual harassment. In June, the Navy asked to be reimbursed for bathrobes White House staff had purloined during their stay onboard the USS *George Washington*. Clinton did not know yet that worse, including an impeachment trial, was yet to come.

Intense media scrutiny beset Clinton's personal life. In 1993, the press revealed that his father had been married three times before marrying his mother Virginia, and had fathered two children Clinton did not know about.[43] Hillary's father Hugh Rodham, family friend Vincent Foster, Jr., and Clinton's mother Virginia died during the first 12 months of the presidency. The day of Virginia's funeral, Bob Dole went on national television to call in very harsh terms for a Whitewater independent counsel.[44]

The presidency upheld its reputation as a 24-hour fishbowl in which nothing goes unnoticed. In August 1994, when Clinton smacked his lectern for emphasis as he was presenting his health-care plan, gossipers noticed that the presidential seal fell off. They also laughed a few days later when he tripped as he was jogging in front of the Watergate complex. The conservative *American Spectator* kept a cruel monthly chronicle on the travails of the "Boy-Statesman."[45] To their enemies, Bill and Hillary were an ambitious couple with an overwhelming drive for power and no scruples. Ambitious they were, but the criticisms stung nonetheless, as they had stung every president before.

There was no honeymoon period. Republicans, not a single one of whom voted for Clinton's first budget, went immediately on the offensive. The percentage of presidential bills accepted by Congress, as compiled by the *Congressional Quarterly*, was well below average.[46] Even attempts to allow extensive access to two journalists backfired when they published scathing accounts of an inexperienced and chaotic White House.[47]

Doubts concerning the president's foreign policy credentials were the most pronounced. In the popular psyche, presidential manliness is often equated with military and foreign policy prowess. Despite Clinton's extramarital adventures, many conservative voters saw him as a weak husband dominated by a Ms. Rodham refusing to stand by her man. Even though he had been a member of the ROTC during his first two undergraduate years at Georgetown University, Clinton asked for, and obtained, unusually generous deferments that spared him from service in Vietnam. The draft-dodging-pacifist-turned-commander in chief had the bad luck of running against World War II veterans in both of his presidential campaigns, in a country that had sent numerous former soldiers to the White House.[48]

Clinton's *spinmeisters* spent a considerable amount of energy trying to convince the electorate that "Bill" was a man of the people, one who could feel their pain. As he appeared in call-in radio talk shows, town hall meetings, and late-night shows, answered questions about his underwear preferences (boxers or briefs?), and played the saxophone on the *Arsenio Hall Show*, Clinton managed to connect with elements of the electorate that spent little time watching C-SPAN or reading the editorial page of the *New York Times*. By doing so, he also risked endangering his aura as a president. Aides told Clinton to stop talking about foreign policy in his jogging clothes.[49]

His leadership style also came under criticism. During Clinton's first year in office, he took the habit of holding two- or three-hour free-for-all meetings in the Oval Office, during which any staff member could stop by and offer his or her opinion. Decisions were not easily reached in this manner, leaks abounded, and the administration looked indecisive. Clinton might have impressed his close aides with his versatility when he did crosswords, talked on the phone, and tackled foreign policy issues all at once, but, to outsiders, this was merely a proof that the MTV generation, shallow and unfocussed, had taken over.

His native Arkansas was derided in the East as backwater hillbilly country, not a fertile ground for world leaders. In his 1992 acceptance speech at the Republican National Convention, Bush referred to his adversary as "the leader of the Arkansas National Guard—the man who hopes to be Commander in Chief."[50] He later joked that Clinton's only foreign policy experience was at the IHOP (International House of Pancakes, where he liked to dine).[51] Clinton's dreams of bringing democracy to Haiti, according to this view, were little more than white trash's burden. Had the criticism been fair, Clinton would have been only the latest in a long series of statesmen with limited prior foreign policy experience, including William Jennings Bryan, Lyndon B. Johnson, and Ronald Reagan. But Clinton had a background few Americans of his age could match. He was a brilliant student who lived for two years in England as a Rhodes scholar and visited the Soviet Union. He spent the summers of 1965 and 1966 as an intern working for William Fulbright's Senate Foreign Relations Committee.[52]

Clinton's priorities targeted him for blame. During his first ten months in office, he delegated much of his power to Anthony Lake, Warren Christopher, and his national security team in order to focus on his domestic agenda. He used the United Nations as a surrogate for a foreign policy he had no time to devise. After the October 1993 double disaster in Mogadishu and Port-au-Prince, Clinton followed a more hands-on approach. Leon Panetta was asked to reorganize the White House. Meetings became shorter and tighter, participants were screened, and Clinton had his afternoons for himself. Christopher, whom Clinton had momentarily planned to replace, managed to schedule a weekly lunch with the president.

A painful incident reminded Clinton that the chaotic first months had left an indelible mark. In May 1994, the parents of two of the Rangers who died in Mogadishu came to the White House to receive the Congressional Medal of Honor on behalf of their sons. Refusing to shake Clinton's hand, Herbert Shughart, the father of one Ranger, told Clinton: "You are not fit to be President of the United States. The blame for my son's death rests with the White House and with you. You are not fit to command."[53] This was one of Clinton's worst memories as president.

Foreign policy was probably the area in which the press was most biting. Paraphrasing Theodore Roosevelt, the *Wall Street Journal* wrote that Clinton "speaks loudly and carries a twig."[54] The *New York Times* talked about the "administration's almost empty vial of foreign-policy credibility," while the *Progressive* spoke of a "weak and muddled foreign policy."[55] "Dropping the Ball?," "Hurry up and Wait" attacked *Time Magazine.*"[56] "Don't Bother me with Foreign Policy," "U.S. Resolve, Needed Then and Needed Now," "Turning the Other Cheek," and "The Limits to Leadership," answered *U.S. News and World Report.*[57]

Congress was not kinder. In late April 1994, many congressmen took to the floor to lament the state of U.S. foreign policy, citing Haiti, Somalia, Rwanda, and Bosnia.[58] The immediate cause for this outpouring of discontent was Clinton's recent behavior, which congressmen judged unworthy of a president. When the Serbs had attacked UN-protected Gorazde, Clinton had spent his day playing golf, before heading off to a rally of Mustang car owners in Concord, N.C.[59]

In May 1994, as the administration was reviewing its Haiti policy, only 13 percent of Americans thought Clinton had a clear foreign policy vision; 40 percent approved of Clinton's foreign policy, all of this in the absence of any national crisis.[60] On public television, editors of regional newspapers confirmed that, while foreign policy itself was not at the forefront of Americans' everyday thinking, it reflected badly on his overall performance. Cynthia Tucker of the *Atlanta Constitution* said that Atlantans were not "overwhelmed with concern" about Haiti,

> but I do think Atlantans and the public at large are affected by what they see as the President's lack of leadership. . . . I think that they see a President who waffles and who is indecisive on foreign policy, on health care, on Supreme Court Justices. I think the President misunderstands a fundamental psychology of leadership, that the American people expect him to stand up, to say what he thinks the nation ought to do, whether

it's in Bosnia or Haiti or on crime, and stick to it. And he doesn't do that. . . . And I think that affects him in domestic matters as well.[61]

Growing doubts about Clinton's foreign policy credentials were starting to affect his overall approval ratings. In August 1994, two months before midterm elections and two years before Clinton was up for reelection, his approval rating fell below 50 percent.[62] The field of presidential hopefuls was already overflowing, as Republicans, confident that winning in 1996 would be a snap, were getting ready for the kill.[63]

Much has been made of Clinton as the "Comeback Kid." He was defeated as a governor, then reelected. He won the 1992 primaries despite the Gennifer Flowers scandal. He won in 1996 after a disastrous first hundred days. He was impeached, then judged not guilty. But Clinton, who lived through those crises rather than looked at them in hindsight, did not know that he would survive them. What he did know was that he had been elected with 43 percent of the vote and that foreign policy had undermined many a Democratic president, including Wilson, Truman, Johnson, and Carter.[64]

Clinton's easy confidence in domestic matters was absent when he explained his intention to invade Haiti in a televised address on 15 September 1994. He felt the need to repeat the rationale several times, that he had no other choice after the failure of every other option, and that he had an exit strategy—as if the prospect of getting out justified getting in. He wrapped himself in the mantle of previous Republican presidents, explaining that the United States successfully intervened in Panama and Grenada. He even mentioned that Belgium, Bangladesh, and Jordan supported the invasion. His needing to seek reassurance from the Bangladeshi Foreign Ministry indicated that he greatly needed to reassert his presidential authority.

Taking a Stand in Haiti Could Help Clinton Look Presidential

Clinton was not the first president whose early mandate was marred by doubts concerning his leadership abilities. Historical precedents showed that foreign policy ventures have helped presidents demonstrate their toughness. John F. Kennedy (Cuba), Ronald Reagan (Grenada), and George Bush (Panama) proved their foreign-policy assertiveness by intervening in Latin America. In October 1993, as the two were aboard Marine One, Clinton told Lake that he wanted David "Gergen working on this. The Reagan people were much better at the politics of foreign policy than we are. Look at Lebanon. They went into Grenada two days later and fixed it."[65] Doing anything, anywhere, was necessary to prove that he had the stuff real presidents are made of.

Presidents need times of crisis to demonstrate their greatness; without a Great Depression and a World War, Franklin D. Roosevelt might have been little more than a talking Calvin Coolidge. Clinton complained that he never got a chance to prove his presidential abilities and to build a historical legacy because his presidency, coming after the end of the Gulf War and ending months before the start of the war on Terror was a period of relative peace. In October 1993, Clinton met Richard Reeves, the author of a biography of Kennedy. They spent two hours discussing how a young, inexperienced president had rebounded after early reversals at the Bay of Pigs—Kennedy was lucky enough to live during the Cold War, Clinton said.[66] In June 1994, as he toured the Italian World War II battlefields where his father (and Bob Dole) had fought fifty years earlier, Clinton must have longed for a crisis of global proportions. "I would have much preferred being president during World War II," Clinton later told Bob Woodward. "I'm a person out of my time."[67]

Many of the president's key advisers thought that foreign policy successes could help overcome the negative assessments of Clinton's character. Longtime friend and campaign strategist Dick Morris thought that foreign policy tells us "about the personality of our leaders. . . . Obviously, the use of force in foreign affairs can erase an image of weakness and vacillation, leaving an impression of resolution and toughness in its place."[68] A few days before the invasion, Clinton called Morris to ask for some advice.

CLINTON: I've got to speak on TV about invading Haiti, what arguments should I use?

MORRIS [thinking]: What do I know? I don't know anything about Haiti. But this isn't about Haiti; it's about American politics a month before the 1994 election. And you do know elections, so go for it. [Aloud] You shouldn't invade Haiti at all. You're invading the wrong goddam island. Racism and isolationism are the two most deadly, poisonous forces in our politics, and by suffering casualties in Haiti, you will be offending them both at once, and you'll never recover.

CLINTON: [Mentions all the human rights abuses.]

MORRIS [thinking]: It wasn't the real reason. He still remembers the 1979–80 episode where the Cuban refugees sent by Carter cost him his reelection in Arkansas. [Aloud] I know you're afraid of the refugees, but why would you ever invade an island? Just surround it and blockade it. You could force the Dominicans to let us police their side of the border as a condition for letting goods enter their side of the island.

CLINTON: We'd starve too many innocent people whom we want to help. Besides, I don't think the Dominicans would agree, and our allies wouldn't like it.

MORRIS: Look, I'm no expert on Haiti, but there'll be hell to pay if you incur American casualties in Haiti. [. . . .] We need a massive force a few miles out. Then try diplomacy. When they feel the heat, they'll see the light. [For the speech,] you've got to get off the refugee issue and onto the human rights and value issues. You look weak when you are trying to stop refugees from flooding us, but you look strong when you are protecting children abroad.[69]

Political adviser George Stephanopoulos also placed on Clinton's desk a copy of pollster Stanley Greenberg's conclusions that idealism resonated with the American public to "fine-tune our arguments before the president's speech" and "help sell a decision that was already made."[70] When drafting his address to the nation on 15 September 1994, Clinton rejected Anthony Lake's suggestion that he should focus on America's interests. "The case was strongest, he said, on humanitarian grounds. The American public would sympathize with the plight of those whose faces were getting cut for their beliefs."[71] Morris and Greenberg had apparently won their case, giving some credence to Morris' depiction of Clinton as a political Janus divided between his public idealism and his private focus on his own political interests.

The Sunday-morning President Clinton is the one we have all seen so often on television. Pious, optimistic, brilliant, principled, sincere, good-willed, empathetic, intellectual, learned, and caring, he is the President for whom America voted in 1992 and again in 1996. But the Saturday-night Bill who cohabits within him is pure id— willful, demanding, hedonistic, risk-taking, sybaritic, headstrong, unfeeling, callous, unprincipled, and undisciplined.[72]

The accusation that "Clinton was ordering the invasion not to protect national security, but to appease a political constituency," remembered Stephanopoulos, "was the argument that drove us most crazy." But,

> although the invasion was not politically motivated, and full of political risk, it could be a political plus. Clinton was constantly being called 'spineless' and 'wishy-washy'— Doonesbury was depicting him as a talking waffle. Paradoxically, the more the Republicans screamed, the more they helped the president. Taking a lonely stand on a tough issue like Haiti was the best way for Clinton to demonstrate presidential character.[73]

As domestic political advisers, Stephanopoulos and Morris were only consulted intermittently on foreign policy. National Security Adviser Anthony Lake and his deputy, Sandy Berger, were the only ones with daily access to the president on such issues, and they jealously guarded this privilege.[74] Despite Lake's low public profile (a legend on a *New York Times* photograph once described the guardian of the country's national security as an "unidentified" man), he was actively trying behind the scenes to shift Clinton's attention away from politics and towards Lake's own security- and ideals-based priorities.[75] Lake, whose *Our Own Worst Enemy* (1984) lamented the great importance domestic politics plays in foreign policymakers' calculations, remembers

> in the Clinton White House, politics was too often seen as an end in itself. At the 8:30 a.m. senior staff meeting, held every morning in the office of the Chief of Staff, I engaged in almost daily battle with the President's political staff . . . over the relative weight to be given political considerations when they conflicted with our substantive goals. . . .
> Like sex in Victorian times, the political implications of our national security decisions are seldom discussed in the polite company of the President's foreign policy advisors. (Also like sex in Victorian times, that doesn't mean it isn't on their minds.) No doubt, President Clinton was driven in part by calculations of political advantage. He is a great and natural politician. . . . Many worried that intervention in Haiti would be unpopular. This time President Clinton held firm. He knew that if the intervention went well, as it did, his standing as President and Commander in Chief would rise—as it did.[76]

Secretary of State Warren Christopher had extensive political experience in the Johnson and Carter administrations and was sufficiently astute to be given the difficult political task of selecting a suitable vice-presidential running mate for candidate Clinton in 1992. Even though he would have preferred to continue the economic embargo rather than to use force,[77] Christopher saw the political advantages to be obtained from an invasion.

Taken together with the reverses we suffered in Somalia that fall, the Harlan County incident created a perception of lack of resolve that took us some time to shake off. . . . Inside the administration, we were all growing increasingly frustrated with our lack of success and the effect this was having on public opinion, both within the U.S. and around the world.[78]

PDD-25, the Clinton administration framework on peacekeeping, stated "the President believes U.S. support for and participation in UN peace operations can only succeed over the long term with the bipartisan support of Congress and the American people."[79] Despite this, polls showing a public reluctance to intervene were not worrisome. When the president bombed Iraq in June 1993, his approval ratings immediately jumped 15 percent, and the administration was confident the public would rally behind the flag. As Christopher noted, "American public opinion usually opposes military intervention abroad, at least until our troops land. This was decidedly the case with Haiti."[80]

And rally it did. A majority of the public, initially opposed to the invasion, supported it after it started.[81] The day after the invasion, Dole, who had opposed it initially, introduced Senate Resolution 259 to support "the men and women of the U.S. armed forces in Haiti."[82] *Time* magazine columnist Michael Kramer, who had written "The Case Against Invading Haiti" when troops were about to invade Haiti, went back to the drawing board and outlined "The Case for Intervention" a week later.[83] Ratings only started to slip when Clinton, against Morris' advice, stepped down from his presidential pedestal and got involved in the nitty-gritty of midterm campaigning.[84]

Why Haiti?

When Clinton, Lake, Christopher, and U.S. Ambassador to the UN Madeleine Albright outlined their strategy for democracy in a series of September 1993 speeches, Haiti was barely mentioned in passing.[85] None of Clinton's main advisers had any specialization in the history of what Christopher called "that very troubled country."[86] Christopher was a California lawyer, Albright a native of Czechoslovakia, Lake a scholar on Africa, and Assistant Secretary of State Richard Holbrooke a Russia specialist. Special envoy to Haiti Lawrence Pezzullo told administration people that he "didn't know much about Haiti," but got the job anyway.[87] Had they been pressed to name a place to make a stand, many Americans would probably have mentioned Sarajevo, not Port-au-Prince. Cuba, a communist dictatorship, an endless source of refugees, and a greater blow to U.S. credibility, was another logical candidate.[88]

During the December 1993 meeting of the so-called "friends of Haiti" (Canada, the United States, France, and Venezuela) in Paris and the January 1994 Miami conference, U.S. envoys made insistent remarks that Haitians should work out a solution by themselves. Noting the humanitarian side effects of the embargo, they did not propose any solution besides negotiation. To an observer ignorant of what came next, it seemed clear that the international community was preparing itself to quietly drop the issue altogether. Citing internal diplomatic sources, the usually well-informed *New York Times* confided that the international community was about to give up the idea of ever restoring Aristide to power.[89]

According to NSC staff member Richard Feinberg, one reason why Haiti was eventually chosen as the goal of Clinton's first major intervention abroad was "feasibility."[90] The case to intervene in Rwanda and Bosnia might have been more compelling, but such missions in distant countries torn apart by civil war were, as the Somalia debacle had proved, militarily and politically dangerous to carry out.[91] Should a war be fought to reassert presidential power, it would have to be both easy and short. Haiti's credentials were particularly suited for the task.

Haiti was Easy

As early as February 1993, Clinton publicly asserted, "we certainly ought to be able to [restore democracy] in our backyard." Clinton repeatedly accompanied his comments on Haiti with words such as "not hard," "close to our shore," "nearby," "in our neighborhood," "at our door," and "in our region."[92] Throughout the 1990s, regional powers similarly focused most of their interventions in their own spheres of interest. France intervened in her *pré carré* (backyard) in Rwanda and the Central African Republic, Russia in Chechnya, Europe in Bosnia and Kosovo, Australia in East Timor, and Africans in the Congo and Sierra Leone, while Japan sent peacekeepers to Cambodia.

Besides Haiti's proximity, the state of its army, which Stephanopoulos described as "not exactly a fearsome adversary," made Pentagon planners confident they would win.[93] Once able to defeat France, Spain, and England, the Haitian Army proved no match for the small Marine force that took over the country in 1915 with a mere two casualties on its side. The army was disbanded and replaced by a *Gendarmerie* whose task was to provide indigenous auxiliaries to the occupation force.[94] Renamed *Forces Armées d'Haiti* (or FAdH) in 1946, the Haitian armed forces had neither the will nor the capacity to protect the country from an invasion. Soldiers, dispatched in small units throughout the country, were asked to muzzle internal opposition and maintain order. Out of the army's twelve basic units, nine were deployed to each village of Haiti's nine departments, one constituted the police of Port-au-Prince, and one was the presidential guard. The heavy-weapons unit was the only Army unit one could truly label military in nature. The Haitian Army, by and large, was a police force wearing military fatigues (many soldiers had two uniforms, one police blue and one army green, and wore them indiscriminately).

The Haitian Army's recent military record did not bode well for its ability to stop a U.S. invasion. In July 1958, eight men, including five American filibusters, landed in Montrouis, hijacked a *tap tap* (small bus) to the capital, took over the main army barracks in Port-au-Prince, and almost toppled the regime. Duvalier considered fleeing the country, changing his mind when a hostage, sent out by the invaders to buy cigarettes, told him how small the force was.[95] In August 1964, 13 expatriates landed near Jérémie and disappeared in the countryside. The Haitian Army was unable to capture the rebels and only won two months later when soldiers tricked the rebels out of their hideout by capturing and torturing most of their relatives.[96]

The Haitian Army's flagrant deficiencies were most evident in January 1981, when Bernard Sansaricq, a relative of the rebels executed in 1964, raised funds and a force of 39 men to invade Haiti. Sansaricq airlifted eight men to the Haitian island of La Tortue, then rented a boat to send in the remainder of his force. Reluctant to carry out this dangerous mission himself, he destroyed the boat's engines and floorboards when his acolytes forced him to accompany them. Disabled and sinking, the boat was rescued by the U.S. Coast Guard. The eight hungry men on La Tortue, kilometers away from the Haitian mainland, isolated and cut off from further supplies, were in a weak strategic position. Soldiers and *Macoutes* attacked the rebels but withdrew after suffering severe casualties, most of them caused by friendly fire. Jean-Claude Duvalier then sent twenty of his elite troops, the Leopards, who panicked in their first encounter, turned around, and called in sick. The army only had two functioning weapons in its arsenal: time and the hope that the rebels' incompetence would eventually surpass its own. It surrounded the rebel stronghold, set up tables, took game cards out, and waited. When heat, hunger, and thirst took their toll, five of the rebels attempted to force the blockade and were shot. The last three surrendered, were taken to Port-au-Prince, questioned, tortured, and executed.[97]

In 1994, the Haitian Army numbered about 5,200 enlisted men, 1,000 officers, and 1,300 police auxiliaries. It had four patrol boats, two planes, and some lightly armored vehicles, though few of those were fully functional. There were a few heavy guns, but of the kind one would find on the lawn of an American Legion post. After watching the army's training routine, Col. David H. Hackworth concluded, "the 7,600-man Haitian military force doesn't have the skill and dedication to fight its way out of a retirement home." The Americans "would coldcock these swaggering assholes in less time than Mike Tyson could put down Boy George."[98] The derogatory terms left aside, there was no doubt the U.S. Army would win the first encounter. Secretary of Defense Dick Cheney contacted Powell in December 1991 about military options. Powell was straightforward, "We can take over the place in an afternoon with a company or two of Marines," he answered, "But the problem is getting out."[99]

Getting out was indeed what kept U.S. military planners awake at night. According to internal leaks, intelligence reports in May 1994 stressed that the U.S. Army could easily take over Haiti, but that a long, open-ended commitment of troops would be required before order could be fully restored.[100] Under guidelines set by PDD 25 the same month, such "open-ended" peace operations "should not be undertaken."[101] Military planners preparing a Haiti invasion were aware of this limitation.[102] If Haitian soldiers, following the example of Charlemagne Péralte in 1918–1919 and Muhammad Farah Aidid in 1993, took to the hills, the United States would have to fight a costly insurrection. Haiti would be easy as long as one got out quickly.

Haiti Had to be Short

Days before the intervention, the president held an interview with wire-service correspondents. Stephanopoulos waited anxiously for him to mention that troops would leave quickly, but Clinton, even though he had been briefed in advance, forgot to emphasize it. As minutes withered away, Stephanopoulos tried to get the president's attention by staring at him from afar. He mouthed the word *limit* silently, made hand gestures, and even held a sign saying *limit mission*; but the president, who did not have his glasses, failed to react. Stephanopoulos finally wrote a message on a small piece of paper, folded it, and passed it on to Clinton just in time for the last question. As an after word to his final answer, the president finally said the key words: he had "a disciplined and clear" exit strategy.[103]

With the exception of the Civil War, the U.S. Army has always been recognized as a force particularly mindful of its casualty rate. This concern, entirely legitimate in a democratic society, became imperious after the Vietnam War, especially in low-intensity conflicts such as Haiti where stakes were low. The heavy-handed use of air power, an American tradition aimed at limiting American casualties, was of little use in a country such as Haiti where roads were already in ruins, electricity was already intermittent, and the air force was virtually inexistent. A Vietnam-era President had to take the dangerous step of sending ground troops to a country where the previous U.S. occupation had lasted 19 years (1915–1934).

To limit the potential for a military and political quagmire, the administration defined the goals of Operation Restore Democracy very narrowly. The mission was simply to bring Aristide back to Haiti as president of Haiti, and to create an environment secure and stable enough for a UN force to take over.[104] The Carter–Jonassaint agreement did not even require that Cédras leave Haiti. Even though the United States eventually provided technical assistance to elections and pledged development aid, the administration carefully refrained from using the word "nation-building."

Requesting the involvement of the United Nations, which the Clinton administration had previously blamed for the Somalia fiasco and derided as a bloated bureaucracy,[105] was another way to ensure that the U.S. occupation would come to a quick end. The United States, unilaterally or through the OAS, had until 1994 carefully guarded the Western Hemisphere as a special place protected by the Monroe Doctrine, but the United Nations could play a triple role. If things went as wrong as in Mogadishu, it could always be targeted for blame. With polls showing that Americans were more likely to support an intervention if it was multilateral, it gave multilateral backing to an invasion that the OAS refused to endorse.[106] The administration also asked for help from the Caribbean Community (CARICOM). The military contribution was negligible, but the U.S. military representative to the CARICOM was told the goal was to get "as many flags as possible."[107]

Last and most importantly, the United Nations was willing to take over the operation after U.S. troops left. The U.S. Army would invade Haiti, reinstall Aristide, take a few pictures, and go home. A UN-led multinational force would then do the nation-building equivalent of mopping up. Resolution 940, which authorized the use of force, specifically mentioned that a UN mission in Haiti (UNMIH) would take over as soon as a secure and stable environment was established.[108] (In March 1995, when the United Nations expressed doubts that a secure and stable environment had indeed been established, U.S. troops simply insisted that it had, and left).

In June 1994, *ABC News* leaked a May 1994 internal memo to UN Secretary General Boutros Boutros-Ghali from UN Special Envoy to Haiti Dante Caputo and the transcript of conversations between Boutros-Ghali and his advisers.[109] The memo outlined both the political benefits of an invasion and the U.S. desire to get out as fast as possible. Having met with Deputy Secretary of State Strobe Talbott and other State Department officials over the previous two weeks, Caputo concluded that the United States had already decided that "an invasion of Haiti is its best option," but was afraid it could never extricate itself from Haiti.

> The President of the United States' main advisers are of the opinion that not only does this [military] option constitute the lesser evil, but that it is politically desirable. Thus we think that the current opposition of public opinion to an armed intervention will change radically, once it will have taken place. The Americans see in this type of action a chance to show, after the strong media criticism of the administration, the President's decision-making capability and the firmness of leadership in international political matters.[110]

The alleged U.S. goal after a successful invasion was to make room for a multinational occupation force, thus "transferring the political cost on the UN." In the ensuing discussion, Boutros-Ghali's adviser Alvaro de Soto complained, "the Americans will be applauded and the dirty work will come back to the UN." Caputo's informants within the Clinton administration were convinced

> the Americans will not be able to stand for much longer, until August at the latest, the criticism of their foreign policy on the domestic front. They want to do something; they are going to try to intervene militarily. . . . The United States will make the UN bear the responsibility to manage the occupation of Haiti. 'With Aristide as President during two or three years, it will be Hell!' It is not so much the armed intervention itself that we have to avoid. What we do not want is to inherit a 'baby.'[111]

Whether this was official U.S. policy or not, Clinton used his ability to withdraw on schedule as a selling point in his 15 September address to the nation. After interminably making the case that his country should get involved, he pointed out that it would do little and leave. "The United States cannot—indeed, should not—be the world's policemen. . . . When [the invasion] is completed, the vast majority of our troops will come home, in months, not years."[112] The last-minute deal with the junta guaranteed that there would be no combat operations, few American casualties, and that Clinton's political gamble would not backfire.[113] Along with U.S. credibility and immigration pressures, Clinton's political problems—namely, the need to secure congressional support for his legislative agenda and the necessity to silence criticisms that the president was an ineffectual manager of U.S. foreign policy—thus provided a strong incentive to intervene militarily. Meanwhile, another party was also aggressively pursuing a U.S. intervention: Haitians themselves.

CHAPTER EIGHT
HAITIAN LOBBYING

Many scholars have condemned U.S. interventions in Latin America for hegemonic arrogance in imposing the will of the United States on passive, helpless Latin American populations. In reality, most U.S. interventions have been actively promoted by nationals of the very country in which the United States was intervening, by the likes of Guatemala's Castillo Armas, the Dominican Republic's conservative military officers—and Haiti's Jean-Bertrand Aristide.[1] From 1991 to 1994, the U.S. government was assaulted by a veritable Haitian lobbying juggernaut led by Aristide, which clashed, in a prolonged subterranean conflict largely ignored at the time, with the junta's own lobbying efforts.

The triumvirate ruling Haiti managed to convince many in the United States, including the CIA and several Republican congressmen, that Aristide was psychologically unstable, but it generally proved inept when it came to public relations. Aristide, concluding that he could only be restored with international help, was a much more dedicated and effective lobbyist. His first instinct was to turn to France and to fellow Latin American leaders. All were sympathetic and anxious to preserve the hemisphere's fragile new democracies, but they were equally determined to protect national sovereignty, and, despite all the friendly smiles, Aristide understood that the Organization of American States would never support more than an ineffectual embargo.

Aristide thus moved to Washington, DC in early 1992 and increased contacts with the UN and the U.S. government, especially after Bush lost the 1992 election. He made himself more palatable by dropping the word socialism from his vocabulary and preaching national reconciliation. He asked for ever-stricter embargoes, signed the July 1993 Governors' Island accord, lobbied tirelessly while being attacked by the press and his many enemies in Washington, and eventually, pressed by time, went to the verge of treason in promoting a military invasion of his mother country. By September 1994, he had spent dozens of millions of dollars of his starving countrymen's money to convince the Yankee hegemon to invade his own country on behalf on a man most Americans did not know or did not like. How Aristide's lobbying campaign unfolded is one of the strangest stories of recent U.S. diplomatic history.

The Junta's Public Relations Problem

Already infamous for overthrowing Aristide and massacring his supporters, the Cédras regime did little to address its public relations problem. During its tenure in power, the junta treated disrespectfully the very people and institutions it should have tried to assuage, including the OAS, the Black Caucus, the Clinton adminis-tration, and the U.S. media. A week after the 1991 coup, at Port-au-Prince airport, armed men threatened an OAS delegation headed by Secretary General Joao Clemente Baena Soares. The delegation aborted the mission and, one day later, the OAS declared an embargo against the regime.[2] In September 1993, Cédras gave a cold reception to a Black Caucus delegation headed by the influential Rep. Charles Rangel (D-NY).[3] One month later, the FRAPH humiliated the Clinton administra-tion when it prevented the *Harlan County* from landing its troops in Haiti. Cédras frequently refused to grant interviews to foreign journalists. Col. David Hackworth, best selling author and journalist for *Newsweek*, arrived in Port-au-Prince in 1994 wearing his "tropical uniform" (shorts and T-shirt). "General Cédras was a very pompous prick," Hackworth later complained, and "when I went to his headquar-ters to ask for an interview, the vibes I got from everyone were, *How can a beach bum like you see the Man?*"[4] "These were the kind of guys who sent you death threats when you wrote a bad story about them," says a U.S. journalist reporting from Port-au-Prince. "Their way to get good press was to dump bodies in front of the Montana Hotel, where foreign journalists stayed."[5]

Cédras tried unsuccessfully to deflect international criticism by installing puppet civilian governments and claiming that uncontrollable paramilitary groups, not he, were responsible for the political repression. A month after the regime's henchmen killed Justice Minister Paul Malary, he declared, "measures have been taken since the beginning for the protection of the members of the [Aristide] government." He added that he and the armed forces "have spent the seven months of [Aristide's] government in full cooperation with the government and the other institutions"— "full cooperation" which included a coup d'état.[6] Such blatant lies made him appear devious and unreliable abroad and angered domestic associates who would have preferred stronger leadership. An internal memo argued,

> General Cédras, being the most powerful man in the country, cannot afford to remain neutral. . . . The Army has an interest in *orienting* the situation in a well-defined direc-tion in order to put an end to the prevalent confusion. . . . [Aristide] may succeed in sapping the credibility of General Cédras if the silence and the neutrality of the Commander in Chief continue to support the actual worsening of the situation and the corruption that is rampant today.[7]

In October and November 1991, the junta hired public relations specialists, but they pocketed the money and left.[8] Elsie and Charles Joseph (sister and brother in law of police chief Michel François) met Senators Pressler and Helms in an effort to avert a U.S. invasion.[9] Prime Minister Marc Bazin ordered that a report describing the desperate social conditions prevalent in Haiti be distributed to U.S. AID in order to undermine support for the embargo.[10] But the only sustained lobbying effort was due to a mysterious man known as "the Shadow."

The Shadow

The Shadow's existence and role as a key adviser of Raoul Cédras are a confirmed fact, but the details of his life remain difficult to ascertain.[11] Born in Calgary in the late 1940s, the Shadow once was a Canadian Air Force officer. He claims to have then operated an airfield in Ireland where movies such as *Blue Max, Red Baron*, and *Zeppelin* were shot, to have worked with Stanley Kubrick on *Barry Lyndon*, and to have acted as a stunt flyer in *These Magnificent Men in their Flying Machines*.[12]

The Shadow had his first taste of Haiti in 1980 as he prepared a film on Voodoo. One night, while trying to dig up a zombie in a cemetery, the crew was attacked by local peasants who put an end to this cinematographic desecration. He spent one third of his time in Haiti during the 1980s, "wandering around."[13] His wanderings apparently helped him befriend some members of the Haitian military, because days after the 1991 coup he became Cédras' personal adviser. According to him, "Cédras didn't choose me." Someone "at a very high level" in Washington forced the junta to accept a man who would serve as a liaison.[14] Complaining that the U.S. media did not take him seriously when he contacted them, the Shadow asked Cédras to name him Haitian honorary consul in December 1991, in which post he remained until 1994. In 1993, a Toronto daily blew his cover and he was subsequently known by the name Lynn Garrison.[15]

In the days following the coup, Garrison inspected Aristide's private quarters in the presidential palace, where he found a painting representing a necklacing scene, medication, and a private diary belonging to Aristide. These allegedly confirmed what Aristide's Haitian enemies had suspected ever since September 1988, when he remained prostrated for days following the attack on churchgoers at his St. Jean Bosco parish: Aristide was manic depressive.[16] Manic depression, or bipolar disorder, is characterized by long periods of lethargy interrupted by bouts of extravagance and irritability; the implication was that Aristide was an unreliable ruler who could at any time have violent, irrational outbursts. Garrison passed the information on to the U.S. Embassy's military attaché and DIA representative in Port-au-Prince, Col. Pat Collins, an "old friend, a good friend" whom he met with daily.[17] He also gave Aristide's medical information to CIA analyst Brian S. Latell. In an April 1993 trip to Washington, Garrison conferred with Pentagon officials and members of Congress.[18]

In October 1991, he started communicating regularly with the Dole and Helms congressional staffs. Compliments of Garrison, a reproduction of the Père Lebrun painting appeared as a prop for a 20 October 1993 Helms speech.[19] Presenting himself as "the consul in Haiti," he managed to obtain the private telephone numbers of most Senators, Representatives, and administration officials, whom he then inundated with faxes presenting the "Truth About Haiti": Aristide was a manic depressive and a murderer, the economic embargo was slowly destroying the Western Hemisphere's least advanced economy, and the junta did not commit a single human rights violation. The operation was hampered by Haiti's deteriorating phone system. As it often took a full hour to get a dial tone, Garrison had to hire someone to sit by the telephone waiting for the line to open. With only two functioning fax machines, sending out dozens of faxes took days. Garrison sought to arrange meetings with the

Chairman of the Congressional Foreign Affairs Committee, Lee Hamilton, and Secretary of State Warren Christopher, but stopped when Cédras indicated that he was not interested.[20]

Given Cédras' lack of interest in his schemes, most of Garrison's plans, including Operation TRUTH and EXODUS, were never carried out. Operation TRUTH's goal was to disrupt a March 1992 ceremony at Los Angeles' Biltmore Hotel in honor of Aristide. Garrison planned to hire 200 black demonstrators, equip them with signs in French, English, Creole, and Spanish, and even include a few *bona fide* Haitians in case some were interviewed. Hostesses would then direct guests to an adjacent room filled with anti-Aristide pamphlets. TV and newspaper advertisements would also publicize that Aristide had encouraged murderous mobs to burn and hack to pieces his political opponents. The junta never came up with the $100,000 it had promised for the operation.[21] Under operation EXODUS, Garrison hoped to send 10 boats with 1,500 refugees each to the very limit of U.S. territorial waters in Florida. Five days of heightened media attention would allow the junta to make public its claim that the embargo, not political repression, encouraged people to flee. Cash and enthusiasm for the project were lacking, however.[22] Corruption also undermined some projects. A 1994 plan to hire half a million people for a giant pro-junta rally demonstrating Cédras' popularity faltered when officers helped themselves from the $360,000 budget. The plan backfired when the press reported the demonstration's low turnout.[23] "No serious foreign newspaperman took Garrison seriously," remembers the *Los Angeles Times*' Caribbean correspondent. "The place was just full of wackos."[24]

Impact of Anti-Aristide Lobbying

When Lake was asked about what the CIA's position regarding Haiti was, he immediately snapped back: "The CIA isn't involved in policy-making."[25] The CIA claimed that its role in Somalia and Haiti was limited to intelligence assessments.[26] In fact, however, the CIA had a distinctively anti-Aristide political bias.[27] There were rumors that the CIA knew about, or had even encouraged, the 1991 coup and later shipments of U.S. and Brazilian guns to paramilitary forces, but evidence is currently too scarce to confirm such claims.[28] Inaccurate intelligence reports which, publicized at propitious times, sapped Aristide's moral authority were the CIA's tactic of choice. Such reports were largely based on information that supporters of the junta provided to the U.S. Congress and to the intelligence community.

The junta's allegations that Aristide was mentally unfit, which Garrison passed on to CIA and DIA agents in Port-au-Prince, reached CIA National Intelligence Officer for Latin America Brian S. Latell and Sen. Jesse Helms (R-NC). On 20 October 1993, Helms demanded a CIA briefing on Aristide. Within hours, just as Aristide was meeting a group of sympathetic Senators in room S-116 of the Senate, 13 less sympathetic Senators, 10 of them Republican, listened in room S-407 as Latell briefed them on Aristide's secret CIA psychological profile. Latell also briefed the House Intelligence Committee the same day, and on 21 October CIA Director R. James Woolsey confirmed the rumors about Aristide to members of the House and Senate intelligence committees.[29]

On the twenty-first, after mentioning that room S-407 was so secure that no eavesdropping was possible, Helms proceeded to unveil on the Senate floor most of what Latell had revealed in the secret hearing the day before (CNN, the *New York Times* and the *Washington Post* provided additional details). In essence, Latell had stated in his briefing, Aristide was a blood-crazed madman who had condoned necklacing, ordered the murder of Roger Lafontant, and had still not renounced violence; he suffered from manic depression and took 13 kinds of medication, including Lithium and Haldol; he had visited a psychiatric hospital in Canada in 1980.[30] Coming just as the administration was debating whether to invade Haiti in the wake of the *Harlan County* humiliation, and a day before Congress was to vote on a Dole–Helms bill to prevent the administration from dispatching troops to Haiti, this CIA briefing to Congress, forwarding the junta's depiction of Aristide as a madman, was an obvious political coup (the bill passed in a watered-down version).[31]

Impaired by his poor accent and grammar, broken, cryptic sentences, and innumerable references to "death" and "life," Aristide never managed to entirely quell the rumors. Helms (in public) and Undersecretary of Defense Walter B. Slocombe (in private) labeled Aristide "a psychopath."[32] "No one knows whether [the rumors] are true or not," Clinton admitted; but, he rhetorically asked to Republicans, "what's their alternative?"[33] Luckily for Aristide, there was no other viable candidate, which made moot the junta's point that Aristide was unfit to rule. Marc Bazin, Aristide's adversary in the 1990 election and a U.S. favorite, compromised himself by becoming prime minister under the junta.[34]

The Clinton administration was also successful in undermining the accuracy of the CIA's junta-inspired reports. Immediately after Latell's briefing to Congress, pro-Aristide administration officials leaked a 21 July 1992 three-page secret CIA memo in which Latell wrote that Cédras belonged to "the most promising group of Haitian leaders to emerge since the Duvalier dictatorship was deposed in 1986." Latell reported "no evidence of oppressive rule. . . . Gen. Cédras impressed me as a conscientious military leader who genuinely wishes to minimize his role in politics, professionalize the armed services, and develop a separate and competent civilian police force. I believe he is relatively moderate and uncorrupt."[35] Latell's credibility dipped further when an investigative reporter from the *Miami Herald* called Canadian hospitals, all of which denied having ever treated Aristide. Latell had apparently not double-checked the junta's accusations before making them public in Congress.[36] Because Latell's reports on Aristide were based on information fed by the junta, they failed to sway NSC staff member Richard Feinberg.

> At the time, my concern was: what were the sources? Everything came from Aristide's enemies. In retrospect, based on what Aristide has done since then, less favorable comments were probably closer to the truth.[37]

The balance of power in Washington also hindered the junta's attempt to undermine Aristide's appeal. The junta very effectively swayed the CIA and Republican congressmen, but Congress and the CIA took a minor part in the decision-making process that led to the invasion. The vast majority of congressmen paid little attention to the administration's efforts to restore him to power until American credibility was so deeply compromised that an invasion had become a necessity. The CIA lost much of its aura with the end of the Cold War and mole scandals. Aldrich H. Ames (sentenced on 28 April 1994 to prison for life for espionage) did much harm to the agency when he described it as a "self-serving sham carried out by careerist bureaucrats who have managed to deceive several generations of American policy makers and the public about both the necessity and the value of their work."[38]

More generally, the coup leaders did not have their back to the wall. They thought they had won, and, accordingly, made few efforts to manipulate U.S. policy until September 1994. "They always tried to second-guess U.S. motives," says a journalist who met junta leaders repeatedly in 1991–1994. "They thought this was still the Cold War, and that, like under Duvalier, the United States would criticize them publicly but support them because Aristide was a Communist."[39] Aristide, on the other hand, was both out of power and pressed for time. His own lobbying campaign proved much more efficient.

Aristide's Options

On 30 September 1991, as he sat in the plane taking him to Venezuela and exile, many ideas must have gone through Aristide's mind. There was probably anger at the idea that Cédras, the very man he had appointed as commander in chief, had double-crossed him. There was probably shame as well: he was fleeing his people while his supporters were being shot in the streets. As miles passed, two central questions emerged, one of which would haunt him for the following 3 years. Do I try to go back, and, if so, how? When he arrived in Caracas, Aristide, at the urging of President Carlos Andres Perez, had the answer to his first question: he would do all he could to return as president of Haiti. Figuring how to do it took the better part of the next three years. According to Micha Gaillard and Patrick Elie, two close advisers to Aristide (Elie followed him in exile, Gaillard was one of his representatives in Haiti), "as usual, Aristide didn't have a long-term plan."[40] "Aristide is a militant who learned the hard way how to become a statesman," slowly devising solutions as problems emerged.[41] Three options emerged. To come back as president of Haiti, Aristide could negotiate with the junta, trigger a popular revolt in Haiti, or ask for help from the international community.

Even though Aristide publicly favored negotiations, he entertained this option more as a way to polish his image of moderation abroad than as a real possibility. In July 1992, Aristide created the Presidential Commission, a nine-member commission headed by Aristide's friend Father Antoine Adrien.[42] Aristide asked the Commission to represent him in Haiti and to bring him back to power through "a true national consensus" and "a government of national concord."[43] The Commission tried to sponsor a political settlement, but Aristide and Cédras negotiated in bad faith, refusing to make any concessions.[44] Even after they signed the July 1993 Governors' Island accords, both sides tried not to implement its clauses. Robert Malval, Aristide's prime minister and a fervent supporter of a negotiated solution, finally erupted in a December 1993 letter to Aristide that "you regularly kicked me under the belt and stabbed me in the back."[45] After one year of unsuccessful efforts, Father Adrien jotted down a short, revealing sentence in his personal notes: "intransigence on both sides."[46]

Immensely popular among the urban poor and the rural population, Aristide could have tried to go to the Haitian hills and to take advantage of a terrain ideally suited for guerilla warfare. A 1993 letter by Aristide's supporters urged him to start the struggle. "We are asking if we will always live as maroons without ever acting. . . . We want direct contact with the man for whom we are fighting."[47] Antoine Izméry, the financier of Aristide's 1990 campaign, also contacted Elie (in charge of maintaining contact with Haitians living abroad) suggesting that the diaspora support a rebellion in Haiti.[48] Elie agreed with this solution, as did Chavanne Jean-Baptiste, a peasant leader and member of the Presidential Commission. Elie proposed this strategy several times to Aristide, who personally and adamantly rejected it. Not only was the better-armed junta likely to win, Aristide believed, but he would lose all the legitimacy he had accumulated as a democratically elected president if he became yet another deposed leader who tried to fight his way back into power in a civil war.[49]

Having rejected both a negotiated solution and an armed struggle, Aristide only had one option left: to lobby external forces and convince them to act on his behalf. Unlike the junta, Aristide was willing to dedicate millions of dollars to that lobbying campaign. Being out of power, he felt a sense of urgency Cédras lacked. He was willing to grant interviews, adapt his rhetoric to new circumstances, and to place himself in the public spotlight. Given Aristide's dislike of the United States, and his belief that the U.S. government had helped overthrow him, fellow Latin Americans and the French were the ones he first turned to.

Mobilizing Aristide's Friends (1991–1992)

On 30 September 1991, following the coup that overthrew Aristide, the Organization of American States issued a resolution expressing "its most energetic condemnation." It also immediately added that it expressed "solidarity with the people of Haiti in its struggle to consolidate its democratic system without external interference, exercising their sovereign and inalienable will."[50] Ambiguity marked the OAS's stance during the following years, as its support for democracy competed with its deep suspicion of foreign interventions.

Shortly after the coup, the OAS created an *ad hoc* group of foreign ministers, headed by a series of Bolivian foreign ministers (Ronald McLean, Roberto Peña, and Entonio Aranibar Quiroga). The fear that other coups would break out in Latin America if this one were to succeed was the main impetus for action, and most countries denounced the junta.[51] The Dominican Republic was the only notable exception. In addition to the long history of conflict dividing the two occupants of Hispaniola, Dominican President Joaquin Balaguer personally hated Aristide. During his presidency, Aristide raised in a UN speech the case of Haitian canecutters employed in the Dominican Republic, comparing their plight, with some justification, to slavery.[52]

Despite their overwhelming support for Aristide, asking for a foreign intervention was a step few Latin Americans were willing to take. The fact that Haiti was a French- and Creole-speaking black republic created a racial and cultural gap with the rest of the hemisphere. Diego Arria, Venezuelan Ambassador to the UN in 1991, explained that the OAS's desire to help was only half-hearted because:

> this is the only Black society in Latin America, I mean, with the exception of some fundamentally Caribbean countries. They were speaking another language, they were speaking French. They were a highly illiterate population. But fundamentally a very poor Black society. Very foreign, some people thought, to our own region.[53]

OAS Secretary General Joao Clemente Baena Soares and OAS–UN special envoy Dante Caputo warned repeatedly against an intervention.[54] In July 1994, when the UN Security Council passed resolution 940 authorizing the use of force, Brazil abstained. Argentina voted in favor of the intervention, then withdrew its support. Days before the invasion, 14 Latin American heads of state asked for the reestablishment of peace in Haiti by pacific means.[55] Venezuela, with the support of other Latin American countries, also proposed a last-minute mission in the weeks preceding the assault, and the conservative Caracas daily *El Universal* condemned the U.S. intervention.[56]

Clinton was aware of what he euphemistically called Latin American "reservations" about the intervention.[57] As late as 1 September 1994, the "multinational force" he had called for was only composed of 266 troops from Belize, Jamaica, Barbados, and Trinidad. Aside from Canada and the Caribbean Community (CARICOM), most Latin American and Caribbean countries were either neutral or opposed to a military intervention. Three months after the invasion, the thirty-four heads of state (including Aristide) attending the Summit of the Americas in Miami, Florida could only agree on a declaration stating their attachment to "the principles of the sovereign equality of states, non-intervention, self-determination, and the peaceful resolution of disputes."[58] A 1997 OAS resolution even forgot to mention that a U.S. military invasion had been necessary for Aristide to come back to Haiti.[59]

France's initial reaction was more encouraging. Ambassador to Haiti Jean-Raphël Dufour interceded on Aristide's behalf during the most critical hours of the coup, then attacked the junta so violently that he was declared *persona non grata* in Haiti. Aristide was a personal acquaintance of French President François Mitterrand and met him repeatedly after the coup. Turning to France was a way to balance the United States' predominance in Caribbean politics.[60]

But despite all the calls for help, French policy remained cautious. Dufour was called back to France in November 1991. The *lycée français* in Port-au-Prince, which many children of the junta attended, reopened shortly after the coup. Elie, sent to France to negotiate on Aristide's behalf, came to the conclusion that France only favored an embargo and a negotiated solution.[61] Not only was the Caribbean outside her sphere of influence, but France already had her hands full in Bosnia and Rwanda, where the deployment of French troops was being bitterly criticized. *Le Monde*, the daily of reference, editorialized that Paris had neither the means nor the will to send a contingent of soldiers to Port-au-Prince, and French Foreign Minister Alain Juppé declared after meeting Clinton in May 1994 that France was "certainly not" ready to take part in a military intervention in Haiti.[62]

Staying out of the invasion force, France sent a few policemen, judges, and blue helmets for the follow-up UN mission, limiting herself to the role of financial contributor. She did not even manage to send an ambassador in time for Aristide's 15 October 1994 return. More than ever, the Caribbean was and remained an American lake.

Making New Friends (1992–1994)

It took nine months for Aristide to understand that the prospects of returning to power through mild OAS and French support were dim. In June 1992, he wrote to UN Secretary General Boutros Boutros-Ghali that the OAS, while active, had proved unable to restore democracy to Haiti and that he was requesting the UN's help.[63] Boutros responded that he would ask Soares if the UN could get involved in the Haitian situation, which he did, prompting Soares to protest that the UN was stepping outside of its turf.[64] In a clear shift from the previous 50 years of its existence, the UN nevertheless involved itself in this American crisis. Yet, once again, Aristide's hopes went unmet, for the United Nations only favored an embargo and a negotiated settlement. Even if it had pushed for an invasion, it would have been in no position to influence the United States given the antagonistic nature of U.S.–UN relations at the time.

Always prompt to emphasize his contributions to world peace in his memoirs, *Unvanquished* (1999), Boutros-Ghali wrote little about Haiti. This reflected the United Nation's lack of persuasive power in the area. In the days immediately preceding the invasion, for example, the junta refused to meet Swedish diplomat Rolf Knutsson in a last-minute UN attempt to avert an invasion, preferring to meet former U.S. president Jimmy Carter instead. When Carter struck a unilateral deal, the OAS–UN special envoy, former Argentine foreign minister Dante Caputo, resigned in protest, and the Security Council expressed reservations about the Carter–Jonassaint agreement.[65]

Throughout the 1990s, the United States and the United Nations squabbled over arrears and dues. Besides a common taste for well-tailored suits, Boutros-Ghali, Warren Christopher, and Madeleine Albright had bad personal relations with one another. Boutros-Ghali, in his bitterly anti-American memoirs, complained that Christopher and Albright denied him the right to pursue an independent policy. "It would be some time before I fully realized that the United States sees little need for diplomacy; power is enough."[66] Republican accusations that the Clinton administration delegated its foreign policy to the United Nations also obliged the administration to reassert its independence by criticizing the United Nations.

Aristide had fled to Caracas, then Paris, then New York. But Venezuela, France, and the UN had neither the will nor the means to invade Haiti. Reluctantly, Aristide came to the conclusion that he needed the help of the 82nd Airborne, and that to obtain it he had to ask for it. In 1992, contrary to the wishes of his entourage, who preferred New York, Montréal, or Paris, he set up his headquarters in Washington. His goal was not to visit the Smithsonian but to set up a lobbying base from which he could ask for a more generous refugee policy, a stricter embargo against the junta, and, eventually, a military intervention. The difficulties he faced were tremendous, first and foremost his host country's dislike for Aristide, dating back to previous Republican administrations.

During the November 1987 and January 1988 Haitian general elections, which Aristide denounced as a fraud, Ronald Reagan and the NSC authorized a covert CIA operation to finance several "acceptable" candidates in the hope of undermining Aristide's summons to boycott.[67] During the December 1990 elections, in which Aristide participated, the United States supported Aristide's opponent Marc Bazin. The day of the elections, former Defense Secretary Robert S. McNamara, former House Speaker Jim Wright, former Deputy Secretary of State John Whitehead, former UN Ambassador Andrew Young, and former NSC member Robert Pastor met with Aristide. The 90-minute meeting was hostile and tense.[68] Aristide claims that the U.S. delegation asked him to concede the election to Bazin.[69] Pastor, who remembers that meeting "vividly," rejects Aristide's allegation as "a total lie." According to him, widespread Army fraud on election day raised the possibility that Aristide would lose in the official tally, and that his supporters would riot in the process. When members of the U.S. delegation asked Aristide to call on his supporters to reject violence, he cut them off. "I know who all of you are. But you don't see what's happening. They're stealing the elections. I am not going to restrain my people."[70] The accusations, harsh tone, and mutual incomprehension were characteristic.

The Bush administration condemned the 1991 coup that overthrew Aristide, but official statements hint that it was also considering an alternative to Aristide. Repeatedly questioned in October 1991, State Department Deputy Spokesman Richard Boucher argued in favor of a "constitutional government," refusing to say whether that meant a return of Aristide.[71] The absence of potential replacements doomed this policy from the start, but Bush confessed a lack of enthusiasm for Aristide. "Our policy has been . . . to get this man back, not because of a great love for any individual but because of a commitment to democracy."[72] During the Bush administration, the State Department sent an FBI team to Haiti to investigate the murder of Roger Lafontant, whom, the junta said, Aristide had ordered murdered when he was overthrown in 1991. The FBI reported some evidence linking Aristide to the murder.[73] Roger Lafontant's widow Gladys sued Aristide for $10 million in the United States, but Aristide successfully claimed diplomatic immunity.[74]

Clinton administration officials, while supportive of Aristide's attempt to regain the presidency, were far from showering praise upon their champion. Asked in October 1993 to comment on rumors that Aristide was mentally unfit, Clinton answered, "well, but you know, some of those guys, they like the government they got, I think."[75] Arguing that he could not go against the Haitian people's wishes was Clinton's only line of defense. Anthony Lake, Aristide's most forceful supporter in the administration, described him as "a controversial figure . . . He is at one and the same time deeply, even mystically attached to 'the people' and their welfare; a coldly calculating politician; a charming and warm interlocutor; and a democrat, but one who plays by the winner-takes-all rule of Haiti's political culture."[76] Robert Pastor, who met the Haitian exile numerous times while working with Jimmy Carter to restore Aristide to power, similarly alleges, "one Aristide was a gentle, kind, quiet-spoken, saintly individual, while the other was cruel, tough, angry, and uncompromising."[77]

In 1993 and again in 1994, Aristide was left out of two key negotiations, then accused of being intransigent when he balked at the concessions made in his name.

Cédras was already on his way back to Haiti when Aristide finally had a chance to see a copy of the July 1993 Governors' Island accord and tried unsuccessfully to change some points. Nor was he consulted about the Carter mission. Aristide was so angry about the September 1994 Carter–Jonassaint agreement that he waited three days to say "thank you" publicly. "Aristide was not happy with us," recalled Lake.[78]

Aristide's friend Elie gave a bleak description of relations between the Haitian president-in-exile and his host country. "The United States lied to us. For three years, Aristide was a prisoner. Every guest coming in was filmed. The apartment and the phone lines were probably tapped."[79] They were. In August 1994, administration officials provided transcripts of telephone conversations between Aristide and his friends for a House briefing. Aristide allegedly complained in the tapes of being "pushed around" by the United States.[80] Luckily from a U.S. point of view, Aristide was barred from running for reelection under the Haitian constitution. Since the Clinton administration insisted that the three years spent in exile should be counted as part of his mandate, this meant that Aristide would leave office shortly after the intervention, in February 1996.

The Clinton administration's public stance towards the junta was almost sympathetic by comparison. In public, Clinton failed to mention that the junta was involved in drug trafficking. He waited until 15 September 1994 to call the dictators "thugs." Even then, he was willing to send the Carter team to negotiate an agreement with them, and the administration did all it could to preserve the Haitian army as the nucleus of the "new" police force. In that context, convincing the United States to support Aristide's return to Haiti, even at the cost of risking U.S. lives for that purpose, was a difficult task. Aristide set out to win over a few influential members of the Clinton administration by toning down his public rhetoric, hiring well-connected lawyers, and raising enough funds to pay them, then telling his new American friends that they ought to sponsor an invasion of his own country.

Talking to the Right People

In contrast to the cloistered Cédras, Aristide spent his three years in exile meeting heads of state, administration officials, diplomats, parliamentarians, journalists, sympathetic liberals, Hollywood celebrities, and Haitian supporters, swirling from New York to Paris, Washington, Los Angeles, Montréal, and Miami. Such extensive travels were a novelty for Haitian presidents. His predecessors had avoided visits abroad for fear of being overthrown (Aristide himself was overthrown two days after his September 1991 trip to New York). Traveling and meeting other heads of state was probably a way to occupy the years of exile and to prove to himself and to others that he was still president. Still, by maintaining a busy diplomatic schedule, Aristide was able to defend his case in countless meetings with influential heads of state.

Immediately after the coup, Aristide met Venezuelan President Carlos Andres Perez in Caracas, flew to Paris (1 October), then to the United States (4 October), where he met Bush and addressed the UN Secretary Council and the OAS General Assembly. On 23 October, he went from Caracas to Paris, Switzerland, Brussels, then Paris again. Dominica, St. Lucia, Grenada, and St. Kitts and Nevis followed on 1–6 November. He attended the summit of French-speaking countries in Paris

(19–21 November 1991), came back to meet Mitterrand (3 April 1992), visited French Guyana (15 June), Martinique (18 June), then Paris again (6 September), as a part of a European tour that took him to Bonn, the Hague, and Brussels. In August 1993, he announced that he would go on another ten-day tour of Europe to promote his new book *Tout homme est un homme.*[81]

Aristide met Boutros-Ghali for the first time on 15 September 1992, addressed the General Assembly on 29 September 1992 and 28 October 1993, and met Boutros-Ghali again on 5 March 1994. He met Warren Christopher (5 February 1993), Clinton (16 March, 1 July, 22 July, 6 December 1993), and Al Gore (27 October 1993). This was in addition to international conferences such as the one on New and Restored Democracies (Nicaragua, 4 July 1994) and meetings with other heads of state, such as Prime Minister Brian Mulroney of Canada (January 1994), and lesser U.S. officials, including members of the NSC and the State Department. "Over time," Christopher wrote,

> Aristide and I became quite well acquainted, as I contacted him to discuss developments or to ask his support on specific issues. National Security Adviser Anthony Lake devoted long hours to developing a relationship with him and seemed to earn his confidence.[82]

Saying the Right Words

Days after the 27 September 1991 speech in which he encouraged his supporters to kill his political opponents, Aristide spoke to the UN Security Council. Aristide was now out of power, and adopted a tone in striking contrast with his earlier speech. Dressed in a conservative gray suit, talking calmly about justice and democracy, all of this in excellent French, he no longer desired to "give the *Macoutes* what they deserve."[83] During his exile, Aristide adapted his ways to the new environment in which he found himself surviving, with Darwinian efficiency.

Faced with a superior enemy, Aristide reacted the way his slave ancestors had. Unable to overtly disobey their masters, Haitian slaves could physically escape from the plantation, becoming maroons; or they could agree with their master in public, then work to undermine his orders behind his back.[84] Aristide started his life as an intellectual maroon during the Duvalier years, when a frontal attack on the dictatorship was tantamount to suicide. In his memoirs, he explained how, as a radio show host in 1979, he was asked to tone down his criticisms: "I obeyed sometimes . . . in a tricky manner. I stopped my comments to quote texts of the Bible that were much more violent."[85] A December 1985 sermon was characteristic. Aristide quoted an apparently innocuous passage of the Bible (Isaiah 3:12), but what he meant was clear to any Haitian angry at Baby Doc and his wife Michèle: "O my people, the tyrant is a child and he is governed by women."[86] In 1991, he advocated mob lynching by using deliberately ambiguous terms. Marooning, Elie said, was what Aristide did in exile. "When you dance with a blind man ten times taller than you are, you learn how to move your toes out of the way."[87]

Aristide dropped references to imperialism, "cold country to the north,"[88] and socialism from his public rhetoric. Instead, he promised national reconciliation and "justice," not "reprisals," and political amnesty for the coup leaders.[89] He also chose Robert Malval, a business figure, as prime minister of the interim government the Governors' Island accords called for. In interviews with the media, he accused the junta of drug trafficking, of killing orphans, and of increasing immigration pressures, cleverly pushing all the buttons that might warrant an American reaction. He dismissed concerns about his lack of democratic credentials by denying the violence of his "necklacing" speech. "Let's put the text in its context. The coup had started [in fact, it started two days later]. I was using words to answer bullets."[90] Blessed with a gift for languages, he improved his English, which was at first very hesitant (Cédras, even though he was also multilingual, spoke through an interpreter in his rare interviews).[91]

Aristide kept his distance from Fidel Castro, even accepting a prize by a Miami anti-Castro group.[92] The two met only twice, briefly, during his exile. During one of these chance encounters, at Nelson Mandela's inauguration in Pretoria, Castro told Aristide that "I could speak on your behalf, but I am not sure that my support would be of much help to you."[93] Aristide waited until 6 February 1996, hours before leaving office, to recognize the Cuban regime.[94]

The Aristide who spoke after meeting Clinton at the White House in March 1993 had changed much in less than two years. "We realize how beautiful it is to work in a non-violent way for the restoration of democracy. The Haitian people today hear your voice and, on behalf of them, I can say, in the past, we wanted to be with you—we are with you; in the future, we will be with you, and you will be welcome in Haiti when I will be there after the restoration of democracy."[95] The three-paragraph statement mentioned "non-violent" and "peaceful" four times, "people" and "democracy" eleven times.

In the spring of 1994, Aristide became more aggressive, as he realized that his time was running out and that the administration, under the weight of the Black Caucus and Randall Robinson's protests, was reviewing its Haiti policy. On 21 April, he denounced the U.S. refugee policy as "a cynical joke. It's a racist policy. It's really a way to say we don't care. . . . It's true it's a genocide, it's true it's a holocaust. It's true it's a cynical joke."[96] Lake and Talbott immediately asked to meet him and promised to tighten the embargo; 400 Haitian refugees were allowed to enter the country. Christophe Wargny, who lived in exile with Aristide, recalls, "after throwing some hardballs, Aristide followed with soft ones. Well advised by his American lawyers that the new, more humane refugee policy marked a promising sign of a radical change of policy, he became more conciliatory."[97]

The speech Aristide delivered three days before the invasion, in the presence of Clinton, Gore, Christopher, Gray, Chairman of the Joint Chiefs of Staff John Shalikashvili, and many foreign government officials, was a political masterpiece sure to please his hosts. In less than ten minutes, he managed to support the intervention in vague terms, to come out against vengeance, to announce that he would not run for reelection, to advocate "an open market," and to promise that "our refugees will stay at home." He mentioned "democracy" seventeen times, "peace" thirteen times, "reconciliation" eight times, "hope" and "stability" four times each, "justice," "respect," "liberty" (or "freedom") three times each, and had enough time left to say a word or two about "amnesty" and "equity."[98] J. Brian Atwood, administrator for the USAID, proudly confided, "when we first met him when he was running for president [1990], he was a person with a real attitude about the United States and the West. But I think he has really grown. He knows all the practical issues now."[99]

Using the Right Intermediaries

Once in Washington, Aristide proved to be talented at networking. Aside from meeting administration officials and securing the support of the Black Caucus, he befriended, or hired, well-connected individuals who defended him. Some, including black activists, liberals, and members of the clergy, took up his cause because they felt a personal and ideological kinship to Aristide. Others, most prominently lawyers who lobbied on his behalf, also received financial compensation for the professional services they performed.

The Robinsons were helpful friends. Hazel Ross-Robinson, the foreign policy adviser to Rep. Ronald V. Dellums (D-CA), the Chairman of the House Armed Services Committee and one of the six members who were arrested for demonstrating in front of the White House, had also advised William Gray III, future U.S. special envoy to Haiti, when he was on the House Foreign Affairs Committee.[100] Hazel Ross-Robinson became a paid lobbyist for Aristide after the U.S. intervention, earning $227,396 in her first year alone.[101] Her husband, head of TransAfrica Randall Robinson, had been a legislative assistant for Rep. William L. Clay (D-MO) and Charles C. Diggs Jr. (D-MI).[102] Famous for his fight against apartheid in South Africa, Robinson staged a well-publicized 27-day hunger strike that forced the Clinton administration to ease its refugee policy; he knew Lake, a fellow scholar on Africa.[103]

In August 1993, Aristide hired Stephanie Owens, a California public relations specialist who had been special assistant during Clinton's transition (1992–93), then senior policy adviser to Commerce Secretary Ron Brown. Paid $125 an hour, her job was to "mobilize the current celebrities/entertainers that have supported or expressed an interest in supporting the Haitian campaign."[104] Owens organized fundraisers for Aristide among his Hollywood supporters, which included Susan Sarandon and Ed Glover, as well as Michael and Patricia Medavoy and Mary Steenburgen, all three of them friends of the Clintons and very generous political contributors to the campaign funds of the Clintons, Dodd, Gore, Joseph and Ted Kennedy, and the Democratic National Committee.[105] Sarandon and Tim Robbins used the 1993 Academy Awards ceremony to attack the U.S. refugee policy in Haiti, and the exiled priest became, if not a *cause célèbre*, at least a *cause du jour* among California liberals.[106] In March 1994, a long list of 95 Hollywood stars, singers, members of Congress, NAACP executives, friends of Bill Clinton, and clergymen published a full-page ad in the *New York Times* asking that the U.S. refugee policy, presently "driven by considerations of race," become "colorblind."[107]

On the media front, Babeth and Rudi Stern's documentary, *Haiti: Killing the Dream*, first broadcast on PBS on 29 September 1992, gave millions of Americans their first, ardently pro-Aristide summary of the ongoing crisis.[108] Christophe Wargny, Aristide's hagiographer, lived with him in exile, coauthored his books, and wrote favorable editorial pieces in the French media.[109] Taylor Branch, author of a Pulitzer Prize-winning biography of Martin Luther King, was a friend of Lake, Aristide, and Clinton.[110] Complaining about the Aristide camp's successful use of the U.S. media, the U.S. Embassy in Haiti concluded in an April 1994 cable that reports of human rights abuses were "a propaganda tool" that Aristide used to "cement his influence in Washington," later alluding to "the exploitation of the tragedy by Aristide and his Washington lobbying apparatus."[111] Jean Casimir, Aristide's Ambassador to the United States, even claimed to control American editorialists, though he did not substantiate his claim.

> We need friends all over the United States to suggest favorable articles to the Constitutional government. . . . To obtain such services one must pay. Today that's the only method known to make the White House and the State Department listen to you. It is not by mere chance that the large circulation newspapers have been publishing editorials favorable to the restoration of democracy in Haiti. We pay.[112]

As a priest, Aristide had many Catholic and Protestant supporters, whose main contribution was to write letters and to stage protests. In March 1993, 40 people, including such religious leaders as Rev. Jesse Jackson, were arrested in front of St Patrick's Cathedral in New York City as they were demonstrating in the middle of Fifth Avenue.[113] U.S. Catholic and Protestant leaders also planned to accompany Aristide to Haiti to ensure the implementation of the Governors' Island accords.[114] In May 1994, 33 Catholic bishops and 262 heads of Catholic religious orders signed a letter asking Clinton for a tightened embargo and the end of forcible returns of Haitian refugees to Haiti.[115] On the other hand, the conservative Vatican hierarchy proved to be Aristide's most dedicated enemy. The Catholic Church opposed liberation theology, as well as the political ambitions of its clergy as a matter of general policy (canon 285 par. 3, 287 par. 2).[116] The Vatican was the only government in the world to recognize the Cédras regime and opposed both the embargo and the intervention.

Lawyers have often dominated the American political landscape; in 1994, the legal profession could count the president, his wife, and the secretary of state among its ranks.[117] Aware that well-connected lobbyists could argue his case to administration insiders, Aristide hired a small army of lawyers, whose role was not to provide legal counsel, but to oversee Aristide's public relations campaign.[118] They failed to convince the general public and Aristide's many Washington enemies, but these men and women, who often happened to be major contributors to Democratic causes, opened doors to the few people who really counted and helped push Haiti higher on the administration's agenda. This was a tactic François and Jean-Claude Duvalier had successfully adopted while in power.[119]

Former Maryland congressman and Clinton fundraiser Michael D. Barnes was Aristide's best pick. Aristide hired Barnes, then a partner at the Washington law firm Arent, Fox, Kintner, Plotkin, and Kahn, in October 1991, barely 10 days after he was overthrown.[120] When Barnes moved to Hogan and Hartson in May 1993, Aristide became a client of Barnes' new firm as well.[121] Barnes had represented Maryland's 8th district from 1979 to 1987 and chaired the House Western Hemisphere Affairs Subcommittee. He had also been Clinton's fundraiser in wealthy Montgomery County (Maryland) in 1992.[122] Apparently sympathetic towards Aristide's cause, he initially offered his services at minimal cost.[123] After Aristide gained access to Haitian government funds, Arent, Fox received $372,680 for its support in the first six months of 1993.[124] When Barnes moved to Hogan and Hartson, Aristide paid him a monthly fee of $55,000, which he cut in half in 1994 due to Haitian financial difficulties.[125]

Barnes appeared at congressional hearings and gave interviews, but his political contacts were what mattered most. Barnes knew Deputy NSA Sandy Berger, who was a partner at Hogan and Hartson before joining the NSC. Barnes also knew Lake, with whom he had worked on the 1972 Edmund Muskie presidential campaign, as well as U.S. Ambassador to the United Nations Madeleine Albright, who later became Muskie's assistant, then worked for the Center for National Policy, a Democratic think tank, along with Barnes. Vic Johnson worked for Barnes when he was a Congressman and remained the staff director of the House Subcommittee on Western Hemisphere Affairs. Barnes contributed generously to the Clinton campaign, the Montgomery County Democratic committee, Chris Dodd, Joe Kennedy, Al Gore, the Hogan and Hartson political action committee, and multiple Democratic candidates nationwide.[126] The law firms he worked for made political contributions of $10,000 to $20,000 a year each.[127]

Barnes was one of those exceedingly well-connected Washington insiders who could, and did, pick up the phone and call NSC officials Lake, Berger, Richard Feinberg, and Nancy Soderberg. In the State Department, he kept in contact with Assistant Secretary of State for Interamerican Affairs Bernard Aronson, his successor Alexander Watson, Michael Kozack (who worked for the State Department's Bureau of Interamerican Affairs), Assistant Secretary for International Narcotics Matters Robert S. Gelbard, Albright, U.S. Ambassador to Haiti William L. Swing, and U.S. special envoy to Haiti Lawrence Pezzullo. He kept in constant contact with Aristide's allies in Congress, particularly Joseph P. Kennedy III and members of the Black Caucus such as Charles Rangel and Major P. Owens, as well as Vic Johnson and Alan Fleischman, both of whom worked for the House Subcommittee on Western Hemisphere Affairs.[128] He met or called all the journalists writing the Haiti articles for major media outlets. Bill Clinton and Al Gore were also on his call log, although more rarely.

Barnes worked for Aristide during the Bush administration, but his activism increased exponentially after Clinton's election. The money he spent lobbying for Haiti (phone calls, photocopies), which averaged a few hundred dollars a month in 1992, jumped to $2,367 in February 1993.[129] By 1994, Barnes' telephone bills alone totaled almost $9,000 a semester.[130] Barnes would place calls five to six times a day on Aristide's behalf, contacting most senior officials at least every other week. From February to August 1993, Barnes and other lawyers at Arent, Fox, and Hogan and Hartson placed no fewer than 318 phone calls and attended 107 meetings with administration officials and congressmen on the situation in Haiti.[131]

After Barnes left Arent, Fox in May 1993, the firm remained on Aristide's payroll at $10,000 a month.[132] Burton V. Wides, a partner of Barnes' old firm, was the reason why. Wides' overbearing personality and liberal views made him many enemies, but, as former administrative assistant to Sen. Paul Sarbanes, a member of the Senate Foreign Relations Committee, he came with a thick Rolodex.

Under various names (Burton, Burton V., and Burton Y.), Wides contributed to Clinton's 1992 campaign and others', including Ted Kennedy's and Chairman of the House Subcommittee on Foreign Affairs Robert G. Torricelli's (D-NJ). In addition to Wides' personal contributions, Arent, Fox continued to contribute heavily to political campaigns, to the tune of $34,000 for 1994 alone.[133] Wides met mostly with members of the Black Caucus as well as Hazel Ross-Robinson, but his contacts also included Berger, Feinberg, and Larry Rossin, a Latin America specialist on the NSC.[134]

Ira J. Kurzban, the husband of former congressional candidate Magda Montiel Davis, contributed large sums to Clinton, Charles Rangel, Carrie Meek, Carol Moseley Brown, Ted Kennedy, and Alcee L. Hastings, all important Aristide supporters. In his efforts to publicize the plight of Haitian refugees, and to mobilize Florida politicians, Kurzban repeatedly met, or called, Pezzullo, Swing, NSC staff member Eric Schwartz, Attorney General Janet Reno, Gelbard, Strobe Talbott, as well as members of Congress.[135] Kurzban, an immigration lawyer, also appeared regularly on TV on immigration issues. His work, which included managing part of Aristide's government funds, earned Kurzban almost $130,000 in 1992, over $150,000 in 1993, and over $370,000 in 1994.[136] Aristide also employed the Washington public relations firm McKinney and McDowell Associates to oversee press briefings and media interviews.[137] Prime Minister Malval had his own U.S. lawyer, who opened channels to Joseph Kennedy, Sam Nunn, and Chairman of the Senate Foreign Relations Committee Richard Lugar.[138]

Finding the Money

For Aristide, the ousted president of a destitute country, living in exile was as much a financial challenge as a political one. Lawyer fees mounted up to several million dollars. Despite his image as a priest of the poor, living in a barren hotel room, Aristide enjoyed a comfortable life in exile.[139] He rented large apartments in Washington's expensive Georgetown section and frequently traveled abroad, always with a large entourage. During the negotiations of the Governors' Island accords, Cédras was lodged on the island, courtesy of the U.S. government. Aristide, refusing to be anywhere near his enemy, stayed at the UN Plaza Hotel with 18 people, while another 23 members of his entourage slept at Hemsley Palace on Madison Avenue.[140] He also had to pay Haitians diplomats who had remained loyal to him and the Presidential Commission representing him in Haiti. The U.S. government, aside from providing security, refused to pay for anything.

The Government of Haiti's deposits abroad represented the most important source of income. Fifty-three million dollars were frozen in the wake of the 1991 coup, then made available to the government in exile.[141] In order not to violate the embargo, anyone owing money to Haiti was required to deposit the money in the account. These sums, which included offsets from international calls to Haiti, could be substantial.[142] The Federal Reserve Bank of New York managed the funds (Blocked Government of Haiti Account #021083909), which were then transferred to Riggs National Bank on Dupont Circle (account #170067666) for use by the government in exile. One newspaper managed to obtain a copy of a budget request representing expenses for a three-month period in 1993, which came to a total of $5.7 million. Not devoid of a certain sense of humor, the budget estimated PR costs at $0, but asked for over $130,000 monthly for law firms and travel. Aristide's salary, presumably a part of the $642,000 quarterly costs of the secretariat of the presidency, was a secret. There were over half a million dollars of "unexpected expenses" for the quarter, estimated down to the cent[143] (appendix V).

Embezzlement most likely took place. The Presidential Commission in Haiti presented a budget of $10,910 for July-September 1992 (including one-time set-up costs).[144] By January 1993, the quarterly budget had jumped to $48,437, including a vague $8,000 per month for "costs."[145] The same year, the government in exile asked for $67,000 per quarter for this commission. So attractive were the funds that when Aristide nominated Malval to be interim Prime Minister in 1993, the junta immediately asked him for access to the funds (allegedly to modernize the army).[146] In 1993, when the frozen funds were still abundant, the trust fund Kurzban managed showed payments of $400 to $700 a week to Haitian-sounding names such as Obed Dorceus, Mario Louis, Sasha Mercier, and Judith Alcindor in compensation for unspecified "services."[147]

The exact services performed by Haitian American lawyer Mildred Trouillot were equally obscure. Aristide hired her in January 1993, not as a lobbyist but as a close assistant whose role was to advise "the president of Haiti, accompan[y] the president in meetings," and generally stay close to him.[148] Her monthly retainer, starting at $3,000 plus expenses, increased regularly even as that of lawyers as crucial as Barnes diminished due to budgetary restrictions. Even after the intervention, when Trouillot moved to Haiti and stopped being registered as a Washington lobbyist, her salary kept increasing, reaching a peak of $15,000 a month in the fall of 1995.[149] Payments only stopped in February 1996, when Aristide married Trouillot, and when continuing to subsidize his significant other at government's expense would have become overly scandalous.[150]

Haitian Americans, already accustomed to sending money to their relatives in Haiti, helped Aristide financially. In one pro-Aristide rally, supporters filled whole bags with cash in a matter of minutes. The organizers of the march and representatives of Aristide then quarreled over who should take control of the funds.[151] How the Haitian Diaspora's substantial cash contributions to Aristide's government-in-exile were used will forever remain a mystery.

After frozen funds, offsets, and private donations, foreign contributions were the most important, and most controversial, source of income for Aristide. On 28 October 1993, as he spoke to the UN General Assembly, Aristide included some pro-Taiwan comments that seemed out of place in a speech focusing on his restoration. This political *faux-pas* was also a bizarre mistake for a usually astute politician, for it angered Communist China, a permanent member of the Security Council, armed with a veto power that could block any UN mission to Haiti. An 8 October 1993 check drawn on account #202010034579 of the International Commercial Bank of China gave the answer. A month before Aristide's speech, Taiwan's ambassador to Haiti, Lee Nan Hsing, had signed a $1 million check to Aristide's government-in-exile.[152] Taiwan, a rich but diplomatically isolated country, routinely uses aid to poor countries to obtain diplomatic support in the UN (Haiti had been promised $6 million in 1991, only $2 million of which was paid before the coup). Aristide's friend Patrick Elie acknowledged that "Taiwan follows a policy towards countries that recognize its existence which we may have profited from," justifying the move by saying that this was a form of "tactical flexibility" that was standard in diplomacy (he mentioned the Anglo-Soviet World War II alliance) and that "for us it was a vital matter."[153]

Based on conversations with State and Treasury officials, the *Wall Street Journal* estimated that by June 1994 Aristide had spent $30 million and was spending money at the rate of $5.6 to 5.9 million a quarter.[154] Kurzban, who managed a Haitian trust fund, initially received payments from the Haitian Embassy well in excess of the $600,000 the fund spent in a year.[155] But by late 1993, expenses had jumped to over $1 million a semester, and the fund was drawing red ink, forcing Aristide to curtail expenses drastically; the fund lost money throughout 1994.[156] Aside from exasperation after almost three years in exile, Aristide's deteriorating financial situation must explain his increasingly militant tone in the spring of 1994. Wargny recalled the gloomy mood that dominated during that period. "Seeing time go by so fast, President Aristide's entourage worried [that further delays would bring about the] elimination of the constitutional president of Haiti."[157]

Asking for a U.S. Intervention

Meeting heads of state, phrasing requests in inoffensive terms, hiring lawyers to lobby on his behalf, and ensuring that he had the financial wherewithal to keep doing so were important; but, even more than the medium, what mattered most was the message. Until late 1993, Aristide merely demanded that economic sanctions be more severe and better enforced, and that the United States intervene diplomatically on his behalf. He emphatically rejected an invasion in public comments.[158] Interviewed in October 1991, he stressed that a U.S. "military intervention is not [an option] we even consider. . . . Military intervention raises ugly memories in Haiti."[159] When Vice President Al Gore told Aristide in the wake of the *Harlan County* incident that an invasion would not take place, Aristide was reportedly "ecstatic."[160]

Aristide frequently told his representative in Haiti, Micha Gaillard, that he wanted the United States to solve the crisis the coup initiated, because "the white man [*le blanc*] must undo what he did,"[161] but he initially opposed an intervention because he held deep suspicions against what he called "the cold country to our north."[162] His many books are distinctly anti-American, and Aristide, in public and private, suspected the United States of having backed the 1991 coup that threw him out of power.[163] Aristide's friends were even more vocal, especially during the Bush administration. When Bush lost the 1992 elections, Antoine Izméry wrote to him, "you have made my day. . . . Your ex-Ambassador to Haiti, the well-known terrorist Alvin P. Adams Jr., orchestrated the destabilization of Haitian democracy leading to the coup. . . . Your vice-president Dan Quayle, an utter disgrace to humanity, accentuated the magnitude of your racist policies."[164] Father Adrien wrote to Aristide in December 1992, "*undoubtedly* one of the many centers of power in Washington gives the putsch leaders some signals to encourage them to harden their position. . . . [Promises of negotiations] are part of a well thought-out scenario to put us to sleep."[165]

By late 1993, however, the repression had claimed many Lavalas supporters, including prominent ones such as Antoine Izmery and Paul Malary. As became clear during the October 1993 *Harlan County* incident, negotiations and sanctions had failed. His presidential mandate was nearing its end and money was running out. Aristide, his back to the wall, took a second look at a U.S. intervention.[166]

During a 22 October 1993 PBS interview, Aristide was asked if he was ready to advocate a U.S. military intervention, an option he had previously rejected. Aristide's incoherent response was the first sign that he was reevaluating his position. "As the head of it [the Haitian state], if I ask for military intervention, I will be impeached by my constitution, so I fully—that if at the same time I see the folks out of the country tonight or even more today, right now, I will feel happy because all of us want life. We give our life for having life, not death."[167] On 9 November, he pointed out at a small press conference with French-speaking journalists that "the people of Haiti would be happy" to see a foreign military intervention, but that the Constitution prevented him from asking for one himself.[168] The *Miami Herald* was the only U.S. newspaper to pick up the story.[169] At the Miami International Conference on 14 to 17 January 1994, it was Aristide's supporters' turn to propose a U.S. intervention, while Aristide insisted the United States should get him back in Haiti by 7 February 1994 (the third anniversary of his inauguration).[170] The conference had little impact outside the circle of devoted Haiti watchers. The general public was much more interested in the Los Angeles earthquake and the trial of Lorena Babbitt.

In early June 1994, Aristide's calls for an intervention became more open. Asking for "a surgical action" to remove the junta, he referred in a *New York Times* interview to the 1989 intervention in Panama as a model. "Haiti is not the first case. When things were like that in another country, something was done. Why not in Haiti?"[171] A day later, at a TransAfrica conference in Washington, he argued, "swift and determined action should be taken to remove the coup leaders within the framework of the GI [Governors' Island] agreement. I will not waste time describing what this action would be. The international community knows how to proceed."[172] He repeated the same words to Latin American foreign ministers three days later.[173] This salvo, coming, as it did, in short order, at carefully chosen venues and in nearly identical terms, had obviously been carefully weighed to provoke a U.S. response.

The response came quickly, but it came from Haiti. On 9 June, the Capois-la-Mort right-wing organization accused Aristide of high treason. Formal legal proceedings began in August, charging Aristide with violations of Art. 58 of the penal code (which banned secret dealings with enemies of the state) and of Art. 21 and 135–1 of the 1987 Constitution, which obliged the president to preserve the nation's independence under penalty of forced labor for life. Aristide's entourage also had misgivings about the use of force. A 1993 Lavalas memo had complained about an "overpowering" international community that showed a willingness to push "*le souverain*" (the sovereign, i.e., Aristide) aside. "Can we accept that a foreign force on the national territory is not under the direction of the government? Isn't there a risk that the international force (that is, Americans) will monopolize effective political power?"[174] In June 1994, some Aristide advisers were uneasy as he invited Americans in Haiti.

In Aristide's defense, this was not the first time a Haitian leader had betrayed his country for political gain. In the intensely competitive political climate preceding the 1915 U.S. invasion, both sides repeatedly called for a U.S. intervention. François Duvalier, another self-styled nationalist, welcomed the arrival of a Marine training group in 1958 to shore up his regime; as two of his predecessors had done before him, he also offered Môle St. Nicolas to the U.S. Navy in 1961 (the Navy refused).[175] During the Governors' Island negotiations, Cédras, afraid that anti-Army riots would follow Aristide's return, insisted that a large UN force be sent to Haiti along with Aristide (Aristide had demanded the same thing five months earlier).[176]

Because of the uproar his remarks had created, Aristide started backpedaling. On 25 June 1994, he denied ever having asked for a U.S. intervention. "I always said it, and today I will repeat it again: I am against a military invasion. I am against a military occupation." Asked if he would ever agree to be brought back to power by means of an invasion, Aristide emphatically repeated "never, never, and never again."[177] Afraid that Aristide would later accuse UN troops of invading Haiti, Boutros-Ghali enjoined him to commit in writing to UNSC Resolution 940 authorizing the use of force, but Aristide's letter only indicated, "I feel that the time has come for the international community . . . to take prompt and decisive action, under the authority of the United Nations."[178] He deliberately refused to make any clearer endorsement of an invasion. Haiti's permanent representative to the United Nations Fritz Longchamp, finally wrote a laconic note "to inform you of the agreement of the *Government of* President Jean-Bertrand Aristide with draft resolution S/1994/904 [draft of resolution 940 authorizing the use of force]."[179]

This U-turn was mere public posturing; in private, Aristide continued to ask for an invasion. Caught between a fiercely independent people and his desire to return to power, Aristide cultivated an ambivalence that irritated supporters such as Anthony Lake. "On the one hand, he [Aristide] privately welcomed [an invasion] as a solution to the problem. On the other, given the memories in Haiti of the American occupation earlier in the century, he would not publicly endorse another entry of American forces, whatever its purpose."[180] In the meetings NSC staff member Richard Feinberg attended, Aristide and his American lawyer Michael D. Barnes "kept pressuring us to take a tougher stand against the junta. As time went on, Aristide was increasingly in favor of the use of force. But he very cleverly remained ambivalent in public because of Haitian nationalism."[181]

Aristide's many conversations with high-level administration officials, and his public and private requests for U.S. military intervention, must have had an effect, which declassification will one day allow us to weigh with more precision. Barnes, who had a knack for contacting the right people at the right moment, met or called Pezzullo, who had just started as U.S. special envoy to Haiti, 17 times in two months from mid-March to mid-May 1993 alone.[182] In October 1993, when the *Harlan County* left Haiti, Barnes was able to schedule a teleconference with Lake (14 October) and Berger (14 and 18 October). During the ensuing crisis, Barnes met or called administration officials up to 13 times a day (20 October 1993).

When Latell accused Aristide of being mentally unbalanced, Barnes contacted congressional aides "regarding members [of the Black Caucus] acting as surrogates to defend against character assassinations directed towards Aristide."[183] He also granted interviews to all the most influential media sources in the country, from the *New York Times* to *Time Magazine*, NPR, PBS, CNN, ABC, the *Wall Street Journal*, the *Washington Post*, and *Associated Press*. One of these reporters was Christopher Marquis of the *Miami Herald*, who investigated charges leveled against Aristide's mental health and undermined the credibility of Latell's allegations.[184]

In the spring of 1994, at the critical time when the Clinton administration was reviewing its Haiti policy, Barnes called or met Clinton (once), Lake (4 times), Berger (7 times), Feinberg (3 times), Rossin (3 times), Pezzullo (6 times), Fleischman (6 times), Ross-Robinson (12 times), Kozack (5 times), Watson (2 times), and Swing, in addition to daily contacts with the press and members of Congress and their assistants, particularly Joseph Kennedy and Charles Rangel.[185] In March 1994, Lake and Deputy Secretary of State Strobe Talbott also met Aristide numerous times in his Washington suite to seek his opinion. Lake recalls,

> At Strobe's suggestion, I began by asking Aristide for *his* views on the situation, since it was entirely possible that he knew more about Haiti than a foreigner like me did. This helped us begin a dialogue of somewhat greater trust, since he had been treated earlier only to constant lectures from the American side. We developed standing pleasantries—for example, taking turns serving coffee to the others attending our meetings.[186]

Lake also recalls that Aristide was asking for an invasion in such private conversations. In a telephone interview, Lake nevertheless insisted that U.S. policy was not influenced by Aristide's demands. "*We* were deciding what to do. He was making his policy, and we were making ours."[187] Feinberg concluded otherwise. "Aristide and [his lawyer Michael D.] Barnes had very good access to the President. Aristide used the political system—the media, the Black Caucus, Hollywood, human rights activists—with great sophistication. There were people within the administration that were influenced by Aristide."[188]

Who these people were Feinberg did not say, but Aristide's supporters eventually included some of the most influential people in the Clinton administration. On the NSC, Lake and Berger eventually favored an intervention, along with many staff members, including Nancy Soderberg. So did Gore and his national security adviser, Leon Fuerth. White House political advisers were initially cautious, but Stephanopoulos and others eventually favored the intervention when they realized that it could be politically rewarding for the president to look strong and courageous. The Black Caucus steadfastly supported Aristide. Warren Christopher was on Aristide's side, even though he would have preferred to continue the embargo. Talbott, Undersecretary of State Peter Tarnoff, and State Department Policy Planning Chief James B. Steinberg favored an intervention. These people often had direct access to the president, and dominated the issue when it was still considered secondary by others. Such allies were more helpful than the discredited CIA analyst and the members of the congressional minority the junta could count on its side.

Aristide believed that his supporters played a central role in prompting the United States to intervene. Half of the speech he delivered the day he came back to Haiti thanked "the Haitian people's many defenders" without whom his return could not have taken place. Among others, Aristide named U.S. congressmen, including Joseph Kennedy, members of the Black Caucus such as Charles Rangel and Major Owens, activists such as Randall Robinson, clergymen such as Jesse Jackson, intellectuals such as Taylor Branch, and artists such as Jonathan Demme and Harry Belafonte.[189]

Hoping to restore U.S. and presidential credibility, to prevent Haitian boat people from leaving Haiti, and to satisfy key political constituencies, but also influenced by Aristide's lobbying campaign, and—nominally at least—committed to Haitian democracy, the administration finally sent an expeditionary force to Haiti, the first elements of which landed in Port-au-Prince in the morning of 19 September 1994.

CHAPTER NINE
INVADING HAITI, EVADING RESPONSIBILITIES (19 SEPTEMBER–15 OCTOBER 1994)

Shelton Comes In

On 19 September 1994, Henry "Hugh" Shelton, commander of the U.S.-led Multinational Force (MNF), stepped out of the helicopter that had carried him from the command ship USS *Mount Whitney* and set foot on Port-au-Prince airport.[1] His mission: meet junta leader Raoul Cédras and determine what form the U.S. occupation would take. Shelton's task was awkward at best. The institution he represented, the Pentagon, had opposed the invasion, while his commander in chief had issued mixed signals, first claiming that the cause of Haitian democracy justified putting U.S. lives at risk, then authorizing Carter to sign an agreement with dictators to limit losses of life. In light of the intervention's sudden shift from a unilateral U.S. military offensive to a collaborative effort by the United States and the Cédras regime to orchestrate a peaceful transfer of power following the signature of the Carter–Jonassaint agreement, Shelton had to restore democracy in collaboration with autocrats.

Even though Haiti had been enemy territory less than 24 hours before, Shelton, who had initially hoped to parachute in with his troops during the night assault, insisted on carrying no weapon or protective armor of any kind. Knowing that Cédras would be watching the CNN broadcast of his arrival, he wanted to make one point clear: "it was all designed to show him, number one, that I wasn't the least bit afraid of what the hell he had in that country."[2] The attitude, a mix of bravado, courage, and shrewdness, was typical of Shelton.

The 6' 5" son of North Carolina farmers, Shelton joined the ROTC in college, then spent the 1960s as a Green Beret, training Montagnard tribesmen in Vietnam (he earned a Purple Heart when a poisoned stake pierced his leg). A Gulf War veteran as well, Shelton commanded the 82nd Airborne Division, the XVIIIth Airborne Corps, and Special Forces units.[3] He initially opposed the Haiti intervention, but this soldier's soldier, tall, abrupt, and no-nonsense, was determined to obey orders. His tactic was simple: "if you decide to use force, you should use a force that is well-prepared, well-equipped, and you should use it overwhelmingly."[4] Had the invasion taken place, his son Jeff, a helicopter pilot for the 82nd Airborne, would have been on the front lines.[5]

Regarding Cédras, Shelton "expected to put the bastard in cuffs and detain him at best," but the Carter–Jonassaint agreement changed all this. Forced to collaborate with the "bastard," he fell back on his understanding of the Haitian mind. "One thing that came loud and clear as I looked at the culture of the Haitians is that there are two things that they understood; one was force and one was fear."[6] In his first meeting with Cédras, Shelton thus described himself as a hard-liner who expected to inform the Haitians of what ought to be done, not to receive orders from local authorities. On the other hand, should the Haitian Army collaborate with the U.S. Army on matters such as law enforcement, Shelton promised that he would treat its members with respect.

The conversation set the tone for the first month of the occupation. Inadequate military planning and Clinton's shifting policies obliged U.S. commanders on the ground, first Shelton, then General David C. Meade, to improvise. The invading force, whose military superiority was overwhelming, was in a position to impose its will in every area it deemed fit, but in order to avoid an extensive, casualty-prone mission, Shelton and Meade showed their willingness to establish a collaborative, not adversarial, relationship. As a result, the U.S. soldiers' main mission became force protection, not restoring democracy; the Haitian Army remained as a law-enforcement body and continued to commit human rights abuses; and U.S. courts prosecuted U.S. soldiers overzealous in their democratic idealism, not members of the junta. The military rank-and-file and the U.S. media wondered what exactly U.S. troops had come to achieve, but the invading force's low profile proved successful in one regard: not a single American life was lost in combat during the first weeks of the occupation.

Inadequate Planning

Planning for the invasion, even though it started almost a year before U.S. troops landed in Haiti, left soldiers unprepared for the challenges of occupying a country under the framework set by the Carter–Jonassaint agreement. Following the October 1993 *Harlan County* incident, the U.S. Atlantic Command (USACOM) in Norfolk, Va. had created a working group, code-named "Jade Green," whose task was to plan an invasion of Haiti—a "forcible entry," in military jargon—that received the code-name "Dragon's Blood" or OPLAN 2370. Only a handful of key officers, including USACOM commander Adm. Paul David Miller and senior planner Maj. Gen. John J. Sheehan, knew about the plans. Others learned what their mission was only days before landing in Haiti.[7]

The actual detailed military planning, which Adm. Miller transferred to the XVIIIth Airborne Corps in January 1994, appears almost amateurish in retrospect. Because of excessive security concerns, two men, Major Kevin Benson and Major William Burke Garrett, did all the preparatory work, operating in what was deemed the only secure location in Fort Bragg: a refurbished closet on the third floor of the Corps headquarters. During the first month of planning, secrecy was so tight that they did not even have access to intelligence reports or satellite pictures. Lacking the proper clearance, they obtained the necessary information through a friend who happened to know someone working in the Analysis and Collection Element.[8]

After 95-hour weeks, the two met with superiors in a bare basement in Norfolk during four-day weekends to hammer out details.

On 2 June 1994, the Pentagon ordered that a second plan, based on a nonforcible entry, be prepared; this plan received the name OPLAN 2380. On 2 September, planners met in Washington to draft yet another plan, OPLAN 2375, which incorporated elements of both existing options. Probably puzzled by the erratic itinerary followed by U.S. policy, the Pentagon thus had three different options: the first, 2370, asking for Joint Task Force 180 (the 82nd Airborne) to fight its way into Haiti; the second, 2380, planning to employ Joint Task Force 190 (the 10th Mountain Division) as a purely peacekeeping force; and the third, 2375, incorporating elements of both plans.[9]

In contrast to the secretiveness of the first few weeks, security measures unraveled rapidly as the invasion date approached. Interagency planning began on 11 September, greatly increasing the number of people privy to classified information. Selected reporters, who promised that they would not publish their stories until the troops actually landed, had access to all the secret documents of the 82nd Airborne, including satellite imagery, maps of the attack, and the list of targets each unit was set to take over.[10] The administration also briefed reporters. Within days, the detailed framework—which unit would attack which target—of the invasion was public knowledge.[11]

At Shelton's insistence, the forcible entry option made use of overwhelming force. Five entire battalions of paratroopers, traveling on 60 C-130 and 45 C-141 transport planes, were to take over 41 different targets in Port-au-Prince, the capital, and Cap Haïtien in the north. With 8,000 paratroopers, this was the largest U.S. airborne operation since World War II. Marines would simultaneously launch an amphibious attack against Cap Haïtien, while AC-130 Specter planes towered overhead.[12] Adm. Paul David Miller made the radically novel suggestion that two aircraft carriers, the USS *America* and the USS *Eisenhower*, be entirely stripped of their planes (there was no Haitian air force to speak of) and transformed into landing pads from which helicopters could quickly ferry troops in and out of Haiti.[13] Within days, the force was to peak at 20,000 troops, equipped with everything from helicopter gun ships to M-2 Bradley fighting vehicles, to face a mere 7,000 Haitians. The military overkill was designed to limit casualties on both sides by reducing the entire invasion to a swift night assault. Americans would control all the country's strategic locations before the Haitian Army even woke up.

No one ever feared that the invasion would fail. The plan called for an airdrop during a night of the full moon, which made U.S. paratroopers as easy to shoot from the ground as their grandfathers were at Ste-Mère Eglise in June 1944. But planners did not expect Haiti's defenders to fire a shot; what they feared was that paratroopers might sprain their ankles if they landed in the dark. Dismissing the Haitians as irrelevant, planners spent most of their time improving air traffic patterns to avoid collisions, protecting troops from the only fire they were likely to encounter (friendly fire), and preparing an exit strategy.[14]

After nearly a year of frantic planning, the forcible entry was perfectly fine-tuned. Paratroopers were even able to rehearse their flights with computer simulations, a luxury unheard of previously. But all of this careful planning proved useless. When the invasion was called off at the last minute, the Pentagon suddenly had to shift from the forcible entry plan to the peacekeeping option, while keeping in mind that the environment was only semi-permissive. Planes filled with paratroopers turned around, then remained on standby for 24 hours (in case fighting did occur), then were unloaded and refitted with the material needed for the peacekeeping mission. In the meantime, the 10th Mountain Division was rushed to the scene, finding none of the facilities the 82nd Airborne should have secured previously. Because the invasion was peaceful, taking over enemy barracks was no longer possible. Soldiers settled in at the airport and the industrial complex near the port, both of which had been idled by the embargo, and worked feverishly to make them inhabitable.

Logistical shortcomings marred the first two weeks. No one was there to welcome and orient soldiers at the airport, so troops typically arrived after nightfall, slept outside, during rainstorms if necessary (September is the rainy season in Haiti), and spent the following morning finding their units.[15] They then commandeered a warehouse, rid it of goats, human feces, spider webs, and rats, and called it home (medical units found it particularly challenging to establish a sterile environment). Portapotties and showers were in short supply. Soldiers made do by rushing outside, naked, during tropical showers.[16] For lack of hot meals, they lived off a diet of preservative-laden ready-to-eat meals. Then, they started wondering what their mission actually entailed now that they were to collaborate with, not kill, every Haitian soldier they would encounter.

Ambiguous Orders, Reluctant Soldiers

U.S. commanders in Haiti, when they tried to devise an occupation policy in the wake of the Carter–Jonassaint agreement, suffered from the dearth of precise instructions from Washington, DC. The exact goals of the operation, as set out by the commander in chief, were ambiguous. During the days immediately preceding the invasion, Clinton delivered two addresses to the American people. The first, on 15 September, was highly idealistic, describing in minute detail the human rights abuses the United States ought to combat. The second, on the eighteenth, justified the Carter agreement by stressing that it "minimize[d] the risks for American forces and the forces of the 24 nations of the international coalition." The first speech would have warranted an ambitious, active occupation policy, conducted in opposition to former human rights abusers Clinton labeled "thugs," while the second implied that force protection was paramount and that the thugs—upgraded to "military leaders of Haiti"—were now friends.[17] To use the military's nomenclature on peace operations, the intervention started as a Peace Enforcement Operation (PEO), that is, "the application of military force . . . to compel compliance with resolutions or sanctions designed to maintain or restore peace and order," then shifted to a peacekeeping operation (PKO), that is, "military operations undertaken with the consent of all major parties to a dispute, designed to monitor and facilitate implementation of an agreement . . . and support diplomatic efforts to reach a long-term solution."[18]

On a more practical level, the last-minute switch from a forcible entry to a "peaceful" invasion left U.S. military units wondering what the rules of engagement

(ROEs) were. Soldiers had been issued three different ROE cards, color-coded white, yellow, and blue, each of which corresponded to a different environment.[19] Inevitably, snafus occurred, and soldiers who had been scheduled to land ten days after the invasion had destroyed the Haitian Army were rushed to Haiti with an ROE card designed for a peaceful environment. As a result, some U.S. soldiers ignored that the rules of engagement allowed them (rule #4) to stop members of the military "if they appear to threaten essential civic order" and to detain "persons observed committing serious criminal acts" (rule #7).[20]

Because of the ambiguity of Clinton's agenda, and because existing contingency plans did not correspond to the political situation created by the Carter–Jonassaint agreement, it was up to commanders on the ground, first Hugh Shelton (September–October 1994), then David C. Meade (October 1994–January 1995), to determine policy. When offered two options, one emphasizing the restoration of a democratic order at any cost and the other aiming to limit U.S. combat casualties, they chose the latter. This emphasis on force protection was particularly felt in the capital, Port-au-Prince, which was under Meade's direct supervision, less so in Cap Haïtien and rural areas.

The reasons for this reluctance to take risks were numerous. Ever since Colin Powell's anti-interventionist "doctrine" set forth in 1992, the Pentagon had been wary of getting bogged down in peacekeeping operations such as the one in Haiti.[21] After the 1992 election, the commander in chief, whom his opponents described as a draft-dodging, anti-gun Democrat who supported the presence of gays in the armed forces, was often seen as an interloper by a conservative institution emerging from 12 years of Republican presidents. The rank-and-file, wary of Clinton's intentions, frequently, and approvingly, quoted Bob Dole's comment that Haitian democracy was not worth a single American life.[22] The Somalia debacle further reduced interest in such missions.

American officers were more than willing to adopt a conciliatory attitude toward fellow soldiers who constituted the only counterweight to a radical populist priest they abhorred. Intelligence officers, probably influenced by the junta's accusations relayed through the CIA, likened the pro-Aristide Lavalas supporters to an anti-American lynch mob. During the week following the invasion, Primary Intelligence Requirements (PIRs) required intelligence officers to track potential threats to U.S. troops; pro-Aristide violence came second; human rights abuses against Aristide supporters only came third.[23] The Defense Intelligence Agency (DIA) even told U.S. troops that the murderous FRAPH was merely a political party.[24] According to a counterintelligence officer who participated in the Haiti mission, army intelligence officers "were very much anti-Aristide. . . . We only received anti-Aristide information."[25]

In the case of JTF 190 (the peacekeeping force), combat fatigue was also to blame for the refusal to undergo dangerous missions. In addition to regular training missions, the 10th Mountain Division, which formed the bulk of JTF-190, had been deployed to Florida after Hurricane Andrew struck (August–September 1992), then to Somalia for two difficult tours of duty, before it set up its headquarters in Port-au-Prince. Constant deployments created severe family problems, including divorces. In the words of a civil affairs officer from JTF 180, "the thing that all of us have noticed, that's really been alarming to all of us . . . the 10th Mountain Division seems to have come out of their experience in Somalia with a siege mentality."[26] Soldiers, who had expected the Haitian Army to wither away within hours of the invasion, acted with circumspection upon landing in a Port-au-Prince where the Haitian Army still patrolled the streets.

A U.S. force actively involved in local affairs would also be more difficult to extricate, so soldiers viewed their passivity as a guarantee that they would leave quickly. A mere one month into the invasion, Col. James L. Campbell, Chief of Staff of JTF 190, argued that the U.S. force had already achieved its mission and that the time had arrived to call in the United Nations. "Just by the nature of the beast, every day longer we're here, we're going to embrace more neat ideas in terms of the safe and secure environment."[27]

Many soldiers doubted that anything could be achieved anyway. The political adviser to the 10th Mountain Division commander confided, "I still believe that we should not have intervened in Haiti. . . . Haiti has a way of defeating the best of our intentions."[28] Col. James S. Gulick, as director of the civil military operations center of JTF-190, could have helped rebuild Haiti, but did not for lack of trust. Noticing the high level of corruption in Haiti, as well as casual disregard for basic mainte-nance, he saw no reason to improve infrastructures, preferring "to help the Haitians help themselves."[29]

Culture shock also made American troops wary of even having contact with the local population. An information packet on Haitian culture and history distributed to American soldiers aimed at increasing cultural awareness, but it contained so many inaccuracies that it proved counterproductive. As a result, many soldiers saw all Haitians as Voodoo sorcerers ready to throw magic powders in their face and to attack them with HIV-infected syringes.[30] Haitians were partly to blame for U.S. circumspection regarding Voodoo. The junta's puppet president, Emile Jonassaint, had already threatened to make use of his Voodoo powers.[31] U.S. soldiers deployed to the countryside were often taken aback when faced with accusations that a former *Macoute* was also a zombie. In the island of La Gonâve, locals asked a GI to arrest a 70-year-old woman accused of being a werewolf.[32] Surgeons had to learn how to treat machete and arrowhead wounds. Haitian American Creole linguists were a knowledgeable and appreciated subsidiary to intelligence units, but even they found it difficult to communicate with the population. They were afraid that paramilitary units linked to the junta would retaliate against the family members of anyone collaborating with an invading force, and many translators opted to take off their name tags.[33] Aside from Haitian Army officers and mulatto businessmen providing logistical support to U.S. forces, few Haitians had extensive contacts with Americans.

Racism, prevalent on both sides during the 1915–1934 U.S. occupation of Haiti, was much less a factor in 1994. A psychological operations officer found his task easy because "when you're talking about the Haitian culture, you're not talking about a sophisticated people to begin with," but such disparaging comments were relatively rare.[34] The 1994 U.S. military, home to many Blacks, women, and minorities, reflected the increasing diversity of American society, and it was initially welcomed as a liberating, not invading force.[35] Blaming racism for the Army's failure to establish contact with locals would overlook the fact that culture shock also besets diplomats, teachers, and NGO workers, many of whom, after years in Haiti, admit having barely any contact with the local population. Due to the language barrier, violence, widespread suspicion of foreigners, and extreme poverty, they find it easier to live in the hills of wealthy Pétionville, zooming by the native population in locked, armored, and air conditioned sport-utility vehicles.[36]

Primacy of Force Protection

Unsure of what the mission exactly was, and afraid of getting bogged down in a hostile country, the military hierarchy made force protection the most important, or even the only, objective of what remained, nominally at least, an operation to restore democracy. Orders were strict. Despite the tropical heat, soldiers had to wear full body armor at all times. The military hierarchy went berserk whenever it spotted a soldier with sleeves rolled up on CNN. It was not uncommon for senior officers on an inspection tour to personally implement the dress code, rather than delegating such tasks to lower-ranking servicemen. Green Berets were particularly targeted.[37] Soldiers working in the port argued at length that falling in the water while clad in Kevlar and a helmet was dangerous before they were allowed to adapt their gear.

General David C. Meade, who commanded the 10th Mountain Division, which formed the bulk of U.S. troops in Port-au-Prince, and who took over as head of the entire multinational force in October 1994, insisted that his troops stay inside heavily protected barracks, and that they not talk or give food to anyone outside. Peacekeeping limited itself to a few mobile patrols, conducted by troops with orders not to stop, step off their vehicle, or establish roadblocks.[38] Even though the invasion plans made heavy use of the U.S. Army's ability to fight at night, it took two weeks before American soldiers organized night patrols. Such strict orders contradicted FM 41–10, the standard field manual on civil–military affairs, which encourages "direct involvement with the civilian populace" and lists among an occupying force's main duties the protection of law and order and the prevention of human rights abuses.[39]

An attempt to reduce the availability of weapons among the local populace also met with limited success for lack of proactive policies. The multinational force raided some Haitian Army compounds, including the heavy weapons unit at Camp d'Application, but stopped short of attacking every weapons cache and conducting widespread body searches. All too frequently, Haitians accused their personal enemies of owning weapons, further diminishing the U.S. desire to carry out such raids.[40] A weapons buy-back program, which offered a financial compensation to any individual turning in a functioning weapon, was a way to avoid having to look for the weapons, but the cash offered was initially set below the guns' market value.[41] Weapons seized in that manner were put aside for the new Haitian National Police (HNP), kept as museum pieces, or, most often, sent to Pennsylvania to be melted down. Twenty thousand weapons were seized during the first three months of the occupation, but an estimated 200,000 guns remained in circulation.[42] Success was unlikely, as Americans had not managed to rid their own country of guns, nor even to decide whether such a policy was appropriate in the first place.

The force's extreme caution was less marked in rural areas, where Special Forces, not 10th Mountain Division light infantry troops, were deployed. Displaying the braggadocio associated with their *esprit de corps*, Green Berets often refused to wear body armor, showed little respect for the dress code, and sneered at the troops barricaded in Port-au-Prince, who did little and feared everybody.[43] Far away from the scrutiny of their superiors, obliged to control thousands of square kilometers with small 12-man A-teams, they did not hesitate to mingle with the local population and to take sides—often against local Haitian Army tyrants. They prided themselves on doing stuff, resenting that some sissy from headquarters would criticize them for violating the dress code or alcohol policy. When Meade visited Camp d'Application, Green Berets rose from their bench in sequence in a wave-like motion (Meade delayed their deployment as a punishment).[44]

This undisciplined, take-charge, take-sides attitude directly contradicted Meade's orders, prompting him to punish troublemakers. In Fort Liberté, Special Force team leader Stan Goff, who was known for his strong anti-Haitian Army bias, his refusal to implement the dress code, and his leftist, anti-American political views, was relieved of his command on 10 December. He and Team commander Capt. Mike Gallante narrowly escaped a court-martial.[45]

Collaborating with the Haitian Armed Forces (FAdH)

Law enforcement was a particularly thorny issue. Asking U.S. troops to patrol the streets and to arrest criminals would most certainly have put U.S. lives at risk, so Shelton and Meade shied away from it. On the other hand, a complete breakdown of law and order would have been even more likely to undermine the goal of force protection, so one needed to find someone, preferably not American, willing to police Haiti until a new police force could be trained. Luckily for U.S. soldiers, there was already a force present in Haiti willing to, and experienced in, quelling demonstrations and arresting troublemakers. Unfortunately for Haitian civilians, this force was the Haitian Army.

Despite Haitian soldiers' poor human rights record, U.S. troops proceeded to rely on their services for day-to-day law enforcement. The first weeks of the occupation were thus marked by an odd business-as-usual atmosphere: the Haitian Army policed the streets, occasionally shooting pro-Aristide demonstrators, while American troops, thousands-strong but cloistered in their barracks, remained largely idle. "We are not in the business of doing the day-to-day law and order," explained the Chairman of the Joint Chiefs of Staff at a 20 September–White House briefing.

> For that matter, they [Haitian soldiers] are resolving or quelling any demonstrations unless these demonstrations or this level of violence becomes so great that it threatens the overall stability and the security of multinational forces and then we will intercede.[46]

The first major human rights violation occurred one hour later, when Haitian soldiers, who were dispersing a crowd that had come to welcome U.S. troops in the harbor, beat Benykel Dédé, a coconut vendor and father of five children, to death.

Foreign TV crews were there to record the murder. American soldiers were also present, but, believing that they were bound by their rules of engagement, did not intervene.[47] Adding insult to injury, State Department spokesman Michael McCurry announced that the multinational force had no intention of prosecuting the culprits. "When the duly elected government is in place, they can follow up on those types of abuses and prosecute them to the full extent that the Haitian law provides. That is not a question, again, that is within the province of the multinational force."[48]

Following the incident, Shelton and Meade met Cédras and Haitian Army Chief of Staff Philippe Biamby and warned them that cooperation would end if the police acted in that manner.[49] The Haitian Army immediately scaled down the repression, as well as everything else. Units stayed in their barracks and rarely ventured out. This created a dilemma for U.S. commanders. If they wanted to avoid patrolling and incurring casualties, they had to resort to some native force. However great its limitations were, the Haitian Army was the only credible, organized police force. Its demise would result in popular unrest, thus requiring an extensive American presence, as a shootout in Cap Haïtien soon made clear.

Marines landed in Cap Haïtien on the twentieth, finding a city marred by extreme tensions.[50] Relations between Col. Tom Jones, commander of the U.S. Marine occupation force in Cap Haïtien, and Lt. Col. Josaphat, commander of the Haitian military force in Cap Haïtien, were bad from the beginning.[51] Pro-Aristide crowds frequently held demonstrations, which Haitian soldiers put down ruthlessly. To prevent such violence, 14 U.S. Marines surrounded a police station on the afternoon of the twenty-fourth.[52] A large crowd formed, throwing insults and various pieces of garbage at the policemen occupying the post. Even though the soldiers spent the day playing dominoes and cards, rumors swirled that they had prepared an ambush. Aware that a prolonged gunfight would provoke a bloodbath among surrounding civilians, the Marines decided that, should a shooting occur, they would not duck for cover but immediately open fire on the policemen. Each Marine loaded his M16, picked one opponent, aimed his gun at him, and waited. Insults continued to rain, while the policemen feigned indifference. The sun set.

The tension that had accumulated throughout the day and the week exploded at 7 p.m., when two Haitian soldiers got into an argument. One reached for his gun, and the other raised his Uzi. Feeling threatened, Lt. Virgil Palumbo shot both of them in the chest and his fellow Marines immediately unleashed a deluge of fire, spraying the building with 1,000 rounds. No Haitian soldier had time to shoot. On the U.S. side, only one Haitian American Navy linguist, José Joseph, was wounded, but ten Haitian policemen lay dead. It took another three hours of negotiating to convince the six terrified survivors, some of them wounded, that they could safely surrender. Under the cover of darkness, remaining Haitian soldiers in the city, 400 in all, fled.[53]

At Josaphat's request, Cédras met Jones, accused him of war crimes, and unsuccessfully demanded that he be dismissed and court-martialed.[54] In less time than it takes for a trigger-happy NYPD officer to be acquitted, Jones concluded that his troops had acted in self-defense. Roadblocks cordoned off the area until the morning of the twenty-fifth, after which pro-Aristide crowds ransacked this and other police stations in Cap Haïtien, turning over the weapons to any American they encountered (journalists included).[55]

The incident could have created a rift between the U.S. and Haitian armed forces and marked the beginning of a forceful occupation policy, but it had the exact opposite effect. As the Haitian police fled Cap Haïtien, the Marines were obliged to take over all law enforcement duties, and commanders in Port-au-Prince foresaw the day when the complete breakdown of the Haitian Army would force them to become Haiti's reluctant nanny. Becoming pro-consul of Haiti was Shelton's greatest nightmare.

> I almost had to worry more about the complete collapse of the FAD'H [Haitian Army] . . . because, for all their faults, they still were an institution that had some organization to it that you could, in fact, hold accountable for some things and could provide . . . some amount of stability in the country which you wouldn't have if you had nothing, to whit, Cap Haïtien. And I thought to myself, if we got that throughout the country, Port-au-Prince with 1.2 million for example, versus 60 to 85 thousand people up in Cap Haïtien . . . 1.2 million people with no police force and no military and no nothing here then we're the only thing left. And so I had a personal interest in trying to keep the FAD'H from collapsing totally and complete anarchy taking over.[56]

U.S. troops thus did their best not to humiliate their Haitian counterparts and encouraged them to leave their barracks, patrol the streets, and maintain order. Unfortunately, the muscular way in which the Haitian Army and its supporters understood law enforcement again led to some well-publicized excesses. On the twenty-ninth, Aristide supporters held a demonstration in Port-au-Prince to commemorate the return of the capital's mayor. Right-wing gunmen launched a grenade at the demonstrators, killing 5 and wounding 60.[57] The following day, Haitians again demonstrated to celebrate the third anniversary of the 1991 coup. Emboldened by the sight of American military vehicles they hoped would protect them, they approached the headquarters of the FRAPH. But the vehicles were only passing by, on their way to establishing roadblocks on Ave. John Brown (the main road to the wealthy suburb of Pétionville, also known as Route de Pétionville) in order to prevent violence against the elite, and FRAPH members shot and killed at least six of the demonstrators before the crowd retaliated and killed two members of the FRAPH.[58]

Restoring democracy while collaborating with supporters of the junta proved confusing for U.S. troops. On 3 October soldiers of the 10th Mountain Division launched a raid on FRAPH headquarters. Meanwhile, as the U.S. force had encouraged them to do, members of the Haitian Army patrolled the neighborhood, unaware that a raid was on. When the Haitian soldiers approached a U.S. roadblock and insisted that they be allowed to go through, they were promptly arrested, disarmed, and handcuffed. Their mouths taped, they were placed back in the truck they had come in.[59] When U.S. soldiers finally realized that the men that they had arrested were good, friendly supporters of the former regime assigned to police duties, as opposed to the bad, unfriendly supporters of the regime they were supposed to arrest, they freed the Haitians; some of them, in tears, asked to be escorted back to their headquarters lest the surrounding crowd kill them. Shelton once again feared this would force his men to take on law enforcement missions. "We should not have done that. I mean, that was uncalled for. [Our troops] had become a little adversarial in the relationship with the police. But that almost destroyed the police."[60] Shocked by the U.S. Army's reliance on human rights abusers for law enforcement missions, one U.S. captain decided to act on his own.

The Strange Case of Lawrence P. Rockwood

Had the intervention in Haiti really been dedicated to restoring democracy, Capt. Lawrence Peck Rockwood would have been one of its heroes.[61] A soldier, as his father, grandfather, and great-grandfather had been, he believed in the code of honor of professional warriors. His father, a World War II veteran, had even taken Rockwood as a child to visit Dachau.[62] Rockwood, 36 years old in 1994, belonged to a generation that had grown up in the shadow of Vietnam and My Lai. On his desk in Fort Drum, Rockwood kept three pictures, one of Hugh C. Thompson (famous for ordering his helicopter gunner to fire on U.S. troops massacring Vietnamese civilians at My Lai), one of Col. Claus von Stauffenberg (a Nazi officer who tried to kill Hitler on 20 July 1944), and one of Col. Georges Picquart (a French officer who opposed his superiors' efforts to frame Alfred Dreyfus as a German spy).[63] He was also a Buddhist who once considered Catholic priesthood and an idealist.

Joining the army in 1977, Rockwood became an intelligence officer in 1989. He served in Germany, Honduras, and Panama, but never saw combat, which may explain his enthusiasm as he left for Haiti. Arriving in Port-au-Prince on 23 September he took up the night shift as counterintelligence officer in the office of the assistant Chief of Staff for intelligence (G2). His superior, Lt. Col. Frank B. Bragg, told him that his main mission was to gather intelligence on potential threats to U.S. soldiers. There was much to be done, as intelligence reports, before and during the invasion, were of dubious quality. Standard procedure required that every bit of information be graded with a letter-number combination assessing the reliability of the source (A: always; E: never; F: not checked), and whether the information had been double-checked (1: confirmed; 5: proved false; 6: not checked). Most human intelligence reports were classified F6 (neither source nor facts checked), which was troubling given the number of rumors swirling around Port-au-Prince.[64]

Rockwood claims that threats to the U.S. force were nonexistent, and that Clinton's 15 September speech and Field Manual 41–10 should have warranted a more proactive stance, particularly with regard to prisoners.[65] Rockwood thus collected intelligence reports on human rights abuses by Haitian military personnel, murders, torture, and disappearances, many victims of which seemed to come from Haiti's infamous prisons. One particularly troubling report he came across described a prison in Les Cayes, where cells were so crowded that prisoners' skin peeled off. This is where the infamous Mondelus Norelus, a.k.a "Saddam Hussein," operated.[66] Bragg dismissed such stories as rumors, and Rockwood's reports on human rights abuses did not make their way into the daily intelligence summary distributed to senior officers. Bragg also denied Rockwood's request to inspect the *Pénitencier National*, Haiti's central prison. Rockwood appealed to his superiors, the provost marshal officer, the allied release coordinator, the chaplain, the Staff Judge Advocate, the Civil Military Operations Center, the Military Police, and the UN military observer, but to no avail. Visiting the national penitentiary was too dangerous and too low a priority.

On the morning of 30 September Rockwood filed an inspector general's complaint. The move was potentially career-threatening, and, concluding that "my career was over anyway," he decided not to wait for a response but to act immediately.[67] That same night, at 5 p.m., Rockwood prepared himself to do something unthinkable to soldiers: disobey. He wrote a note on which he pinned a tiny American flag upside-down.

> I am doing something that is clearly legal to stop something that is plainly illegal. Action required: All means necessary to implement the intent of the United Nations and U.S. president intent on human rights. Take this flag. It is soiled with unnecessary blood. You cowards can court-martial my dead body.[68]

Rockwood put on a flak jacket, seized his M-16 and a full load of ammo, left his room, and climbed over the barbed wire surrounding the U.S. barracks. Wandering for an hour through the dark streets of Port-au-Prince, he finally found the penitentiary (there are very few street signs in Port-au-Prince, and the names of the streets appearing on maps do not always correspond to the ones commonly used by Haitians). Twenty FRAPH members stood outside the prison, whose door was left ajar. Rockwood came in and announced to the warden, Maj. Serge Justafor, that he was the vanguard of a U.S. inspection team. Justafor, a graduate of the infantry school in Fort Benning, Ga., spoke English and allowed Rockwood to visit military prisoners. These being Haitian soldiers that the multinational force had placed under the custody of Haitian soldiers, they, not surprisingly, were very well treated.[69] The two dozen other prisoners sleeping on the infirmary's concrete floor, on the other hand, were shockingly emaciated. Several of them were amputees due to gangrene, while others suffered from dysentery. An excrement-filled trench running through the room was the only sanitation facility.

Justafor never let Rockwood visit the several hundred prisoners living in the main cells, but one can extrapolate their conditions from other testimonies. Paul J. Browne, an international police monitor who visited the prison in October 1994, described conditions as "medieval. . . . Most of the prisoners relied on daily visits from family members or friends to get fed. . . . No records, no accounts of why they were there, how long they were there, when they were due to be released."[70] Even after the main cell, which had held 500 prisoners standing in six inches of excrement, was cleaned up, Rep. Dan Burton (R-IN) testified in Congress that "the prison's conditions were subhuman. . . . Most noticeable was the terrible stench. It was overpowering."[71]

Rockwood refused to leave until he could inspect the main cell, which Justafor steadfastly refused, so both men called for U.S. authorities to intervene and to break the gridlock. The U.S. Embassy was a few blocks away, but it took three hours for the military attaché, Maj. Roland Spencer Lane, to arrive on the scene—he had presumably never visited the National Penitentiary. Lane sided with the warden and ordered Rockwood back to his barracks, where he was read his rights. Two psychological evaluations and one day later, Rockwood had another stormy conversation with his superior, Bragg, then was sent back to the division's headquarters in Fort Drum, N.Y.

Rockwood could have resigned or accepted nonjudicial punishment. Ever the martyr, he preferred to undergo a court-martial. His obvious insubordination, and the fact that all five officers on the jury were under Gen. Meade's command, left little doubt as to the outcome of the trial. In May of 1995, Rockwood was found guilty on three of the five counts: failure to report to duty, disrespectful attitude toward a superior, and disobedience. The sentence, which could have been up to ten years in prison, was dishonorable discharge. Appeals to a U.S. court of appeals and to the Supreme Court were inconclusive, and Rockwood is still trying to convince the Secretary of Defense to reopen his case. In 2000, he became an adjunct professor of history at California State University at San Marcos.[72] He also ran for U.S. representative in the November 2004 election.

Coming in the wake of various attacks against Haitian civilians in which the Haitian Army and FRAPH were involved, the lone captain's single-handed inspection of the National Penitentiary and his subsequent arrest and trial attracted much public attention.[73] Proving more responsive to media criticism than to the Haitians' plight, the multinational force started paying more attention to prisons. Col. Michael Sullivan, who entered the penitentiary on 1 October as he searched for weapons, told Meade that conditions were appalling.[74] So did UN police monitors after they paid a visit two weeks later.[75] Finally, three months after the invasion, U.S. troops entered the prison and requested a list of prisoners. Gen. James Hill, who succeeded Meade as commander of the multinational force, personally inspected every prison in Haiti. Undersecretary of Defense Walter Slocombe and several congressmen also visited the penitentiary.[76] Rockwood's *coup d'éclat* helped justify Operation Restore Democracy's name.

Emmanuel Constant and the FRAPH

To avoid U.S. casualties, U.S. commanders in Haiti Shelton and Meade followed a policy regarding Emmanuel Constant, one of the junta's most prominent supporters, similar to the one they had followed with Haitian policemen and prisons: do not rock the boat. The head of a paramilitary group, the FRAPH, that claimed a membership of 300,000 people, Constant, who had led the October 1993 demonstration against the *Harlan County*, represented a serious threat to the multinational force. In order to obtain a pledge that Constant would not attack U.S. troops and that he would help diminish levels of political violence, U.S. commanders held an important bargaining chip: immunity from prosecution.

On 3 October, the U.S. occupation force conducted a raid against the headquarters of the FRAPH in Port-au-Prince. Thirty low-ranking FRAPH members were arrested.[77] Despite appearances, this did not mark the beginning of a countrywide crackdown against paramilitary groups associated with the junta, however. During the raid, a DEXTRA (Documents Extraction) unit seized thousands of pages of internal documents, which the U.S. government subsequently refused to make available to the public, hindering later efforts to document the FRAPH's crimes and its links with the U.S. intelligence community.[78] Shortly after the raid, U.S. commanders Meade and Shelton met FRAPH leader Emmanuel Constant in the VIP lounge of the Port-au-Prince airport.[79]

Meade and Shelton carefully staged the meeting. Meade first met Constant and transmitted a U.S. request that Constant endorse democracy publicly, advocate reconciliation with Aristide, and urge his followers to renounce political violence. In return, Meade promised that the U.S. occupation force would stop its crackdown against FRAPH members. When Constant tried to negotiate terms, Meade told him he would have to talk to Shelton, the top dog, and a mean one too. Constant, aware that U.S. troops had previously raided his party's headquarters, was left alone for ten minutes while a Navy SEAL team loudly inspected the building, slamming doors, toting guns, and trying to scare Constant. The 6'5" Shelton finally entered the room.

> So I walked in and . . . I just said to myself "remember two things force and death they understand." So I looked at him and I said "sit down!" And he immediately sat down and the smile left his face and his eyes were big. [Constant started negotiating for better conditions.] I let him get about ten seconds into that and I cut him off and I told him very curtly that I was not interested in hearing any of that right now. . . . I really wanted him to understand in no uncertain terms that if he would not cooperate, that if he did not meet all the conditions laid out, that we would hunt him and the members of his organization like dogs, like rats.[80]

Constant accepted the deal. That night, Constant called fellow FRAPH members and encouraged them to maintain a low profile. The following day, the U.S. Embassy announced that Constant would hold a press conference, and Constant, speaking in English, read a speech that Meade had helped to draft. "We accept Aristide's return and are willing to work as a constructive opposition force so that we can reestablish order and dignity in the country."[81] Less than six months before, Constant had declared that "if Aristide were to return, he would die."[82] Haitians were so outraged by this sudden turnaround that U.S. soldiers had to protect Constant from a lynch mob as he left the press conference.[83]

The following day, U.S. Defense Secretary William Perry announced that he had "not set out to eliminate the FRAPH as an organization." Asked why U.S. forces had not arrested Constant, he answered that "we only went after the people where we had some reason to believe that they were provoking violence and that they had the weapons to do that," which was a fairly accurate description of Constant and the FRAPH.[84] U.S. Special Forces in the field also received orders from the Pentagon to stop harassing FRAPH members.[85] The occupation force had struck the same Faustian bargain with the FRAPH that it had with the Haitian Army: forgiveness and collaboration, even with human rights abusers, in exchange for a no-fight pledge.

Public Criticism

Emphasizing force protection, delegating dangerous police duties to the Haitian Army, and cutting deals with human rights violators kept the intervention casualty-free, but it generated a lot of bad press in the United States. Images of U.S. soldiers standing by helplessly as their Haitian allies beat supporters of Aristide to death, splattered across U.S. newspapers and TV newscasts, contradicted Clinton's portrayal of Operation Restore Democracy as an idealistic crusade and undermined the credibility of a force afraid to step out of its fortified compound at the Port-au-Prince airport. Shelton's close relationship with Cédras also left Haitian civilians wondering whether they should treat the U.S. invader as a friend or a foe. Knowing that tepid public support for the operation could lead to a repetition of the Vietnam and Somalia fiascoes, U.S. forces expended a great amount of energy catering to the media and to the Haitian people.

OPLAN 2370, the original invasion plan, incorporated a day-by-day timetable of what the public relations offensive would entail. Even soldiers at the unit level were briefed on how to respond to the media. Joint Task Force 180's Joint Information Bureau alone employed 23 public affairs specialists. Probably out of fear that the media would prove more fearsome than the Haitian military, they were scheduled to be air-dropped along with other paratroops during the first hours of the invasion.[86] With his superiors' approval, the commanding officer of the 10th Mountain Division's helicopter brigade, Col. Lawrence E. Casper, spent the last two days before his troops left Norfolk, Va. aboard the U.S.S. *Eisenhower* fielding interviews. On 19 September, when it finally came time to ferry 10th Mountain Division troops into Port-au-Prince airport, Meade ordered Casper to delay the carefully fine-tuned helicopter schedules by 60 seconds because CNN had announced that the first troops would land at 9:30 a.m.—not 9:29.[87]

The media were given access to even the most sensitive facilities. With approval from the White House, TV and radio crews traveled along with paratroopers during the aborted night assault.[88] Others were present in the command center of the USS *Mount Whitney*, from which Shelton monitored the invasion. Afraid that the restrictive pooling adopted during the Gulf War would generate bad press, and that it was difficult to keep journalists away from the front lines in such a fluid situation, the Army ferried delegations of journalists by helicopter throughout Haiti. So quickly were journalists informed that soldiers typically left CNN on at all times to keep abreast of latest developments. CNN alone had five crews in Haiti with the capability to broadcast from anywhere, anytime. Journalists were so competitive that they flocked en masse to the few armed confrontations between U.S. forces and Haitians, often outnumbering U.S. soldiers in the process.[89]

U.S. forces also tried to garner public support in Haiti itself by spreading their message: we come in peace, do not attempt to resist, do not try to emigrate to the United States. Before the invasion even started, U.S. planes had dropped 18 million leaflets over a nation of 8 million people, more than half of whom were illiterate.[90] After they landed in Haiti, U.S. troops took over Haiti's national TV channel and radio station, bought advertisements on private channels and stations, hired town criers, rented billboards, and attached loudspeakers to cars and helicopters. So important were these "psy-op" operations that they were directly overseen by the National Security Council.[91] The military's *spinmeisters* succeeded in the short term. U.S. soldiers generally encountered throngs of thankful Haitians wherever they went, even though, given the isolation of the Haitian countryside, U.S. troops came across a few inhabitants of rural areas who, weeks after the U.S. occupation force's arrival, still did not know that their country had been invaded.[92] Anti-American resentment did not surface in full force until the fall of 1995 (see chapter twelve).

Low Morale

American journalists were not the only ones wondering what the exact goals of Operation Restore Democracy were. U.S soldiers were, too. The uncertainty and lack of purpose born of the operation's shifting goals, along with the strain typically associated with deployments abroad, resulted in low troop morale.

Canceling the assault literally in midair carried a cost that was not only diplomatic and political, but human as well. Soldiers updated their will and life linsurance policies, put war paint on, boarded the planes, took off, and prepared for combat, excited that the entire 82nd Airborne was involved, only to learn that the operation was off. The emotional letdown was tremendous. Encumbered by their parachutes and equipment, and secretly hoping that the plane was going to turn around again, some paratroopers refused to unrig until they were back on the ground. Everyone had drunk a lot to avoid dehydration, and there was nothing but little plastic bags to relieve oneself during the long ride home. Dreams of glory and hopes of medals faded away.[93] Aboard an amphibious assault force, a mere 20 miles from its target, Cap Haïtien, 1,800 Marines learned that the invasion was cancelled just as, painted with camouflage, they were receiving their loads of ammunition. "We were so pumped up and ready to go," Lance Cpl. Rian Smith complained. "Now this!"[94] What was supposed to be a shoot'm up invasion turned into a complex cohabitation with human rights abusers.

The former thugs were now friends. There was no fighting, but troops had to remain in full body armor in Haiti's scorching heat. Boredom, lack of purpose, and homesickness were prevalent. Cédras was a petty tyrant, not a totalitarian dictator, but soldiers felt as if Dwight D. Eisenhower had cancelled D-Day, met Hitler every day to coordinate occupation policies, refused to inspect concentration camps, and ordered GIs to be friendly with the Nazis because they were the main law enforcement body.

Interviews conducted for an Army oral history project typically ended with a question that threw every soldier off balance: what did you think was a humorous episode? Soldiers either struggled to relate an anecdote that was everything but funny, or responded that there never was a humorous moment. Strangely, even though a total of 23,000 troops landed in Haiti when the initial plans had called for only 15,000 in the post-fighting phase,[95] and even though they were told to do as little as feasible, soldiers complained of being overworked and of never getting enough sleep. They also resented the poverty, the filth, the heat, and the lack of basic facilities. The situation improved when the Army sent in Morale, Welfare and Recreation equipment (MWR), including ice cubes, Coke, satellite televisions, ice cream, and showers.[96]

Given the widespread availability of deadly weapons, low morale quickly translated into human losses. Within a month of the invasion, by which time the size of the U.S. expeditionary force had already dropped to 16,000 troops, three American soldiers, Pvt. Gerardo Luciano, 22, Spec. Alejandro Robles, 20, and Marine Cpl. Maurice A. Williams, 21, had committed suicide. Self-inflicted death, more than enemy fire, was the threat Americans faced.[97]

Psychiatrists attached to the 10th Mountain Division blamed the aborted invasion and subsequent uncertainty for the high suicide rate. "People were geared up to do a lot of fighting, and then they didn't," said Capt. Donald Hall. "That left a lot of aggressive energy with no place to go."[98] It is "not clear to the average soldier why we're here," argued Maj. Eric D. Cipriano, adding that constant deployments also took their toll. "When you continuously deploy soldiers, you get tired soldiers. . . . They're away from families, they don't get to see children grow up, they miss significant life events." Cipriano received so many interview requests that public affairs specialists from the Department of Defense coached him on how to handle the media.[99] Two of the soldiers who killed themselves belonged to a company in the 10th Mountain Division that had spent most of its time locked up in a Port-au-Prince barrack, so 10th M.D. commander Meade received most of the blame for the low morale, the mindless enforcement of rules, and the failure to achieve much with such a large force. The 25th Infantry Division replaced the 10th Mountain Division ahead of schedule, on Christmas 1994. When Meade left the multinational force in January 1995, he received no promotion and retired.[100]

Cédras Exits

The Carter–Jonassaint agreement only called on the military junta to step down, not to leave the country. Still, Cédras' continued presence was likely to inflame political passions, especially if Aristide only awarded him political, not criminal, amnesty. The administration thus dropped ever more pointed hints that he ought to go, and, in early October, Shelton met Cédras, warned him that he might get mobbed and killed, and enjoined him to leave before Aristide's planned return on 15 October.[101] The safety issue was more than just a rhetorical device. When Cédras delivered his resignation speech, on 10 October, a large crowd surrounded the Army headquarters, insulted him, and threw rocks at his car as he departed.[102] Port-au-Prince police chief Michel François had already left for the Dominican Republic on 4 October. Apparently swayed by the safety argument, Cédras told Shelton that he was seriously considering the idea, but that his wife, the business-minded element of the couple, was worried about their financial situation.[103]

Secretary of Defense Perry flew to Haiti to hammer out the departure arrangements. Negotiations lasted until 12 October, when the U.S. government offered to rent Cédras' three villas. Officially, the payback only amounted to a one-year, $60,000 lease, but the package included several valuable nonmonetary side benefits as well. U.S. troops would protect Cédras' goods as he moved them away and the boat he left behind (Cédras even arranged to store his china and artwork in the U.S. Embassy, but he eventually found an alternate warehouse). Protecting Cédras' villas turned out to be a 24-hour job as locals tried to loot them.[104] The United States provided medical attention to Cédras' brother Alex after he suffered a heart attack.[105] Bank accounts from supporters of the coup, totaling one million dollars, were unfrozen (Cédras had withdrawn most of his money before the sanctions took effect). The United States also agreed to pay for Cédras' entourage's trip and living expenses in exile for one year. Upon arriving in Panama, Cédras commandeered an entire floor of a Panama City palace, then moved to Contadora Island, an island 37 miles south of Panama that had previously been the shah of Iran's private retreat.

Even though no direct cash handout was involved beside rent for the villas, the Caribbean correspondent for the *Los Angeles Times* calculated that the various incentives added up to a one million-dollar bribe, a considerable figure considering how weak Cédras's bargaining position was.[106]

Late on 12 October, as military escorts picked up Cédras, Biamby, and their relatives, the multinational force waited for the radio code indicating that the exile had begun. "First base" was the signal that the convoys had departed. "Second Base" indicated that they had arrived at the airport. Seven people, including Cédras, his wife, his three children, a maid, and Biamby, boarded a U.S.-chartered B757 bound for Panama. Cédras went to the second plane to check that his ailing brother and 22 other friends and relatives, whose destination was Miami, were well taken care of. Finally, at 3 a.m., his plane took off. The radio announced "Third Base," then "Home Run," as both aircraft left. After refusing boatloads of Haitians for the previous three years, the U.S. government, presumably hoping that the dictators' departure would facilitate the political transition, had just offered a golden exile to 30 very special Haitian refugees.

This accommodating policy was typical the first month of the invasion. Over and over again, the U.S. command in Haiti, to whom Clinton's wavering policies had given a large amount of leeway, refused to undertake dangerous missions, going as far as relying on the hated Haitian Army to carry out the day-to-day law enforcement it was unwilling to take over. This cautious attitude kept the U.S. body count at zero, but it also suggested that the idealistic rationale for Operation Restore Democracy was of lesser importance than political imperatives, namely, avoiding a new Mogadishu disaster, and administrative infighting, namely, the Pentagon's opposition to the intervention.

The U.S. military's close collaboration with the junta, however useful on the short term, could not go on forever. With Aristide's return on 15 October, the remnants of the Haitian Army rapidly melted away. Unable to use representatives of the old order to maintain peace on the cheap, the U.S. force now had to design a longer-term, less questionable solution.

Chapter Ten

Peacekeeping (15 October 1994– 31 March 1995)

Aristide Returns

On 15 October 1994, a black American limousine carrying Aristide, U.S. Secretary of State Warren Christopher, and U.S. special envoy to Haiti William Gray III arrived on the tarmac at Andrews Air Force Base.[1] The mood was upbeat. "In a few moments, we will depart on a joyous and historic journey to accompany President Aristide on his triumphant return to Haiti," Christopher announced.[2] "A wonderful day of peace, democracy, respect," responded Aristide.[3] Aristide's party—U.S. and Haitian officials, congressmen, journalists, and friends—boarded three planes and took off.

However joyous, the flight could not match the atmosphere in Haiti, where enthusiastic crowds were getting ready to welcome *Titid*—Aristide's Creole nickname—back home after three years in exile. Port-au-Prince Mayor and Aristide supporter Evans Paul had called upon the population to clean up the city. Garbage mounds temporarily disappeared, Haitians swept the streets, and the presidential palace and Aristide's private residence in Tabarre, both of which soldiers had looted, received fresh coats of paint. After the 1991 coup, Cédras had repeatedly mentioned that, once an egg is laid, one cannot put it back inside the hen. The Creole proverb was an allusion to Aristide's symbol, the rooster, and to Cédras' belief that Aristide would never come back to Haiti. Now that Aristide was on his way back, murals triumphantly flowered all over town with an ironic motif: a hen, an egg, and a finger pushing the egg back to where it came from.[4] When his plane landed in Port-au-Prince, Aristide entered history as the first Haitian president to ever return to power after being overthrown.

Thousands of Haitians greeted Aristide at the airport and in front of the presidential palace, but the U.S. presence was even more overwhelming. A U.S. helicopter ferried Aristide from his plane to the palace, where a Delta Force unit took over his personal protection. U.S. troops closed the airport to commercial traffic, patrolled the streets, and draped the capital in barbed wire, while U.S. sharpshooters positioned themselves on rooftops. Upon his arrival in the presidential palace, Aristide delivered a speech behind a thick piece of bulletproof glass and spent half of the address thanking the U.S. supporters who had made his return possible.[5]

Haiti's woes were as obvious as the U.S. military presence. The children were potbellied, the streets potholed, and the presidential palace, though freshly painted, had no telephones, no running water, and no electricity.[6] A mere one day after Aristide's return, the *telediol* (Haiti's rumor mill) already claimed—falsely, as it turned out—that a coup was under way, led by interim Army Chief of Staff Jean-Claude Duperval. Aristide waited three days before venturing out of the presidential palace, and a month before meeting journalists.[7]

As Aristide's return made clear, he and his successor would have to face two main problems over the years to come. The first was the omnipresence of the U.S. force on Haitian soil. Foreign troops kept Aristide in office, but military occupation might trigger a nationalistic backlash after the excitement surrounding Aristide's return had worn off. The second problem was the magnitude of Haiti's underdevelopment. The international community's help, which had been decisive in bringing Aristide back to power, was just as crucial to draw Haiti out of poverty, but giving in to foreign economic and political requests would be an unacceptable infringement on Haitian national sovereignty. Continuing to secure international support while portraying himself as a proud Haitian patriot: this was the delicate balancing act required of Aristide.

On the U.S. side, Aristide's return created even more problems than it solved. The ambiguous collaboration with the Haitian Army came to an end, but dealing with Aristide, a historically anti-American president whose democratic legitimacy prevented the kind of get-tough attitude Shelton had adopted with Cédras, could prove even more difficult. The Haitian Army's rapid disintegration in October-December 1994 also meant that the U.S. Army, in the absence of a functioning Aristide government, had to take over police-keeping responsibilities, while avoiding such an extensive role that withdrawal would become impossible. Before the invasion, Clinton had clearly warned that U.S. soldiers would "not be involved in rebuilding Haiti or its economy. . . . When this first phase [restoring Aristide and creating a police force] is completed, the vast majority of our troops will come home—in months, not years."[8]

As Clinton hinted at in his speech, creating a local, independent Haitian National Police (HNP) was the solution to this conundrum. Haitian policemen could take over policing duties that the Haitian Army had previously been responsible for. The existence of a local police force, aside from keeping Haitian nationalists quiet, also allowed the U.S. Army to claim that Haiti had become "a secure and stable environment," which meant, under UN Security Council resolution 940, that the UN force could step in.[9] Last, a "neutral" police force—composed in large part of recycled Haitian Army soldiers—could be a useful counterweight to Aristide's political ambitions. As during the first month of the occupation, policing by proxy kept the U.S. casualty rate low. As during the first month of the occupation, the emphasis on making the occupation quick and painless resulted in a democratization process that was almost as imperfect and superficial as during the first U.S. occupation.

Historical Precedents for the Haitian National Police

Latin Americans frequently describe their northern neighbor as imperialist, but U.S. policy in Latin America has often been characterized by its reluctance, rather than its eagerness, to place foreign peoples under direct U.S. administration.[10] One of the first tasks the Marines undertook in Haiti in 1915 was to disarm the local factions vying for power, to demobilize the Port-au-Prince garrison, and to train an indigenous police force (the *gendarmerie*); the force became operational in February 1916.[11] During the 1910s and 1920s, the United States trained similar police forces in Nicaragua (*Guardia Nacional*) and the Dominican Republic (National Constabulary) whose role was to take over policing after U.S. troops withdrew.[12] Nominally apolitical, these forces quickly became a prized asset in the struggle for power; they allowed Anastasio Somoza and Rafael Trujillo to take over Nicaragua and the Dominican Republic, respectively. Cédras, interim commander in chief of the *gendarmes* (renamed Haitian Army in 1946), overthrew Aristide in 1991.

The *gendarmes'* nefarious record as policemen was as discouraging as their habit of entering the political fray. The role of rural *gendarmes* (known as *chefs seksyon*, or section chiefs), as spelled out in the *Moniteur*, Haiti's *Federal Register*, was to protect people and property, fields, animals, maintain order, present any people arrested to the nearest army post within 24 hours, along with a detailed report, and obtain an arrest warrant unless the person was caught in the act—a role that they never fulfilled. On the other hand, the *Moniteur* emphasized, the section chief should not act as a judge, impose fines, impose extralegal taxes, accept bribes, or mistreat residents—which was a fair summary of their actual job description.[13] Unpaid assistants seconded section chiefs. To make a living, these assistants extorted the local peasantry, which earned them the nickname of *souket lawouze*, those who collect the dew, the last drops of money.[14] The *gendarmes'* only notable achievement, from a U.S. point of view, was the help they provided in pacifying Haiti during the first U.S. occupation and in facilitating the withdrawal of U.S. troops in 1934.

From the Haitian Army (FAdH) to the Haitian National Police (HNP)

Despite the political and professional shortcomings of the *gendarmerie* created during the first U.S. occupation of Haiti, the 1994 U.S. occupation force again set out to create a national constabulary that, it was again hoped, would focus on law enforcement and remain politically subordinate to the 1987 constitution. Presidential Decision Directive 71, based on lessons learned in Haiti in 1994, explained that the creation of a local police was essential to guarantee the U.S. troops' quick withdrawal. "Ultimate responsibility to conduct law enforcement should not be taken away from local police forces as this may breed dependency," the directive warned. "The responsibility for local law enforcement will remain with the indigenous police forces."[15] Because dependency on U.S. troops and mission creep were anathema to the 1994 U.S. command in Haiti, training of a Haitian constabulary was the first long-term mission undertaken by the multinational force, one that was characterized by hasty, insufficient training of police cadets and the use of former Haitian soldiers in the new police force.

The creation of this police force began in a haphazard manner. The *Harlan County* detachment had only been charged with training the Haitian Army, not with creating an entirely new force. During Aristide's three years in exile, neither he nor the U.S. government trained cadres in preparation for his return to Haiti. The United States hoped that the Haitian Army would remain in place even after Aristide's return, and be progressively scaled down to a purely military force of 3,500 until a national police would be ready to take over. In fact, Aristide pruned the ranks of the army with such rapidity that a mere 1,500 men remained by January 1995.[16] The few remaining soldiers rarely ventured out of their barracks after Aristide's return, fearing that his supporters would lynch them. The professional incompetence of the *gendarmes'* descendants, already obvious to a U.S. training mission sent to Haiti in the late 1950s,[17] shocked Commander of the 16th Military Police Brigade Col. Michael L. Sullivan.

> The daily operations of the Haitian police went something like this: they would come to work in the morning, somewhere between eight and ten o'clock in the morning; some in civilian clothes, some in uniform. There didn't seem to be any pattern as to arriving or whether they were in uniform or not; they just kind of wandered in [in fact, many came in civilian clothes because they feared retribution from the outraged citizenry]. When they got in, there was no accountability; there was no formation of any kind; there was no roll call; there was nothing. They just kind of hung out at the police station playing dominoes, or cards, or talking, or eating. Sometime in the afternoon between fifteen hundred and seventeen hundred [3 and 5 p.m.], they would kind of wander home. No one would come to the police station to make a complaint; no phone calls would come in asking them to do anything.[18]

The rapid breakdown of the Haitian military forced U.S. forces to act. As a stopgap measure, U.S. military police maintained order during the weeks following Aristide's return, gave the Haitian Army rudimentary training in law enforcement, and encouraged Haitian soldiers to step out of their barracks.[19] The USAID even hired a private security company as Aristide's interim personal guard for a three-month period.[20] International Police Monitors, whose mission was to train the new police and to monitor its human rights record, started arriving in Haiti in October 1994. Former New York City Police Commissioner Raymond W. Kelly headed this multi-national group, 1,300-strong at its peak. To facilitate the transition from the army to the new police, they and a U.S. Department of Justice program, ICITAP, set out to train an Interim Public Security Force (IPSF).[21]

The name change, from Haitian Army (FAdH) to interim force (IPSF), was deceptive.[22] Despite the nominal change, Haitian Army soldiers formed the bulk of the interim force. Thirty-four hundred of Haiti's Seven Thousand soldiers made their way into the interim force after a three-layered screening process. Haitian Army officers first weeded out some soldiers. The U.S. Embassy and Aristide's government then carried out a second screening based on the human rights record of each soldier. Both tried to gather individual data based on UN, OAS, and DIA reports, but lack of information made it difficult to guarantee that no human rights violator joined the ranks of the interim force. In the third stage of screening, members of the interim force could be expelled if Haitians denounced them for past crimes, which created a dangerous precedent in which the composition of the police force was subject to the whims of public pressure. Five days of remedial training was deemed sufficient to turn these former members of an oppressive force into defenders of Haitians' human rights.

Nine hundred refugees repatriated from Guantánamo formed the remainder of the interim police force. The State Department expressed fears that former asylum-seekers would be too supportive of Aristide, which explains their limited numbers and inferior status. Despite the fact that they were not tainted by their association with the junta, and that they had undergone a longer, 21-day training in addition to the week-long regular training, the Guantánamo refugees were subordinated to former soldiers, wore a different uniform, and carried no weapons. The interim force was first deployed to Cap Haïtien, where the Haitian Army had disintegrated following the September shootout with the Marines. Unconvinced that a new uniform signified redemption, Haitians threatened to kill former soldiers. Police monitors thus had to ship soldiers-turned-policemen to other cities where no one knew them (in 1991–1994, the junta had similarly transferred local strongmen when they proved too sadistic).

Members of the permanent national police, known as Haitian National Police (HNP), started training in February 1995. To expedite the process, each month a class of 375 cadets (raised to 750 by August) started their short four-month preparation. Because this rhythm quickly overran the U.S. Department of Justice's training capacities in Haiti, policemen did half their training in Fort Leonard Wood, Missouri. Aristide protested: Haitian soldiers (including Cédras, François, and Biamby) who had undergone training in the United States had returned with renewed political ambitions, and, many alleged, CIA contacts. Minister of Justice Léon Jeune resigned after agreeing to permit the overseas training, and Aristide finally obtained an agreement that the last half of the training would take place in Haiti.[23] Members of the National Police were deployed starting in July 1995, and the interim police was completely phased out by December 1995. Fifteen hundred former Haitian soldiers made their way into the supposedly new and apolitical police force, the *Police Nationale d'Haïti* (PNH), which numbered 5,000 people.[24] The rapidity with which policemen were trained and deployed marred the police force for years to come, as did the fact that many Haitian soldiers with little respect for human rights joined its ranks.

Disbanding the Haitian Army

What to do with the Haitian soldiers who had not joined the police force was an issue that pitted Aristide, who was understandably wary of showing mercy for the soldiers who had overthrown him three years earlier, and the U.S. government, which made public its interest in the continued existence of the Haitian Army. Clinton had publicly denounced the military junta as "thugs," but U.S. officials feared that firing all soldiers would destroy the only force powerful enough to check Aristide's potential excesses. It would also leave a large group of armed, disgruntled, unemployed soldiers, potentially willing to launch an armed insurgency in Haiti. In October 1994, Haitian officers fled the country, taking with them the funds that had been put aside for the health care and retirement benefits of their troops.[25] A deadly 26 December 1994 riot, in which four soldiers died as they were protesting lack of pay, stood as a stern remainder that one could not ignore the Haitian Army's financial woes.[26] The USAID acknowledged "moral objections" to helping former soldiers while letting other Haitians fend for themselves, but the threat represented by discontented soldiers prompted a $8.67 million U.S. program to give practical training, along with a set of tools, to demobilized soldiers in order to facilitate their transition to civilian life.[27] Showing mercy for the Haitian Army pleased Shelton and Meade, who had maintained frequent and generally cordial relations with Cédras and other Haitian Army officers. Speaking in late October 1994, Meade said,

> the FAd'H [Haitian Army] continues to exist as an institution (both the military side and the police) and that's what we want. We did not want to have the circumstance, and do not want to have the circumstance, where there would be no police and no military force in this country. . . . And strange as it may sound, we found General Cédras and General Biamby professional, and proper to work with. We had what we called a proper relationship with them.[28]

"Proper to work with" and "professional" were not words Aristide would have used to describe Cédras and Biamby. When he was still in exile in the United States, Aristide had promised he would keep a 1,500-soldier army, but he changed his plans after he came back to Haiti.[29] In November 1994, former Costa Rican President Oscar Arias Sanchez traveled to Haiti to advocate the entire suppression of the Haitian armed forces (as was the case in Costa Rica and Panama), an idea that Haitians embraced with enthusiasm.[30] Accordingly, the December 1994 law creating the Haitian National Police attributed most Army resources (including barracks) to the new police.[31] Aristide then proceeded to cut funds to the army, a move contrary to prior promises to his U.S. ally. According to Aristide, in December 1994, "a foreign general came to see me. He threatened violence in no uncertain terms if we continued on this path."[32]

Aristide's position as president of Haiti allowed him to win this first political skirmish with his U.S. friends. When the United States requested in February 1995 that three pro-Aristide officers accused in a July 1991 murder be fired, Aristide obliged, but he also fired 39 other officers, including every officer above the rank of major, and chose a friend of his, Dany Toussaint, as commander in chief.[33] With the exception of the presidential band, Aristide finally disbanded the army altogether in April 1995, and transferred the 1,500 soldiers remaining in the army at that time to the interim police. The decision was unconstitutional: ART. 263 of the 1987 Constitution stipulates that there must be a police, an army, and no other armed group, instead of a police-army seconded by paramilitary factions (as was the case when the junta ruled Haiti) or a police, no army, and an army of occupation (as was now the case). It also eliminated the most powerful, organized group opposed to Aristide's rule.

Military Success of the U.S. Occupation

Collaborating with the Haitian Army, then creating a national police with many of its former members, paid off militarily. In contrast to the first U.S. occupation, when the Marines invaded the island with great ease, only to find themselves faced with a rural insurrection that was only subdued five years later, the first six months of the 1994 occupation only saw five armed confrontations between U.S. and Haitian soldiers, resulting in a mere four casualties on the U.S. side—including one dead. The 24 September Cap Haïtien shootout left 10 Haitians dead and one Marine wounded. On 2 October, an unidentified Haitian shot at, and wounded, a Special Operations soldier in Les Cayes.[34] Twelve days later, one Haitian soldier was wounded in a confrontation in Belladère. U.S. troops, assisted by Haitian soldiers, killed four demobilized soldiers as they protested in front of Haitian Army headquarters on 26 December.[35]

On 12 January, 1995, a two-man Special Forces team manned a road checkpoint near Gonaïves. A white pick-up truck carrying two Haitians, including former soldier Aurel Frédéric, refused to stop. When the two U.S. soldiers, Staff Sergeant Tommy Davis and Sergeant First Class Gregory Dale Cardott, chased the vehicle in their Humvee, Frédéric opened fire, wounded Davis, and killed Cardott before being shot dead himself. The incident was tragic for both Frédéric and Cardott, who left a wife and two daughters in Fayetteville, NC but political repercussions were extremely limited. Cardott's death was only briefly mentioned in the U.S. media outside of North Carolina, where he was stationed, and California, where he was born.[36] Cardott was the only U.S. soldier to die in combat in Haiti. This low body count, due in part to the reliance on Haitian forces, first the Haitian Army, then the National Police, was essential. Because Haiti appeared "secure and stable," U.S. forces could claim that they achieved the goals set by UN Resolution 940, and the U.S.-led multinational force could prepare for the UN takeover planned for 31 March, 1995.

Resumption of Political Violence: The Mireille Durocher-Bertin Case

However successful from a military standpoint, Operation Restore Democracy failed to end political violence in Haiti, as the case of Mireille Durocher-Bertin, a famous anti-Aristide lawyer who had supported the junta in 1991–1994 and attacked Aristide as a traitor, made tragically clear.[37] On 28 March, 1995, three days before the departure of the U.S. force, as Durocher-Bertin and a client, Eugène Baillergeau, sat in their car in one of Port-au-Prince's infamous traffic jams, two gunmen shot them dead.[38] Aristide immediately condemned the murder, but allegations that he or his close associates were involved in the murder—never proved nor refuted— plagued U.S.–Haitian relations for the following six months.

Weeks before the murder, Claude Douge, an interpreter working for the U.S. occupation force, had been contacted by a gunman asking Douge to help him kill Durocher-Bertin, allegedly under orders from Mondésir Beaubrun, Aristide's Minister of the Interior. Douge tipped his superiors, and U.S. troops arrested the gunman and four of his accomplices as they were on a reconnaissance tour near Durocher-Bertin's house and workplace. The gunmen drove a gray Isuzu trooper registered to the Ministry of the Interior and carried Beaubrun's phone number. Once arrested, they confessed that Beaubrun had personally given the car keys to them.

General George A. Fisher, the commander of the multinational force, wrote to Aristide and Justice Minister Jean-Joseph Exumé to notify them of the plot, and asked Exumé to warn Durocher-Bertin that her life was in danger.[39] Exumé and Durocher-Bertin met twice, but the husband of the victim asserted that Exumé never talked about the murder plot to his wife.[40] Durocher-Bertin died on 28 March. Probably concluding that the Aristide cabinet was a poor message carrier, the Pentagon later leaked to the *New York Times* a list of 27 Aristide opponents who, according to rumors circulating in Port-au-Prince, were in danger of being shot.[41]

Because of the victim's high profile, and because she died three days before the official ceremony marking the end of direct U.S. occupation, the case immediately attracted great attention. By 5:30 a.m. the day following the murder, the FBI had four men working on the case in Haiti (the Haitian police, still in its infancy, had no investigative unit at the time). The inquiry proved difficulty. Among other things, the FBI team, operating in a foreign country, lacked legal powers, including the right to subpoena witnesses. FBI investigators also complained that Haitian government officials did all they could to slow the investigation.[42]

By June 1995, the controversy over the Durocher-Bertin case focused on the rights of interviewees. FBI agents wanted to interview members of the interim police force and Haitian administration officials. Aristide complained to U.S. Ambassador to Haiti William Lacy Swing that the FBI team was infringing on Haitian national sovereignty and demanded that the FBI investigate crimes committed against Aristide supporters as well.[43] The Haitian government also requested that it be notified ahead of time whenever an interview took place, and be allowed to sit in on interviews. On 3 July, Swing, State Department Haiti coordinator James F. Dobbins, Deputy Assistant Director of the FBI William E. Perry, and Associate Deputy Attorney General Seth P. Waxman met Aristide and his U.S. lawyers and reached an agreement: no Haitian official would be notified of, or present at, interviews; the government of Haiti could provide an attorney to indigent witnesses; the Durocher-Bertin investigation would proceed independently from any other murder case.[44]

Rancor nevertheless persisted. All 13 witnesses were represented by the same U.S. attorneys, who were all paid by the Haitian government, and were hosted by Haitian authorities while in Haiti.[45] The attorneys also insisted on having an independent court reporter keep a verbatim transcript of the interviews, which the FBI claimed was contrary to standard FBI practices.[46] In August 1995, one of the witnesses' attorneys asked to interview a number of U.S. military personnel believed to have exculpatory evidence that the FBI had overlooked.[47] Failing to resolve their dispute with the Haitian government, FBI investigators simply abandoned the case. They started leaving in July 1995; the last FBI members left Haiti in October. A September 1995 cable from the U.S. Embassy in Port-au-Prince concluded that:

> the FBI investigation of the Bertin assassination is at a standstill due to lack of GOH [Government of Haiti] cooperation. Individuals around the president who are thought to be implicated in execution-style killings continue to hold their official and quasi-official positions.[48]

When asked whether members of Aristide's presidential guard were involved in the murder, Dobbins categorically replied: "Yes, and also members of the police."[49] The State Department also received intelligence reports in early 1995 linking many murders to a small group of people in Aristide's security forces, suggesting that there was a death squad.[50] Aristide's lawyer, on the other hand, contended that Baillergeau was a partner of Mr. Durocher in the drug business, and attributed the murder to financial, not political, rivalries unrelated to the Haitian government. Alternatively, he argued, the murder had been committed by right-wing thugs linked with the U.S. intelligence community in an attempt to frame Beaubrun and discredit Aristide.[51] Two Haitian suspects arrested by U.S. forces accused congressional Republicans of masterminding the murder to embarrass Clinton.[52]

Who killed Durocher-Bertin will probably always remain a mystery, but the murder's political repercussions are easier to ascertain. Durocher-Bertin died just as Clinton was about to visit Haiti for the first time and to pass the peacekeeping torch, along with a "stable and secure" environment, to the United Nations. The administration suddenly had to devise a public relations strategy to answer accusations that it had restored a murderer to power. Despite his suspicions that Durocher-Bertin's murder was linked to Aristide's guard and police, Dobbins wrote Deputy Secretary of State Strobe Talbott to suggest that the administration should minimize the significance of this and other suspicious murders in public statements, acknowledging only "a limited number of what would appear to be revenge-motivated killings [euphemism for political assassinations], of which Bertin's is the most prominent."[53]

Republicans, who had gained control of both houses of Congress in the November 1994 elections, also sensed that the murder had great political potential. Rep. Benjamin A. Gilman (R-NY), the new chairman of the House Committee on International Relations, declared that "the government we re-installed in Haiti started, or assisted in, murdering some of its political opponents within 3 months of our invasion and then stonewalled the FBI's inquiry."[54] He also accused the Clinton administration of covering up those murders to avoid political embarrassment.

The political shock waves of the murder also hit Aristide, who resorted to U.S. lawyer-lobbyists he had employed during his exile, most prominently Burton V. Wides, to defend Haitian witnesses and to protect his reputation.[55] Wides' aggressive style and the FBI's insistence on keeping him out of interviews led to an increasingly acerbic exchange of letters between Wides and U.S. officials.[56] Another U.S. lawyer working for Aristide, James McGuirk, engaged in similar epistolary quarrels.[57] By October 1995, recriminations on both sides had reached the point where Wides accused the FBI of blaming Aristide for its own failure to find the culprits, while an amendment by Bob Dole threatened to cut U.S. aid to Haiti because of the Durocher-Bertin murder.[58]

Whether Aristide conspired in Durocher-Bertin's murder or not, the case exemplified both the Haitian National Police's limitations—it had proved unable to protect Durocher-Bertin, then to even assign investigators on her case—and the renewal of tensions between Aristide and U.S. officials. U.S.–Haitians tensions stemmed in part from long-standing Haitian suspicions of U.S. motives, as well as a long history of political violence, both of which the multinational force could hardly be blamed for. The police's limitations, on the other hand, were the fruit of a tendency on the U.S. side to eschew any policy that could result in U.S. casualties or an extended stay in Haiti. Short-term improvisation based on political and military expediency ended on 31 March, 1995, with the transition from the U.S.-led multinational force (MNF) to the UN mission in Haiti (UNMIH).

CHAPTER ELEVEN

NATION BUILDING: GREAT EXPECTATIONS
(31 MARCH 1995–JUNE 1997)

The UN Comes In

To uninformed observers, UN Security Council Resolution 975 (30 January 1995), which stated that a "secure and stable" environment now reigned in Haiti, was barely worth noticing.[1] To the 6,000 U.S. troops still in Haiti, on the other hand, the resolution was momentous, for it indicated that the transition to a UN force would take place, even setting a date: 31 March. Only 2,400 U.S. troops, drawn from the 2nd Armored Cavalry Regiment in Fort Polk, La., stayed in Haiti to participate in the 6,000 troop–strong UN Mission to Haiti (UNMIH). An American, Maj. Gen. Joseph Kinzer, remained as the UN force's military commander, while UN special envoy to Haiti Lakdar Brahimi of Algeria became the top foreign civilian official. Nine hundred international police monitors also stayed in Haiti.[2]

On 31 March, Clinton arrived in Haiti to oversee the transition. The visit, Clinton's first, boded well from a public relations perspective. Despite Mireille Durocher-Bertin's troubling murder, Operation Restore Democracy was still viewed as an overwhelming success, and U.S. troops were withdrawing on schedule. Mondésir Beaubrun, Aristide's Minister of the Interior and the prime suspect in Durocher-Bertin's murder, was conspicuously absent from the podium where prominent Haitian officials stood during the transition ceremony. "This is a day of celebration, and nothing can cast a cloud on it," Clinton told reporters.[3] UN Secretary General Boutros-Ghali remembered the scene vividly.

> Soon Aristide, Clinton and I were led to a newly built podium in front of the presidential palace. Photographers and cameramen were to the left of the stand, the best place to get pictures, but the American president had to be on the right for reasons of precedence. I was oblivious to this teleprotocol until made aware of the frantic but vain efforts the Americans had made to avoid this situation. The White House wanted to make this ceremony an American victory celebration; my entourage wanted to feature the United Nations. The Americans, of course, won the contest. Even so, Madeleine Albright was overheard complaining about the number of "UN people" on the platform.[4]

The fact that Clinton only visited Haiti to celebrate the departure of U.S. troops could have suggested that the United States would become disengaged with Haitian affairs (ironically, this was the first visit of a U.S. president to Haiti since Franklin D. Roosevelt arrived in 1934 to oversee the departure of U.S. troops at the end of the first U.S. occupation of Haiti). There was indeed a strong incentive to do little in Haiti. Restoring Aristide to the presidential palace and instating a modicum of law and order in Haiti were two clear objectives, both of which had been achieved in the first six months of the U.S. occupation. Creating a vibrant, prosperous democracy, on the other hand, was a vague, open-ended mission whose success, difficult to quantify in any case, was unlikely given Haiti's historical record. Previous attempts to start anew, following the war of independence in 1804, during the first U.S. occupation in 1915, and after Aristide's election in 1990, had all ended in failure. On the UN side, financial problems militated against an ambitious nation-building agenda.[5] Resolution 940, which authorized the use of force, specifically mentioned that countries participating in the multinational force would do so at their own expense. Later resolutions contained insistent requests for monetary contributions from international donors.[6]

Despite the many good reasons that could have justified abandoning Haiti to its fate, both Clinton and Boutros-Ghali, even as they insisted that the Haitians must play the central role in building their country's future, pledged to give Haiti a helping hand. "Your government, the United Nations, and the United States will do all we can to guarantee free, fair, and secure elections," Clinton declared upon his arrival in Haiti. "We, your neighbors, your allies, and your friends, will support your efforts to create jobs, to attract investment from beyond your borders, and to rebuild and repair your injured land."[7] During the transition ceremony, Boutros-Ghali added that "as the multinational force departs and the United Nations take over, two factors remain vital: the people of Haiti must maintain their commitment to rebuild their society, and the member states of the United Nations must continue to support this revitalization of the multilateral idea."[8]

Administration officials remember that this stated commitment to Haiti's political and economic betterment was more than mere public posturing. According to NSC staff member Richard Feinberg, "there was a commitment of time, money, and effort. A lot of senior people spent a lot of time on Haiti. Stotzky's thesis that the administration walked away from Haiti was bullshit.[9] "A lot was done," Lake insisted. "The U.S. greatly increased public aid. The army employed many Haitians. The Peace Corps went there. We did police training. Exiles were brought back and trained for the police. Now you could say that the planning for the civilian effort was good but not excellent. But you'd be wrong to say we didn't do much."[10]

For political reasons, Clinton and Boutros-Ghali stopped short of calling for nation building, but U.S.–UN policies in Haiti in 1995–1997 came very close to it. First and foremost, the goal was to restore—or, rather, create—democracy, which required foreign help ranging from police training to technical assistance for elections and judicial reform. A democratic Haiti would mean little to Haitians if they remained hungry, so the international community also pledged substantial development aid and called for economic reforms.

Operation Create Democracy

In light of U.S. policies prior to, and immediately following, the 1994 intervention, the sudden U.S. renewal of interest in Haitian democracy seemed astonishing. Why, after collaborating with dictators, should U.S. troops now commit to democratic reforms they had demonstrated little enthusiasm for previously? The changing political environment in Haiti was part of the explanation. There was no more Haitian Army to collaborate with. The United Nations and Aristide now had a greater say in occupation policies. There were fewer U.S. troops in the field, so the fear of casualties could take a backseat to nation-building efforts.

The changing political environment in the United States was just as essential. Following their victory in the November 1994 elections, Republicans took control of both houses of Congress in January 1995. The Republicans' steadfast opposition to anything Clintonian, their long-standing dislike for Aristide, and the administration's claim that Haiti was its greatest foreign policy success to date warranted that U.S. policy in Haiti be criticized in one way or another. Since Clinton had publicly stated that the intervention's main goal was the restoration of democracy, Republicans desiring to attack his Haiti policy asserted that no democracy had been restored.

Accordingly, a Dole amendment to the foreign aid bill for FY 1996 froze all aid to Haiti until Clinton certified that political killings, including Durocher-Bertin's murder, had been solved.[11] In April 1996, Rep. Robert S. Walker (R-PA) and Jim Nussle (R-IA), two close allies of Newt Gingrich in the House, sent a secret memo to Republican committee and subcommittee chairmen, asking them to use their committees as pulpits from which they could attack the Clinton administration.[12] Rep. Benjamin A. Gilman (R-NY), the new chairman of the House Committee on International Relations, organized a series of hearings accusing the Clinton administration of covering up political murders committed by Aristide.[13] Criticized for the shortcomings of Haitian democracy, the Clinton administration now had a vested political interest in seeing democracy flourish. The political tit-for-tat had come full circle. Initially, Clinton's commitment to Haitian democracy may have been secondary, but, as he was now held accountable for it, the administration set out to ensure that Haiti was indeed democratic.

The first U.S. occupation of Haiti had rarely bothered with registration drives, so one could not design a democratization plan based on historical precedents. In 1918, the United States had simply drafted a Haitian constitution, then organized a plebiscite on the constitution that resulted in the Soviet-style landslide of 98,225 for, 768 against.[14] Ninety-seven percent of the electorate was illiterate; some voters thought they were electing a president, one, a pope. The occupation force, which controlled disbursement, also stopped paying Haitian deputies whenever they refused to endorse U.S. policies. In December 1938, a mere four years after the end of the first U.S. occupation of Haiti, President Sténio Vincent announced that the Haitian people's mentality was too "arrested" for democracy and declared himself a dictator.[15]

In 1995, the UN force designed a more elaborate, three-pronged plan whose goals were to elect a democratic Parliament and president to draft laws; to build an effective police force to enforce them; and to create a fair justice and prison system to punish those who broke them. The new Haitian national police was already being trained, which left electoral fraud, corrupt courts, and squalid prisons as the remaining obstacles on the path to democracy.

With extensive financial and technical assistance from foreign countries, Haiti held legislative elections in June and September 1995, presidential elections in

December 1995, partial elections to fill House, Senate, and local seats in April 1997, and run-offs in July and August 1997. The December 1995 elections were the most controversial. Aristide could not constitutionally run for a second consecutive term and had promised, while he was in exile, that he would abide by the Constitution and step down in February 1996,[16] but his Haitian supporters argued that his mandate should be prolonged by three years to make up for the time he spent in exile, a move that American officials opposed as a dangerous precedent.[17] As late as a month before the scheduled presidential election, Aristide remained ambiguous as to his intentions, telling a crowd of five to ten thousand supporters yelling "three more years" that "I must acknowledge what you request, listen to what you request, and to understand it. . . . I have seen, I have heard, and I have understood."[18] Following another such speech in November, Anthony Lake made a rare television appearance to insist that despite Aristide's "very ambiguous" remarks, "the elections are scheduled and we expect them to take place."[19] After much uncertainty and several public U.S. warnings that Aristide should not run, the election finally went on as planned and Aristide's friend and former Prime Minister René Préval, along with the pro-Aristide *Organisation Politique Lavalas*, swept the presidential and legislative elections, earning 88 percent of the vote.[20] In February 1996, Préval was inaugurated president.

Contrary to Aristide, whose father was a peasant of moderate means, Préval, the son of an agriculture minister, grew up in a relatively affluent family, studied in Europe, and lived in the United States for five years.[21] An agronomist and a businessman, Préval met Aristide at *lafanmi selavi* (family is life), the shelter for homeless children Aristide operated in the 1980s. Both men, fervent opponents of Duvalier, developed such a close friendship that they were described as *marassa*, twins. Préval served as Aristide's prime minister in 1991, then followed him into exile from 1991 to 1994. The bond that united the two men loosened when Préval finally decided to step out of Aristide's shadow and run for the presidency in 1995. He won largely on the strength of his past association with Aristide, but even that failed to convince more than 30 percent of the electorate to go to the polls. When Préval was inaugurated in February 1996, Aristide earned more applause than the new president did.[22] From 1996 to 2001, Aristide considered Préval to be, at best, a surrogate, at worst, an usurper—in private, he described Préval as "closer to zero than to mediocre."[23]

The transition from Aristide to Préval symbolized how, despite Haiti's ostensible move toward democracy, very little had changed. Préval and *lavalas* candidates won in a landslide, but they had no organized constituency of their own and Haiti remained characterized by its populist bond between the masses and the former priest they idolized. Never had Haiti voted so often and so cleanly, and never before in Haitian history had a peaceful transition taken place between two democratically elected presidents, but elections quickly became too much of a good thing. Because the 1987 Constitution called for the election of numerous local and national officials, many of which required run-off elections, and because Aristide did not run for any of these positions, Haitians quickly tired of voting. A mere 10 percent of the electorate voted in the April 1997 legislative, senatorial, and local elections.[24]

The international community successfully focused on the surface trappings of democracy, such as elections, but more substantial components of a genuine democratic system remained absent. There was no real political change when Préval took over, for Aristide, who alone could summon thousands of supporters on the streets of the capital in a mere radio speech, continued to sway considerable political power even after leaving office. With Aristide at the apex of his popularity, there was no viable opposition party, which left factionalism within *Lavalas* itself as the imperfect substitute for a real democratic debate. Breaking with his former allies, Aristide created a new political organization, *lafanmi lavalas* (the Lavalas family), in November 1996. Political infighting and popular opposition to the international community's demands for neoliberal reforms produced three different prime ministers in the first 18 months: Smark Michel, a neoliberal businessman (November 1994–October 1995), the more leftist Claudette Werleigh (October 1995–February 1996), then Rosny Smarth (February 1996–June 1997), who advocated the privatization of state-owned companies.

Judicial reform was an even more complicated matter. Not only did Haiti need to reform its notoriously corrupt courts, but it also had to decide what to do with human rights abuses conducted in 1991–1994. The new Aristide regime could either favor victors' justice and conduct trials similar to the Nuremberg and Tokyo trials following World War II, or install a truth commission similar to those in El Salvador, Argentina, and South Africa, which would offer amnesty in exchange for a truthful accounting of past crimes. The U.S.-sponsored Governors Island and Carter-Jonassaint accords settled for the latter and offered amnesty to the junta. To please his hosts during his exile in the United States, Aristide thus pledged that he would pass an amnesty law. Days before the invasion, he declared:

> Members of the military—we will create jobs for you. You will not be isolated. You are the sons of the land, the nation's citizens. Stop the violence. Do not be afraid. We say "no" to vengeance; we say "no" to retaliation.[25]

During the first weeks of the occupation, U.S. troops, operating in a legal vacuum, did not address the judicial reform issue. There was no formal state of war, so the basic laws of war, such as the Geneva conventions, did not apply; the United States did not come as a colonizing power, so the occupation force refrained from legislating; U.S. forces were not competent in Haitian law, so they did not implement it. When U.S. troops arrested Haitians, they simply detained them without the benefit of a trial, and waited for the Aristide government to be restored. In the meantime, prisoners were put under the custody of the Haitian Army, which usually looked the other way when fellow soldiers escaped.[26]

Aristide's return to Haiti allowed him to oversee judicial issues, but his first move was to renege on his promises of amnesty. His supporters, who had been the targets of the junta's many human rights violations, were outspoken in their opposition to any amnesty, so the October 1994 amnesty law was very limited in its scope, offering political, not criminal, amnesty, and only covering the period from the 1991 coup to July 1993.[27] Aristide set up *bureaux de doléances*, temporary offices where victims of human rights violations could come to testify and file complaints.[28] Father Adrien, former chairman of Aristide's presidential commission, declared in 1995 that "I don't think there is any kind of reconciliation possible" between *Lavalas* and the elite that supported the coup.[29] A later law on judicial reform (17 August 1998) stipulated that no one could absolve the junta for the crimes it committed while in power (ART. 6–8).[30] *Bay kou bliye, pote mak sonje*, says the Creole proverb: "the one who hits forgets, the one who bears the mark remembers."

A March 1995 decree created the *Commission Nationale de Vérité et de Justice*, whose title was revealing: contrary to the South African truth and *reconciliation* committee, the Haitian truth and *justice* commission aimed to document past crimes for future judicial revenge, not to bring Haitians together in a great national coming out.[31] The decree creating the commission specifically mentioned that it should not offer freedom from prosecution in exchange for confessions.[32] The commission's work was greatly hampered by a lack of funds, which prevented commission members from interviewing junta supporters now living in exile, as well as by the U.S. refusal to release 160,000 pages of FRAPH and Haitian Army documents documenting the political repression in 1991–1994. The commission relied extensively on forms filed by victims, as well as forensic analyses of the bodies the Haitian Army and the Port-au-Prince hospital had dumped at Ti Tanyen, a few miles from the capital (when the commission visited the site in September 1995, the corpses were still there, mixed with garbage).[33]

The final report, released in February 1996 and entitled *Si M Pa Rele* ("if I don't cry out"), was most notable for its detailed account of the 24 April 1994 Raboteau massacre, during which the army killed 20 to 50 Aristide supporters in a shantytown near Gonaïves. Alas, the report's usefulness proved limited. Only Aristide had a copy of the report, which he made little use of, having received it two days before he left office. A first French edition of 60 copies appeared in September 1996, followed by another one of 1,500 copies in 1997. Nongovernmental organizations finally translated the document into Creole to make it accessible to the vast majority of the population. The report listed witnesses, some of whom were immediately harassed by former soldiers.[34]

Investigating human rights abuses was useless unless there was a functioning judicial system to sentence perpetrators, but the pace of judicial reform proved excruciatingly slow. Little was done besides creating commissions and passing laws. After the Truth and Justice Commission handed out its report, another commission, the *Commission Préparatoire à la Réforme du Droit et de la Justice* (preparatory committee for legal and judicial reform) was created, which produced its own report in July 1998. A law on judicial reform finally took effect in August 1998, and the new *Ecole Nationale de la Magistrature* (national school for judges) produced its first 60 graduates in May 1998. They had received 24 weeks of training.[35] An Office of the Ombudsman was created in September 1995 to protect Haitians from abuses by public authorities. Prisons underwent the same slow legal facelift. A National Penitentiary Administration was created in June 1995, followed by a Bureau on Pre-Trial Detention in June 1998. Both issued orders that prisoners be better fed, minors and women separated from men, and prisoners awaiting trial judged without unreasonable delay.[36]

On a superficial level, democratic reform proceeded apace. A new police force appeared, elections were held, a commission investigated human rights violations, and deputies, after a few years' delay, finally passed laws reforming courts and prisons. But Haiti's previous constitutions, which frequently contained equally elaborate procedures calling for the rule of law and democratic processes, had been little more than intellectually gratifying, but unenforced, legal facades that gave meaning to the Creole proverb "law is paper, and bayonets are steel." Should Haiti be reformed on paper only, there was a risk that Haiti would become officially democratic, while little changed below the surface. The people would not abide by laws that the government was unable to enforce. The police force would capture criminals who would never be judged. The judicial system would never try those singled out in the Truth and Justice Commission's investigation. With no amnesty, Aristide's enemies would remain irremediably antagonistic. With no real justice, their victims would remain acrimonious. Aristide might have said yes to reconciliation and yes to justice, but his country would get none. Only the future would determine whether these fears were founded or not. In the meantime, U.S. support for democracy continued, with one particularly damning exception.

Justice, Emmanuel Constant, and the United States

When Emmanuel Constant promised in October 1994 to U.S. commanders Shelton and Meade that he would call for national reconciliation, he managed to stop a crackdown against members of his paramilitary group, the FRAPH.[37] The Aristide government, on the other hand, remained steadfastly determined that Constant should pay for his crimes, and, on 21 December 1994, a Haitian magistrate issued an arrest warrant against him. Constant immediately fled to the Dominican Republic, entering the United States *via* Puerto Rico on Christmas Eve with a six-month tourist visa (B2).[38] Constant's visa was revoked in February 1995, and, on 29 March, U.S. Secretary of State Warren Christopher asked Attorney General Janet Reno to find Constant, to arrest him, and to deport him to Haiti, citing the promotion of democracy in Haiti as "one of our foremost foreign policy priorities." His aim was to "bring to justice those responsible for serious crimes and violations of the fundamental rights of Haitians," including Constant and the FRAPH.[39] Reno responded positively, and it seemed likely that Constant, sharing the fate of other Haitian illegal immigrants, would soon be sent back to Haiti.[40]

It took two months for U.S. authorities to find Constant, who had been living at his mother's house in New York City since his arrival in the United States, and to send him to a Maryland immigration jail, but he was finally sentenced to deportation to Haiti in September 1995.[41] Constant failed to appeal the decision, but he sued the U.S. government for $50 million in compensatory and punitive damages for ruining his chances of ever becoming president of Haiti (he apparently considered the position to be highly lucrative).[42] His legal prospects were dim. Among other things, he argued that he could never be elected president of Haiti if he were deported to Haiti, an assertion whose logic was particularly unclear; he was not even officially registered as a presidential candidate.[43] A State Department legal team aggressively pursued Constant's deportation, describing him as a major human rights violator in 1993–1994.[44] Even if Constant had won this case, he would have received compensation, but would have been deported anyway.

Constant proved legally feeble, but politically savvy. In October 1995, he granted an interview to the *Washington Post* to complain that, when he had informed Clinton of his predicament, he had only received a standard "Dear Emmanuel" form letter thanking him for his "interest in my efforts to restore democracy to Haiti."[45] Two months later, he appeared on a CBS program from his Maryland cell and revealed that he had organized the *Harlan County* demonstration at the very time he was on the CIA payroll. Deciding to resist deportation by embarrassing the CIA publicly, he declared: "I'm in jail. I've been betrayed. I've been humiliated. And I think it's about time for the world and the American public to know that me [sic], Emmanuel 'Toto' Constant, is not what they are saying."[46] The timing was particularly bad for the CIA, which was in the middle of operation "scrub," an attempt to stop using human rights abusers as informers.[47]

Amazingly, after actively seeking Constant's deportation for over a year, the INS suddenly freed him on 14 June 1996. A September 1998 court decision denying Constant's plea for a stay of deportation was not implemented either.[48] In November 2000, a Haitian court finally tried Constant *in abstentia*, along with 36 former members of the military junta, for their role in a 1994 massacre in Gonaïves and sentenced him to forced labor for life, but, despite protests by the Haitian government and the Haitian–American community that the United States, the very proponent of Operation Restore Democracy, was hosting one of Haitian democracy's most devoted enemies, Constant remained in New York, where he lives to this day.[49] Even though he is now a convicted criminal, the U.S. government has not yet extradited Constant. Coming after a 23,000-troop intervention to restore democracy and an 18-month legal battle to deport Constant, the decision to allow him to stay in the United States was most puzzling. Congressman and Aristide friend Joseph P. Kennedy (D-MA) wrote Clinton to "express grave concern over the release of Emmanuel Constant from jail" and hinted that Constant's past as a CIA informer was the main reason for the special treatment he received.

> As for concerns that a trial may expose embarrassing links between FRAPH and our intelligence services, I contend that the interests of democratic rule are better served by exposing any such connections to the light of public scrutiny.[50]

In its response to Kennedy, the Department of Justice, after consulting with the NSC and the State Department, argued that the United States could not extradite Constant because Haiti had not filed an extradition request in the proper form and because Constant's return "would have placed an undue burden on the Haitian judicial and penal system."[51] Both were obvious lies. Six months before, the U.S. government's own lawyers had argued in court that it was "essential to proceed with efforts to deport Constant independent of any extradition efforts," and that his return to Haiti was a prerequisite, not an impediment, to the establishment of the rule of law in Haiti.[52] The key to this mystery was a "settlement agreement" the immigration court and Constant alluded to.[53]

According to government documents obtained under the Freedom of Information Act, top U.S. officials held a White House deputies meeting on 23 May 1996 to discuss Constant's case.[54] Associate Deputy Attorney General Seth Waxman, Deputy Attorney General Jamie S. Gorelick, and Deputy Secretary of State Strobe Talbott, whose respective departments had up to that point handled deportation proceedings against Constant, attended the meeting, as did Deputy National Security Adviser Sandy Berger, CIA Operations Deputy Director David Cohen, and CIA Deputy Director George S. Tenet. Transcripts of the White House deputies meeting remain classified, but the decision to free Constant most likely originated with two traditional enemies of Aristide during his years in exile, the U.S. Embassy in Port-au-Prince and the CIA. One memo indicates that, at the suggestion of U.S. Ambassador to Haiti William Lacy Swing, Talbott proposed that "conditions" be offered to settle the case.[55] The CIA, already criticized for employing human rights violators in the past, was increasingly concerned by Constant's willingness to go public about his past ties to the CIA and probably suggested that he be given an incentive to remain silent. In its efforts to convince the INS to abandon deportation proceedings, the CIA also transmitted intelligence reports to the INS, Constant, and the Department of Justice warning that there were death plots against Constant in Haiti. According to the CIA, Constant would be imprisoned, a prison riot would be "staged as a diversion, during which an attempt to kill [him] w[ould] be made."[56]

The deputies agreed on a settlement proposal that Constant's attorney signed on 14 June, the day Constant was released. The settlement ended deportation proceedings against Constant. In exchange, he promised to put an end to his hopeless lawsuit against the U.S. government, to stay in New York, and to report to the INS weekly. Most importantly, he would "neither make public oral or written statements about Haitian politics nor engage in political activities concerning Haiti," and keep the terms, as well as the existence, of the settlement secret.[57] This agreement, silence in exchange for freedom, was only valid for 120 days, but Constant's continued presence in the United States and his later complaint about a "gag order," suggest that the deal remains valid by tacit understanding.[58] Impunity for past crimes was the price the United States paid to keep its past association with human rights abusers secret.

Economic Development

In 1960, South Korea and Haiti had the same gross domestic product (GDP) per capita, about $900. By 2000, South Korea's GDP per capita had jumped to $10,550, while Haiti's had shrunk to $460.[59] Haiti's average annual GDP growth was 0 percent during the 1980s and −1.3 percent during the 1990s, while its population grew by 2 percent a year from 1980 to 2000.[60] By the late 1990s, 80 percent of Haitians lived in dire poverty. The number of workers employed in the assembly sector, estimated at 65,000 people in 1991, neared zero when the embargo came to an end in 1994; by 1997, this number had only rebounded to 18,000, in a nation of 8 million people where there was little other industrial activity.[61]

Haiti's startling descent further into the abyss of underdevelopment prompted the international community to pursue ambitious economic policies in parallel with its democratization efforts. Compassion and greed were not the deciding factors; democratization itself demanded prosperity. Haitians would never support the democratic transition if it did not bring immediate financial benefits. Illiterate citizens living on the margins of survival made a poor support base for democratization. A bankrupt state could not pay its policemen or judges, finance elections, or feed its prisoners. Conversely, in South Korea and Taiwan, democracy had followed economic development, and the Clinton administration was betting that the same would happen in China. In 1996, Clinton concluded that "countries making the transition from authoritarian regimes to democracy are unstable and prone to conflict, especially if they are not also making economic progress."[62] Lifting Haiti out of poverty was a consensual, compassionate way to ensure democratization's success, but devising a method to do it was more problematic.

U.S. policy during the 1915–1934 occupation had succeeded in stabilizing Haiti's currency, the *gourde*, retiring public debt, and building roads, airstrips, irrigation canals, and hospitals, but success had come at a price. Forced labor gangs (*corvées*) built and maintained the roads, while U.S. officials took over the customs receivership and other key financial posts. Because economic success was U.S.-imposed and U.S.-led, it did not survive the U.S. troops' departure in 1934. Within 20 years, most of the infrastructures built by the Marines were in a tragic state of disrepair. A car trip from Port-au-Prince to Jacmel, which took two hours in 1934, took nine in 1957.[63] Such heavy-handed forced-development policies, aside from not being sustainable, were politically unpalatable in 1995, 40 years after a wave of de-colonization swept Asia and Africa.

The UN force could not draft a development framework based on the first months of the 1994 intervention either, for the U.S. Army refrained from acting as a colonial power and limited itself to a few small projects that were clearly insufficient to trigger Haiti's long-awaited economic resurrection. Soldiers dug wells, repaired buildings, cleaned sewers, and built bridges only when these were useful to the occupation force.[64] If anything, the beginning of the occupation reinforced existing economic structures. The U.S. Army rented the industrial complex, a sprawling area next to the Port-au-Prince airport formerly home to the world's largest baseball factories, from the Mevs, one of Haiti's richest families. In addition to paying rent, U.S. soldiers cleaned and fixed these buildings.[65] Lt. Col. Edward J. Anderson, a civil affairs officer for JTF-180 remembers that "all the way through our intention was, clearly, to limit military civic action" such as infrastructure programs. Days before the invasion, Anderson added,

> some little shit head from the State Department stood up . . . and said, "wouldn't it be wonderful if we could go in and get all the power ready to turn on, and when Aristide comes back he walks in and symbolically turns on the light switch and all the lights come on in the country?" Any of us that have ever been involved in anything like this, looked at each other and said, "what does this guy smoke? Do they feed them strange things in the State Department?" This little shit head was the Deputy Assistant Secretary of State! And I'm sitting there thinking to myself, you guys are just totally out to lunch! The objective here is not for the United States government to look good.[66]

The international community, most notably the United States, the United Nations, the World Bank, the IMF, and the Inter-American Development Bank, devised much more ambitious plans for the long term. Their development strategy emphasized private enterprise and free trade, backed by a massive infusion of foreign aid. This neoliberal agenda, which the USAID had put forward as early as 1991,[67] was finalized at an informal meeting between the Government of Haiti and international donors held in Paris on 26 August 1994, then put forward officially at a formal international gathering in Paris on 30–31 January 1995. The Paris program emphasized improved tax collection, privatization of public companies, a leaner, more effective government, the use of nongovernmental organizations to channel funds, and lower tariffs.[68] The White House had unveiled a similar plan on 14 December 1994.[69] The World Bank cited similar objectives in 1998.[70]

The impetus to adopt this neoliberal agenda was strong. First and foremost was the widely held view that capitalism was the most effective way to achieve economic growth. Following the fall of the Soviet Union and the failure of top-down development strategies in the 1960s and 1970s, free-market ideology dominated money-lending agencies such as the IMF and the World Bank. A 1997 study for Port-au-Prince's USAID office associated freedom in the political arena with freedom in the marketplace, saying that "the legacies of elitism, exploitation, dictatorship, state predation and crony capitalism must be destroyed in Haiti. . . . A free and stable democracy requires an open, participatory, and competitive economic framework."[71]

Relying on private investments also diminished the need for costly public aid. In the words of Rep. Dan Burton (R-IN), "I would rather get the private sector involved, as one Member of Congress, rather than have the American taxpayer pay the freight for what appears to be an endless amount of expenses down there."[72] Petty U.S. commercial interests, on the other hand, played a minor role. Internal USAID documents never alluded to the interests of the few U.S. companies doing business in Haiti (American Airlines, Shell, and Texaco). Far from plotting a giant conspiracy to reduce Haiti to a state of economic bondage, reports usually started with a summary of the horrendous economic situation faced by everyday Haitians, and recommended setting money aside for health and education projects.[73] Total direct U.S. investments in Haiti amounted to only $18 million in 1997 and $32 million in 1999.[74]

Last, but not least, there was a strong feeling that the Haitian government was thoroughly incompetent, and should thus be left out of economic development. A study commissioned by the USAID concluded, "the Haitian government has shown itself to be profoundly incapable of organizing and executing a coherent and firm response to even the most trivial of challenges."[75] The World Bank less cruelly recommended "to assess realistically what the Haitian state can and cannot do and to redefine the role of the state in society."[76] A project to repair roads characteristically noted that the transportation ministry was "seriously overstaffed," while lacking "qualified engineers and specialists. . . . The most pervasive problem in Haiti is the weak institutional capacity of the public sector."[77] So profound was the Haitian government's alleged ineptitude that donors pledged $218 million for 1994–1997 just for "governance projects" aimed at reforming the government. The Inter-American Development Bank's project #HA/94/012 even offered $1.2 million to teach the Ministry of Cooperation the proper way to ask for and manage foreign aid![78]

Given the widespread distrust of Haiti's government, encouraging the growth of the private sector was the most important priority, requiring the removal of legal barriers to foreign investments. In 1918, the U.S. officials who drafted the Haitian Constitution had repealed the ban that had prevented foreigners from holding land in Haiti since the nation's independence.[79] A few obstacles remained, namely, ART. 55 and 55-2 of the 1987 Constitution, forbidding foreigners from holding land along the border with the Dominican Republic, and a law preventing foreigners from owning more than 1.29 hectare in towns and 6.45 hectares in rural areas, but both of these could be circumvented by relying on local partners.[80] On the other hand, Haiti's nine "parastatals," state-owned companies controlling such sectors as flour and cement production, were a clear impediment to free competition and the U.S. State Department asked for their privatization.[81] During an October 1995 visit to Haiti, Vice President Gore presented "the promotion of investment through privatization" as very important to the creation of a sound economic future for all Haitians.[82]

Creating a favorable climate—decent infrastructures, no public monopolies, no corruption, legal protection, minimal risk, low taxes—was what businessmen demanded,[83] and the Clinton administration relayed those demands.[84] One administration proposal called for the U.S. Overseas Private Investment Corporation to offer $100 million in insurance and financial guarantees to offset the risks associated with investing in Haiti.[85] Administration officials brought more than 200 U.S. businessmen to tour Haiti.[86] In one such tour, Deputy Secretary of State Strobe Talbott declared,

> in addition to the security situation, there are also practices, and in some cases absence of practices, in place in Haiti that have made it an uninviting environment for Americans and others to do business. This has to do with regulatory procedures, customs procedures, that kind of thing. We've been working very closely with the Haitian government to see if there aren't some improvements that could be made along those lines. . . . Corruption and inefficiency are the two endemic problems there.[87]

Free trade, which the Clinton administration was advocating on a worldwide basis, was the second priority. In December 1994, 34 American presidents and prime ministers met in Miami for the Summit of the Americas. As is generally the case with multilateral treaties, the final agreement was vague—proposition #15 courageously asserted that tourism was "important."[88] But proposition #9, which called for a free-trade zone in the Americas, included a precise timetable and a list of actions to undertake within months. Ministerial meetings in Denver (summer 1995), Cartagena (March 1996), and Belo Horizonte, Brazil (May 1997) worked out the details. Clinton's loss of his fast-track authority impaired negotiations thereafter, but the push for freer trade resulted in the U.S.–Caribbean Basin Trade Partnership Act, signed into law in May 2000, which lowered tariffs on textile products and handicrafts.[89]

Aristide himself advocated free trade. Trade barriers imposed under Baby Doc had resulted in high prices that further impoverished the poor (Aristide's supporters) while enriching a few public and private monopolies run by the elite (Aristide's enemies). In order to reduce the high cost of living (*la vie chère*), tariffs thus dropped following Duvalier's fall in 1986, then again in 1994 and 1995. A member of the World Trade Organization (1996) and CARICOM (1999), Haiti imposed low tariffs of 0 to 3 percent on basic staples and 15 percent for the most heavily taxed products; the average duty was 8 percent, with half of all products entering Haiti tax-free. Haiti "currently ranks among the most open economies worldwide," the IMF noted approvingly.[90]

Business-oriented laws, smaller government, and lower tariffs were only part of the equation. Haiti's destitution was so severe that foreign governments and institutions had to pledge hard cash in addition to technical assistance. Given the Haitian opposition to some of the reforms, most notably the privatization of public companies and the reform of the public service, aid also provided political leverage for the international community. No one wanted to repeat the experience of the 1970s and early 1980s, when Duvalier had received almost $1 billion, continued political repression despite promises, diverted most of the money to his own accounts, and left the country poorer than it was when he took over.[91] Among other examples, a 1983 audit showed that hundreds of bags of food donated by the United States to feed hungry Haitians ended up in markets where they were sold; $500,000 worth of food distributed through Catholic Relief Services also disappeared from warehouses.[92] To prevent waste and oblige Haitians to carry out economic reforms, aid packages left no room for improvisation. A 1996 program had no less than 12 pages of small-print instructions on how to spend the money, with timetables for precise reforms to be implemented at each stage of the process.[93]

Aid, even with strings attached, poured with unprecedented abundance. The August 1994 and January 1995 Paris meetings resulted in pledges of $1.2 billion, less than 25 percent of it provided by the United States, the rest by an array of 19 international organizations and 14 governments; by 1996, pledges reached almost $2 billion[94] [appendix IV]. The Inter-American Development Bank offered $329 million for 1995–1997, almost as much as the $357 million it had spent in Haiti from 1961 to 1991.[95] Seventy percent of the pledges were outright grants; 49 percent of the loans were offered on generous terms. In May 1995, Canada, France, and the United States wrote off two-thirds of Haiti's existing debts and rescheduled the rest with a six-year grace period.[96] The amount pledged was so great that Boutros-Ghali expressed fears that this was more than Haiti could possibly absorb.[97] With an external debt reduced to less than $1.1 billion in 1998, Haiti could not even qualify for the heavily indebted poor countries (HIPC) program.[98]

Gathering Clouds

Despite encouraging progress, particularly on the economic front, the first signs of a rising Haitian anti-Americanism appeared in September 1995, when Haitians demonstrated for the first time to oppose the presence of foreign troops in Haiti.[99] Later that month, opponents of Aristide created the *Nouvel Altenativ Fos Popile yo Kont Okipasyon ak FMI* (the People's New Alternative against the IMF and the Occupation) and accused Aristide of being a puppet. On 15 October, U.S. Vice President Al Gore's celebratory visit to Port-au-Prince was tarnished when a crowd pelted his wife Tipper's motorcade with rocks, chanting "Go Home Yankees."[100]

In November 1995, when Aristide's cousin and former bodyguard, Deputy Jean-Hubert Feuillé, was gunned down, the police accused former right-wing president Prosper Avril of masterminding the murder.[101] A State Department cable showed that, two weeks before the murder took place, the United States knew that Avril was "planning harassment and an assassination campaign directed at the Lavalas party and Aristide supporters."[102] Hours before the police came to arrest Avril, a U.S. Embassy official visited him, and Avril subsequently avoided arrest by fleeing to the Colombian Embassy. Both incidents gave way to widespread speculation in Haiti that the evil hand of the CIA was once again at work.[103]

His friend's murder and anti-American popular resentment pushed Aristide to abandon his peace and reconciliation mantra and return to his pre-exile, 1991 persona. Diplomats attending Feuillé's 11 November 1995 funeral in Port-au-Prince's beautiful, pleasantly cool National Cathedral, perched on a breezy hill over-looking the capital's bustling iron market, heard soothing words from Aristide—in French. Those few who were fluent in Creole, on the other hand, could notice that the Creole sentences that interspersed the speech had little to do with the French balderdash designed to fool the innocents from abroad. The Creole sections, much more aggressive, were aimed at Aristide's domestic constituency.

> [Creole] I am reminding you that until further notice there are not two or three heads of state, but just one. [applause] The head of state has spoken. [applause]. . . . I order you to arrest anyone who wants to block this legal, total, and complete disarmament operation if he is a Haitian. [applause] If he is not a Haitian [applause], if he is not Haitian [applause], if he is not Haitian, we will send him back to his country. · [applause]
>
> [French] The month of November 1995 must be a month of peace, a month of success. . . . Gratitude is the heart's memory, we said more than once. We are grateful to our friends, to those who helped us restore democracy in Haiti.
>
> [Creole] I ask the Haitian people to do the following: do not sit idly by, do not wait; accompany the policemen when they are going to enter the homes of the people who have heavy weapons, do not be afraid of them. When you do that, tell the policemen not to go only to the poor neighborhoods, but to go to the neighborhoods where there are big houses and heavy weapons. [applause] The game of hypocrisy is over.
>
> [French] It is time for both the rich and the poor, the men in high places as well as the poor, to enjoy this peace.
>
> [Creole] Freedom or death! [6 times]. . . . It is not a question of sitting idly and waiting for the foreigners to give us security. [applause]
>
> [French] I have come to renew my willingness to move jointly with the international community in mutual respect.

"It is the first time that I have spoken like that since my return to Haiti," Aristide concluded.[104] The speech was indeed reminiscent of Aristide's irresponsible pre-exile diatribes and, as in 1991, it encouraged his supporters to go on a rampage. Violent demonstrations followed the speech, as well as a *dechoukaj* ("uprooting," or manhunt of former Duvalierists) that left more than ten people dead.[105]

In the meantime, Emmanuel Constant's case aside, the United States and the international community pursued a policy clearly intent on deepening Haitian democracy and developing its economy. Political reforms tended to be superficial and overly focused on legal and bureaucratic minutiae, such as organizing elections and creating commissions, but their democratic intent was unmistakable. The economic agenda, which the international community supervised more closely because it provided most of the funds, was a coherent, if neoliberal, program backed by a generous aid package. The unequaled attention and funds lavished on Haiti singled it out as "most likely to succeed" on the Third World yearbook. It took about two years for another one of Haiti's trademark political crises to shatter all the hopes that had been placed in the country's future.

CHAPTER TWELVE

NATION BUILDING: HARD TIMES
(9 JUNE 1997–7 FEBRUARY 2001)

Rosny Smarth Goes Out

On 6 April 1997, Haiti held another round of elections to fill nine Senate seats, two House seats, and thousands of local posts. The great winner of the elections was Aristide's new party, *Lafanmi Lavalas* (the *Lavalas* family), not to be confused with *Organisation Politique Lavalas*, Aristide's former party, now rebaptized *Organisation du Peuple en Lutte* or OPL, which still held a majority in the House. The OPL immediately charged that three of *Lavalas'* victories had been fraudulent. When calculating the threshold for an absolute majority, the electoral commission had omitted to take into account blank ballots, which was contrary to the letter of the law. *Lafanmi Lavalas'* victorious Senators thus won a first-round victory when a run-off election should have taken place. Even though only 10 percent of the electorate voted, some precincts reported vote counts exceeding 100 percent of registered voters. Allegations that members of the electoral commission were corrupt further aggravated the electoral controversy.[1]

To make matters worse, President Préval's prime minister, Rosny Smarth, faced widespread protests in the streets as Aristide's supporters opposed his neoliberal economic policies, most notably his decision to reduce government spending and to prepare state-owned companies for privatization. With popular opposition to his policies, hostility on the part of the still-influential Aristide, a now fractious Parliament, and the sentiment that the April elections had been rigged, Smarth announced that he could no longer govern. He resigned on 9 June, 1997 (he remained as the head of a caretaker government until October).[2] Haiti was now without a government, and would remain so for another 20 months (1997–1999), until Préval illegally nominated a prime minister and dissolved the Parliament by presidential decree. The country then had a government, but no Parliament for another 15 months (1999–2000), until fraud-plagued legislative elections took place. The opposition boycotted the November 2000 presidential election in protest and nominated its own president, which left Haiti with one government and one Parliament, but two presidents (2000–2001). Two failed coup attempts preceded (August 1996) and followed (December 2001) the period.[3]

Haitian politics, complete with betrayals, murders, and plot twists, were as captivating as a particularly brutal soap opera, but the protracted political crisis was nothing to laugh about. Consumed by petty political squabbles, the political class failed to oversee the basic missions of the state. With no functioning government, Haiti would not implement the reforms necessary to secure continued international funding, while political instability scared away potential investors and tourists. The international community, angered by the Haitians' inability to seize this unique opportunity to lift their country out of poverty, froze foreign aid, removed troops, and abandoned Haiti to its fate. Despite all the great hopes raised after Aristide's return, Haiti remained a desperately poor nation run by a government known more for its fractiousness and its ineptitude than for its devotion to the teachings of Thomas Jefferson and Adam Smith.

Haitian "Democracy" Restored

After Smarth left office in June 1997, President Préval, whom Aristide now criticized, the Chamber of Deputies, dominated by the OPL, and the Senate, now dominated by *Lafanmi Lavalas*, failed to agree on a new prime minister acceptable to all sides.[4] Deputies accepted Hervé Denis, a leftist economist and the rector of Haiti's state university, but senators rejected him. The OPL proposed former prime minister, Smarck Michel, former minister of agriculture, Gerard Mathurin, and former ambassador to the United Nations, Jean Casimir, but Préval rejected them all. As 1998 drew to a close, the second consecutive year without a budget, over $2 billion in aid pledged by foreign donors sat idly, waiting for a government to administer it.[5]

After almost two years without a running government, Préval finally nominated Jacques-Edouard Alexis as prime minister in a January 1999 decree, then dissolved the Parliament in February. Both moves were unconstitutional. One day after Préval named Alexis prime minister, Alexis's sister, Marie-Claude Calvin, narrowly escaped an assassination attempt.[6] Negotiations between Préval and the OPL on how to organize legislative elections dragged on for months, with the OPL accusing Préval of complicity in the March 1999 murder of OPL Senator Jean-Yvon Toussaint and Aristide of supporting political chaos to facilitate his return as national savior.[7]

Political instability increased as other measures sponsored by the occupation force, including a new police and judicial and prison reform, proved their limitations. As the number of foreign troops declined, the deficiencies of the quickly trained, poorly funded Haitian police became more evident. Young and inexperienced, or veterans of the murderous Haitian Army (FAdH), and aware that sending criminals to the judicial system would not result in a rapid and fair judgment, policemen took the habit of shooting first and asking questions later. By October 1999, no fewer than 673 police officers (out of a force of 5,300) had been dismissed on corruption, human rights, and other charges.[8] In the first 18 months of its existence, the police killed at least 46 civilians.[9] The death toll was 31 in 1998 and 66 in 1999, few of them killed in self-defense.[10]

Jean-Bernard Charles, one such victim of police abuse, was handcuffed, then shot dead by four Haitian policemen in 1996. Policemen then physically threatened family members who dared complain about their relative's wrongful death. Similar reports of human rights abuses became so numerous that the United States created the Human Rights Fund in the spring of 1996. The fund, whose existence remained secret to avoid public embarrassment, reimbursed the funeral expenses of victims of police abuse, paid for the medical care of the wounded, and provided a safe haven for those harassed by police officers. This was no panacea: when one of Charles's relatives fled to one of the Fund's safe houses, four policemen seized him, broke his knees, lashed his back with a razor, cut his ear, and dumped him in front of the Fund's headquarters.[11]

In November 1997, former chief of the interim police force Léon Jeune, who had become an opponent of Aristide and run for president in 1995, was beaten by the police, arrested, accused of plotting against the state, then released three weeks later under intense international pressure.[12] In October 1999, Vice Minister for Public Security Robert Manuel, who oversaw the police and insisted on his neutrality, resigned after being heavily criticized by Aristide and his supporters—because of his inability to reduce crime, as Aristide said, or because he refused to let Aristide control the police, as Aristide's enemies said. Days later, gunmen killed Aristide's friend and Manuel's likely successor, Jean Lamy. Manuel, whom Aristide supporters accused of ordering Lamy's murder, escaped to Guatemala. The judge investigating Lamy's murder narrowly escaped an assassination attempt himself.[13] Who ordered what, and with which goal, remained uncertain, as is often the case in Haiti, but it was clear that the police, the country's sole legal armed body since the disappearance of the Haitian Army, was the object of an intense subterranean battle for political control.

The judicial system's twin problem of low pay (and, accordingly, corruption) and low level of instruction (and, accordingly, incompetence), were equally intractable. Of the many instances of police abuse, only the 1999 murders of 11 civilians by policemen in Carrefour Feuilles led to a trial, in August 2000.[14] Of the many political crimes committed in 1991–1994, only the 1994 Raboteau massacre, in which the army killed numerous Aristide supporters, led to a trial, in November 2000 (half of the defendants, living in exile, did not attend the trial).[15] Internal documents from the Haitian Ministry of Justice show that extra-judicial procedures remain the norm. In at least two instances, François Séverin, President Préval's Chief of Staff, asked Justice Minister Pierre Max Antoine to free friends of his.[16]

Because the judicial system proved unable to bring inmates to a quick trial, the prison population rose from 1,500 in 1995 to 3,700 in 1999. For lack of funds, training of new prison guards ended in 1998, and the budget remained stable despite the rapidly rising number of detainees, resulting in severe food shortages, malnutrition, and ensuing diseases, which guards worsened by stealing the funds set aside for inmates' food. Due to court delays, 75 percent of the detainees at the National Penitentiary were in pretrial detention. One such prisoner was former general of the Haitian armed forces Claude Raymond, arrested in July 1996 and accused of conspiring against the state, then kept in pretrial detention for so long that he died in February 2000 before he could be judged. In September 1999, 25 inmates at Haiti's national penitentiary went on a hunger strike to protest their being jailed for up to two years without a trial for such charges as "subversion," which included demonstrating in front of the Ministry of Finance to receive their pension. Twenty-one of them were freed in December 1999.[17]

To end the long period of extra-constitutional rule, during which the government, in the absence of a Parliament, ruled by decree, legislative elections were finally scheduled for 21 May 2000. The campaign was anything but peaceful. Fifteen political murders marred the election run-up, the most famous of which occurred on 3 April, when two gunmen killed Jean Leopold Dominique, the founder of Radio Haiti Inter, a longtime opponent of Duvalier, and a supporter of Aristide. Twenty thousand people, including Aristide and Préval, attended Dominique's funeral in the capital's stadium. A hundred *chimères* (chimaera), armed *Lafanmi Lavalas* supporters named after the part-lion, part-dragon, part-goat mythological monster, disrupted the ceremony, chanting "Aristide or death" and "elections or not, Aristide is already our president."[18] The mob pledged to kill Evans Paul, spokesman for the inaptly named opposition coalition *espace de concertation* (space for dialogue.) Protesters burned down the coalition's headquarters, whose spokesman they luckily did not find.[19] Investigation for Dominique's murder was still ongoing as of 2004, with OPL deputy Dany Toussaint a prime suspect.[20]

On election day, among other irregularities, election workers left ballot boxes outside overnight for lack of room; the following day, the ballots, by then scattered on the streets, were picked up and counted.[21] *Lafanmi Lavalas'* probable victory was marred by its attempt to make its victory even more lopsided. The *Lavalas*-controlled electoral commission insisted on declaring *Lavalas* the winner when its candidate had gathered a majority among the 5 or 6 main candidates, rather than all the votes cast, and refused to hold run-off elections in such cases. Thanks in part to this criterion, 72 of 83 deputies, 18 of 19 senators, and two-thirds of 7,500 local mandates elected on 21 May were *Lavalas*. Fearing for his life after he refused to approve the official election results, Léon Manus, Haiti's top election official, fled Haiti for the Dominican Republic on 16 June, then on to Miami and Boston.[22] Numerous opposition candidates, including 30 from the OPL, were arrested after they protested the election results.[23] Policemen were not there, on the other hand, when *Lavalas* supporters attacked the Port-au-Prince headquarters of the opposition party *Rassemblement des Citoyens Patriotes* (Rally of Patriotic Citizens), nearly killing one man and badly injuring another.[24]

Because of the May 2000 election's numerous flaws, the OAS refused to provide observers for run-offs held later that summer, and opposition members refused to take part in the presidential election scheduled for November 2000. Under the 1987 Constitution, the president of Haiti can hold a maximum of two nonconsecutive mandates. As a result, Préval, the incumbent, could not run, but Aristide, who had been out of office since February 1996, could run one last time. Thanks to the opposition's boycott, Aristide ran as the only major candidate, won in a landslide, and was inaugurated as president of Haiti on 7 February 2001, ten years to the day after his first inauguration. In a form of diplomatic protest, foreign governments only sent minor officials to both Aristide's and Prime Minister Jean-Marie Cherestal's inauguration.[25]

The same day, the *convergence démocratique* (democratic convergence), the main opposition coalition, inaugurated its own president, law professor Gérard Gourgue. In an effort to divide his opponents, Aristide welcomed some former Duvalierists in his government, including Trade Minister Stanley Théard (who, among other things, had been implicated in a Duvalier era embezzlement scheme), and met *Macoute* ideologue Serge Beaulieu.[26] Aristide later hinted to policemen that criminals should be summarily shot if caught in the act, rather than jailed and tried. Policemen "do not need to take [a robber caught in the act] to court to answer to the judge," Aristide declared with customary vagueness. "You do not need to wait for that *zenglendo* [criminal] to appear before the judge, you can prevent that murderer from taking action."[27] To fulfill his campaign promises, including hundreds of thousands of jobs, the end of illiteracy, and electricity 24 hours a day, Aristide immediately requested international aid. The answer was emblematic of the growing enmity between Haiti and the international community: no, unless you solve the political impasse first.

Growing Enmity Between Haiti and the International Community

During the first few months following the invasion, U.S. troops typically had to make their way through throngs of thankful Haitians, while murals and signs read "*merci*, America."[28] Despite the outpouring of support, however, one could already discern the seeds of future dissent. The leading French-language daily noted that Haitians were "humiliated" by the invasion, while its Creole counterpart made mention of the "sadness that [had] invaded its heart" when even self-described patriots such as Cédras "who never lost an occasion to make nationalistic propaganda" were now collaborating with the invader.[29] Contrary to U.S. expectations, Aristide showed little gratitude upon his return to Haiti. "He believes the United States helped remove him in 1991 and then brought him back, so they are even" one of Aristide's aides said. "It's like if I steal $20 from you, then give it back to you, you are not grateful, you just think justice has been done."[30]

As the political situation in Haiti deteriorated, so did relations between Haiti and its foreign friends. Haitian opposition to U.S.-sponsored economic reforms was the first catalyst, even though Haitian government officials welcomed the reforms in private. In June 1992, while he was in exile, Aristide had signed a document pledging "to promote the conditions for a true market economy to flourish" in Haiti.[31] After he came back to Haiti, members of his government attending the January 1995 Paris meeting with international donors endorsed, rather than opposed, foreign demands. Prime Minister Smarck Michel criticized parastatals (bureaucratese for state-owned companies), "transformed into milk cows for corruption. . . . [whose] lack of legitimacy is already a given." Minister of Planning (and future Prime Minister) Jean-Marie Cherestal added that "the government encourages the involvement of the nation's private sector, trade unions, and NGOs." Minister of Finance Marie-Michèle Rey reaffirmed, "each of the economic agreements and pledges" made at the previous August 1994 Paris meeting.[32]

But, in public, Aristide remained as liberal as ever, because refusing to cave in to foreign requests was popular, and because the right-wing elite, which alone had the financial means to buy state monopolies, was most likely to benefit from privatization. For plausible deniability's sake, Aristide did not sign the Paris agreement himself and later wrote that it "was never a signed agreement, rather it was a strategy paper. It included many of the elements that the international community was pressing as conditions for financial support of Haiti."[33] In October 1995, Aristide warned on television that "If I learn now, while I am talking to you, of somebody who dares sell the state's possessions on behalf of privatization, I will have him arrested immediately."[34] Because of popular opposition to privatization fanned by Aristide's speeches, Prime Minister Smarck Michel and Rosny Smarth, both of whom supported privatization, resigned.[35] Only two of Haiti's nine public companies had been privatized by 1999.[36]

Aristide's book *Eyes of the Heart* (2000) demonstrated his return to a militant left-wing rhetoric he had temporarily shelved during his exile in the United States: the IMF's neoliberal requirements were unacceptable, Haitian patriots should not yield to foreign *diktats*, and foreign troops should leave. Denunciations of the impact of slavery, of the French tribute of 1823, of the U.S.-engineered slaughter of Haiti's pigs in the 1980s, and a reaffirmation of his attachment to liberation theology completed the list.[37] The criticisms were mostly demagogy on Aristide's part (he had invited foreign troops and capital in), but they found a ready audience in a people historically suspicious of foreign motives.

The presence of foreign troops on Haitian soil was the second main sticking point. Once again, private negotiations directly contradicted public posturing. In June 1995, Aristide asked the UN secretary general to extend the UN mission's mandate until February 1996, and Préval did the same for later extensions of the UN mandate.[38] In March 1999, Louis Harold Joseph, *chargé d'affaires* at the Haitian Embassy in Washington, wrote to Haitian Minister of Foreign Affairs Fritz Longchamp to express his *concern* that U.S. troops were about to leave and advocated that Prime Minister Alexis travel to Washington to convince U.S. officials and editorialists that foreign troops should stay in Haiti.[39] Two months after the last UN troops left Haiti in February 2001, Aristide demanded—privately and unsuccessfully—that they return.[40]

In public, however, Aristide and other Haitian politicians could not afford to go against the anti-American tide, which an August 1997 incident in which New York policemen arrested, beat, and sodomized Haitian American Abner Louima and a March 2000 incident in which a New York policeman shot an unarmed Patrick M. Dorismond dead helped swell.[41] After he left office in February 1996, Aristide's hypocritical attacks on countries that had brought him back to power, then bankrolled his government, grew louder. Criticizing UN troops and neoliberal reforms, Aristide warned that Haiti would not be "indebted to imperialism."[42] In September 1997, the chamber of deputies adopted a resolution demanding the departure of all "foreign armed corps" from Haiti, while Art. 10 of the August 1998 law on judicial reform specified that "as soon as this law is published, the State is under the obligation of obtaining the departure of all foreign armed forces."[43]

An old territorial dispute between Haiti and the United States also flared anew.[44] *La Navase* (Navassa), a 2-square mile, uninhabited Caribbean island 40 miles off Haiti's coast, was discovered by Christopher Columbus in 1504, then given to France along with the rest of Haiti (Treaty of Ryswick, 1697), then claimed as Haitian in subsequent legal documents, including the 1987 Constitution (ART. 8). Meanwhile, following the 1856 Guano Islands Act, the United States authorized its navy to claim every abandoned land with substantial deposits of bird dung, which merchant captain Peter Duncan did in *La Navase* a year later. The United States operated a lighthouse on the island from 1916 to 1996. Controversy resumed in 1999 when Interior Secretary Bruce Babbitt selected *La Navase* as a national wildlife refuge and declared it off limits. A dung-covered islet had little value in and of itself, but its fauna and flora's rare chemical components had a potential value for U.S. pharmaceutical companies. Haitians also suspected that the U.S. insistence on claiming ownership of a historically Haitian territory stemmed from the discovery of gold, uranium ore—or, according to the most extravagant piece of *telediol* (rumor)—a gateway to Atlantis. To Haitians, one thing was clear: U.S. economic imperialism was alive and well.

Haiti continued to pay U.S. lobbying firms, but these were much less effective in swaying public opinion in the United States. When Aristide left office in February 1996, Préval did not renew the $600,000 a year contract with Michael Barnes' firm, Hogan and Hartson.[45] Barnes had been less active after the U.S. intervention took place, placing few calls, "usually at the instigation of the contact person," but he had been Aristide's most precious ally during his exile and he proved irreplaceable.[46] Burton V. Wides received a monthly salary of $14,500, reduced to $7,500 when he set up his own law firm in October 1998, but his contacts were lesser officials for the most part, and his confrontational tone was counterproductive.[47] Aristide hired Hazel Ross-Robinson, whose husband had proved so influential in 1994, as a lobbyist, but she had few contacts outside the Black Caucus, and her monthly pay, reflecting her limited effectiveness in influencing the U.S. political arena and Haiti's increasing financial problems, diminished regularly from $12,500 (1996) to $6,500 (2000).[48] Ira Kurzban remained as a lobbyist, but his seven-figure salary, paid in part with funds from Haiti's telephone company, Teleco, seemed out of proportion to the few phone calls he placed.[49] Another immigration lawyer, Irwin P. Stotzky, also worked as an attorney and adviser to the Aristide and Préval administrations after 1994.[50] (See appendix V.)

Weariness with Haiti's woes set in abroad. Aristide's inflammatory speeches, his calculated ambiguity and hypocrisy, and the political elite's internecine squabbles were nothing new, but they now undermined the nation-building effort. Prospects for democratization were eroding fast. Economic reforms pledged in 1994 and 1995 were not implemented, and the absence of a functioning government made such simple matters as sending a check difficult. As a result, foreign countries first expressed their growing annoyance, then delayed the disbursement of foreign aid, then simply threw up their hands.

Until 1995, the U.S. administration remained officially optimistic. Gore's speech as he was touring Haiti in October 1995 was so enthusiastic as to be funny—a booster in the midst of poverty. "Today, as I stand before you, the representatives of the Haitian family, democracy is flowering in a soil once made barren by the greed and callousness of the thugs and bullies who ruled from these halls [National Palace]," Gore declared. "Democracy and prosperity and opportunity no longer are just a dream, but are becoming a way of life. The world marvels at your progress."[51] By December 1997, when pressed to give his opinion of Aristide, State Department Haiti Coordinator David Greenlee could not utter anything more positive than "I am neither pleased nor displeased."[52] In her famously straightforward style,

Secretary of State Madeleine Albright explained at a Port-au-Prince press conference in April 1998 that "frankly, we have been disappointed that Haiti's political leaders have taken so long to resolve their differences. Democracy requires leaders who will compromise and who are willing to put the needs of the nation above those of party and faction."[53] In February 1999, General Charles E. Wilhelm, head of the Southern Command, recommended withdrawal in a closed House committee hearing.[54] In April 2000, Assistant Secretary of State for Western Hemisphere Affairs Peter F. Romero made a long list of grievances: "the seriously irregular 1997 election which has resulted in the resignation of the Prime Minister, the subsequent cancellation of 1998's legislative and local elections, January 1999's dismissal of the Parliament by President Préval, and extra constitutional rule in Haiti since then."[55]

Public support for the intervention, already tepid to begin with, unraveled as well. Even the liberal *New Republic* published a Six-page cover story entitled "Island of Disenchantment" in September 1997, complete with allegations that Aristide and his entourage organized political killings, comparisons between Aristide and Papa Doc, and a picture of Aristide as the archetypical corrupt dictator: white suit, black sunglasses, full regalia, and uniformed bodyguards.[56] The influential *Time Magazine* and *Le Monde* published similar accounts.[57] Republicans remained steadfastly opposed to the intervention, as they had been since 1994. Beneath the veneer of diplomatic statements, UN Security Council resolution 1212 (25 November 1998), expressing "its deep regret" that the political stalemate had so far prevented the United Nations from leaving Haiti, was equally negative.[58] Such disappointment was ominous: the source of foreign aid started to dry up.

Economic Failure

Haiti suffered its fair share of natural calamities. When tropical storm Gordon (14 November 1994) and hurricane George (22 September 1998) hit Haiti, they dropped heavy rains that washed away the country's already thin top soil. The most accurate study to date revealed that 8–10 percent of the adult population (12 percent in urban areas, 5 percent in rural areas) suffered from AIDS, the highest rate in the world outside of sub-Saharan Africa.[59] But political factors, namely, the growing enmity with foreign donors and internal gridlock, were the single most important explanation for Haiti's economic failure in the late 1990s.

Economic reforms, most notably the privatization of state-owned companies and the introduction of market competition, were not carried out.[60] Because these reforms were prerequisites for the disbursement of foreign aid, international donors refused to follow through on the large financial pledges made in 1994 and 1995. Of the almost $3.5 billion pledged for the period 1994–1997, less than $1.5 billion actually made its way into Haiti (appendix IV). In April 1997, IMF President Michel Camdessus erupted with a frankness unusual in the world of international technocracy. "If there is a scandal in Haiti today, it is that so much money is available to be spent, but is not spent because the parliament of Haiti, due to its factional disputes, has not yet been able to pass the necessary legislation to allow the money to be spent. I say that with a degree of vehemence, because I have put a lot of my personal conviction and energy to trying to put together . . . a solid, credible program for Haiti."[61]

But putting all the blame on foreign aid's skimpiness would be erroneous. A $1.5 billion infusion of cash, even if it fell short of earlier promises, was a lot of money for a country with an annual GDP of $2 billion (this was the equivalent of a $5.25 *trillion*–aid package to the United States). Haitians also had to blame themselves, including their apparent lack of entrepreneurial spirit. The economically oriented elite, who alone had the skills and capital required for industrialization, preferred the safe and steady profits of import licenses to the production of products of substitution. Lowering free-trade barriers, far from forcing Haitian producers to be efficient, thus simply destroyed whatever industrial and agricultural base existed. Government-subsidized U.S. rice imports, for example, simply wiped out production of Haitian rice, a basic staple for the Haitian poor that could have been produced locally, though at a higher price.[62]

Lack of political leadership was equally damning. Aristide, in 2001 as in 1994 and 1991, pledged, not to end poverty, but to move from misery to poverty (with dignity, he added).[63] He limited himself to *petits projets de la présidence*, small paternalistic presidential social projects. On 10 April 2001, for example, Aristide hosted a delegation of a few hundred poor Haitians, fed them, and gave them an envelope containing a thousand gourdes.[64] Such symbolic acts of charity came closer to clientage than development, a subtlety his most devoted supporters did not fully grasp. When Aristide announced in June 2001 that he would personally help any person with financial problems (which, in Haiti, includes most of the population), a throng of hungry Haitians swarmed the gates of the presidential palace, thinking that Aristide would give them money and a job. A presidential aide had to explain to the disappointed devotees what a metaphor was.[65] Government employees' economic expertise was not striking either. A government action plan for 1999 presented a long list of projects with a total cost of 5.3 billion gourdes. The Haitian government could only offer 800 million gourdes as its share, and thus made a request for a 1.6 billion gourdes grant, oblivious to the 2.9 billion gourdes mathematical mistake.[66]

The endless political crisis scared away potential investors. Low wages were not enough to attract investors; political stability and reliable infrastructures were equally essential. The cost of loading a container in Port-au-Prince's harbor was the highest in the hemisphere. Despite Haiti's ravishing vistas, balmy climate, impressive historical monuments, and attractive crafts, the tourism boom that was transforming the neighboring Dominican Republic completely ignored Haiti as the country's periodic bouts of street violence did little to shed its bad reputation abroad as a center of AIDS, poverty, and black magic.

The economic impact of political instability was devastating. From 1995 to 1999, economic growth averaged 2–3 percent a year, barely enough to keep up with population growth. The human development index, a statistic including social elements such as literacy and health resources in addition to net economic wealth, was 0.4 (out of a possible 1) in 1998, which put Haiti last in the Western Hemisphere and one hundred and fiftieth worldwide, down from one hundred and thirty-seventh in 1990. So limited was the trust in the national currency that by 2000, U.S. dollars represented 38 percent of all deposits in Haitian banks.[67]

The assembly sector (clothing, electric products, handicrafts), Haiti's most profitable industry, employed a mere 20,000 people, down from over 100,000 in the

1980s.[68] Even these jobs were unlikely to spread wealth throughout Haiti. Despite an Aristide-mandated rise in the minimum wage from 15 to 36 gourdes a day (approximately 30 cents an hour) in May 1995, the inflation-adjusted minimum wage was 50 percent lower than under Duvalier. Half the firms were paying their employees less than the minimal rate anyhow. On an hourly basis, workers producing Pocahontas pajamas for the Walt Disney Co. earned 325,000 times less than Disney CEO Michael Eisner.[69] These pitiful jobs were the ones Haitians, suffering from an unemployment rate above 50 percent, were fighting to get.

A Failed State: Haiti's Rising Drug and Immigration Problem

Politically deadlocked and economically bankrupt, the Haitian state failed to carry out such basic duties as infrastructure maintenance, law enforcement, education, and health services. By 2000, water was not drinkable. Electricity was available a few hours a day. A few potholed roads connected the largest cities. The police could not halt the rise in violent crimes, nor could courts judge suspects within a reasonable amount of time. Banks and the rich resorted to private militias. Eighty percent of the schools were private, often run by foreign NGOs and churches, which also provided 50 percent of health services. Even public schools charged a fee for lack of funds, so that the Government of Haiti only paid for 7 percent of the country's education expenses.[70] This complete breakdown in public authority was significant for the United States because it resulted in a worsening situation on the drug and immigration front.

Largely ignored prior to the 1994 intervention, Haiti's rising role as a transit area for Colombian cocaine traffickers worried the Clinton administration so much that in 1995 Haiti, along with 28 other countries, became subject to certification, an annual process by which the White House assesses whether foreign countries receiving aid under the Foreign Assistance Act are collaborating in the drug war.[71] The Haitian government's inability, rather than its unwillingness, to stop the drug trade was the most important hurdle. Haiti signed the 1988 UN Convention on Drug Trafficking in 1995 and an October 1997 Maritime Counterdrug Agreement with the U.S. Coast Guard, and a law banning money laundering passed in 2000. A police counternarcotics unit (known as BLTS after its French acronym) appeared in February 1997, but it only employed 24 policemen in a country of 8 million people. Lacking radars, an air force, and a navy, the country could not control its airspace or its coastline. Public officials' poverty fed corruption. Twenty-one justice and police officials were arrested for drug dealing in 1997, but courts rarely condemned the deep-pocketed traffickers. "There were no successful criminal prosecutions of narcotics cases in 1996," a U.S. government report complained.[72]

The United States, considering the Haitian state unable to meet its patrolling duties, took over much of the antidrug effort. A (DEA) office opened in Port-au-Prince in 1997, while U.S. custom officials conducted searches in the capital under the 1997 maritime agreement.[73] Even drug seizures credited to the Haitian government often took place as U.S. Coast Guard cutters, hosting a few token Haitians, intercepted Colombian boats.[74] The DEA administered polygraph tests to all members of the U.S.-funded and -trained BLTS in December 1998 to determine whether its members were involved in drug trafficking (six officers failed the test).[75] The United States demonstrated little enthusiasm for punishing human rights violators such as Cédras, Biamby, and Constant, but it went after Col. Michel François, a former member of the junta widely believed to have dabbled in drug trafficking in the 1980s and 1990s. After the 1994 intervention, François had fled to the Dominican Republic, then to Honduras in April 1996. In March 1997, a Miami court indicted him for helping to smuggle 33 metric tons of cocaine and heroin into the United States from 1987 to 1994.[76] The Honduran government briefly jailed François, then refused to extradite him.

U.S. efforts did not bring an end to the Haitian drug trade. The U.S. Bureau for International Narcotics and Law, which qualified Haiti as a "significant" transit area in its 1996 and 1997 reports, upgraded its assessment to "major" transit area in 1998 and 1999.[77] According to U.S. estimates based on drug seizures, the amount of cocaine transiting through Haiti rose from 46 metric tons in 1997 to 54 tons in 1998 and 67 tons in 1999, or 14 percent of all the cocaine imported from South America.[78] The drug flow finally ebbed in 2000, "but little of this is attributable to the efforts of the Haitian Government," a report pointed out.[79] The local populace simply mobbed Colombian planes as they landed, hoping to grab a share of this manna from heaven, and scared away some traffickers. In 1999, and again in 2000, 2001, 2002, and 2003, Haiti was certified on national security grounds only, one step away from being branded a narco-state.[80] This was a step that Chairman of the House International Relations Committee Benjamin A. Gilman (R-NY) was willing to take. "The Government of Haiti is not only moving to seize absolute power, it is also becoming a consolidated narco-state," he declared in July 2000.[81] In addition to democratic requirements it had routinely included in foreign aid bills since 1995, Congress specified that no aid could be disbursed to Haiti under the 2000 Foreign Operations, Export Financing, and Related Programs Act unless the U.S. government certified that Haiti was collaborating in the drug war.[82]

Immigration concerns also resurfaced. Following the 1994 intervention, the United States had immediately sent home all the refugees detained in Guantánamo. The number of boat people diminished following Aristide's return, but it returned to its pre-intervention level when Haiti's political and economic quandary turned into an overt crisis in 1997. A boat filled with 416 Haitians, which the U.S. Coast Guard intercepted in November 1997, marked the beginning of a new wave of departures.[83] Polls conducted by the U.S. Information Service and the State Department in 1998 and 2000 indicated that two-thirds to three-fourths of Haitians would happily leave Haiti if they had a chance.[84] Aristide refused to renew the 1981 treaty allowing the United States to repatriate refugees when it expired in October 1994, but boat people, labeled economic refugees because they came from a democracy, were sent back nonetheless.[85]

The only bright spot for the Clinton administration was that, in stark contrast to 1991–1994, immigration pressures did not send political wave shocks. The Haitian boat peoples' plight, however horrendous, received only scant media coverage in the United States.[86] Haitian immigrants had few allies in Congress. The 1997 Nicaraguan Adjustment and Central American Relief Act allowed Nicaraguans and Cubans to apply for permanent residency even if they did not qualify and had been ordered deported.[87] Despite many complaints that they were once again discriminated against, all Haitians could obtain was the much more restrictive 1998 Haitian Refugee Immigration Fairness Act.[88]

As the Préval presidency drew to a close, the United States and the United Nations could see that their efforts to bring political stability and economic growth to Haiti had fallen far short of their objectives. As the Haitian government floundered, problems that had temporarily disappeared in 1994, most notably the drug trade and the boat people, reappeared in full force. The continuing political crisis left little room for hope that lavishing more time and money on Haiti would solve anything. U.S. policy had moved from helping a friend in need to preventing the drug-dealing, unstable, recriminating Haiti from becoming too much of a nuisance. With anti-Americanism on the rise in Haiti, this seemed to be the right time to quietly pull foreign troops out.

The United States and the United Nations Depart

Clinton had initially pledged that direct U.S. occupation would end in March 1995, and that the U.S. participation in the UN mission would end in February 1996. To fulfill this promise, U.S. troops temporarily withdrew early in 1996. They were immediately replaced by a 500-man U.S. support group that, for political reasons, Clinton described as an independent, non-UN U.S. presence.[89]

At Aristide's and Préval's request, and out of fear that the Haitian police was not ready to take over law enforcement, the United Nations also maintained troops beyond the original February 1996 deadline. Still resentful over Aristide's support for Taiwan, the People's Republic of China balked at any extension. A series of Security Council resolutions thus extended the UN mission by a few months, each time, officially at least, for the last time—the UN then circumvented the no-extension pledge by creating another mission with a different name, first UNMIH, then UNSMIH, then UNTMIH, then MIPONUH, then MICAH, scheduled to end with Aristide's return in February 2001 (appendix IV). Following the U.S. example, the Security Council withdrew its last troops, Canadian and Pakistani blue helmets, in November 1997, then held that its last two missions, MIPONUH and MICAH, were not technically UN missions but small contingents of police advisers. The charade lasted until the end of the Préval presidency, when the United States and the United Nations finally gave up.

From its base in Camp Fairwinds, in Port-au-Prince, the U.S. support group that stayed in Haiti after most U.S. troops' departure in 1996 conducted a small-scale humanitarian operation, offering free doctor visits to Haiti's poor, repairing schools, and digging wells.[90] By 2000, the group's numbers had dwindled to 130 troops, most of whom left on 18 January 2000, leaving a sign on the door that read "So long, Haiti! The Provost Marshall."[91] Two days later, a U.S. C-141 jet picked up 15,000 pounds of equipment and one lone soldier who constituted the last U.S. military presence in Haiti. "It's a great feeling" to leave, said the man, Green Beret Sgt. Maj. Philip Sloniger from Fort Bliss, Texas. Asked if his mission had been a success, he was less than categorical. "Maybe they're not ready for democracy. Maybe what they need is a benevolent dictator, if such a thing can exist."[92] Operation Restore Democracy had come to an end.[93]

The United Nations mission (MICAH) remained.[94] After one of its members, a Barbadian transport chief, was shot dead by a mob in August 2000, UN Secretary General Kofi Annan announced that, because of rising violence and the political impasse, MICAH, scheduled to end with Aristide's inauguration in February 2001, would not be renewed.[95] By early February, only a few dozen UN representatives remained in Haiti. The Hotel Oloffson and the Hotel Montana, their favorite hangouts, were deserted, and their white four-wheel-drive vehicles disappeared from the streets of Port-au-Prince. Mission Chief Alfredo Lopes Cabral, who stayed so that he could represent the United Nations at Aristide's second inauguration on 7 February, was the last to leave. Kofi Annan had not bothered to come. No one from the United States had either, so U.S. Ambassador Brian Dean Curran was the sole U.S. representative at the swearing-in ceremony. When Cabral left on the eighth, the only people staying behind were the 130 Haitians who had worked for MICAH. They were now jobless, as were most of their fellow countrymen.

CHAPTER THIRTEEN
CONCLUSION

Motives

Anyone with money to spare would have bet, before 1994, that President Bill Clinton would avoid military interventions in Third World countries at all costs. Several of his Democratic predecessors—Wilson, Roosevelt, Truman, and Johnson—had led the United States into its four largest conflicts of the twentieth century, while Republicans complained that wars increased taxes and threatened state tyranny. Nevertheless, the Democrats who came of age during the Vietnam War, Clinton among them, regarded war as a threat to domestic reform and to American purity—or even, as Johnson's demise and Carter's botched hostage rescue operation in Iran showed, a threat to their political survival. Republicans—the Reagan of Grenada and Nicaragua, the Bush of Panama and the Gulf War—were now the warmongers. For someone intent on building his historical legacy on a foundation of domestic reforms, as Clinton was, a risky Vietnam-style intervention in a small Third World trouble spot had no appeal whatsoever.

Intervening in Haiti itself seemed equally unlikely. The CIA, the Pentagon, former President Bush, and many congressmen disliked Aristide intensely, and the Clinton administration was aware of this anti-American populist's dark reputation. Haiti, aside from being of no significant value to the United States economically or strategically, had a discouraging historical record of continuous political strife and economic decay. Aristide seemed destined to follow many other overthrown Latin American leaders into history's dust bin. Who now remembers Leslie Manigat, elected president of Haiti in 1988, then overthrown five months later? No Haitian president, including Jean-Claude Duvalier, had ever come back from exile, and no sensible bookmaker would have bet that Aristide would follow a different path.

And yet, on 19 September 1994, U.S. troops landed in Haiti, followed a few weeks later by Aristide.

Aristide's return was made possible in part by the unique political window of opportunity that opened from January 1993 to November 1994. From September 1991 to January 1993, the Bush administration showed no interest in reinstalling Aristide to power through the use of force. Had Bush been reelected as president of the United States, which his stratospheric approval rates following his victory in the Gulf War seemed to predict, a U.S. military intervention on Aristide's behalf would have been highly unlikely. Clinton's 1992 upset victory, however, made a change in Haitian policy possible.

This window of opportunity only remained open for 20 months. After the Republicans' political tidal wave in the November 1994 off-year elections, Clinton adopted Dick Morris' tactic of triangulation, embracing a conservative agenda to steal the thunder from his enemies in Congress. Invading Haiti in the post-1994 context, when anti-Aristide Republicans controlled both houses of Congress, and when the Contract with America U.S. voters had championed monopolized political debates, would have been improbable. The end of Aristide's five-year constitutional term as president in February 1996, along with his dwindling funds, could easily have brought a final end to the issue altogether.

From January 1993 to November 1994, however, Clinton ruled in a peculiar political environment. His congressional majority was slim, which forced him to pay attention to the demands of his liberal allies, including members of the Black Caucus. His personal credibility was even slimmer, in part because he had proved unable to follow through on his 1992 campaign promises regarding Haiti. His political prospects were somber, which helped turn minor issues like the *Harlan County* incident and the Haitian exodus into crises for the administration when a more secure president could have simply brushed them aside without further thought. For Clinton, 1993–1994 was a time for doubt, policy reviews, and new departures.

When asked why the United States intervened in Haiti, the NSC's Latin America specialist, Richard Feinberg, responded that only historians can afford to draw a clear list of ranked priorities, not policymakers deep in the midst of day-to-day politics. "There was a mix of motives," he said. Democracy was "a major theme," as were migratory issues in Florida and "the need to satisfy political constituencies" such as the Black Caucus.[1] The ease with which the Clinton administration left aside democratic goals in the immediate aftermath of the invasion would seem to suggest that "restoring democracy" was, in fact, not a major factor in the intervention. Nevertheless, motives as disparate as idealism, ending illegal immigration, restoring presidential and U.S. credibility, and responding to the demands of the Black Caucus and Aristide for a U.S. intervention were not mutually incompatible. All of these factors pushed in the same direction: ousting the junta. As a result, no choice had to be made, and no hierarchy of priorities established.

Also, there were so many reasons why the United States should *not* have intervened in Haiti that it took many separate incidents to convince Clinton that he should support the military option. Taken separately, Randall Robinson's hunger strike, the *Harlan County* humiliation, Michael Barnes' high-level lobbying efforts, the stomach-churning reports of human rights abuse coming out of Cédras' Haiti, and the sight of bloated corpses washing ashore on Florida beaches were not enough to justify sending over 20,000 troops and two aircraft carriers. Taken together, they provided a much stronger incentive to act.

It is always difficult to weigh a foreign statesman's influence on U.S. decision-making, which makes the issue of Aristide's role in the intervention particularly problematic. In the United States, Aristide did not vote, did not hold any elected mandate or official position, and occupied a spot—that of a slightly bothersome guest—not defined in the Founding Fathers' constitutional processes. Aristide's power could only come through U.S. intermediaries—members of the Black Caucus, NSC members, editorialists, and lobbyists—who were unlikely to acknowledge their subservience to Haitian interests. But Aristide's importance can more easily be demonstrated counterfactually: what would have happened if Aristide had not settled in Washington, had not pressed his case, had not met U.S. officials, and had not insisted on being restored to his rightful place as president of Haiti? Had Aristide decided to follow Manigat's example and become a professor of international relations at the Sorbonne, or Duvalier's example and retire to a luxurious villa on the French Riviera, there would have been little urgency on the U.S. side to find a solution to the Haitian turmoil. *What* to do—intervene militarily, impose a blockade, or negotiate with the junta—may have been determined by internal U.S. factors, but *whether* to take any action at all had much to do with Aristide's continued presence in the United States.

Despite the Clinton administration's many twists and turns of policy, and the widespread perception at the time that no one in charge knew what they were doing, the overall U.S. policy in Haiti followed a logical pattern. Bush and Clinton started with the least costly, and most consensual, policies. They imposed an embargo, weakened it with many loopholes, protested through diplomatic channels, and encouraged both sides to negotiate a way out. Bush had little at stake in that obscure conflict and was happy to leave it there when no solution emerged from his country's efforts. For the reasons outlined above, Clinton was not willing to leave it there. He thus increased U.S. involvement, strengthened the embargo, directly sponsored negotiations in Governors' Island, N.Y., and offered to send U.S. peacekeepers to enforce the ensuing accords.

When this failed to restore Aristide to power in Haiti, U.S. policy moved up another notch of activism. The war of words escalated—negotiate, or we might invade (May 1994); negotiate, because the UN sanctions an invasion (July 1994); negotiate, or we will invade (September 1994). This bellicose rhetoric carried in it the seeds of the last, and final step. When the United States and the junta came eyeball to eyeball, and the junta refused to blink, the Clinton administration was forced to follow up on its threats and invade Haiti or look hopelessly weak. Clinton may have vacillated on the refugee issue and agonized for months over the fear of U.S. casualties, but the overall shift from sanctions and negotiations to intervention was limpid. In the end, Clinton, the liberal antiwar protester from the 1960s, conducted the United States' last Caribbean intervention of the American century.

The 1994 Intervention: Failure or Success?

That Operation Restore Democracy was a failure is one of the few things Americans (both Democrats, in private, and Republicans), Haitians (both supporters and enemies of Aristide), and international organizations agree on. Haiti is more democratic than it was under Cédras, if one can dub a regime in which a few dozen political murders occur every year more democratic than one in which a few hundred such murders occurred annually, but this slight improvement fell far short of the hopes raised in 1994. On 29 February 2004, a coup d'état once again Forced Aristide into exile. By this point, the U.S. government was so disappointed with Aristide's democratic record that it welcomed the overthrow of the man it had done so much to bring back to power in 1994. Economically, Haiti is now poorer than it was when Aristide first became president in 1991. Post-intervention aid produced a short period of economic growth, followed by a long stagnation compounded by rapid population growth, but a three-year embargo against a desperately poor nation heavily reliant on foreign imports and aid had ruined the Haitian economy beforehand.

The widespread perception that Operation Restore Democracy was a failure is accurate if one sees democratic and economic progress as the main goals to be achieved—and, indeed, these *were* the goals that U.S. and UN officials repeatedly articulated in public statements. If one begins from a different starting point, however, and asks "what did the Clinton administration *really* hope to achieve in Haiti?" a different conclusion emerges. Haiti clearly did not become a strong trading partner, but there is no evidence that this was the objective to begin with. Democracy was not restored—but if democracy was a mere rhetorical device used to sell the intervention, then Haiti's ongoing political crisis was only bothersome inasmuch as it provided political ammunition to Clinton's Republican enemies.

The mere sight of U.S. troops sent the Haitian Army packing up for exile, and the impressive ballet of U.S. Black Hawk helicopters shuttling between the Port-au-Prince airport and aircraft carriers anchored a few miles away erased the perception, born during the *Harlan County* humiliation, that the United States was a weak-kneed superpower. Boat people have resumed their dangerous sea journey to Florida, but they now come from an officially democratic country, and there is no longer any political cost associated with sending back black Haitians while welcoming lighter Cubans. Haitians are now economic refugees, not victims of a racist double standard. The Black Caucus was grateful, and gave the Clinton administration a useful, if temporary, advantage in Congress until the 1994 midterm elections made the issue of holding together a Democratic majority irrelevant. African Americans, 82 percent of whom had voted for Clinton in 1992, remained Clinton's most steadfast supporters. Clinton's approval rate among African Americans remained over 80 percent for most of his presidency, rising to 90 percent *during* the impeachment crisis, at a time when most of Clinton's supporters stayed away from him.[2]

Clinton's image as an ineffectual manager of U.S. foreign policy faded away. Along with the U.S. interventions in Bosnia and Kosovo, statesmanship in Israel, and bombing attacks against Iraq, Afghanistan, and the Sudan, the Haitian invasion undermined one of Dole's strongest campaign arguments in the 1996 election and silenced foreign policy critics during Clinton's second term. Aristide turned anti-American again, but he was in Port-au-Prince, out of Washington, DC and the eye of the international media, and few cared to know what he said in *Le Nouvelliste* now that he had disappeared from the editorial pages of the *Washington Post* and the *New York Times*. Haiti remained a hungry nation and a political mess, but, from the perspective of the Clinton administration, the 1994 intervention was far from being an unremitting disaster.

Why Operation Restore Democracy failed to meet its official objectives is much more controversial. Haitians and their friends blamed the international community that, they say, abandoned Haiti after the intervention, neglected to disburse the money it had promised to give, insisted on a neoliberal agenda dictated by economic imperialism, and prolonged the political crisis by supporting Aristide's opponents. "The dilemma is, I think, the classic dilemma of the poor; a choice between death and death," wrote Aristide in 2000. "Either we enter a global economic system, in which we cannot survive, or we refuse, and we face death by slow starvation."[3] Aristide was convinced that the United States brought him back, then set him up to fail.[4]

International support was indeed less than steadfast. When U.S. troops landed in Haiti, the various factors that had pushed Clinton to intervene began pulling in different directions. When the invasion unfolded successfully, the need to restore presidential and U.S. credibility, which had played a central role in pushing Clinton to intervene, took second place to the fear that a long-term commitment would bring few rewards and, possibly, U.S. combat casualties. The basic reality of Haiti's low strategic value resurfaced when the Clinton administration had to decide how many lives, and how many billions of dollars, the United States was willing to spend for Haitian democracy's sake. For financial reasons, the United Nations was equally anxious to avoid being drawn into too ambitious a mission.

Nation building was thus carried out superficially and imperfectly. Cutting a deal with dictators decreased risks of political strife in the short term, but it sent a message that political expediency was more important than human rights. Sending observers to monitor an election was not enough to ensure that 200 years of a political history in which coups, not democratic debate, brought political change, would disappear. Providing policemen with four months of training before sending them to rural areas—where dictatorship of the strong (*Macoutes*, 1957–1986, 1987–1990, 1991–1994) and dictatorship of the weak (*Père Lebrun*, 1986, 1991) had up until then been the main methods of law enforcement—was not enough to guarantee that law and order and impartial justice would subsequently reign in Haiti.

Foreigners, particularly Americans, saw the problem differently. Putting the blame squarely on Haitian shoulders, they accused Haitians of rigging elections, refusing negotiations, failing to make good use of the aid they received, and more generally wallowing in a political crisis that allowed them to blame everyone but themselves for their own shortcomings. U.S. interest in Haiti, according to this perspective, merely declined after Haiti proved to be a great disappointment. Because this was the second time in a century that well-intentioned Americans had failed to turn Haiti around, criticisms implied—subtly, because no one wanted to suggest racial inferiority—that the United States had failed in the face of a 200 year history of Haitian incompetence, and that Haitians were culturally unable to govern themselves effectively. When the NSC's Richard Feinberg was asked why Haiti did not become democratic and prosperous, he answered that "this is a question an anthropologist should answer," implying that the problem was cultural, not political. "Have you been to Haiti? Then, you know what I mean. The only other possible step would have been to set up a protectorate, but this is not politically feasible nowadays."[5]

U.S. policymakers had a point. Haitians seemed to expect foreigners to provide the money, the expertise, and the manpower to change Haiti, and to do so with a total and disinterested dedication, while Haitians were to sit by idly and criticize the *blan* for his innate imperialism. Such refusal to acknowledge Haitians' own responsibility for Haiti's past shortcomings and future development is one of the main factors in the country's underdevelopment. The plan Aristide unveiled in 2003 to solve his country's economic woes was highly representative of this attitude: France, he argued, should reimburse the 90 million francs indemnity Haiti had paid her in 1823. Thanks to the magic of compounding interests, he calculated that France now owed Haiti exactly $21,685,155,571.48. Haitian jokesters had a ready-made explanation for Aristide's insistence that the sum not be rounded to the nearest dollar: "otherwise, what would be left for the people?"[6]

Lessons Learned During Operation Restore Democracy

There are three main lessons to be taken from Operation Restore Democracy, each of which can be applied to other peacekeeping operations. First, shallow motives do not make for a successful intervention. Extensive, long-term international involvement is essential to solve the immense challenges faced by conflict-torn nations, but feel-good operations, as in Somalia, or look-strong operations, as in Haiti, are unlikely to invest the time and human and financial sacrifices necessary to secure substantive achievements. Even if the 1994 intervention's sole purpose had been to restore democracy, an avowedly worthier aim than propping up sagging presidential polls, long-term popular support for that goal would have been improbable. Most people unhesitatingly profess their sincere interest in seeing world peace reign, democracy flourish, and hungry children eat to their heart's content, but they expect these abstract, unrealistic ideals to remain dreams, not to represent the bulk of their nation's diplomatic agenda. Should a politician appeal to the American people's idealistic instincts to obtain support for his foreign policy goals, he would receive nominal public approval initially, only to face widespread popular rejection later on if there was no hard, concrete national interest justifying the human and financial sacrifices U.S. citizens were asked to make.

For this reason, interventions motivated by short-term political interests, even when their promoters drape themselves in an idealistic mantle, are unlikely to succeed, unless these poor, divided nations also present a real strategic value, as was not the case in Haiti. Where key security interests were at stake, as in former Yugoslavia (1995) and Afghanistan (2001), popular willingness to endure casualties, remain involved for years, and spend billions of dollars made U.S. policymakers' task easier.

Ensuring that one's means are adapted to a peacekeeping operation's specific needs is the second important lesson. U.S. troops, who later defeated Serbian and Serbian-backed forces in Kosovo and Bosnia, were effective in scaring the junta from power and allowing Aristide's return. As a military force trained to defeat armored divisions in the plains of Central Europe, however, the U.S. Army proved much less effective when it came to disbanding the Haitian Army, ending human rights violations, and initiating the democratic and economic transitions. Even the 10th Mountain Division, a light division theoretically well suited for this type of mission, proved unapt. All the U.S. Army could offer was violence, which Haiti already had plenty of, and even that it was unwilling to provide given its fear of casualties.

Republican conservatives' systematic opposition to peacekeeping diplomacy did not simplify Clinton's task in that regard. On the one hand, they staunchly resisted using U.S. forces in nontraditional roles (including peacekeeping) and keeping them deployed abroad for a long period. At the same time, they harshly criticized the only institution able to take over such missions should the U.S. military remain focused on fighting conventional wars, the United Nations, underfunded it, and refused to allow it to create an international army. Despite the multiplication of low-level internal conflicts worldwide, there is still no force bridging the gap between the well-equipped, but cautious, national armies, and the well-intentioned, dedicated, and patient humanitarian NGOs that lack the military and diplomatic leverage, along with the large financial resources, necessary to bring about substantial political change. Such a force would have been particularly helpful in Haiti.

Finally, the age of white men burdened with their *mission civilisatrice* having ended, the eventual success, or failure, of a peacekeeping operation rests in the hands of the local government and population. The United Nations insists that, by dedicating a mere 0.7 percent of their national revenue, rich countries could finance aid programs large enough to jump-start many poor economies such as Haiti's. But such programs, if directly managed by international lenders, would be useless, breeding dependency, inciting local resentment at foreign meddling into internal affairs, and failing to address the problem at the heart of many poor countries' initial economic problems: poor political management.

Aid programs can only succeed if local elites are willing and able to make the most out of foreign money and to take over their nation's destinies after foreign assistance is phased out, as was the case in Europe during the Marshall Plan. In that regard, Aristide, who had been so resourceful in inviting a U.S. intervention, proved much less competent when the time came to make the intervention succeed, preferring to strengthen his populist credentials by attacking foreign donors and securing his power base by shutting out the opposition rather than working to alleviate Haiti's poverty. Peaceful people governed by competent and conscientious administrators rarely need to be peace-kept and nation-built in the first place, so the need for strong local political leadership presents the greatest challenge to the success of future peacekeeping operations, as well as the main reason for the political and economic failure of the 1994 U.S. intervention in Haiti.

Appendix I
Economic Statistics[1]

AI.1 U.S. trade with Haiti, in millions of dollars

Year	U.S. exports to Haiti	U.S. imports from Haiti	Trade balance
1986	387	375	+ 12
1987	459	395	+ 65
1988	475	382	+ 92
1989	472	374	+ 97
1990	477	343	+ 134
1991	395	284	+ 111
1992	209	107	+ 102
1993	229	154	+ 74
1994	205	59	+ 146
1995	550	130	+ 420
1996	475	144	+ 331
1997	499	188	+ 311
1998	549	272	+ 277
1999	614	301	+ 313
2000	527	271	+ 256

AI.2 U.S. trade in 1994, in millions of dollars

Country	U.S. exports to . . .	U.S. imports from . . .	Balance
Cuba	5	0	+ 5
Haiti	205	59	+ 146
Jamaica	1,066	747	+ 319
Dominican Republic	2,799	3,091	− 292
Mexico	50,844	49,494	+ 1,350
World	633,164	931,894	− 298,731

AI.3 U.S. trade with Haiti in 1996, in millions of dollars

Category	U.S. exports to Haiti	U.S. imports from Haiti
Food	165	7
Misc. manufactured articles	76	114
Total	474	144

Appendix II

Political Contributions from the Clothing Industry[2]

AII.1 Political contributions from the clothing industry, 1990–1998, in $

Election cycle	Total contributions	Soft money contributions	Republicans (total)	Democrats (total)
1998	2,255,191	1,222,234	1,323,639	902,642
1996	2,256,169	1,187,930	1,073,694	1,181,475
1994	868,769	356,470	394,669	473,100
1992	1,569,730	329,050	634,375	932,630
1990	311,766	0	81,962	229,804

AII.2 Contributions to presidential campaigns from the clothing industry, 1992–2000, in $

Candidate	1992 election	1996 election	2000 election
Bill Clinton (D)	16,350	32,150	
Al Gore (D)			30,500
Bill Bradley (D)			52,000
George Bush (R)	50,815		
Bob Dole (R)		35,730	
Alexander Lamar (R)		10,150	4,000
Pete Wilson (R)		10,000	
George W. Bush (R)			100,776
John McCain (R)			5,850

AII.3 Top recipients of contributions from the clothing industry, 1992–1996, in $ (with Senate and House ranking of top beneficiaries)

Recipient	1992	1994 (rank)	1996
Robert Torricelli (D), HR, S	8,500 (4) House	7,500 (3) House	21,600 (4) Senate
Christopher Dodd (D), S	3,750 (20)	0	0
Bob Dole (R), S	1,000 (34)	0	0
Jesse Helms (R), S	850 (38)	0	19,500 (5)
Les Aspin (D), HR	3,000 (16)	0	0
Joseph Kennedy (D), HR	900 (85)	2,000 (15)	3,158 (22)
Robert Menendez (D), HR	1,800 (37)	1,660 (23)	0
Benjamin Gilman (R), HR	1,000 (53)	600 (51)	1,000 (68)
Major R. Owens (D), HR	0	500 (52)	0
Lee Hamilton (D), HR	1,000 (53)	250 (110)	1,000 (68)

Appendix III
Immigration Data[3]

AIII.1 Total number of immigrants admitted to the United States, 1984–1994

Country	1984	1988	1992	1993	1994
Haiti	9,389	34,806	11,002	10,094	13,333
Jamaica	19,822	20,966	18,915	17,241	14,349
Cuba	10,599	17,558	11,791	13,666	14,727
Dominican Republic	23,147	27,189	41,969	45,420	51,189
Mexico	59,557	95,039	213,802	126,561	111,398
Total	545,903	643,025	973,977	904,292	804,416

AIII.2 Immigrants admitted in FY 1994, by type

Country	Family-sponsored	Relatives of U.S. citizens	Refugees	Total
Haiti	8,367	3,713	664	13,333
Jamaica	7,047	6,189	1	14,349
Cuba	1,674	906	11,998	14,727
Dominican Republic	24,343	25,996	8	51,189
Mexico	39,136	30,146	15	111,398
Total	211,961	249,764	121,434	804,416

AIII.3 Estimated population of illegal immigrants in the United States, 1992–1996

Country	Illegal immigrants, October 1992	Country	Illegal immigrants, October 1996
1-Mexico	1,300,000	1-Mexico	2,700,000
2-El Salvador	327,000	2-El Salvador	335,000
3-Guatemala	129,000	3-Guatemala	165,000
4-Canada	97,000	4-Canada	120,000
5-Poland	91,000	5-Haiti	105,000
7-Haiti	88,000	13-Dom. Rep.	50,000
14-Jamaica	42,000	15-Jamaica	50,000
Total	3,400,000	Total	5,000,000

APPENDIX IV
HAITI AFTER 1994

AIV.1 Money pledged as of 1996, for 1995–1997 (in $ million)[4]

Donor	Amount
European Union	380
World Bank	359
Inter-American Development Bank	329
USAID	265
France	97
Canada	74
Others (including IMF)	485
Total	1,989

AIV.2 Actual disbursement of funds to Haiti as opposed to commitment, 1994–1997 ($ million)[5]

Donor	Commitment	Disb.: 1994–1995	Disb.: 1995–1996	Disb.: 1996–1997
Canada	268	35	34	34
France	168	26	16	23
USA	696	250	113	101
IMF	150	23	0	21
Total	3,484	625	415	420

AIV.3 Disbursement of aid to Haiti, 1996–1999 ($ million)[6]

Donor	1996	1997	1998	1999
U.S.	115	145	N/A	N/A
Other	266	428	N/A	N/A

AIV.4   UN missions in Haiti, 1994–2001[7]

Resolution	Date	Mission created or extended	Personnel	Deadline
940	31 July 1994	UNMIH	60	30 January 1995
975	30 January 1995	UNMIH	6,000 + 900 police	31 July 1995
1007	31 July 1995	UNMIH	6,000	29 February 1996
1048	29 February 1996	UNMIH	1,500	30 June 1996
1063	28 June 1996	UNSMIH	900	30 November 1996
1085	29 November 1996	UNSMIH	900	5 December 1996
1086	5 December 1996	UNSMIH	800	31 July 1997
1123	30 July 1997	UNTMIH	300	30 November 1997
1141	28 November 1997	MIPONUH	300	30 November 1998
1212	25 November 1998	MIPONUH	300	30 November 1999
1277	30 November 1999	MIPONUH	300	15 March 2000
1277	30 November 1999	MICAH	300	6 February 2001

APPENDIX V

HAITIAN LOBBYING

AV.1 Quarterly budget for Aristide's government-in-exile, 1993 (rounded to the next dollar)[8]

Category	Monthly total	Quarterly total
Foreign service (outside U.S.)	315,767	947,301
Secretariat of the president	214,233	642,700
Ministerial cabinet	740,567	2,221,700
Meeting	11,667	35,000
Presidential commission	22,333	67,000
Governmental commission	40,000	120,000
Public relations	0	0
Travel	23,333	70,000
Law firms	110,000	330,000
Unexpected expenses	142,196	426,589
Foreign service (inside U.S.)	241,061	723,183
Unexpected expenses (foreign service inside U.S.)	33,333	100,000
Total	1,894,491	5,683,473

AV.2 Haitian payments to U.S. lobbying firms and lawyers, August 1994–June 1996, in $[9]

Lobbying firm	1994–1995	1995–1996
Arent, Fox	137,000 (August 94–August 95)	90,000 (September 95–February 96)
Hogan, Hartson	480,197 (August 94–August 95)	300,000 (September 95–February 96)
Kurzban	3,152,891 (December 94–December 95)	801,371 (January 96–February 96)
Williams & Connolly	147,986 (September 94–September 95)	None reported
Ross-Robinson	None reported	141,381 (September 95–February 96)
Mildred Trouillot	59,798 (September 94–February 95)	Amount unspecified

Notes

Chapter One   Introduction

1. George Stephanopoulos, *All Too Human: A Political Education* (NY: Little Brown, 1999), 113–115.
2. William J. Clinton, "U.S. Interests in Haiti," *USDOS Disp.*, vol. 5, no. 38 (19 September 1994), 605–607. See also *Status on Haiti: Communication from the President of the U.S. Transmitting a Report Regarding Action to Support Multilateral Efforts to Restore Democracy in Haiti and to Protect Democracy in our Hemisphere* (Washington, DC: U.S. Government Printing Office, 1994).
3. Lawrence E. Casper, *Falcon Brigade: Combat and Command in Somalia and Haiti* (Boulder, CO: Lynne Rienner, 2001), 186.
4. "US Plan to Seize Haitian Ruler is Reported but then Denied," *NY Times* (21 September 1994): A15.
5. Interviewed in "Eye to Eye with Connie Chung," *CBS News* (15 September 1994).
6. "Envazyon se dra," *Libete* no. 102 (17–23 August 1994): 7; Rick Bragg, "Haiti's New Militia Drills with Sticks," *NYT* (11 August 1994): A8.
7. Haitian troops once fought in the U.S. itself. In 1779, 1,550 French–Haitian colonial troops led by the Vicomte de Fontanges and the Marquis du Rouvray tried to seize Savannah from the British. Robert D., Nancy G. and Michael Heinl, *Written in Blood: The Story of the Haitian People, 1492–1995* (NY: U. Press of America, 1996), 34–35.
8. Quoted in Nicolas Jallot and Laurent Lesage, *Haïti: dix ans d'histoire secrète* (Paris: Editions du Félin, 1995), 171; Howard W. French, "Is Voodoo the Weapon to Repel the Invaders?" *NYT* (24 June 1994): A4.
9. Quoted in Jean-Michel Caroit, "Le vaudou sauvera-t-il les putschistes?" *Le Monde* (9 August 1994): 7.
10. "Manifestation à PAP contre l'intervention américaine," *Le Nouvelliste* (9 September 1994): 1.
11. Larry Rohter, "In PAP, the Signs of Invasion Are in the Air," *NYT* (15 September 1994): A8.
12. Anthony Lake telephone interview with the author (18 May 2001).
13. "Meet the Press," *NBC* (11 September 1994).
14. Robert Pastor telephone interview with the author (10 December 2001); Bill Clinto, *My Life* (NY: Knop, 2004), 616.
15. Pastor, who accompanied Carter during that mission, remembers that there was "a great deal of unease" among State Department and NSC staff members participating in the mission. Robert Pastor telephone interview with the author (10 December 2001).
16. The original draft of the press release announcing the mission read "with President Clinton's approval, Jimmy Carter . . ." Stephanopoulos insisted that a president should "order," not "approve," and the press release was changed accordingly. David Halberstam, *War in a Time of Peace: Bush, Clinton, and the Generals* (NY: Scribner, 2001), 280.

17. Clinton told Powell that Carter was "a wild card. . . . the next thing you know, he's negotiating a deal." Colin L. Powell and Joseph E. Persico, *My American Journey* (NY: Random House, 1995), 598.

18. The following overview of the Carter mission is drawn from Powell and Persico, *My American Journey*; Lynn Garrison, *Voodoo Politics: The Clinton-Gore Destruction of Haiti* (Los Angeles: Leprechaun Publishing, 2000); Lynn Garrison telephone interview with the author (10 May 2001); Robert Pastor telephone interview with the author (10 December 2001); Elaine Sciolino et al., "On the Brink of War, a Tense Battle of Wills," *NYT* (20 September 1994): A1; David Gergen, *Eyewitness to Power: The Essence of Leadership, Nixon to Clinton* (NY: Simon and Schuster, 2000).

19. Warren Christopher, *In the Stream of History: Shaping Foreign Policy for a New Era* (Stanford: U. of California Press, 1998), 180–181.

20. The following profiles of Cédras, Biamby, and François are drawn from Dominique Levanti, "Haitian Military Leaders from Variety of Backgrounds," *AFP Wire* (19 September 1994); "Thumbnail Sketches of Key Players in Haitian Drama," *AP Wire* (18 September 1994).

21. Lynn Garrison telephone interview with the author (10 May 2001).

22. "Cedras Says Aristide Cannot Return," *FBIS* (3 October 1991), 5.

23. Quoted in Powell and Persico, *My American Journey*, 598.

24. Quoted in Rick Bragg, "Mission to Haiti: In the Background; Varying Views on Role Of Haiti General's Wife," *NYT* (26 September 1994): A11.

25. Lois Romano, "The Reliable Source," *WP* (27 September 1994): D3.

26. Gergen, *Eyewitness to Power*, 321–322.

27. Elaine Sciolino et al., "On the Brink of War, a Tense Battle of Wills," *NYT* (20 September 1994): A1.

28. Powell and Persico, *My American Journey*, 600.

29. Garrison, *Voodoo Politics*, 4; Col. David H. Hackworth with Tom Mathews, *Hazardous Duty: America's Most Decorated Living Soldier Reports from the Front and Tells it the Way it is* (NY: William Morrow, 1996), 236; Powell and Persico, *My American Journey*, 597–602. A local TV station in Fort Bragg also showed live footage of planes taking off.

30. Kenneth Freed, "US Gives Cedras a Lucrative Deal to Get Out of Haiti," *LA Times* (14 October 1994): A1. See chapter 9 for further details.

31. Bob Shacochis, *The Immaculate Invasion* (NY: Penguin Books, 1999), 75–77; Stan Goff, *Hideous Dream: A Soldier's Memoir of the U.S. Invasion of Haiti* (NY: Soft Skull Press, 2000), 93.

32. Quoted in John Tierney, " 'The Press was Here,' but not the Enemy," *NYT* (20 September 1994): A12.

33. *White Paper, Presidential Decision Directive 25, Reforming Multilateral Peace Operations* (U.S. Department of State Bureau of International Organization Affairs: 3 May 1994), www.fas.org/irp/offdocs/pdd/index.html.

34. *White Paper, Presidential Decision Directive 56, Managing Complex Contingency Operations* (May 1997), www.fas.org/irp/offdocs/pdd/index.html. Based on lessons drawn from Haiti, PDD 71 advocated the deployment of a civilian police, most of it non-American, to accelerate the disengagement of U.S. military forces in future peacekeeping operations. *White Paper, Presidential Decision Directive 71, Strengthening Criminal Justice Systems in Support of Peace operations and Other Complex Contingencies* (U.S. Department of State Office of International Information Programs: (24 February 2000)), www.fas.org/irp/offdocs/pdd/index.html.

Chapter Two   Haiti Before the U.S. Intervention

1. Robert D., Nancy G., and Michael Heinl, *Written in Blood: The Story of the Haitian People, 1492–1995* (NY: U. Press of America, 1996); Herbert Gold, *Best Nightmare on Earth: A Life in Haiti* (NY: Simon and Schuster, 1991).

2. The following overview of Haiti's history until the first U.S. occupation is drawn from Heinl, *Written in Blood*; and Jacques Barros, *Haïti de 1804 à nos jours* (Paris: L'Harmattan, 1984; 2 vols.).

3. Aristide and Christophe Wargny, *Jean-Bertrand Aristide: An Autobiography* (NY: Orbis Books, 1993), 153.

4. Among others, see Barros, *Haïti de 1804 à nos jours*, vol. 1: 171–196, 246–300.

5. Quoted in Heinl, *Written in Blood*, 120.

6. Lawrence E. Harrison, *Underdevelopment is a State of Mind: The Latin American Case* (1985; reprint, NY: Madison Books, 2000), 81.

7. U.N. Food and Agriculture Organization, Département des forêts, *National Tropical Action Programme, Haiti, FAO/FO/HAI/89/026* (1995).

8. Heinl, *Written in Blood*, 172, 385.

9. The following overview of the first U.S. occupation is drawn from Suzy Castor, *La ocupación norteamericana de Haití y sus consecuencias, 1915–1934* (Mexico City: Siglo Veinteuno Editores, 1971); and Hans Schmidt, *The United States Occupation of Haiti, 1915–1934* (New Brunswick, NJ: Rutgers, 1971).

10. Quoted in Schmidt, *The U.S. Occupation of Haiti*, 48, 111. The U.S. official was John A. McIlhenny, who later became the top U.S. civilian official in Haiti.

11. The following overview of the Duvaliers' presidencies is drawn from Elizabeth Abbott, *Haiti: The Duvaliers and Their Legacy* (1988; reprint, NY: Simon and Schuster, 1991); and Bernard Diederich and Al Burt, *Papa Doc: Haiti and Its Dictator* (1969; reprint, Maplewood, New Jersey. Waterfront Press, 1991).

12. Abbott, *The Duvaliers and Their Legacy*, 263.

13. George P. Shultz, *Turmoil and Triumph: My Years as Secretary of State* (NY: Scribners, 1993), 622.

14. The following overview of the period following Duvalier's fall is drawn from Amy Wilentz, *The Rainy Season: Haiti since Duvalier* (NY: Simon and Schuster, 1989).

15. There is no standard biography of Aristide. The following overview of Aristide's life is drawn from Aristide's autobiographical works, including Aristide, *La vérité en vérité* (PAP: Le Natal, 1989), Aristide, *In the Parish of the Poor* (NY: Orbis Books, 1993); Aristide and Christophe Wargny, *Tou moun se moun: tout homme est un homme* (Paris: Seuil, 1992); published in the United States as *Jean-Bertrand Aristide: An Autobiography* (NY: Orbis Books, 1993); Mark Danner, "Haiti on the Verge," *NY Review of Books* (4 November 1993): 25–30; "The Prophet," ibid. (18 November 1993): 27–36; "The Fall of the Prophet," ibid. (2 December 1993): 44–53; "Profile–Who is Aristide?"; *MacNeill-Lehrer News Hour* (10 October 1994); Wilentz, *The Rainy Season*.

16. Aristide and Wargny, *Tout moun se moun*, 45.

17. Aristide and Wargny, *An Autobiography*, 53.

18. World Bank, *Country at a Glance Tables: Haiti at a Glance* (DC: World Bank, October 2001), 1, 2; World Bank, *World Development Indicators Database*, http://devdata.worldbank.org/data-query/.

19. Garrison, *Voodoo Politics*, 58.

20. After John F. Kennedy died on 22 November 1963, many Haitians concluded that Papa Doc, whom Kennedy had stigmatized for his human rights abuses, had killed Kennedy by pricking his Kennedy doll 2,222 times. Gold, *Best Nightmare on Earth*, 141.

21. Aristide, *In the Parish of the Poor*, 52.

22. Quoted in Christian Lionet, *Haiti: l'année Aristide* (Paris: L'Harmattan, 1992), 203.

23. The following overview of Aristide's election and first presidency is drawn from *Le Nouvelliste*, Haiti's daily of reference, and Roland I. Perusse, *Haitian Democracy Restored, 1991–1995* (NY: U. Press of America, 1995).

24. Quoted in "Le Père Jean-Bertrand Aristide officiellement candidat à la présidence," *Le Nouvelliste* (18 October 1990): 2.

25. Aristide and Wargny, *An Autobiography*, 34, 60.

26. Rodney Saint-Eloi, "Une séance de déchoucage," *Le Nouvelliste* (7–9 January 1991): 5.
27. The name derived from a tire commercial in which the salesman, Claude Lebrun, put his head through a tire of the Kuhmo brand. Robert Fatton, Jr., "The Rise, Fall and Resurrection of President Aristide," in Robert I. Rotberg, ed., *Haiti Renewed: Political and Economic Prospects* (DC: Brookings Institution Press, 1997), 151.
28. Rodney Saint-Eloi, "Une séance de déchoucage," *Le Nouvelliste* (7–9 January 1991): 5. The expression "made-to-order" should not be taken too literally, as it is unlikely that the tires were manufactured expressly for the purpose of necklacing political opponents.
29. Michèle Wucker, *Why the Cocks Fight: Dominicans, Haitians, and the Struggle for Hispaniola* (NY: Hill and Wang, 1999), 134.
30. "L'ex-Président Ertha P. Trouillot détenue au pénitencier," *Le Nouvelliste* (2–4 April 1991): 1.
31. "Lawyers Refuse to Handle Lafontant Defense," *FBIS* (22 January 1991): 8.
32. "L'actualité en question," *Le Nouvelliste* (5 August 1991): 1.
33. Quoted in "L'actualité en question," *Le Nouvelliste* (5 August 1991): 1.
34. "Aristide Address 27 Sep After Visit to U.N.," *FBIS* (7 October 1991): 17–19.
35. Gérard Bissainthe, "Adieu Sylvio," *Haïti Observateur* (6–13 November 1991): 9; "Mob Reportedly Kills and Burns One-Time Populist Hero," *AP Wire* (30 September 1991).
36. "Army Leader Cédras Address," *FBIS* (2 October 1991), 7.
37. Quoted in "A Place Called Fear," *Vanity Fair* (February 1994): 74.
38. Quoted in ibid., 76.
39. Quoted in Garrison, *Voodoo Politics*, 125–126, 128, 130.
40. "Le film des événements" and "La proclamation du commandant en chef des forces armées, le général Cédras," *Le Nouvelliste* (9 October 1991): 2, 4, 7; "Army Leader Cédras Address," *FBIS* (2 October 1991), 7.
41. Quoted in A. Fr., "Le Général Cédras 'a bien caché son jeu,'" *Le Monde* (4 October 1991): 4.
42. Aristide, *Dignity* (Charlottesville: U. Press of Virgina, 1996), 41; Garrison, *Voodoo Politics*, 129.
43. Pierre Mouterde and Christophe Wargny, *Apre bal, tanbou lou: cinq ans de duplicité américaine en Haïti, 1991–1996* (Paris: Austral, 1996), 79–80.
44. Aristide himself accused the United States of overthrowing him. Aristide, *Dignity*, 46, 49, 56, 61. Haitians believe the U.S. masterminded the coup because the U.S. military attaché met with Haitian officers the night the coup started. Kenneth Freed personal interview with the author (10 April 2002).
45. Garrison, *Voodoo Politics*, 137–140, Jallot and Lesage, *Dix ans d'histoire secrète*, 123–124.
46. Michael Norton, "Army Chief Denies Leading Coup, Seeks a Way Out Amid International Pressure," *AP Wire* (4 October 1991); Dominique Levanti, "PAP Residents Stay Off Streets," *AFP Wire* (3 October 1991); Commission Nationale de Vérité et de Justice, *Si M Pa Rele* (1996; reprint, PAP: Min. of Justice, 1997).
47. "Army Leader Cédras Address," *FBIS* (2 October 1991), 7.
48. James Baker, *The Politics of Diplomacy* (NY: Putnam's Sons, 1995), 601–602.
49. For a detailed, behind-the-scenes account of the negotiations, see Robert Malval, *L'année de toutes les duperies* (PAP: Regain, 1996), 117–145.
50. UNSC, S/RES/867 (23 September 1993), 2.
51. For an eyewitness account, see Marie Cervetti and Emmanuelle Ott, *Des bleus sans casque: chronique d'une mission civile de l'ONU en Haïti* (Paris: Austral, 1994), 179–183.
52. G. Berggren et al., *Sanctions in Haiti: Crisis in Humanitarian Action, Working Paper* no. 93.07 (Harvard U. Center for Population and Development Studies: November 1993); Howard French, "Study Says Haiti Sanctions Kill up to 1,000 Children a Month," *NYT* (9 November 1993): A1.
53. UNSC, S/RES/940 (31 July 1994).
54. Anthony Lake telephone interview with the author (18 May 2001).
55. *Public Papers: Clinton* vol. II (1994), 1558.

Chapter Three   Economic Interests

1. James Ridgeway, *The Haiti Files: Decoding the Crisis* (DC: Essential Books, 1994); Paul Farmer, *The Uses of Haiti* (Monroe, ME: Common Courage Press, 1994); Deidre McFadyen and Pierre La Ramée, *Haiti: Dangerous Crossroads* (Boston, MA: South End Press, 1995).

2. Bill Clinton and Al Gore, *Putting People First: How We Can All Change America* (NY:Times Books, 1992), 13, 129–130, 118.

3. Bill Clinton, "American Leadership and Global Change," *USDOS Disp.*, vol. 4, no. 9 (1 March 1993), 113–118.

4. Mickey Cantor, "U.S. Trade Policy and the Post-Cold War World," *USDOS Disp.*, vol. 4, no. 11 (15 March 1993), 143–148.

5. *Nomination of Warren M. Christopher to be Secretary of State, Hearing before the CFR, USS, 13 and 14 January 1993* (DC: USGPO, 1993), 22.

6. Anthony Lake, "Tying Power to Democracy," *NYT* (23 September 1994): A35.

7. *United States Policy and Activities in Haiti, Hearing before the CIR, HR, 24 February 1995* (DC: USGPO, 1995), 9.

8. Aristide, *In the Parish of the Poor*, 9; Aristide and Wargny, *An Autobiography*, 126.

9. Mouterde and Wargny, *Apre bal, tanbou lou*, 63.

10. Aristide and Wargny, *An Autobiography*, 67.

11. Ibid., 143. For other anti-American comments, see ibid., 47, 56, 76, 87, 116, 123; and Aristide, *Dignity*, 49, 56, 61, 79.

12. "Aristide Delivers Labor Day Speech," *FBIS* (10 May 1991), 12–14. See also "Aristide Interview on Economy, Foreign Relations," *FBIS* (21 March 1991), 21.

13. World Bank, *Haiti: List of Priority Investment Projects* (1991), 1, 13, microenterprise collection, USAID Library, PAP.

14. Michael Tarr, "International-PAP," *UPI Wire* (19 February 1988); Kenneth Whiting, "After Two-Year Odyssey, Ship Unloads Toxic Cargo," *AP Wire* (26 November 1988).

15. IMF, *Press Release no. 95–14: IMF Approves Stand-By Credit for Haiti* (DC: IMF, 8 March 1995), 1.

16. U.S. Department of State, *1993 Country Reports on Economic Policy and Trade Practices* (DC: USGPO, 1994), 379.

17. World Bank, *Haiti: External Financing* (December 1997), 1, microenterprise collection, USAID Library, PAP.

18. George Bush, "Executive Order 12779, 28 October 1991," *Federal Register*, vol. 56 (30 October 1991): 55975.

19. Clinton, "Executive Order 12917, 21 May 1994," *FR*, vol. 59 (24 May 1994), 26925.

20. *Haiti: The Agreement of Governor's Island and its Implementation, Hearing before the SWHA of the CFA, HR, 21 July 1993* (DC: USGPO, 1993), 41, 72.

21. Micha Gaillard, "Communiqué de presse no. 2," folder "Commission présidentielle," box 320.01 COM, Collège St. Martial library. The visit prompted the OAS Secretary General to protest to the U.S. Assistant Secretary of State for Interamerican Affairs. "The Secretary General to his Excellency Bernard Aronson (17 July 1992)," "Bernard Aronson to the Secretary General (24 July 1992)," OEA/ser. F/ V.1 MRE/ INF 16/92, OAS library.

Chapter Four   Restoring Democracy

1. UN General Assembly resolution 43/157 (December 1988) also defended democracy as the ideal form of government. See also Boutros Boutros-Ghali, *An Agenda for Peace: Preventive Diplomacy, Peacemaking and Peacekeeping* (NY: United Nations, 1992), 9, 25, 37; Boutros-Ghali, *An Agenda for Democratization* (NY: United Nations, 1996), 3, 12–13.

2. For example, see John D. Martz, "Democracy and the Imposition of Values: Definitions and Diplomacy," in Martz and Schoultz, eds., *Latin America, the United States, and the Inter-American System* (Boulder: Westview Press, 1980).

3. For example, see Michael H. Hunt, *Ideology and U.S. Foreign Policy* (New Haven: Yale U. Press, 1987).

4. For example, see Kenneth M. Coleman, "The Political Mythology of the Monroe Doctrine: Reflections on the Social Psychology of Hegemony," in Martz and Schoultz, eds., *The Inter-American System*, James Petras, H. Michael Erisman and Charles Mills, "The Monroe Doctrine and U.S. Hegemony in L.A.," in Petras, ed., *Latin America: From Dependence to Revolution* (NY: John Wiley, 1973).

5. For two books, both of them largely based on Clinton's speeches, supporting the thesis that the 1994 intervention's main goal was to restore democracy, see Alex Dupuy, *Haiti in the New World Order: The Limits of the Democratic Revolution* (Boulder, CO: Westview Press, 1997); and Roland I. Perusse, *Haitian Democracy Restored, 1991–1995* (NY: U. Press of America, 1995).

6. David Maraniss, *First in His Class: A Biography of Bill Clinton* (NY: Simon and Schuster, 1995), 108.

7. Roger Morris, *Partners in Power: The Clintons and their America* (NY: Henry Holt, 1996), 1–2.

8. Clinton, "Inaugural Address, 20 January 1993," *USDOS Disp.*, vol. 4, no. 4 (25 January 1993), 45.

9. *Public Papers: Clinton*, vol. 1 (1993), 810.

10. Clinton, "Confronting the Challenges of a Broader World," Warren Christopher, "Building Peace in the Middle East," Anthony Lake, "From Containment to Enlargement," Madeleine K. Albright, "Use of Force in a Post-Cold War World," *USDOS Disp.*, vol. 4, no. 39 (27 September 1993), 649–668. See also Clinton and Al Gore, *Putting People First: How We Can All Change America* (NY: Times Books, 1992), 132, 136, 138–139, 228–229; Clinton, *Between Hope and History: Meeting America's Challenges for the 21st Century* (NY: Times Books, 1996), 163; Lake, "Confronting Backlash States," *Foreign Affairs*, vol. 73, no. 2 (March–April 1994), 45, 55; *Nomination of Madeleine K. Albright to be U.S. Ambassador to the U.N., Hearing before the CFR, USS, 21 January 1993* (DC: USGPO, 1993), 11; Albright, "Use of Force in a Post–Cold War World," *USDOS Disp.*, vol. 4, no. 39 (27 September 1993), 665; *Nomination of Warren M. Christopher to be Secretary of State, Hearing before the CFR, USS, 13 and 14 January 1993* (DC: USGPO, 1993), 23, 24, 28; Christopher, "Democracy and Human Rights: Where America Stands," *USDOS Disp.*, vol. 4, no. 25 (21 June 1993), 441.

11. Steven A. Holmes, "Christopher Reaffirms Leading U.S. Role in World," editorial desk, "A Brand X Foreign Policy," *NYT* (28 May 1993): A1, A28; Daniel Williams et al., "Administration Rushes to 'Clarify' Policy Remarks by 'Brand X' Official"; Lloyd Grove, "Who Was that Masked Official," *WP* (27 May 1993): A45, D1.

12. *National Security Decision Directive 220* (2 April 1986), NLS-NSC-NSDD-220, Ronald Reagan Library; "U.S. Embassy PAP to Secretary of State (6 November 1987)," folder Haiti, box 2, Human Rights collection, NSA.

13. *Public Papers: Bush*, vol. 2 (1991), 1260.

14. For example, see "El Secretario General al excelentísimo señor Boutros Boutros-Ghali (10 July 1992)," OEA/Ser. F/V. 1 MRE/INF. 15/92, OAS.

15. Clinton, "U.S. Interests in Haiti," *USDOS Disp.*, vol. 5, no. 38 (19 September 1994), 605–607.

16. For example, see Warren Christopher, *In the Stream of History: Shaping Foreign Policy for a New Era* (Stanford: U. of California Press, 1998), 184; Clinton, *Continuation of National Emergency with Respect to Haiti: Communication from the President of the U.S., House Document 103–109* (12 July 1993); Anthony Lake telephone interview with the author (18 May 2001); Lake, "Tying Power to Democracy," *NYT* (23 September 1994): A35. Lake's sales pitch might have been more convincing had he not been the coauthor of *Our Own Worst Enemy: The Unmaking of American Foreign Policy* (NY: Simon and Schuster, 1984), in which he claimed that many U.S. interventions were motivated by short-term domestic political interests under the cover of idealism.

17. The following overview of the human rights situation in Haiti in 1991–1994 is drawn from Commission Nationale de Vérité et de Justice, *Si M Pa Rele* (1996; reprint, PAP: Min. of Justice, 1997), Amnesty International, *The Amnesty International Report on Human Rights Around the World* (London: AI, 1993–1994); Human Rights Watch, *World Report* (NY: HRW, 1991–1994); *Silencing a People* (NY: HRW, 1 March 1993); *Rape in Haiti: A Weapon of Terror* (NY: HRW, 1 June 1994); Charles Kernaghan et al., *Haiti after the Coup* (NY: National Labor Committee, 1993); Lawyers Committee for Human Rights, *Haiti: Learning the Hard Way, The UN/OAS Human Rights Monitoring Operation in Haiti, 1993–1994* (NY: Lawyers Committee on Human Rights, 1995); Cervetti and Ott, *Des bleus sans casque*, Jean-Baptiste Chenet personal interview with the author (3 July 2001).

18. CNVJ, *Si M Pa Rele*, chapter 6, 2.2, 2.3.

19. CNVJ, *Si M Pa Rele.*, chapter 4, 2.1, Dan Coughlin, "The Case of Lawrence P. Rockwood," *Haïti Progrès* (20 March 1995): 1; Douglas Farah, "Americans Find Victims of Squalor, Sadism in Jails," *WP* (12 October 1994): A28.

20. CNVJ, *Si M Pa Rele*, chapt. 5, C1, chapt. 6, 2.3; Human Rights Watch, *Rape in Haiti: A Weapon of Terror* (NY: HRW, July 1994).

21. CNVJ, *Si M Pa Rele*, 412, 415.

22. Kenneth Freed, "U.S. Gives Cedras a Lucrative Deal to Get Out of Haiti," *LA Times* (14 October 1994): A1; Elaine Sciolino, "Exile in Style Being Offered to Haiti Chiefs," *NYT* (20 June 1994): 7.

23. *U.S. Policy Toward, and Presence in, Haiti, Hearings and Markup before the CFA, HR, 13, 27, 28 September 1994* (DC: USGPO, 1994), 18.

24. U.S. Department of State, *Country Reports on Human Rights Practices for 1991* (DC: USGPO, 1992), *Country Reports on Human Rights Practices for 1992* (DC: USGPO, 1993); *Country Reports on Human Rights Practices for 1993* (DC: USGPO, 1994).

25. Reproduced in James Ridgeway, *The Haiti Files: Decoding the Crisis* (DC: Essential Books, 1994), 184–190.

26. "1994 Daily Press Briefing no. 129, Tuesday, 9/13/94," in U.S. Dept. of State Bureau of Public Affairs, *U.S. Foreign Affairs on CD-ROM, January 1990–May 1996*, vol. 4, no. 1 (DC: Dept. of State, June 1996).

27. Dick Morris, *Behind the Oval Office: Getting Reelected Against All Odds* (Los Angeles: Renaissance Books, 1999), 247.

28. Stephanopoulos, *All Too Human*, 309. According to a Gallup poll conducted after Clinton's speech, Americans thought that stopping human rights abuses (67%) and promoting democracy (55%) were the most valuable reasons to intervene in Haiti. Only 40% of Americans deemed U.S. credibility a valuable reason to intervene (58% did not). George Gallup Jr., *The Gallup Poll: Public Opinion, 1994* (Wilmington: Scholarly Resources, 1995), 141.

29. In his September 1994 televised address, Clinton alluded to "the wave of democracy that has swept our entire region." Clinton, "U.S. Interests in Haiti," *USDOS Disp.*, vol. 5, no. 38 (19 September 1994), 606.

30. Richard E. Feinberg telephone interview with the author (10 December 2001).

31. Delegates such as Faleomavaega participate in commissions and debates, but, contrary to representatives, they cannot vote on the final passage of a bill. *U.S. Policy Toward, and Presence in, Haiti, Hearings and Markup before the CFA, HR, 13, 27, 28 September 1994* (DC: USGPO, 1994), 30–31.

32. *Situation in Haiti: Hearing before the CAS, USS, 28 September 1994* (DC: USGPO, 1994), 43.

33. *Public Papers: Clinton* (1993), 1926.

34. Anthony Lake, *Six Nightmares: Real Threats in a Dangerous World and How America can Meet Them* (NY: Little Brown, 2000), 130.

35. *CR* (20 October 1993), S13979.

36. Elaine Sciolino, "Aristide Adopts a New Role: From Robespierre to Gandhi," *NYT* (18 September 1994): Section 1, 1.

37. Diederich and Burt, *Haiti and Its Dictator*, 13–20, 81–98; Heinl, *Written in Blood*, 547–549.
38. Félix d'Orsinville personal interview with the author (4 July 2001).
39. Quoted in Mark Danner, "Haiti on the Verge," *NY Review of Books* (4 November 1993): 27.
40. Aristide and Wargny, *Tout moun se moun*, 57–58; Martin-Luc Bonnardot and Gilles Danroc, *La chute de la maison Duvalier: textes pour l'histoire* (Paris: Karthala, 1989), 78. Traditional Haitian folk songs, sung during the communal farming work known as *kombit*, similarly tease people and spread gossip through allusions. Melville J. Herskovits, *Life in a Haitian Valley* (1937; reprint, NY: Doubleday, 1971), 74–76.
41. Calling him a psychopath, Jesse Helms displayed at an October 1993 Senatorial hearing a copy of a painting that allegedly hung in Aristide's presidential office; it showed a neck-lacing scene, complete with matches and gasoline, *CR* (20 October 1993), S13979.
42. There was an average of ten political murders per month from 1986 to 1991, 25 per month under Cédras (1991–1994), and five per month under Aristide (1991 and 1994–1995). CNVJ, *Si M Pa Rele*, 412.
43. Patrick Elie personal interview with the author (11 July 2001).
44. "Aristide Discourages Revenge; Urges Unity, Faith," *FBIS* (10 January 1991), 12–13. See also "Documents pour l'histoire," *Le Nouvelliste* (7–9 January 1991): 13.
45. "President Aristide Addresses Youth Rally," *FBIS* (8 August 1991): 5.
46. Kenneth Freed personal interview with the author (10 April 2002).
47. "Aristide Address 27 Sep After Visit to UN," *FBIS* (7 October 1991), 17–19. For footage of the speech, see "Showdown in Haiti," *PBS Frontline* (14 June 1994).

Chapter Five   U.S. Credibility

1. Robert J. McMahon, "Credibility and World Power: Exploring the Psychological Dimension in Postwar American Diplomacy," *Diplomatic History* (Fall 1991): 455.
2. Ibid.: 457.
3. Quoted in Lee Ann Fujii, "Finding the Middle: An Analysis of Johnson's 1965 Decision to Escalate the War in Vietnam," *International Relations Journal* (Winter–Spring 2000–2001), 72.
4. *Public Papers: Nixon* (1970), 405–409.
5. Lars Schoultz, *National Security and United States Policy toward Latin America* (Princeton: Princeton U. Press, 1987), 279. See also Scott Miller, *Consumed by Credibility: An Analysis of the 1994 U.S. Intervention in Haiti* (M.A. thesis, Ohio University, August 1995), 19.
6. Clinton, "U.S. Interests in Haiti," *USDOS Disp.*, vol. 5, no. 38 (19 September 1994), 605. See also Clinton, *With Regards to Haiti: Communication from the president of the U.S., House Document 103–309* (18 September 1994), 1.
7. For further details on Clinton's dream of a New World Order, see Alex Dupuy, *Haiti in the New World Order: The Limits of the Democratic Revolution* (Boulder, CO: Westview Press, 1997), 7–20.
8. *White Paper, PDD 25, Reforming Multilateral Peace Operations* (U.S. Department of State Bureau of International Organization Affairs: 3 May 1994), www.fas.org/irp/offdocs/pdd/index.html.
9. Elliott Abrams, *Security and Sacrifice: Isolation, Intervention, and American Foreign Policy* (Indianapolis: Hudson Institute, 1995), 1–2, 142.
10. Clinton first traveled to Africa in 1998 (22 March–2 April). In 1994, his administration would not even use the word "genocide" for fear that it would force the United States to intervene in Rwanda. Halberstam, *War in a Time of Peace*, 276–277.
11. In 1994, the UN had peacekeeping missions in the following countries: Angola (UNAVEM), Chad/Libya (UNASOG), Liberia (UNOMIL), Mozambique (UNOMOZ), Rwanda (UNAMIR), Uganda (UNOMUR), Somalia (UNOSOM), El Salvador (ONUSAL), Haiti (UNMIH), former Yugoslavia (UNPROFOR), Western

Sahara (MINURSO), India-Pakistan (UNMOGIP), Cyprus (UNFICYP), Georgia (UNOMIG), Tajikistan (UNMOT), Golan Heights (UNDOF), Iraq-Kuwait (UNIKOM), Lebanon (UNIFIL), Gaza (UNTSO).

12. Charlayne Hunter-Gault, "Divided Nations," *McNeill-Lehrer News Hour* (20 June 1996).
13. Bill Clinton, "Confronting the Challenges of a Broader World," *USDOS Disp.*, vol. 4, no. 39 (27 September 1993), 650, 652.
14. Madeleine K. Albright, "A Strong United Nations Serves US Security Interests," *USDOS Disp.*, vol. 4, no. 26 (28 June 1993), 461–467. In its attempt to unseat Boutros-Ghali, the United States lost the vote in the Security Council (1–14), but he was nonetheless replaced by Kofi Annan of Ghana. All previous secretaries generals had served two terms.
15. Elizabeth Drew, *On the Edge: The Clinton Presidency* (NY: Simon and Schuster, 1994), 153.
16. Quoted in Daniel Williams and Ann Devroy, "U.S. Bombing, Credibility Linked; Christopher Raises Stakes in Bosnia Before Skeptical Panel," *WP* (22 April 1994): A1 Bob Woodward, *The Choice: How Clinton Won* (NY: Touchstone, 1996), 261. The U.S.-sponsored Dayton accords, which ended the Bosnian War, were finally signed in 1995, after the invasion of Haiti.
17. For example, see Trudy Rubin, "The Word is Out Around the World: Clinton Talks Tough but Acts Weak," *Philadelphia Enquirer* (22 April 1994): A27; Karen Elliott House, "Clinton Speaks Loudly and Carries a Twig," *WSJ* (4 May 1994): A14; "Clinton's Rolodex Problem," *US News and World Report* (10 January 1994): 25–27, "After Talking Tough, Getting Tough?;" ibid. (9 May 1994): 48–49; "Don't Bother me with Foreign Policy," ibid. (16 May 1994): 36–38; "The Sweets Sounds of Silence," ibid. (11 July 1994): 68; "Turning the Other Cheek," ibid. (25 July 1994): 20–23; "The Limits to Leadership," ibid. (12 September 1994): 96; "Still a US Invasion. Still Wrong," *NYT* (2 September 1994): A24; Richard Falk, "The Free Marketeers;" Richard Barnet, "Groping for a Security Blanket," *Progressive* (January 1994): 21; George Church, "Dropping the Ball?," *Time* (2 May 1994): 53–57; Bruce Nelan, "Hurry up and Wait," *Time* (20 June 1994): 40–41; Jon Hull; "Anger from the Grassroots," *Time* (29 August 1994): 38–39; Kevin Fedarko, "Policy at Sea," *Time* (18 July 1994): 20.
18. Steven Butler, "U.S. Resolve, Needed Then and Needed Now," *U.S. News and World Report* (13 June 1994): 12.
19. Anthony Lewis, "Whistling Past Weimar," *NYT* (28 January 1994): A27.
20. Clinton, "Explaining Somalia to the Congress," in Alvin Rubinstein, Albina Shayevich, and Boris Zlotnikov, eds., *The Clinton Foreign Policy Reader: Presidential Speeches with Commentary* (London: M.E. Sharpe, 2000), 146.
21. Clinton, "U.S. Military Involvement in Somalia," *USDOS Disp.*, vol. 4, no. 12 (18 October 1993), 714. See also Clinton, "Explaining Somalia to the Congress," in Rubinstein et al., *The Clinton Foreign Policy Reader*, 147.
22. *Current Military Operations, Hearings before the Committee on Armed Services, USS, 6 August, 4–13 October 1993* (DC: USGPO, 1993), 113. Making a suggestion eerily reminiscent of Wilson's desire to install "Good Men" in the Caribbean, Sam Nunn proposed to bring "maybe 20 to 50 of those leaders here, to train them here, and then go back when you have them trained and have that help. I am looking for allies down there. Where are the good guys that are going to help us with their own?" ibid., 131.
23. "This Week with David Brinkley," *ABC News* (10 October 1993).
24. "President of the Republic of Haiti to the Secretary General (24 July 1993)," UN S/26180, 4, Malval, *L'année de toutes les duperies*, 292.
25. Quoted in "One Killed, Another Wounded in Anti-US Demonstrations," *AFP Wire* (12 October 1993).
26. UN Doc. A/48/532, Add. 1, 7–18, "Des manifestants bloquent l'accès du port de PAP à des diplomates américains," *Le Nouvelliste* (11 October 1993): 1.

27. Peter J.A. Riehm, "The U.S.S. *Harlan County Affair,*" *Military Review* (July August 1997): 31–36. On 25 March 1994, the FRAPH also prevented a French ship, the *Galisbey,* from unloading 530 tons of humanitarian aid.

28. *Current Military Operations, Hearings before the Committee on Armed Services, USS, 6 August, 4–13 October 1993* (DC: USGPO, 1993), 132–133.

29. *U.S. Policy toward Haiti, Hearing before the SWHA, CFR, USS, 8 March 1994* (DC: USGPO, 1994), 10, 12.

30. Boutros Boutros-Ghali, *Unvanquished: A US-UN Saga* (NY: Random House, 1999), 109.

31. Folder "Haiti," box 2, *Incoming FOIAs,* NSA.

32. Clinton, *Developments concerning the National Emergency with Respect to Haiti, Message from the President of the U.S., House document 103–246* (25 April 1994), 3.

33. *Roundtable on Haiti, Briefing before the CFA, HR, 20 October 1993* (DC: USGPO, 1993), 2.

34. Drew, *On the Edge,* 334.

35. Anthony Lake interview with the author (18 May 2001); Lake, *Six Nightmares,* 131.

36. Richard E. Feinberg telephone interview with the author (10 December 2001).

37. Quoted in Halberstam, *War in a Time of Peace,* 273.

38. "Showdown in Haiti," *PBS Frontline* (14 June 1994).

39. "Nouvelle manifestation néo-duvaliériste à PAP," *Le Nouvelliste* (1 October 1993): 1; Howard W. French, "Haiti Police Chief Poses Hurdle to Aristide's Return," *NYT* (5 October 1993): A3.

40. Unnamed adviser, "Mémo confidentiel au général Cédras" (c. February 1992), folder "Accord de Governors' Island, 1993," box 320.04 SIT, Collège St. Martial library.

41. "Showdown in Haiti," *PBS Frontline* (14 June 1994).

42. *Current Military Operations, Hearings before the Committee on Armed Services, USS, 6 August, 4–13 October 1993* (DC: USGPO, 1993), 114.

43. Allan Nairn, "The Eagle is Landing," *Nation* (3 October 1994): 346; "Our Man in Fraph," *Nation* (24 October 1994): 458; R. Jeffrey Smith, "Haitian Paramilitary Chief Spied for CIA," *WP* (7 October 1994): 1; Stephen Engelberg, "A Haitian Leader of Paramilitaries was Paid by CIA," *NYT* (8 October 1994): A1. An unnamed administration official also said that "several of the principal players in the present situation were compensated by the U.S. government." Tim Weiner, "Key Haiti Leaders Said to Have Been in the CIA's Pay," *NYT* (1 November 1993): A1. Rep. Robert G. Torricelli (D-NJ), a member of the House Intelligence and Foreign Affairs Committees, confirmed that supporters of the junta were on the CIA payroll.

44. Ed Bradley, "Toto Constant," *CBS 60 Minutes* (3 December 1995). Lynn Garrison, who advised Cédras at the time, agrees that the CIA knew of the demonstration ahead of time, but he insists the CIA told Constant to call it off. Garrison telephone interview with the author (10 May 2001).

45. The following overview of Constant's life and role in Haiti is drawn from Baltimore Immigration Court, "In the Matter of Emmanuel Constant, Respondent (11 September 1998)," 2–3; *personal collection* (INS FOIA request); Allan Nairn, "The Eagle is Landing," *Nation* (3 October 1994): 346; "Our Man in Fraph," *Nation* (24 October 1994): 458; R. Jeffrey Smith, "Haitian Paramilitary Chief Spied for CIA," *WP* (7 October 1994): 1; Stephen Engelberg, "A Haitian Leader of Paramilitaries was Paid by CIA," *NYT* (8 October 1994): A1; David Grann, "Giving 'the Devil' his Due," *The Atlantic Monthly* (June 2001): 54.

46. A U.S. journalist who spoke regularly with CIA officials in Port-au-Prince thinks otherwise. "The CIA hoped that Constant had a chance of beating Aristide in a popularity contest and that he would one day replace Aristide as President of Haiti." Kenneth Freed personal interview with the author (10 April 2002).

47. "Defendants' Memorandum in Support of their Motion to Dismiss, Constant vs. Christopher and Reno, Civil Action WMN95–3814 (11 May 1996)," 9, *personal collection* (DOJ FOIA request). Constant claimed DIA attaché in Haiti Col. Patrick Collins

encouraged him to found FRAPH. Allan Nairn, "The Eagle is Landing," *Nation* (3 October 1994): 346; Nairn, "Our Man in Fraph," *Nation* (24 October 1994): 458.

48. CNVJ, *Si M Pa Rele*, chapter 7, 1.2.

49. CNVJ, *Si M Pa Rele*, chapter 7, 1.2.B; David Beard, "Haitian Homeless from Big Arson Fire Predict More Violence," *AP Wire* (28 December 1993).

50. Quoted in "Defendants' Memorandum in Support of their Motion to Dismiss, Constant vs. Christopher and Reno, Civil Action WMN95–3814 (11 May 1996)," 13, *personal collection* (DOJ FOIA request).

51. Kenneth Freed personal interview with the author (10 April 2002).

52. Tim Weiner, " '93 Report by CIA Tied Haiti Agent to Slaying," *NYT* (13 October 1996): A9.

53. *FR*, vol. 58, no. 209 (1 November 1993), 58, 480; *FR*, vol. 59, no. 67 (7 April 1994), 16, 552.

54. Unsigned Lavalas document, "Mémoire" (c. Fall 1992), folder "Accord de Governors' Island, 1993," box 320.04 SIT, Collège St. Martial library.

55. G. Berggren et al., *Sanctions in Haiti: Crisis in Humanitarian Action Working Paper No. 93.07* (Harvard U. Center for Population and Development Studies: November 1993). Howard French, "Study Says Haiti Sanctions Kill up to 1,000 Children a Month," *NYT* (9 November 1993): A1.

56. Garrison, *Voodoo Politics*, 151. Contemporary observers concurred. Elizabeth D. Gibbons, *Sanctions in Haiti: Human Rights and Democracy under Assault* (Westport, Conn.: Praeger, 1999), 28–46, Mouterde and Wargny, *Apre bal, tanbou lou*, 123.

57. "Executive Order 12853, 30 June 1993," *FR*, vol. 58 (2 July 1993), 35843; "Executive Order 12872," 18 October 1993), in *FR*, vol. 58 (20 October 1993), 54029. White House Office of the Press Secretary, *Press Briefing* (18 October 1993).

58. *Humanitarian Relief Efforts in Haiti, Hearing before the SWHA, CFA, HR, 9 February 1994* (DC: USGPO, 1994), 1.

59. Lake, *Six Nightmares*, 132–133; Rowland Evans and Robert Novak, "Clinton Talked Out of Haiti Invasion," *Chicago Sun-Times* (19 May 1994): 31.

60. Quoted in Elaine Sciolino et al., "Failure on Haiti: How US Hopes Faded," *NYT* (29 April 1994): 1.

61. Quoted in Halberstam, *War in a Time of Peace*, 279.

62. Clinton, "U.S. Interests in Haiti," *USDOS Disp.*, vol. 5, no. 38 (19 September 1994), 605. See also Clinton, *With Regards to Haiti: Communication from the President of the US, House Document 103–309* (18 September 1994), 1.

63. Kevin Fedarko, "This Time we Mean Business," *Time Magazine* (19 September 1994): 30–33.

64. "Few Options left for US in Haiti Crisis," *NYT* (4 September 1994): A17, "Preaching to Skeptics," in *NYT* (16 September 1994): A1. See also "Backing into a Corner," *US News and World Report* (27 June 1994): 38–39.

65. Quoted in Marshall Ingwerson, "Saving Face," *Christian Science Monitor* (15 September 1994): 2.

66. Quoted in Doyle McManus, "Clinton's Call to Arms based on Credibility," *LA Times* (16 September 1994): A1, Fred Barnes, "Oh, All Right Then," *New Republic* (10 October 1994): 12. One must note the adjective "seriously," which implied that Haiti represented no actual strategic interest besides credibility.

Chapter Six   National Security

1. For a rare case in which an administration official used this line of argument, see William H. Gray, III, interview, "Face the Nation," *CBS NEWS* (3 July 1994).

2. Regarding the lack of traditional strategic interests, see Ernest H. Preeg, "What are the Real US Interests in Haiti?," in Georges A. Fauriol, ed., *Haitian Frustrations: Dilemmas for US Foreign Policy* (DC: CSIS, 1995); *CR* (1994), S12163.

3. For substantial excerpts leaked by a dissenting administration official, see "Excerpts from Pentagon's Plan," *NYT* (8 March 1992): 14.

4. "Intelligence Capabilities" (c. 15 November 1991), fiche 438, item 02125, Presidential Directives on National Security from Truman to Clinton, NSA.

5. "Scope of the Commission's Inquiry, 6 June 1995," 1; document 1117, fiche 461, "Preparing for the 21st Century, 1 March 1996," 24; document 1118, fiche 463, Office of Naval Intelligence, "DNI Posture Statement, 1994," 19; document 336, fiche 871, US Espionage and Intelligence microfiche collection, NSA; John J. Sheehan, "Foreword," in John R. Ballard, *Upholding Democracy: The United States Military Campaign in Haiti, 1994–1997* (Westport, CT: Praeger), xi.

6. "NSDD-221 (1986)," item 01957, fiche 452, "Fact Sheet (c. 8 April 1986)," item 01958, fiche 413, *Presidential Directives on National Security from Truman to Clinton*, NSA.

7. *Statement by General George A. Joulwan, USA, Commander in Chief US Southern Command before the Senate Committee on Armed Services* (5 March 1992); *Statement by General George A. Joulwan before the House Committee on Armed services* (17 March 1992); folder "military," box 3, Congressional Hearings on Drugs, NSA.

8. *U.S. International Drug Control Policy: Recent experience, future options, seminar proceedings prepared for the use of the Committee on the judiciary, USS, 2 February 1994* (DC: USGPO, 1994), 11; *Drugs, Law Enforcement and Foreign Policy: A Report of the Subcommittee on Narcotics, Terrorism and International Operations, USS, 13 April 1989* vol. 1 (DC: USGPO, 1989), 32.

9. Warren Christopher and Robert S. Gelbard, "A New International Strategy to Combat Drugs," *USDOS Disp.*, vol. 5, no. 8 (21 February 1993), 89–90. See also *Statement of Assistant Secretary of State for International Narcotics Matters Robert Gelbard before the Senate Foreign Relations Committee* (29 April 1994), Box 2, Congressional Hearings on Drugs, NSA.

10. George Kourous, *Bush vs. Noriega: The Noriega Challenge to George Bush's Credibility and the 1989 U.S. Invasion to Panama* (M.A. Thesis, Ohio University, November 2000), 262–263.

11. David Maraniss, *First in His Class: A Biography of Bill Clinton* (NY: Simon and Schuster, 1995), 154, 283, 419–423.

12. *Review of the Anti-Drug Abuse Act of 1986: Joint Hearing Before the Subcommittee on Federal Spending, Budget and Accounting of the Committee on Governmental Affairs, USS and the Senate Caucus on International Narcotics Control, 4 May 1987* (DC: USGPO, 1988), 11–14, 70–75.

13. Abbott, *The Duvaliers and Their Legacy*, 257–259.

14. Ibid., 279–280.

15. Prospel Avril, *Vérités et révélations, Tome II: L'armée d'Haïti, bourreau ou victime?* (PAP: Le Natal, 1997), 192.

16. *Drugs, Law Enforcement and Foreign Policy: A Report of the Subcommittee on Narcotics, Terrorism and International Operations, USS, 13 April 1989,* vol. 1 (DC: USGPO, 1989), 194.

17. "Aristide Implicates *Macoutes* in Drug Dealings," *FBIS* (16 January 1991), 8.

18. Quoted in Paul Lewis, "Aristide Asks UN to Place a Total Embargo on Haiti," *NYT* (29 October 1993): A6.

19. Patrick Elie personal interview with the author (11 July 2001).

20. *Recent Developments in Transnational Crime Affecting U.S. Law Enforcement and Foreign Policy, Hearing Before the Senate Subcommittee on Terrorism, Narcotics and International Operations of the CFR, USS,* 21 April 1994 (DC: USGPO, 1994), 107–108.

21. Bureau of International Narcotics Measures, *1993 International Narcotics Control Strategy Report* (DC: USGPO, 1 April 1994), 191–194. See also *Review of the 1992 International Narcotics Control Strategy Report, Hearings before the CFA and the SWHA, HR* (DC: USGPO, March 1992), 211–212.

22. "State Department Daily Press Briefing no. 80: Monday, 5/23/94," Dept. of State Bureau of Public Affairs, *U.S. Foreign Affairs on CD-ROM, January 1990-May 1996*, vol. 4, no.1 (DC: Department of State, June 1996).
23. Bureau of International Narcotics Measures, "1991 International Narcotics Control Strategy Report (3/92)," in Dept. of State Bureau of Public Affairs, *US Foreign Affairs on CD-ROM, January 1990-May 1996*, vol. 4, no. 1 (DC: Department of State, June 1996).
24. Tim Weiner, "A Leader of Former Haitian Junta is Charged with Smuggling Tons of Drugs to US," *NYT* (8 March 1997): A6; William Branigin, "INS Inspector Charged in Drug Scheme; Indictment Says Smuggling Ring Headed by Haitian Fugitive Exploited Ethnic Ties," *WP* (2 May 1998): A2.
25. World Bank, *Haiti: List of Priority Investment Projects* (1991), 5, microenterprise collection, USAID Library, PAP.
26. Heinl, *Written in Blood*, 501.
27. Abbott, *The Duvaliers and Their Legacy*, 172.
28. Ibid., 235–235, Heinl, *Written in Blood*, 677.
29. See also Heinl, *Written in Blood*, 680–681. After the fall of the Duvalier regime, the need to continue the Haitian Migrant Interdiction Operation was specifically mentioned in *National Security Decision Directive 220* (2 April 1986), NLS-NSC-NSDD-220, Ronald Reagan Library.
30. Hérold Jean-François, *Le coup de Cédras* (PAP: L'Imprimeur II, 1995), 451, 463; Clinton, "U.S. Interests in Haiti," *USDOS Disp.*, vol. 5, no. 38 (19 September 1994), 606.
31. "Showdown in Haiti," *PBS Frontline* (14 June 1994). A former Aristide aide, now his political enemy, even accused Aristide of financing some of the boats, which he allegedly called "missiles" aimed at Florida. Micha Gaillard personal interview with the author (9 July 2001).
32. In 1992–1993, screening centers operated temporarily in Les Cayes and Cap Haïtien as well.
33. Clinton and Gore, *Putting People First*, 116–120.
34. Clinton, "Protecting US Borders Against Illegal Immigration," *USDOS Disp.*, vol. 4, no. 32 (9 August 1993), 561.
35. Quoted in Elaine Sciolino, "Clinton Says US Will Continue Ban on Haitian Exodus," *NYT* (15 January 1993): A1; Clinton, *My Life*, 463. Intelligence agencies had warned Clinton that as many as 200,000 Haitians would take to the seas if he eased the U.S. refugee policy. Christopher, *In the Stream of History*, 175.
36. Robert Pastor telephone interview with the author (10 December 2001).
37. Howard W. French, "Few Haitians Test U.S. Sea Barricade," *NYT* (21 January 1993): A8.
38. *Sale vs. Haitian Centers Council* 61 U.S.L.W. (21 June 1993); Harold Hongju Koh, "Closed-Door Policy for Refugees," *New Jersey Law Journal* (23 August 1993), 26.
39. Stephanopoulos, *All Too Human*, 309. Emphasis in text.
40. *Current Military Operations, Hearings before the Committee on Armed Services, USS, 6 August, 4–13 October 1993* (DC: USGPO, 1993), 135–138.
41. DeWayne Wickham, *Bill Clinton and Black America* (NY: Ballantine Books, 2002), 19.
42. As a law clerk to Supreme Court Justice William O. Douglas in 1949–1950, Christopher helped write two 5 June 1950 Supreme Court decisions holding that graduate schools could not be segregated. His first big case in the Los Angeles firm O'Melveny & Myers, in 1957, was to defend a black woman at the Supreme Court. Christopher also investigated the 1965 Watts riots, handled the 1967 Detroit and Newark riots for the Johnson administration, and chaired a commission on police abuse after the beating of Rodney King.
43. "Affidavit, Antoine Eustache (19 February 1992)," folder Haiti, box 2, Human rights collection, NSA.
44. "Affidavit, Jennie Smith (10 February 1992)," folder Haiti, box 2, Human rights collection, NSA.

45. "DOJ Limited Official Use: Haitian Situation Report (c. 1992)," "DOJ Limited Official Use: Special Intelligence Report: Haiti (24 February 1992)," folder Haiti, box 2, Human rights collection, NSA.
46. State Department, *Country Reports on Human Rights Practices for 1992* (DC: USGPO, February 1993), 425.
47. Reproduced in Ridgeway, *The Haiti Files*, 184–190.
48. American Immigration Lawyers Association, *The AILA Human Rights Delegation Report on Haiti* (DC: American Immigration Law Foundation, March 1993), 22–23.
49. *U.S. Human Rights Policy Towards Haiti, Hearing before the Legislation and National Security Subcommittee of the Committee on Government Operations, HR, 9 April 1992* (DC: USGPO, 1993), 57–94. See also Gilles Danroc and Daniel Roussière, *La répression au quotidien en Haïti, 1991–1994* (PAP: HIS, 1995), 50.
50. Gary Pierre-Pierre, "407 Haitians Are Returned in Just one Day," NY (9 July 1994): A6.
51. *US Human Rights Policy Towards Haiti, Hearing before the Legislation and National Security Subcommittee of the Committee on Government Operations, HR, 9 April 1992* (DC: USGPO, 1993), 4, *US Policy toward Haiti, Hearing before the SWHA, CFR, USS, 8 March 1994* (DC: USGPO, 1994), 16.
52. *US Policy toward Haiti, Hearing before the SWHA, CFR, USS, 8 March 1994* (DC: USGPO, 1994), 9. See also ibid., 5.
53. *CR* (22 November 1993), H10985; *CR* (1 February 1994), E44, "Opponents of Policy on Haiti Begin Fast," *NYT* (13 April 1994): A15.
54. UN A/48/867, S/1994/150, Steven Greenhouse, "Aristide Condemns Clinton's Haiti Policy as Racist," *NYT* (22 April 1994): A1.
55. The administration unsuccessfully tried to claim that only Premier Robert Malval, who had resigned five months before, could legally nullify the agreement. During the summer of 1994, Aristide and the United States also clashed over the content of radio broadcasts to Haiti. The United States wanted Aristide to call on his compatriots to stay in Haiti, which he refused; each side eventually made half of the broadcasts, with a right to veto each other's message.
56. Roberto R. Aleman, "Haiti is Washington's Dirty Little Secret, No Panama Reversal," *NYT* (26 July 1994): A18.
57. Clinton, "U.S. Interests in Haiti," *USDOS Disp.*, vol. 5, no. 38 (19 September 1994), 606. See also Clinton, *With Regards to Haiti: Communication from the President of the US, House Document 103–309* (18 September 1994), 1. Christopher wrote that the intervention "finally resolv[ed] the refugee problem in a humane and sustainable way." Christopher, *In the Stream of History*, 182.
58. Quoted in Maraniss, *First in His Class*, 379.
59. Dick Morris, *Behind the Oval Office: Winning the Presidency in the Nineties* (NY: Random House, 1997), 5. The other defeat was a failed Congressional bid in 1974. Castro eventually reneged on an agreement to take the Cubans back, and they never left (most got residency in 1985). In a less-known side issue, most of the 25,000 Haitians who had taken to the sea at the same time were sent back to Haiti.
60. *Gallup Poll*, 228.
61. Richard E. Feinberg telephone interview with the author (10 December 2001).

Chapter Seven   Domestic Politics

1. For another work stating that Clinton's foreign policy in Haiti and elsewhere was shaped by domestic political concerns, see David Halberstam, *War in a Time of Peace: Bush, Clinton, and the Generals* (NY: Scribner, 2001).
2. *Gallup Poll*, 123–124, 235.
3. U.S. Department of State, *Interagency Review of US Government Civilian Humanitarian and Transition Programs* (January 2000), 6–7, Electronic Briefing Book no. 30, NSA.

4. Bruce W. Nelan, "Is Haiti Worth It?," *Time* (1 November 1993): 26. In the first four months of 1994, *Time* carried only one short article on Haiti. Cathy Booth, "Still Punishing the Victims," *Time* (11 April 1994): 55–56.

5. "Clinton, Under Pressure, Presses Haiti," *US News and World Report* (2 May 1994): 15.

6. Selden Rodman, "First Test for Democracy," *National Review* (11 February 1991): 26, Ambrose Evans-Pritchard, "Getting to Know the General," William F. Buckley, Jr., "Forget Democracy in Haiti," *National Review* (29 November 1993): 26, 79.

7. John Canham-Clyne, "Haiti Betrayed," *Progressive* (April 1994): 18–23; "How about Haitigate," *Nation* (11 April 1994): 469.

8. *CR* (1993), S13979.

9. On 20 September, 1994, Louisiana Representative Robert Livingston described Aristide as a "radical leftist who has spewed anti-American venom for years. . . . [a] fanatic. . . . [with] brutal dictatorial tendencies of his own," *CR* (1994), E1880.

10. Clinton also proved he was attuned to the political rhythms of Haiti, where coups are traditionally staged on Sundays. On Sundays, politicians and the army brass are often on vacation, and the streets of Port-au-Prince are not clogged by traffic. The three coup attempts during the 1991 Aristide presidency took place on Sunday, 6 January (Lafontant coup), Sunday, 28 July (Navy mutiny), and Sunday, 29 September (Cédras coup).

11. "Preaching to Skeptics," *NYT* (16 September 1994): A11; Stephanopoulos, *All Too Human*, 308.

12. *CR* (5 October 1994), H10972-H10994; *CR* (6 October 1994), H11020–11036.

13. Haiti is divided into nine *départements*, or administrative regions. The "Tenth Department" symbolized Haitians living abroad.

14. Philip Hilts, "FDA Set to Reverse Blood Ban," *NYT* (24 April 1990): C11; Seth Faison, Jr., "Thousands of Haitians Protest Coup," *NYT* (12 October 1991): A31; "25,000 Join Central Park Rally to Back Ousted Haitian Leader," *NYT* (27 April 1992): A3; "Haitians, in March to UN, Demand Democracy," *NYT* (30 September 1992): A1; Jean-François, *Le coup de Cédras*, 432–433.

15. Adam Clymer, "Democrats Promise Quick Action on a Clinton Plan," *NYT* (5 November 1992): B6.

16. Monica Borkowski, "High Fever to No Pulse," *NYT* (27 September 1994): B10.

17. Robert Pear, "$1 Trillion in Health Costs Is Predicted," *NYT* (29 December 1993): A12.

18. "Transcript of 2nd Debate Between Bush, Clinton, and Perot," *NYT* (16 October 1992): A11. Sixty six % of Americans trusted Clinton to implement universal coverage, the issue they trusted him the most for. Adam Clymer, "American Have High Hopes for Clinton," *NYT* (19 January 1993): A13.

19. As of February 1994, five were from New Jersey (Robert J. Torricelli, Donald M. Payne, Robert E. Andrews, Robert Menendez, Christopher H. Smith), five from New York (Gary L. Ackerman, Eliot L. Engel, Charles E. Schumer, Benjamin A. Gilman, David A. Levy), and five from Florida (Harry Johnston, Alcee L. Hastings, Peter Deutsch, Ileana Ros-Lehtinen, Lincoln Diaz-Balart).

20. They were Reps. Torricelli, Menendez, Smith (NJ), Deutsch, and Ros-Lehtinen (FL). Torricelli first suggested there should be a military intervention in February 1993. *The Future of US Foreign Policy, Regional Issues, Hearings before the CFA, HR, February-March 1993* (DC: USGPO, 1993), 58.

21. *Humanitarian Relief Efforts in Haiti, Hearing before the SWHA, CFA, HR, 9 February 1994* (DC: USGPO, 1994), 10.

22. *Haiti: Views from Congress and Legislative Approaches: Hearing before the SWH, CFA, HR, 27 July 1994* (DC: USGPO, 1994), 34.

23. 21 July, 13, 19, 21 October and 16 November 1993, 1, 9—twice—February, 26, 28 April, 23 May, 8 June, 14, 27 July, 2 August, 27, and 28 September 1994.

24. Larry Rohter, "Foreign Policy: Florida Has One," *NYT* (22 May 1994): section 4, 1.

25. Florida Office of Planning and Budget, *The Unfair Burden: Immigration's Impact on Florida* (Tallahassee, Fla.: Executive Office of the Governor, March 1994), opening page, iii, 9. Dade County manager Joaquin Aviño, urged the federal government to take "very strong, aggressive action to send a message that there must be a settlement in Haiti so as to relieve the pressure there for emigration." Joaquin Aviño, "Commentary: Views from an Affected Community," in Georges A. Fauriol, ed., *The Haitian Challenge: US Policy Considerations* (DC: Center for Strategic and International Studies, 1993), 38.

26. "The 1992 Elections: State by State," *NYT* (4 November 1992): B8.

27. On 8 March 1994, for example, Reps. Carrie Meek (D-FL), Joseph P. Kennedy (D-MA), Charles Rangel (D-NY), Sen. Tom Harkin (D-IA), and Aristide lobbyist Michael D. Barnes were invited as star witnesses, while Lawrence Pezzullo and Walter Slocombe were relegated to the afternoon session.

28. There were 39 Black members of the House of Representatives (including the delegate from the District of Columbia, Eleanor Holmes Norton, who could not vote) and one Black Senator (Carol Moseley-Brown). Ronald Smothers, "Black Caucus in Congress Gains in Diversity and Experience," *NYT* (10 November 1992): A17.

29. DeWayne Wickham, *Bill Clinton and Black America* (NY: Ballantine Books, 2002), 102–104, 145.

30. Ibid., 131.

31. *US Human Rights Policy Towards Haiti, Hearing before the Legislation and National Security Subcommittee of the Committee on Government Operations, HR, 9 April 1992* (DC: USGPO, 1993), 57.

32. Patrick Elie personal interview with the author (11 July 2001).

33. Mouterde and Wargny, *Apre bal, tanbou lou*, 156–157.

34. *Humanitarian Conditions in Haiti, Hearing before the Select Committee on Hunger, HR, 11 June 1992* (DC: USGPO, 1992), 28.

35. The letter found its way to Aristide's Presidential Commission archives. "Members of the Black Caucus to Pdt. Bill Clinton, 29 January 1993," folder "Situation politique en Haïti, 1994," box 320.04 SIT, Collège St. Martial library.

36. They were Major Owens of Brooklyn, Donald M. Payne of New Jersey, Barbara-Rose Collins of Michigan, Ronald V. Dellums of California, Joseph P. Kennedy II of Massachusetts, and Kweisi Mfume of Maryland. They were released shortly thereafter.

37. Karen De Witt, "Hunger Strike on Haiti: Partial Victory at Least," *NYT* (9 May 1994): A7.

38. Quoted in Elaine Sciolino et al., "Failure on Haiti: How US Hopes Faded," *NYT* (29 April 1994): 1.

39. "Showdown in Haiti," *PBS Frontline* (14 June 1994). Aristide Prime Minister Robert Malval wrote about Aristide's "dragoons of the Black Caucus." Robert Malval, *L'année de toutes les duperies*, 400.

40. Quoted in Stephanopoulos, *All Too Human*, 216.

41. The following overview of Clinton's first year in office is drawn from Bob Woodward, *The Agenda: Inside the Clinton White House* (NY: Simon and Schuster, 1994); Elizabeth Drew, *On the Edge: The Clinton Presidency* (NY: Simon and Schuster, 1994).

42. Susan Schmidt, "Rose Law Firm to Close its DC Outpost," *WP* (25 November 1994): A21.

43. David Maraniss, *First in His Class: A Biography of Bill Clinton* (NY: Simon and Schuster, 1995), 26.

44. Dole later apologized for the poor timing. Woodward, *The Choice*, 423–424.

45. R. Emmett Tyrrell, Jr., "The Continuing Crisis," *American Spectator* (October 1994): 10.

46. Clinton saw only 47% of the bills he promoted passed, compared with Kennedy (84%) LBJ (81%), Carter (76%) and Eisenhower (72%). The percentage sunk to 36% after the Republican 1994 victory, the lowest for any president.

47. Woodward, *The Agenda*; Drew, *On the Edge*.

48. Perot's 92 running mate was Adm. James Stockdale, held prisoner in Vietnam for Seven years. George Washington, Andrew Jackson, William Harrison, Zachary Taylor, Ulysses

S. Grant, and Dwight D. Eisenhower were professional soldiers. James Monroe, Franklin Pierce, Abraham Lincoln, James A. Garfield, Benjamin Harrison, William McKinley, Theodore Roosevelt, Harry S. Truman, John F. Kennedy, Richard Nixon, and George H. W. Bush were veterans.

49. Drew, *On the Edge*, 336.
50. "In their Own Words: Transcript of Bush Speech Accepting the Nomination for Another Four Years," *NYT* (21 August 1992): A14.
51. Thomas L. Friedman, "Issues: Foreign Policy—Looking Abroad: Clinton and Foreign Policy," *NYT* (4 October 1992): A1. The Bush campaign also shot an ad in an IHOP restaurant. Michael Wines, "The Ad Campaign; Bush: Trying a Subtler Approach," *NYT* (14 October 1992): A22.
52. Maraniss, *First in His Class*, 93, 145–146.
53. Quoted in Fred Barnes, "Oh, All Right Then," *New Republic* (10 October 1994): 11; Clinton, *My Life*, 554.
54. Karen Elliott House, "Clinton Speaks Loudly and Carries a Twig," *WSJ* (4 May 1994): A14.
55. "Still a US Invasion. Still Wrong," *NYT* (2 September 1994): A24; Richard Falk, "The Free Marketeers," Richard Barnet, "Groping for a Security Blanket," *Progressive* (January 1994): 21.
56. George Church, "Dropping the Ball?" *Time* (2 May 1994): 53–57; Bruce Nelan, "Hurry up and Wait," *Time* (20 June 1994): 40–41; Jon Hull, "Anger from the Grassroots," *Time* (29 August 1994): 38–39; Kevin Fedarko, "Policy at Sea," *Time* (18 July 1994): 20.
57. "Clinton's Rolodex Problem," *US News and World Report* (10 January 1994): 25–27; "After Talking Tough, Getting Tough?"; ibid. (9 May 1994): 48–49, "Don't Bother me with Foreign Policy," ibid. (16 May 1994): 36–38; "US Resolve, Needed Then and Needed Now" ibid. (13 June 1994): 13, "The Sweets Sounds of Silence" ibid. (11 July 1994): 68, "Turning the Other Cheek" ibid. (25 July 1994): 20–23, "The Limits to Leadership," ibid. (12 September 1994): 96.
58. *CR* (1994), H2401, H2407, H2496–2503, H2588, H2617–2618, S4593, S4599, S5126–5129. They were Reps. Porter J. Goss (FL), Cass Ballenger (NC), Robert K. Dornan (CA), Robert S. Walker (PA), David E. Bonior (MI), Frank McCloskey (IN), and Eliot L. Engel (NY), and Sen. Hank Brown (CO), Alfonse D'Amato (NY), and Bob Smith (NH).
59. Douglas Jehl, "A Mustang and a Man Named Bill," *NYT* (18 April 1994): A8.
60. Dan Balx and Richard Morin, "Public is Losing Confidence in Clinton Foreign Policy," *WP* (17 May 1994): A1.
61. "Focus: Editors' Views," *MacNeill-Lehrer News Hour* (20 May 1994).
62. Richard Morin, "Clinton' Ratings Decline Despite Rising Economy," *WP* (9 August 1994): A1.
63. "Early Birds on Parade," *Time* (26 September 1994): 34–36. Over the course of the campaign, Sen. Bob Dole (KS), Phil Gramm (TX), Richard Lugar (IN), Arlen Specter (PA), columnist and television commentator Pat Buchanan, Cal. Governor Pete Wilson, former Tenn. Governor Lamar Alexander, Rep. Robert Dornan (CA), businessman Morry Taylor, publisher Steve Forbes, and former State Dept. official Alan Keyes entered the race for the Republican presidential nomination. Former Sec. of Defense Dick Cheney, House Speaker Newt Gingrich, NY Congressman Jack Kemp, former Vice President Dan Quayle, Mass. Governor William Weld, and former chairman of the JCS Colin Powell also considered running.
64. A losing Dukakis had won 46% of the vote in 1988. Gore earned 48% of the vote in 2000.
65. Anthony Lake mentioned this tirade to Sandy Berger and George Stephanopoulos. Stephanopoulos, *All Too Human*, 217.
66. Al Kamen, "For Lunch, A Course on JFK," *WP* (22 October 1993): A21.
67. Quoted in Woodward, *The Choice*, 65. "It was painful for him," said one person who saw Clinton shortly after the 11 September 2001 attacks. "He has prepared all of his life for

something truly big like this." Quoted in Jonathan Alter, "Citizen Clinton Up Close," *Newsweek* (8 April 2002): 34.

68. Dick Morris, *The New Prince: Machiavelli Updated for the Twenty-First Century* (Los Angeles: Renaissance Books, 1999), 163.
69. Dick Morris, *Behind the Oval Office* (1999), 4–6. See also Morris, *The New Prince*, 165–166.
70. Stephanopoulos, *All Too Human*, 310; Clinton, *My Life*, 645.
71. Lake, *Six Nightmares*, 137.
72. Morris, *Behind the Oval Office* (1999), xiv.
73. Stephanopoulos, *All Too Human*, 308. For similar comments on Bosnia (1995), see ibid., 383.
74. Morris complained that they were separated by a "castle moat" and that Lake, "deeply idealistic but highly territorial, thought political advice was unchaste." Morris, *Behind the Oval Office* (1999), 245–246.
75. Jason DeParle, "The Man Inside Bill Clinton's Foreign Policy," *NYT* (20 August 1995): section 6, 33.
76. Lake, *Six Nightmares*, 259–261.
77. Anthony Lake telephone interview with the author (18 May 2001).
78. Christopher, *In the Stream of History*, 176, 178.
79. *White Paper, PDD 25, Reforming Multilateral Peace Operations* (State Department Bureau of International Organization Affairs: 3 May 1994), www.fas.org/irp/offdocs/pdd/index.html. Christopher argued that "today, foreign policymakers cannot afford to ignore the public.... From Vietnam to Iran-Contra, we have too often witnessed the disastrous effects of foreign policies hatched by experts without proper candor, and without proper consultation with the public and their representatives." *Nomination of Christopher to be Secretary of State, Hearing before the CFR, USS, 13 and 14 January 1993* (DC: USGPO, 1993), 21. Madeleine Albright used almost the same words a week later at her own nomination hearing.
80. Christopher, *In the Stream of History*, 179, 181. Talbott said: "the American people are almost always reluctant to see force used.... It is the administration's hope that as they see this drama unfold . . . they will feel what those of us in the administration feel." *US Policy Toward, and Presence in, Haiti, Hearings and Markup before the CFA, HR, 13, 27, 28 September 1994* (DC: USGPO, 1994), 45. Panetta said that "once combat is joined the nation will rally behind the president." "Preaching to Skeptics," *NYT* (16 September 1994): A11.
81. *Gallup Poll*, 234.
82. *CR* (1994), S13035.
83. Michael Kramer, "The Case Against Invading Haiti," *Time* (19 September 1994): 34; "The Case for Intervention," *Time* (26 September 1994): 28. See also Anthony Lewis, "Resolution Matters," *NYT* (19 September 1994): A17; "Relief, not Victory," "Clinton Wins and Learns," *NYT* (20 September 1994): 22, 23; "Commander in Chief," Owen Harries, "The Case for Clinton's Diplomacy: My So-called Foreign Policy," *New Republic* (10 October 1994): 7, 24–31. Jesse Helms and periodicals on both extremes of the political spectrum remained adamant. *CR* (1994), S13074–13075; Christopher Caldwell, "Barnes-Storming," *American Spectator* (November 1994): 90; Joanne Landy, "Born-Again Interventionists" *Progressive* (September 1994): 23; "Imposing Democracy in Haiti"; 'Patrick Bellegarde-Smith," ibid. (November 1994): 7, 28.
84. Morris, *Behind the Oval Office* (1999), 15–16.
85. Clinton, "Confronting the Challenges of a Broader World," Christopher, "Building Peace in the Middle East," Lake, "From Containment to Enlargement," Albright, "Use of Force in a Post-Cold War World," *USDOS Disp.*, vol. 4, no. 39 (27 September 1993), 649–668.
86. *Nomination of Christopher to be Secretary of State, Hearing before the CFR, USS, 13 and 14 January 1993* (DC: USGPO, 1993), 23, 24, 28.

87. "Showdown in Haiti," *PBS Frontline* (14 June 1994).

88. For a remarkably unclear explanation of why one should invade Haiti, not Cuba, see the Christopher interview in "Meet the Press," *NBC* (11 September 1994).

89. Kenneth Freed, "US Said to Drop Bid to Reinstate Haitian President," *NYT* (17 December 1993): A1.

90. Richard E. Feinberg telephone interview with the author (10 December 2001).

91. Somalia hung such a large shadow that Clinton's advisers never even put a proposal for an intervention in Rwanda on his desk. Jane Perlez, "The Clinton Legacy," *NYT* (28 *December* 2000): A1.

92. *Public Papers: Clinton*, vol. 1 (1993), 56, 162, ibid., vol. 1 (1994), 954, ibid., vol. 2 (1994), 1549, 1560, Bill Clinton, "US Interests in Haiti," *USDOS Disp.*, vol. 5, no. 38 (19 September 1994), 606. In a hearing, Strobe Talbott, admitted that "obviously geography is a factor here." *US Policy Toward, and Presence in, Haiti, Hearings and Markup before the CFA, HR, 13, 27, 28 September 1994* (DC: USGPO, 1994), 17.

93. Stephanopoulos, *All Too Human*, 308. The intervention was set to begin on a clear, moon-lit night. The risk that U.S. paratroopers might hurt themselves in the dark was apparently thought to be greater than the risk of being shot by Haitian sharpshooters.

94. The following overview of the Haitian Army is drawn from Kern Delince, *Quelle armée pour Haïti?* (PAP: HIS, 1994).

95. Abbott, *The Duvaliers and Their Legacy*, 82–85; Diederich and Burt, *Haiti and Its Dictator*, 115–122.

96. Abbott, *The Duvaliers and Their Legacy*, 122–131.

97. Ibid., 245–247.

98. Col. David H. Hackworth, "A Soldier's-Eye View," *Newsweek* (22 August 1994): 33; Hackworth with Tom Mathews, *Hazardous Duty: America's Most Decorated Living Soldier Reports from the Front and Tells it the Way it is* (NY: William Morrow, 1996), 229–230.

99. Quoted in Powell and Persico, *My American Journey*, 544.

100. Michael R. Gordon et al., "Weighing Options, US Aides Assess Invasion of Haiti," *NYT* (30 May 1994): A1.

101. *White Paper, PDD 25, Reforming Multilateral Peace Operations* (Dept. of State Bureau of International Organization Affairs: 3 May 1994), www.fas.org/irp/offdocs/pdd/index.html.

102. "Maj. William B. Garrett interview," in Cynthia L. Hayden, *JTF-180 Operation Uphold Democracy: Oral History Interviews* (Fort Bragg, NC: XVIII Airborne Corps, 1995).

103. *Public Papers: Clinton*, vol. 2 (1994), 1552, Stephanopoulos, *All Too Human*, 310.

104. UNSC, S/RES/940 (31 July 1994).

105. Madeleine K. Albright, "A Strong United Nations Serves U.S. Security Interests," "Myths of Peace-keeping," *USDOS Disp.*, vol. 4, no. 26 (28 June 1993), 461–467; Albright, "The Clinton's Administration's Policy on Reforming Multilateral Peace Operations," *USDOS Disp.*, vol. 5, no. 20 (16 May 1994), 315. Talbott, Christopher and Clinton made similar comments. *US Policy Toward, and Presence in, Haiti, Hearings and Markup before the CFA, HR, 13, 27, 28 September 1994* (DC: USGPO, 1994), 23; *Nomination of Christopher to be Secretary of State, Hearing before the CFR, USS, 13 and 14 January 1993* (DC: USGPO, 1993), 24; Bill Clinton, "Confronting the Challenges of a Broader World," *USDOS Disp.*, vol. 4, no. 39 (27 September 1993), 650, 652.

106. A CNN/Time poll showed that only 17% of Americans supported a unilateral U.S. action. The percentage climbed to 50% if the intervention was multilateral. Jill Dougherty, "Poll Says Americans Against Unilateral Intervention in Haiti," *CNN International News* (1 July 1994).

107. Quoted in Walter E. Kretchik, Robert F. Baumann, and John T. Fishel, *Invasion, Intervention, "Intervasion"* (Fort Leavenworth, KS: US Command and General Staff College Press), 85.

108. UNSC, S/RES/940 (31 July 1994).

109. John McWethy, "UN Memos Say US Plans to Invade Haiti," *ABC World News Saturday* (11 June 1994), Steven Greenhouse; "A Haiti Invasion Wins Hemisphere Support," *NYT* (13 June 1994): A10, "UN View of Haiti Intervention," *WSJ* (16 June 1994): A16; "UN Documents say America is Ready to Invade Haiti," *London Times* (16 June 1994): Overseas News Section, *US Policy Toward, and Presence in, Haiti, Hearings and Markup before the CFA, HR, 13, 27, 28 September 1994* (DC: USGPO, 1994), 24. The State Department immediately denounced the documents as a forgery, but UN special envoy to Haiti Dante Caputo, the purported author of the memo, only denied that there was a precise deadline to invade Haiti, not that he wrote the memo and that conversations took place.

110. Reproduced in *CR* (1994), 18451–18453. The alleged conversation was consistent with an 18 May, 1994 meeting between Boutros-Ghali, Albright and Undersecretary of State Peter Tarnoff reported in Boutros Boutros-Ghali, *Unvanquished: A US-UN Saga* (NY: Random House, 1999), 151.

111. *CR* (1994), 18451–18453.

112. Clinton, "US Interests in Haiti," *USDOS Disp.*, vol. 5, no. 38 (19 September 1994), 606. In February 1996, all U.S. forces withdrew from the UN force (UNMIH). But 450 soldier-engineers immediately came back: the goal was to fulfill Clinton's pledge that the army had left Haiti on schedule.

113. Bill Clinton, "President Clinton Sends Diplomatic Mission to Haiti Bill," *USDOS Disp.*, vol. 5, no. 38 (19 September 1994), 611.

Chapter Eight   Haitian Lobbying

1. Regarding world leaders' attempts to influence U.S. foreign policy, see Jarol B. Manheim, *Strategic Public Diplomacy and American Foreign Policy: The Evolution of Influence* (New York: Oxford U. Press, 1994).

2. Garrison, *Voodoo Politics*, 146–147.

3. Malval, *L'année de toutes les duperies*, 21.

4. Hackworth and Mathews, *Hazardous Duty*, 225.

5. Kenneth Freed personal interview with the author (10 April 2002).

6. "Charting the Course, Raoul Cédras Interview," *MacNeill-Lehrer News Hour* (18 October 1993).

7. Unnamed adviser, "Mémo confidentiel au général Cédras" (ca. February 1992), folder "Accord de Governors' Island, 1993," box 320.04 SIT, Collège St. Martial library. Underlined in original.

8. Jean-François, *Le coup de Cédras*, 308–309. Foreign businessmen also regularly came to Haiti and pocketed payments in exchange for embargoed goods that they never delivered. Kenneth Freed personal interview with the author (10 April 2002).

9. Jill Smolowe, "With Friends like These," *Time* (8 November 1993): 44.

10. Gouvernement de consensus et de salut public de la République d'Haïti, *Livre blanc: conséquences de l'embargo décrété par l'OEA contre la république d'Haïti* (PAP, Aug. 1992), I, microenterprise collection, USAID Library, PAP. See also Lynn Garrison, "For Haitians, A Countdown to Death," *Miami Herald* (3 December 1993); 35A.

11. The following overview of the Shadow's life and role in 1991–1994 is drawn from Lynn Garrison telephone interview with the author (10 May 2001); Garrison, *Voodoo Politics*, "Cédras' Adviser: Aristide 'Will Never Return,' " *FBIS* (26 September 1994), 14; Mouterde and Wargny, *Apre bal, tanbou lou*, 106–107.

12. *Red Baron* (1971) and *Blue Max* (1966) were indeed shot at Weston Aerodrome in Leixlip, Ireland, but he was not mentioned in the credits. Production of *Barry Lyndon* was indeed moved from Ireland to England after Kubrick received threats from the Irish Republican Army, but credits do not mention the Shadow; nor do those of *These Magnificent Men*. Internet Movie Database at www.imdb.com.

13. Lynn Garrison telephone interview with the author (10 May 2001).
14. Ibid.
15. Linda Diebel, "Canadian Connection Working Tirelessly to Denounce Aristide," *Toronto Star* (19 October 1993): 1. See also Phil Davison, "Shadow Plays Dirty Tricks in Haiti" *London Independent* (2 November 1993): Jill Smolowe, "With Friends like These," *Time* (8 November 1993): 44–46.
16. "Le Père Aristide respectera la constitution, s'il est élu," *Le Nouvelliste* (13 November 1990): 1. In November 1991, Aristide's former doctor, Michel-Ange Monplaisir, revealed that he had been diagnosed as a manic depressive in 1977–1978 and prescribed lithium carbonate. Letter reproduced in Monplaisir, "Rapport médical hautement confidentiel sur le cas du Révérend Père Jean-Bertrand Aristide, 3 novembre 1991" in Garrison, *Voodoo Politics*, 558–563.
17. Lynn Garrison telephone interview with the author (10 May 2001). Emmanuel Constant also claimed to have passed on medical information on Aristide to the CIA. Ed Bradley, "Toto Constant," *CBS 60 Minutes* (3 December 1995).
18. Garrison, *Voodoo Politics*, 273–282.
19. Helms declared that "intelligence sources assured me [this painting] was hanging in Aristide's office." *CR* (20 October 1993), S13979.
20. Garrison, *Voodoo Politics*, 184–185, 376.
21. Ibid., 165–166, 171–178.
22. Ibid., 190–191. Interestingly, Aristide supporters planned a similar project that also fell through. At a November 1993 meeting with Bernard Kouchner (founder of Doctors Without Borders), Aristide representative in Haiti Father Adrien discussed the "Boat for Democracy" project, in which Aristide, Kouchner and others would approach Haitian waters in a boat from which they would broadcast radio addresses, thus mobilizing Haitian and international opinion. "Memo pour le rendez-vous de Bernard Kouchner" (ca. 8 November. 1993), folder "Correspondance reçue," Box 320.01 COM, Collège St. Martial library.
23. Garrison, *Voodoo Politics*, 377.
24. Kenneth Freed personal interview with the author (10 April 2002).
25. Anthony Lake telephone interview with the author (18 May 2001).
26. Director of Central Intelligence, "Annual Report FY 1994, September 1995," 2, Document 1088, fiche 445, US Espionage and Intelligence microfiche collection, NSA.
27. CIA station chief John Kambourian told the *LA Times* Caribbean correspondent that he hoped the political crisis would last so long Aristide's presidential term would end before he could be restored. Kenneth Freed personal interview with the author (10 April 2002).
28. George J. Church, "Lying down with the Dogs," *Time* (17 October 1994): 29; Allan Nairn, "Haiti under the Gun," *Nation* (8–15 January 1996): 11–15.
29. Former Secretary of Defense Dick Cheney also did so on television on the twenty-fourth. "This Week with David Brinkley," *ABC News* (24 October 1993); "Charlie Rose," *PBS* (28 October 1993).
30. Latell claimed these were "inaccurate (and cursory) newspaper accounts," but refused to discuss the content of his briefing further due to classification concerns. Brian Latell e-mail message to the author (7 February 2002). For purported excerpts of the report, see *CR* (21 October 1993), S14050, "The World Today," *CNN* (22 October 1993); Steven A. Holmes, "Administration is Fighting Itself on Haiti Policy," *NYT* (23 October 1993): A1; R. Jeffrey Smith, "Hill Briefing about Aristide Renews Debate on CIA Role," *WP* (24 October 1993): A28; Robert D. Novak, "Allegations about Aristide," *WP* (28 October 1993): A23.
31. A year later, Republican Senators such as Larry Pressler (R-SD) also accused Aristide of having received payoffs by Colombian drug dealers (the sole witness failed a polygraph test and only the *Washington Times* picked up the story). Jerry Seper, "Escobar Aide Tells DEA of Aristide Bribe," *Washington Times* (3 October 1994): A1; " 'Some Deception'— But Whose?" ibid. (6 October 1994): A1; "Pressler to Clinton: Why no DEA Questioning of Aristide?" ibid. (7 October 1994): A1.

32. *CR* (20 October 1993), S13979, Halberstam, *War in a Time of Peace*, 279.
33. *Public Papers: Clinton*, vol. 2 (1993), 1810. In a typical quote, Rep. Mitch McCollum's (R-FL) declared that the CIA reports "have affected [my thinking] in a sense, that I know that President Aristide is not the perfect person that everybody might like to have down there. . . . On the other hand, there's really no option though." "Focus: What Now? McCollum interview," *MacNeill-Lehrer News Hour* (29 December 1993).
34. Bazin's own democratic credentials were uncertain. In 1955, as Bazin and Matthieu Galey were studying at the elitist Sciences Po in Paris, Bazin confided to Galey that he intended to become president for life in Haiti. "I will win through an election," he said. "But when I am elected, I will remain president until I die." Quoted in Matthieu Galey, *Journal, I, 1953–1973* (Paris: B. Grasset, 1987), 69.
35. Quoted in Steven A. Holmes, "Administration is Fighting Itself on Haiti Policy," *NYT* (23 October 1993): A1; Tim Weiner, "CIA Formed Haitian Unit Later Tied to Narcotics Trade," *NYT* (14 November 1993): A1; Christopher Marquis, "CIA Memo Discounts 'Oppressive Rule' in Haiti," *LA Times* (19 December 1993): A21.
36. Christopher Marquis, "Spies, Lies and Subversion," in *Miami Herald* (3 December 1993): 34A. See also Roland I. Perusse, *Democracy Restored, 1991–1995* (NY: U. Press of America, 1995), 8–9. His career in the CIA ruined, Latell now teaches at Georgetown University.
37. Richard E. Feinberg telephone interview with the author (10 December 2001).
38. Quoted in David Johnston, "Spy Voices Shame and Defiance," *NYT* (29 April 1994): 16.
39. Kenneth Freed personal interview with the author (10 April 2002).
40. Micha Gaillard personal interview with the author (9 July 2001).
41. Patrick Elie personal interview with the author (11 July 2001).
42. Jean-François, *Le coup de Cédras*, 454–455. The members of the commission were Father Antoine Adrien (chairman), Jean J. Molière, Wesner Emmanuel, Micha Gaillard, Georgette Omero, Chavanne Jean-Baptiste, Michel Lominy, Evans Paul, Pierre Michel Sajous, and Fred Joseph.
43. "Secrétariat privé du Président Aristide, 14 juillet 1992," folder "Commission présidentielle," box 320.01 COM, Collège St. Martial library.
44. Gaillard, a member of the Commission, explained that "we have a culture of all or nothing . . . Aristide didn't want to make a pact with the enemy." Micha Gaillard personal interview with the author (9 July 2001).
45. "PM Robert Malval à Son Excellence Jean-Bertrand Aristide, 14 Décembre 1993," in Malval, *L'année de toutes les duperies*, 423.
46. Père Adrien, untitled document, folder "Manuscrits commission présidentielle," box 320.01 COM, Collège St. Martial library.
47. "Komité Rezistans nan lut Demokrasi a pè Jan Bran Aristid la ak Antoine Adrien," folder "Manuscrits commission présidentielle," box 320.01 COM, Collège St. Martial library.
48. "Patrick Elie à Père Gérard Jean-Juste, 1ᵉʳ juin 1993," Folder "Situation politique en Haïti, 1994," box 320.04 SIT, in Collège St. Martial library.
49. Patrick Elie personal interview with the author (11 July 2001).
50. OAS, "Apoyo al gobierno democratico de Haiti," 30 September 1991, CP/RES 567 (870/91).
51. OAS, "Acta de la séptima sesión," 15, 6 June 1994, OEA/Ser. F/V. 1 MRE/ ACTA 7/94.
52. "Never, never again shall our Haitian brothers be sold so that their blood be converted to bitter sugar," Aristide said in his September 1991 UN speech. Quoted in Jerry Gray, "Haitian's Visit to New York is a Celebration," *NYT* (29 September 1991): A1. Aristide was referring to the title of a book that first raised the issue of Haitian cane cutters, Maurice Lemoine's *Bitter Sugar: Slaves Today in the Caribbean* (Chicago: Banner Press, 1985), which he had read. Aristide and Wargny, *An Autobiography*, 57. See also Michèle Wucker, *Why the Cocks Fight: Dominicans, Haitians, and the Struggle for Hispaniola* (NY: Hill and Wang, 1999), 130–132.

53. "Showdown in Haiti," *PBS Frontline* (14 June 1994).
54. For Soares, see "Informe del secretario general a la reunion ad hoc de ministros de relaciones exteriores sobre Haiti" 14 May 1992, OEA/Serv. F/V.1 MRE/Doc.4/92, for Caputo, see "Acta de la séptima sesión," 16, 6 June 1994, OEA/Ser. F/V. 1 MRE/ ACTA 7/94, for the OAS, see "Promotion of Democracy," 10 June 1994, OAS, AG/RES. 1280 (XXIV-)/94).
55. "Proponen suspensión de embargo a Cuba y restitución de la democracia en Haití," *El Universal* (11 September 1994): 6.
56. Hilarión Cardozo, "Carta a Bill Clinton: es al pueblo haitiano al que le corresponde decidir su futuro," *El Universal* (19 September 1994): 4.
57. *Public Papers: Clinton*, vol. 1 (1994), 1245.
58. Reproduced in "Declaration of Principles," *USDOS Disp. Supplement*, vol. 6, no. 2 (May 1995), 10.
59. "International Presence in Haiti," 5 June 1997, OAS, AG/RES. 1502 (XVII-O/97).
60. A November 1991 speech attributed to Aristide violently attacks France and Dufour, but its authenticity is dubious. "Aristide on French, US 'Hypocritical Behavior,'" *FBIS* (2 December 1991), 15–16.
61. Patrick Elie personal interview with the author (11 July 2001).
62. Quoted in "Haïti: la France n'est pas disposée à participer à une intervention militaire," *Le Monde* (14 May 1994): 5.
63. "Presidente de la Republica de Haiti al excelentísimo señor Boutros Boutros Ghali," 3 June 1992, OAS, OEA/Ser. F/V. 1 MRE/INF. 15/92. See also "President Aristide to Secretary-General Boutros-Ghali (3 June 1992)," UN Doc. S/24340 (22 July 1992), 4–5.
64. "Secretary General to the President of Haiti," UN S/24340 (18 June 1992), 2: "Secretary General to the Secretary General of the OAS," UN S/24340 (19 June 1992), 6: "Secretary General of the OAS to the Secretary General," UN S/24340 (10 July 1992), 7–10. In October 1991, Aristide had first turned to the OAS, asking for democracy to be restored "by pacific means." "Requête formulée par le président de la république d'Haïti," 7 October 1991, OAS, OEA/Ser. F/V.1 MRE/doc. 3/91.
65. "Le médiateur de l'ONU pour Haïti a démissionné," *Le Monde* (21 September 1994): 4. Lakdhar Brahimi of Algeria replaced Caputo.
66. Boutros-Ghali, *Unvanquished*, 198. See also ibid., 98–99, 118–120, 122.
67. The Senate's Select Committee on Intelligence blocked the payments. Jim Mann, "CIA's Aid Plan Would Have Undercut Aristide in '87–'88," *LA Times* (31 October 1993): A1.
68. "It was the most frustrating hour I ever spent. None of us seemed to be able to establish any communication whatsoever," said one of the American participants. Quoted in Lee Hockstader, "US Weighs Hopes and Fears About Haiti," *WP* (19 December 1990): A27.
69. Mouterde and Wargny, *Apre bal, tanbou lou*, 37–38,: Malval, *L'année de toutes les duperies*, 42–43.
70. Robert Pastor telephone interview with the author (10 December 2001). Aristide won despite the fraud, and he apologized to the U.S. delegation the following day for his harsh tone.
71. "U.S. Department of State Daily Press Briefing no. 150: Monday, 10/7/91," in U.S. Department of State, *US Foreign Affairs on CD-ROM, January 1990-May 1996*, vol. 4, no. 1 (DC: Department of State, June 1996).
72. *Public Papers: Bush*, vol. 2 (1992–1993), 1,954. See also *Public Papers: Bush*, vol. 2 (1991), 1,494.
73. Ron Howell, "FBI Probe of Aristide Questioned; Congressman Labels Tactics in Slay Inquiry Watergate-Like," *Newsday* (15 March 1993): 13.
74. "Today's News Update," *NY Law Journal* (14 December 1993): 1.
75. *Public Papers: Clinton*, vol. 2 (1993), 1810. In private, Clinton mentioned that Aristide's alleged mental problems did not preclude his being a good ruler. "Lincoln might have been crazy, but he was a hell of a president," Clinton said. Quoted in Stephanopoulos, *All Too Human*, 219.

76. Lake, *Six Nightmares*, 130.
77. Robert Pastor telephone interview with the author (10 December 2001).
78. Lake, *Six Nightmares*, 138.
79. Patrick Elie personal interview with the author (11 July 2001).
80. Quoted in Elaine Sciolino, "Aristide Adopts a New Role: From Robespierre to Gandhi," *NYT* (18 September 1994): Section 1, 1.
81. Malval, *L'année de toutes les duperies*, 195–196.
82. Christopher, *In the Stream of History*, 177.
83. "Showdown in Haiti," *PBS Frontline* (14 June 1994) has footage of both of Aristide's speeches.
84. Marc-Ferl Morquette, *Les nouveaux marrons: essai sur un aspect de la crise politique, 1989–1998* (PAP: L'imprimeur II, 1999).
85. Aristide and Wargny, *Tout moun se moun*, 57–58.
86. Sermon reproduced in Martin-Luc Bonnardot and Gilles Danroc, *La chute de la maison Duvalier: textes pour l'histoire* (Paris: Karthala, 1989), 78.
87. Patrick Elie personal interview with the author (11 July 2001).
88. Aristide, *In the Parish of the Poor*, 59.
89. "I Am President of Haiti," *Time* (14 October 1991): 36.
90. "It's not if I Go Back, but When," *Time* (1 November 1993): 28. At a House hearing, Barnes insisted that "President Aristide has never suggested that anybody should be necklaced. The man is a priest who is nonviolent both in his personal nature and in his statements." *Haiti: The Agreement of Governor's Island and its Implementation, Hearing before the SWHA, CFA, HR, 21 July 1993* (DC: USGPO, 1993), 37.
91. Meeting with the editorial board of the *Washington Post* shortly after the 1991 coup, all Aristide could answer to the most complex policy questions was "what the world needs now is love." Quoted in Catherine S. Manegold, "Innocent Abroad," *NYT* (1 May 1994): section 6, 38.
92. Jean-François, *Le coup de Cédras*, 430.
93. Quoted in Mouterde and Wargny, *Apre bal, tanbou lou*, 131.
94. Larry Rohter, "Aristide Hands Power to Successor in Haiti," *NYT* (8 February 1996): A14.
95. Aristide and Clinton, "U.S. Support for Democracy in Haiti," *USDOS Disp.*, vol. 4, no. 12 (22 March 1993), 163.
96. Quoted in Steven Greenhouse, "Aristide Condemns Clinton's Haiti Policy as Racist," *NYT* (22 April 1994): A1.
97. Mouterde and Wargny, *Apre bal, tanbou lou*, 169.
98. Aristide et al., "Meeting of the Multinational Force Coalition in Haiti," *USDOS Disp.*, vol. 5, no. 38 (19 September 1994), 608–609.
99. Quoted in Elaine Sciolino, "Aristide Adopts a New Role: From Robespierre to Gandhi," *NYT* (18 September 1994): 14.
100. Donna Britt, "A Good Man Going Hungry for a Good Cause," *WP* (29 April 1994): D1.
101. "SS (31 August 1995)," 5: "SS (28 February 1996)," 5, folder "Hazel Ross-Robinson" (#4992), FARA. See also *Report of the Attorney General to the Congress of the U.S. on the Administration of the Foreign Agents Registration Act of 1938, As Amended* (DC: USGPO, 1995), 300–305, ibid. (1996), 187–190.
102. Karen de Witt, "At the End of the Day, A Lobbyist Turns into a Woodworker," *NYT* (22 August 1991): C12.
103. Karen de Witt, "Hunger Strike on Haiti: Partial Victory at Least," *NYT* (9 May 1994): A7, Christopher, *In the Stream of History*, 178.
104. "RS (20 August 1993)," exhibit A, folder "Stephanie Owens (#4943)," FARA. Aristide's predecessor had relied on the Beverly Hills firm Fouch Roseboro. *Report of the Attorney General [for] 1988, 1989, 1990, and 1991*, 476.
105. Data on political contributions is drawn from filings with the Federal Electoral Commission (www.opensecrets.org).

106. Tim Robbins and Susan Sarandon, "Our 23 Seconds at the Oscars," *LA Times* (5 April 1993): F3.
107. "An Urgent Message to President Clinton," *NYT* (23 March 1994): A10. Those who signed the letter were Hollywood stars (including Sigourney Weaver, Paul Newman, Julia Roberts, Danny Glover, Gregory Peck, Jack Lemmon, and Robin Williams), singers (including Sting and Harry Belafonte), members of Congress (including Black Caucus members Kweisi Mfume, Charles Rangel and John Conyers), NAACP executives, friends of Bill Clinton (including Quincy Jones and Mary Steenburgen), Randall Robinson, and clergymen (including Jesse Jackson, two rabbis, and three bishops).
108. Even though Aristide's Hollywood supporters (including Harry Belafonte and Jonathan Demme) narrated the documentary, Aristide did not directly produce it. Babeth and Rudi Stern, *Haiti: Killing the Dream* (Crowing Rooster Productions: 1992): Bob Shacochis, *The Immaculate Invasion* (NY: Penguin Books, 1999), 10.
109. Aristide and Christophe Wargny, *Tout moun se moun: tout homme est un homme* (Paris: Seuil, 1992), published in the United States as *Jean-Bertrand Aristide: An Autobiography* (NY: Orbis Books, 1993), Wargny, "Introduction," in Jean Bertrand Aristide, *Dignity* (Charlottesville: U. Press of Virginia, 1996), 32, Wargny, "La dignité d'un peuple," *Le Monde* (3 October 1991): 7.
110. Anthony Lake, *Six Nightmares: Real Threats in a Dangerous World and How America can Meet Them* (NY: Little, Brown, 2000), 135.
111. Reproduced in Ridgeway, *The Haiti Files*, 184–190.
112. Casimir did not give more specific details, making it difficult to assess the truthfulness of this rather fantastic claim. Raymond A. Joseph, "The American Press Corrupted," *Haïti Observateur* (22 December 1993): 7.
113. "Religious Leaders Urge Support for Haiti," *Christian Century* (24–31 March 1993): 315.
114. "Church Leaders Plan to Accompany Aristide," *Christian Century* (6 October 1993): 931.
115. "Churches Keep Pressure on US Haiti Policy," *Christian Century* (18 May 1994): 521.
116. The last previous case of a President-priest occurred in 1960, when Fulbert Youlou became president of Congo-Brazzaville. Jean-Michel Dumay, "La présidence et la prêtrise incompatibles," *Le Monde* (18 December 1990).
117. Among the many politicians with some legal training, one may mention Patrick Henry, Richard H. Lee, James Otis, John Adams, Thomas Jefferson, John Quincy Adams, Andrew Jackson, James Monroe, John C. Calhoun, Henry Clay, James K. Polk, Martin Van Buren, Benjamin Harrison, John Tyler, James Buchanan, Abraham Lincoln, Grover Cleveland, James Garfield, Rutherford B. Hayes, Chester Arthur, Franklin Pierce, William McKinley, William Jennings Bryan, Floyd Olson, Hiram Johnson, Robert M. La Follette, Theodore Roosevelt, William Howard Taft, Woodrow Wilson, William Gibbs McAdoo, J. Edgar Hoover, Warren G. Harding, Calvin Coolidge, John W. Davis, Franklin D. Roosevelt, Sam Rayburn, George W. Norris, Huey Long, Dean Acheson, Joseph McCarthy, Adlai Stevenson, John F. Dulles, George C. Wallace, Ralph Nader, Cyrus Vance, and Walter Mondale.
118. To defend himself in the trial accusing him of murdering Lafontant, Aristide hired another law firm, Rabinowitz and Boudin. The firm was paid $167,692 for its services in 1993–1994. "Supplemental Statement (1 December 1993)," 13–19: "SS (1 June 1994)," 12–15: "SS (31 December 1994)," 12–14: folder "Kurzban and Kurzban (#4604)," FARA.
119. To defend their regime in Washington and obtain foreign aid, François Duvalier collaborated with a PR firm headed by John Roosevelt (son of Franklin) and Jean-Claude Duvalier hired future Commerce Secretary Ronald Brown (then a partner in the Washington law firm Patton, Boggs and Blow). Diederich and Burt, *Haiti and its Dictator*, 105: *Report of the Attorney General [for] 1982, 199, Report of the Attorney General [for]1983,* 208.

120. "SS (1 February 1992)," 13: folder "Arent Fox (#2661)," FARA.
121. "SS (1 August 1993)," 3, 12: folder "Hogan and Hartson (#2244)," FARA.
122. Information on Barnes, Wides, and Kurzban's background is drawn from Tom Masland et al., "How Did We Get Here?," *Newsweek* (26 September 1994), 26; Ruth Shalit, "Flack Attack," *New Republic* (24 October 1994): 13; Catherine S. Manegold, "Innocent Abroad," *NYT* (1 May 1994). section 6, 38.
123. Barnes declared that his activities were performed *pro bono publico*. In fact, his firm received small payments. One document shows that his firm received a $2,000 monthly retainer; others say it earned a total of $10,000 from October 1991 to February 1993. *Report of the Attorney General [for] 1988, 1989, 1990, and 1991*, 475, "SS (1 June 1992)," 16–20, folder "Kurzban and Kurzban (#4604)":"SS (1 February 1992)," 34; "SS (1 August 1992)," 26; "SS (1 February 1993)," 20, folder "Arent Fox (#2661)," FARA.
124. "SS (1 August 1993)," 36, folder "Arent Fox (#2661)," FARA. See also "SS (30 June 1993)," 13–17, folder "Kurzban and Kurzban (#4604)," FARA.
125. "Registration Statement (26 May 1993)," exhibit B, folder "Hogan and Hartson (#2244)," FARA. See also "SS (1 August 1993)," 26; "SS (18 February 1994)," 49; "SS (30 August 1994)," 50; "SS (28 February 1995)," 34.
126. Data on political contributions is drawn from filings with the Federal Electoral Commission (www.opensecrets.org).
127. "SS (1 February 1992)," 43–44; "SS (1 August 1992)," 30; "SS (1 February 1993)," 24–25; "SS (1 August 1993)," 39; folder "Arent Fox (#2661),"; "SS (1 August 1993)," 31–32; "SS (18 February 1994)," 57; "SS (30 August 1994)," 56; "SS (28 February 1995)," 44–45; folder "Hogan and Hartson (#2244)," FARA.
128. For a complete list of Barnes' phone calls, see "SS (1 February 1992)," 18–30; "SS (1 August 1992)" 18–24; "SS (1 February 1993)," 17–19; "SS (1 August 1993);" folder "Arent Fox (#2661)"; "SS (1 August 1993)," 15–20; "SS (18 February 1994)," 20–43; "SS (30 August 1994)," 21–48; "SS (28 February 1995)," 24–32; folder "Hogan and Hartson (#2244)," FARA.
129. "SS (1 February 1992)," 39–40; "SS (1 August 1992)," 28; "SS (1 February 1993)," 22; "SS (1 August 1993)," 37; folder "Arent Fox (#2661)," FARA.
130. "SS (18 February 1994)," 53; "SS (30 August 1994)," 54; folder "Arent Fox (#2661)," FARA.
131. "SS (1 August 1993)," 17–35; folder "Arent Fox (#2661)"; "SS (1 August 1993)," 15–20; folder "Hogan and Hartson (#2244)," FARA.
132. "SS (1 February 1994)," 20; "SS (1 August 1994)," 19; "SS (1 February 1995)," 18; folder "Arent Fox (#2661)," FARA.
133. "SS (1 February 1994)," 22; "SS (1 August 1994)," 21; folder "Arent Fox (#2661)," FARA.
134. "SS (1 February 1993)," 17–19; "SS (1 February 1994)," 17–19; "SS (1 August 1994)," 15–18; folder "Arent Fox (#2661)," FARA.
135. "SS (30 June 1993)," 11–12; "SS (1 December 1993)," 11–12; "SS (1 June 1994)," 11; folder "Kurzban and Kurzban (#4604)," FARA.
136. "SS (1 June 1992)," 16–20; "SS (31 December 1992)," 11–13; "SS (30 June 1993)," 13–17; "SS (1 December 1993)," 13–19; "SS (1 June 1994)," 12–15; "SS (31 December 1994)," 12–14; folder "Kurzban and Kurzban (#4604)," FARA.
137. "SS (25 July 1996)," 3, folder "McKinney and McDowell Associates (#5139)," FARA.
138. Malval, *L'année de toutes les duperies*, 380.
139. Albright, *Madam Secretary*, 158. According to his hagiographer, Aristide lived "in a two-room apartment." Material things had "no importance." "You should not imagine him relaxing in an armchair with a newspaper, coffee on a little table, in the morning. He hardly knows how to sit or taste. . . . Eating is nonexistent." Wargny, "Introduction," in Aristide, *Dignity*, 32.

140. Commission présidentielle, untitled, folder "manuscripts commission présidentielle," box 320.01 COM, Collège St. Martial library.

141. Drawing from these funds was authorized by UNSC Resolution 873 (13 October 1993), but funds in the United States were made available to Aristide shortly after the coup. George Bush, *Message to the Congress Reporting on Economic Sanctions against Haiti* (7 April 1992), http://bushlibrary.tamu.edu/papers/1992/92040703.html.

142. One newspaper estimated that ATT offsets alone represented $2 million a month, but the figure seems inflated. "Les fonds de la AT&T déposés à Panama," *Haïti Observateur* (15 September 1993): 1.

143. "Scandale financier," *Haïti Observateur* (24 November 1993): 7. The newspaper has an anti-Aristide bias, but the figures are plausible.

144. Commission présidentielle, "Budget estimatif, 8 juillet 1992," folder "Commission présidentielle," box 320.01 COM, Collège St. Martial library.

145. Commission présidentielle, "Proposition de budget, 5 janvier 1993," folder "Documents CP (interne)," box 320.01 COM, Collège St. Martial library.

146. Malval, *L'année de toutes les duperies*, 12.

147. "SS (30 June 1993)," 13–17; "SS (1 December 1993)," 13–19; folder "Kurzban and Kurzban (#4604)," FARA.

148. "SS (1 August 1993)," 3, 4; folder "Mildred Trouillot (#4763)," FARA.

149. "SS (30 June 1993)," 13–17; "SS (1 December 1993)," 13–19; "SS (1 June 1994)," 12–15; "SS (31 December 1994)," 12–14; "SS (30 June 1995)," 12–16; "SS (31 December 1995)," 12–18; folder "Kurzban and Kurzban (#4604)," FARA.

150. "SS (28 June 1996)," 11–16, folder "Kurzban and Kurzban (#4604)"; "SS (31 August 1995)," 5, folder "Mildred Trouillot (#4763)," FARA.

151. Jean-François, *Le coup de Cédras*, 434–435.

152. The checks are reproduced in "Le conflit Aristide-Chine," *Haïti Observateur* (3–10 November 1993): 18.

153. Patrick Elie personal interview with the author (11 July 2001).

154. Christopher Caldwell, "From PAP to Gucci Gulch," *WSJ* (16 June 1994): A16.

155. "SS (31 December 1992)," 11–13; "SS (30 June 1993)," 13–17; folder "Kurzban and Kurzban (#4604)," FARA.

156. "SS (1 December 1993)," 13–19; "SS (1 June 1994)," 12–15; "SS (31 December 1994)," 12–14. folder "Kurzban and Kurzban (#4604)," FARA.

157. Mouterde and Wargny, *Apre bal, tanbou lou*, 155–156.

158. *Public Papers: Clinton*, vol. 1 (1993), 873–874; ibid., vol. 2 (1993), 1926; ibid., vol. 1 (1994), 816, 819, 819, Kim Ives, "Haiti's Second Occupation," in Deirdre McFadyen, Pierre LaRamée eds., *Haiti: Dangerous Crossroads* (Boston: South End Press, 1995), 111–112; Perusse, *Democracy Restored*, 97–98.

159. "I Am President of Haiti," *Time* (14 October 1991): 36.

160. Quoted in Stephanopoulos, *All Too Human*, 219.

161. Micha Gaillard personal interview with the author (9 July 2001). Haitians refer to themselves as "Niggers" (French *nègres* or Creole *neg*) and to foreigners as "Whites" (*blancs* or *blan*). Contrary to the English language, "White" has a pejorative connotation in Creole that "Nigger" has not.

162. Aristide, *In the Parish of the Poor*, 59. Haitians are generally suspicious of foreigners, particularly Americans. Tourists admiring the Episcopalian church's splendid murals in Port-au-Prince are often shocked to note that all the protagonists of the Last Supper are Blacks, except for Judas.

163. Aristide, *Dignity*, 47, 49, 56, 61, Patrick Elie personal interview with the author (11 July 2001).

164. "Antoine Izméry to George Bush, 4 November 1992," folder "Correspondance reçue," box 320.01 COM, Collège St. Martial library.

165. "Adrien à Aristide, 29 décembre 1992," folder "Manuscrits commission présidentielle," box 320.01 COM, Collège St. Martial library. Underlined in original.

166. Patrick Elie personal interview with the author (11 July 2001).
167. "Newsmaker Interview, Jean-Bertrand Aristide," *MacNeill-Lehrer News Hour* (22 October 1993).
168. Al. Fr., "Le président Aristide évoque l'idée d'une intervention armée pour chasser les putschistes," *Le Monde* (11 November 1993): 7.
169. Mentioned in "Many Would Welcome Force, Aristide Says," *Miami Herald* (10 November 1993): A23. Aristide confirmed his support for surgical strikes in a later interview. Christopher Marquis, "Aristide is Open to Attack on Haiti," *Miami Herald* (5 January 1994): A1.
170. Warren Christopher immediately rejected Aristide's deadline. Elaine Sciolino, "U.S. Rejects Call by Aristide to Reinstate Him in 3 Weeks," *NYT* (17 January 1994): A5.
171. Quoted in Howard W. French, "Doubting Sanctions, Aristide Urges US Action on Haiti," *NYT* (3 June 1994): A3.
172. "Pdt. Aristide's Address to TransAfrica's 13th Annual Foreign Policy Conference, 3 June 1994," blue folder, box 320.04 SIT, Collège St. Martial library.
173. "Acta de la séptima sesión," 5, 6 June 1994, OAS, OEA/Ser. F/V. 1 MRE/ ACTA 7/94.
174. [Lavalas], "Memorandum pour une rencontre avec le premier ministre" (c. Fall 1993), folder "Accord de Governors' Island, 1993," box 320.04 SIT, Collège St. Martial library.
175. Charles T. Williamson, *The U.S. Naval Mission to Haiti, 1959–1963* (Annapolis: Naval Institute Press, 1999), 10; Diederich and Burt, *Haiti and its Dictator*, 166–167. The predecessors were Florville Hyppolite (1888) and Guillaume Sam (1915); Heinl, *Written in Blood*, 294, 373.
176. Malval, *L'année de toutes les duperies*, 221; "Fritz Longchamp à Dante Caputo, 10 février 1993," folder "Situation politique en Haïti, 1994," box 320.04 SIT, Collège St. Martial library.
177. Scott Simon, "Pres. Aristide Says Haiti Needs Reconciliation," *NPR Weekend Edition* (25 June 1994).
178. "President Aristide to Secretary General," 2, UN S/1994/905 (29 July 1994).
179. "Permanent Representative Longchamp to Secretary General," 1, UN S/1994/910 (30 July 1994) (emphasis added), Boutros-Ghali, *Unvanquished*, 152–153.
180. Lake, *Six Nightmares*, 138–139.
181. Richard E. Feinberg telephone interview with the author (10 December 2001).
182. "SS (1 August 1993)," 17–35, folder "Arent Fox (#2661)," FARA. Barnes declined to respond to the author's request for an interview.
183. "SS (18 February 1994)," 20–43, folder "Hogan and Hartson (#2244)," FARA.
184. Christopher Marquis, "Spies, Lies and Subversion," *Miami Herald* (3 December 1993): 34A.
185. "SS (30 August 1994)," 21–48, folder "Hogan and Hartson (#2244)," FARA.
186. Lake, *Six Nightmares*, 133.
187. Anthony Lake telephone interview with the author (18 May 2001). Lake and Aristide remained on excellent terms; Lake spoke at Aristide's wedding on 20 January 1996 and is Aristide's daughter's godfather. Gary Pierre-Pierre, "Many in Haiti are Troubled by Marriage of Aristide," *NYT* (21 January 1996): section 1, 4.
188. Richard E. Feinberg telephone interview with the author (10 December 2001).
189. Télévision Nationale d'Haïti, "Aristide Addresses Nation Upon Return," *FBIS* (17 October 1994), 15.

Chapter Nine   Invading Haiti, Evading Responsibilities
(19 September–15 October 1994)

1. Due to the presence of a few Caribbean units, the force was dubbed multinational, but until the United Nations took over in April 1995, U.S. troops formed the bulk of, determined the policy of, and were virtually synonymous with, the MNF.

2. "LTG Henry H. Shelton Interview," in Cynthia L. Hayden, *JTF-180 Operation Uphold Democracy: Oral History Interviews* (Fort Bragg, NC: XVIII Airborne Corps, 1995), 62–63. Shelton commanded the MNF until 25 October 1994.

3. Clinton, *My Life*, 618. Tom Clancy and John Grisham, *Special Forces: A Guided Tour of US. Army Special Forces* (NY: Berkley Publishing Group, 2000), 28; Halberstam, *War in a Time of Peace*, 414, "Biography: Gen. Henry H. Shelton, Chairman Nominee," http://www.defenselink.mil/news/Jul1997/ n07171997_9707172.html.

4. Quoted in Elaine Sciolino, "Military Chief Hits the Ground Learning," *NYT* (5 December 1997): A1.

5. Richard B. Stolley, "Our Man in Haiti," *Life* (November 1994): 63.

6. "LTG Henry H. Shelton interview," in Hayden, *JTF-180 Oral History Interviews*, 62–63. Shelton's cultural appraisal was based on a conversation with Ambassador William L. Swing and Deputy Chief of Mission Barry Watson.

7. John R. Ballard, *Upholding Democracy: The U.S. Military Campaign in Haiti, 1994–1997* (Westport, CT: Praeger, 1998), 65–66.

8. "Major William B. Garret Interview," in Hayden, *JTF-180 Oral History Interviews*, 49.

9. The plan that was eventually implemented, dubbed "2380 Plus," was similar to 2375. Ballard, *Upholding Democracy*, 61–84; Kretchik, Baumann, Fishel, *Invasion, Intervention, "Intervasion,"* 78.

10. "LTC Timothy D. Vane Interview," in Hayden, *JTF-180 Oral History Interviews*, 158. Hackworth claims intelligence officers gave him all the details he asked for. Hackworth and Mathews, *Hazardous Duty*, 230–231.

11. John Barry and Douglas Walter, "How U.S. Forces Would Go In," *Newsweek* (19 September 1994): 41–42; Michael R. Gordon, "Top US Officials Outline Strategy for Haiti Invasion," *NYT* (14 September 1994): A1; Bradley Graham, "Paratroopers Carry Out Invasion Drill for Haiti," *WP* (14 September 1994): A16; John F. Harris and Bradley Graham, "U.S. Invaders would Rely on Massive Force, Night Operations," *WP* (17 September 1994): A10; Martin Merzer, "Invasion Likely to be a One-Two Three Punch," *Miami Herald* (17 September 1994): A16.

12. Ballard, *Upholding Democracy*, 106.

13. Bob Shacochis, *The Immaculate Invasion* (1999; reprint, NY: Penguin Books, 2000), 59. Miller's idea, first used in Haiti, was also employed during the war against Afghanistan in 2001.

14. Lee "Major William B. Garret interview," in Hayden, *JTF-180 Oral History Interviews*, 49.

15. See most interviews in Hayden, *JTF-180 Oral History Interviews* and *JTF-190 Oral History Interviews*.

16. Lawrence E. Casper, *Falcon Brigade: Combat and Command in Somalia and Haiti* (Boulder, CO: Lynne Rienner, 2001), 213.

17. Clinton, "U.S. Interests in Haiti" and "Announcement of Military Leaders' Agreement," in *USDOS Disp.*, vol. 5, no. 38 (19 September 1994) 605, 611, 612.

18. Joint Chiefs of Staff, *Joint Pub. 3–07.3; Joint Tactics, Techniques, and Procedures for Peace Operations* (12 February 1999), I–6, I7.

19. Casper, *Falcon Brigade*, 201.

20. Lt. Gen. John J. Sheehan, the Director of Operations at the office of the Joint Chiefs of Staff, later admitted that the "rapid transition . . . overtook JTF capability to distribute the latest revision to rules of engagement (ROE) carry cards force-wide prior to arrival of forces in Haiti," *Situation in Haiti: Hearing before the CAS, USS, 28 September 1994* (DC: USGPO, 1994), 21–23.

21. Colin Powell, "US Forces: Challenges Ahead," *Foreign Affairs* (Winter 1992–1993): 32–45, Powell, "Why Generals Get Nervous," *NYT* (8 October 1992): A35.

22. Quoted in Paula Zahn, "Senate Minority Leader Robert Dole Discusses Impending Military Invasion of Haiti," *CBS This Morning* (14 September 1994), Lawrence P. Rockwood telephone interview with the author (26 February 2001).

23. Lawrence P. Rockwood telephone interview with the author (26 February 2001), Goff, *Hideous Dream,* 191, "CPT Ralph Holstein Interview," in Hayden, *JTF-180 Oral History Interviews,* 183–185.
24. Larry Rohter, "Cables Show U.S. Deception on Haitian Violence," *NYT* (6 February 1996): A8.
25. Lawrence P. Rockwood telephone interview with the author (26 February 2001).
26. "LTC Edward J. Anderson Interview," in Hayden, *JTF-180 Oral History Interviews,* 306.
27. "COL James L. Campbell Interview," in Hayden, *JTF-190 Oral History Interviews,* 51. UNSC Resolution 940 specified that the United Nations would take over after a secure and stable environment had been established.
28. "Douglas Watson Interview," in Hayden, *JTF-190 Oral History Interviews,* 60–61.
29. "COL James S. Gulick Interview," in Hayden, *JTF-190 Oral History Interviews,* 127.
30. "CPT Berthony Ladouceur Interview," in Hayden, *JTF-180 Oral History Interviews,* 170.
31. Nicolas Jallot and Laurent Lesage, *Haïti: dix ans d'histoire secrète* (Paris: Editions du Félin, 1995), 171, Howard W. French, "Is Voodoo the Weapon to Repel the Invaders?" *NYT* (24 June 1994): A4.
32. Kretchik, Baumann, Fishel, *Invasion, Intervention, "Intervasion,"* 154; Tod Robberson, "Are You Now, or Have You Ever Been, a Werewolf?," *WP* (14 November 1994): A12.
33. "COL Richard J. Quirk III Interview," "COL Michael L. Sullivan Interview," in Hayden, *JTF-190 Oral History Interviews,* 101, 353.
34. "CPT Carl G. Ayers Interview," in Hayden, *JTF-180 Oral History Interviews,* 369.
35. "CW3 Jerry M. Hanchett Interview," in Hayden, *JTF-190 Oral History Interviews,* 210.
36. Christophe Martin personal interview with the author (30 June 2001).
37. Stan Goff, *Hideous Dream: A Soldier's Memoir of the U.S. Invasion of Haiti* (NY: Soft Skull Press, 2000), 117.
38. "LTC Linton Graham Interview," in Hayden, *JTF-190 Oral History Interviews,* 35–36.
39. Headquarters, Department of the Army, *Field Manuel 41–10* (11 January 1993), 1/4, 1/9.
40. Casper, *Falcon Brigade,* 221.
41. In September 1995, the price rose to $100 for a handgun and $200 for semi-automatic weapons and grenades. The program stopped in February 1996. In 1915, the U.S. consul in Cap Haïtien had pursued a similar policy, giving 50 gourdes to each soldier (100 gourdes to each officer) who turned in his weapons.
42. Marco Tulio Bruni Celli, UN Economic and Social Council Commission on Human Rights, *Situation of Human Rights in Haiti* (6 February 1995), E/CN.4/1995/59.
43. Casper, *Falcon Brigade,* 219.
44. Kretchik, Baumann, Fishel, *Invasion, Intervention, "Intervasion,"* 157.
45. Goff, *Hideous Dream,* 453–475.
46. "General John Shalikashvili White House Briefing," *Federal News Service* (20 September 1994).
47. John Kifner, "Haitian Police Crush Rally as American Troops Watch," *NYT* (21 September 1994): A1, Garry Pierre-Pierre, "Family Mourns Man Killed by Police," *NYT* (24 September 1994): section 1, 4.
48. "1994 Daily Press Briefing no. 135: Wednesday, 9/21/94," in Dept. of State Bureau of Public Affairs, *US Foreign Affairs on CD-ROM, January 1990-May 1996,* vol. 4, no. 1 (DC: Department of State, June 1996).
49. 16th MP brigade commander Col. Michael L. Sullivan delivered the same message to Michel Francois. "MG David C. Meade interview," "COL Michael L. Sullivan interview," in Hayden, *JTF-190 Oral History Interviews,* 10, 353, "LTG Henry H. Shelton interview," in Hayden, *JTF-180 Oral History Interviews,* 66.
50. The following overview of the Cap Haïtien gunfight is drawn from Eric Schmitt, "How a Tense Standoff in Haiti Erupted into a Deadly Shootout with the Marines," *NYT* (27 September 1994): A16; William Booth, "Crowds Ransack Barracks in Haitian City," *WP* (26 September 1994): A1; Richard A. Serrano, "Marine who Fired First Saw Ambush," *LA Times* (27 September 1994): A1.

51. "Rapport du Lt-Col. Josaphat sur les incidents du Cap Haïtien," reproduced in *Le Nouvelliste* (27 September 1994): 1.

52. The Haitian Army and the police were one and the same. Many soldiers, for fear of retaliation, did not even wear a uniform.

53. William Booth, "Crowds Ransack Barracks in Haitian City," *WP* (26 September 1994): A1.

54. "Rapport du Lt-Col. Josaphat sur les incidents du Cap Haïtien," *Le Nouvelliste* (27 September 1994), 1; Signal FM, "FADH Issues Communiqué on Cap Haïtien Shooting," *FBIS* (27 September 1994), 19; William Booth, "Crowds Ransack Barracks in Haitian City," *WP* (26 September 1994): A1.

55. William Booth, "Crowds Ransack Barracks in Haitian City," *WP* (26 September 1994): A1.

56. "LTG Henry H. Shelton Interview," in Hayden, *JTF-180 Oral History Interviews*, 64, 66.

57. Larry Rohter, "5 Haitians Killed as Explosion Rips Democratic Rally," *NYT* (30 September 1994): A1.

58. John Kifner, "Pro-Junta Gunmen Fire on Rally in Haitian Capital," *NYT* (1 October 1994): section 1, 1. On 7 and 9 October, two trucks drove into Aristide supporters, killing 6 people at Etang Bois-Neuf and 14 in Dimizaine.

59. John Kifner, "To Cheers, U.S. Troops Clear Haitian Gunmen's Clubhouse," *NYT* (4 October 1994): A1.

60. "LTG Henry H. Shelton Interview," in Hayden, *JTF-180 Oral History Interviews*, 64.

61. The following section is drawn from telephone interview with Lawrence P. Rockwood (26 February 2001), "LTC Frank B. Bragg interview," in Hayden, *JTF-190 Oral History Interviews*, 79–87, U.S. vs. Lawrence P. Rockwood, II, no. 98–0488, Crim. App. no. 9500872; *U.S. Policy and Activities in Haiti, Hearing before the CIR, HR, 24 February 1995* (DC: USGPO, 1995); *Human Rights Violations at the PAP Penitentiary, Hearing before the SWHA, CIR, HR, 3 May 1995* (DC: USGPO, 1995); 10th MD, *Civil Military Operations Handbook* (unpublished, 1 February 1992), Headquarters, Dept. of the Army, *Field Manuel 41–10, 11 January 1993* (DC: USGPO, 1994), Kretchik, Baumann, Fishel, *Invasion, Intervention, "Intervasion,"* 171–174, Warren D. Hall, *The Obligation to Protect Human Rights: A New Legal Requirement for Commanders?* (Carlisle Barracks, PA.: US Army War College, 1996).

62. His father had liberated a concentration camp in Czechoslovakia during World War II. In 1990, Rockwood did the same trip with his daughter and stepson.

63. Rockwood was also familiar with the case of Gen. Tomoyuki Yamashita, former commander of Japanese forces in Philippines, sentenced to death in 1945 for failing to protect U.S. prisoners.

64. "COL Richard J. Quirk III interview," in Hayden, *JTF-190 Oral History Interviews*, 96.

65. "For security reasons and the need for US national control, only US assets will perform the following services and functions:. . . . (6) US military prisoner confinement operations (7) Accountability for and security of EPWs [Enemy Prisoners of War] retained in US custody." Troops must also enquire about penal institutions, including number, location and capacity of jails, "adequacy (sanitary and health conditions)" and "treatment of prisoners." Headquarters, Dept. of the Army, *Field Manuel 41–10* (11 January 1993), 10/6, B8. See also 10th MD, *Civil Military Operations Handbook* (unpublished, 1 February 1992), V12.

66. CNVJ, *Si m Pa Rele*, chapter 4, 2.1, Dan Coughlin, "The Case of Lawrence P. Rockwood," *Haïti Progrès* (20 March 1995): 1; Douglas Farah, "Americans Find Victims of Squalor, Sadism in Jails," *WP* (12 October 1994): A28.

67. Lawrence P. Rockwood telephone interview with the author (26 February 2001). Rockwood could have filed an anonymous complaint but chose not to do so. One cannot help but surmise that, like many other idealists, Rockwood longed for martyrdom.

68. Quoted in David Hackworth, "When Duty and Conscience Clash," *Newsweek* (22 May 1995): 38.

69. One month later, 100 such prisoners escaped from Haiti's National Penitentiary. Larry Rohter, "Over 100 Inmates Escape From Haiti's Main Prison," *NYT* (1 November 1994): A16.

70. *Human Rights Violations at the PAP Penitentiary, Hearing before the SWHA, CIR, HR, 3 May 1995* (DC: USGPO, 1995), 5–6.

71. Ibid., 2–3. See also *U.S. Policy and Activities in Haiti, Hearing before the CIR, HR, 24 February 1995* (DC: USGPO, 1995), 13–14.

72. Lawrence P. Rockwood telephone interview with the author (26 February 2001).

73. Rockwood, "Court-Martial: A Soldier's Story," *WSJ* (4 April 1995): A20; Lawrence T. Di Rita, "Court Martial with Haitian Policy Links," *Washington Times* (17 April 1995) David Hackworth, "When Duty and Conscience Clash," *Newsweek* (22 May 1995): 38; Hackworth and Mathews, *Hazardous Duty*, 245–249; Stephen Wrage, "A Question of Duty," *Newsweek* (22 November 1999): 52–54; Sylvie Kauffmann, "La désobéissance humanitaire d'un capitaine de l'armée américaine," *Le Monde* (19 May 1995): 1.

74. "COL Michael L. Sullivan Interview," in Hayden, *JTF-190 Oral History Interviews*, 353.

75. *Human Rights Violations at the PAP Penitentiary, Hearing before the SWHA, CIR, HR, 3 May 1995* (DC: USGPO, 1995), 5–6.

76. *U.S. Policy and Activities in Haiti, Hearing before the CIR, HR, 24 February 1995* (DC: USGPO, 1995), 14.

77. John Kifner, "To Cheers, U.S. Troops Clear Haitian Gunmen's Clubhouse," *NYT* (4 October 1994): A1.

78. FRAPH and Haitian Army documents seized during the invasion, 160,000 pages in all, were sent to DIA headquarters near Washington D.C., then to the U.S. Embassy in Port-au-Prince. The Haitian Foreign Ministry and the Haitian Truth Commissions have made repeated demands to get all the documents back, so far unsuccessfully (the U.S. government will only release an expurgated version of the documents without the names of American citizens, which the Haitian government refuses). The author's demands to access those documents, made under the FOIA, were also turned down. "Françoise Boucard à Al Gore, 14 novembre 1995," in CNVJ, *Si m Pa Rele*, 369–70; Dan Coughlin, "Haiti: U.S. Withholding Documents on FRAPH," *Inter Press Service Wire* (10 October 1995); Irwin P. Stotzky, *Silencing the Guns in Haiti: The Promise of Deliberative Democracy* (Chicago: U. of Chicago Press, 1997), 166–170; Christopher S. Wren, "U.S. Agrees to Return Documents Soldiers Confiscated in Haiti," *NYT* (7 December 1995): A11.

79. Constant also met CIA Haiti station chief John Kambourian on 3 October 1994. Allan Nairn, "He's our SOB," *Nation* (31 October 1994): 481.

80. "LTG Henry H. Shelton Interview," in Hayden, *JTF-180 Oral History Interviews*, 65–66.

81. Quoted in "FRAPH Chief Urges Reconciliation, End to Violence," *FBIS* (6 October 1994), 14. On 27 October 1994, Constant also "humbly request[ed] to meet the president [Aristide] as soon as possible to discuss the possibility of holding a peace conference, which would lead to a national reconciliation pact." "FRAPH Leader Wants to Propose Peace Conference," *FBIS* (31 October 1994), 21.

82. Quoted in "Defendants' Memorandum in Support of their Motion to Dismiss, Constant vs. Christopher and Reno, Civil Action no. WMN95–3814 (11 May 1996)," 12, personal collection (DOJ FOIA request).

83. "FRAPH Leader Calls for Supporters to Lay Down Arms," *AFP Wire* (4 October 1994). For a picture of the scene, see *NYT* (8 October 1994): 4.

84. "Newsmaker Interview, William Perry," *MacNeill-Lehrer News Hour* (5 October 1994).

85. Allan Nairn, "Haiti under the Gun," *Nation* (8–15 January 1996): 11–15.

86. When the invasion was called back, they found themselves back in Fort Bragg, unable to field questions in Haiti. The plane they chartered also encountered hydraulic problems, so they were not operational until 20 September. "LTC Timothy D. Vane Interview," in Hayden, *JTF-180 Oral History Interviews*, 157.

87. Casper, *Falcon Brigade*, 191, 205.

88. "LTC Timothy D. Vane Interview," in Hayden, *JTF-180 Oral History Interviews*, 157.

89. Ibid., 158, Jamie McIntyre, "Journalists, Pentagon in Conflict Over Haiti Coverage," *CNN News* (30 September 1994).

90. Bill Gertz, "U.S. Wages Psychological War on Cédras' Junta," *Washington Times* (13 September 1994): A1.
91. Stephen D. Brown, "PSYOP in Operation Uphold Democracy," *Military Review* (September-October 1996), 57–73; Ballard, *Upholding Democracy*, 112; "CPT Carl G. Ayers Interview," in Hayden, *JTF-180 Oral History Interviews*, 369.
92. "Maj. John M. Kidd interview," in Hayden, *JTF-180 Oral History Interviews*, 357; Eric Schmitt, "A Quick Landing to Cheers of 'Merci, Merci!'" *NYT* (21 September 1994): A14.
93. Shacochis, *The Immaculate Invasion*, 75–76, Goff, *Hideous Dream*, 38–39, 50, 93.
94. Quoted in Richard A. Serrano, "1,800 Marines Poised at Brink of Invasion; Then a Stand-Down," *LA Times* (19 September 1994): A5.
95. Ballard, *Upholding Democracy*, 117.
96. Hayden, *JTF-180 Oral History Interviews*, Hayden, *JTF-190 Oral History Interviews*.
97. In the Gulf War, over the course of 6 months, there were eight suicides in a force of 650,000 troops. One soldier killed himself in Somalia, where a total of 96,000 troops spent 15 months. Casper, *Falcon Brigade*, 240–241, 264.
98. Quoted in Gregory Beals and Marcus Mabry, "Haitian Stress Syndrome?" *Newsweek* (31 October 1994): 38.
99. "Maj. Eric D. Cipriano Interview," in Hayden, *JTF-190 Oral History*, 291, 292, 295.
100. Hugh Shelton, by comparison, later became Chairman of the Joint Chiefs of Staff.
101. "LTG Henry H. Shelton Interview," in Hayden, *JTF-180 Oral History Interviews*, 64.
102. Signal FM, "Cédras Said Wounded Following Resignation," *FBIS* (12 October 1994), 7; John Kifner, "A General Departs, to the Rich and Bitter Sarcasm of the People he Ruled," *NYT* (11 October 1994): A14.
103. "LTG Henry H. Shelton interview," in Hayden, *JTF-180 Oral History Interviews*, 64.
104. Casper, *Falcon Brigade*, 234.
105. Despite reservations about his drug-dealing connections, Alex Cédras was admitted into the United States for treatment.
106. Kenneth Freed personal interview with the author (10 April 2002), Freed, "U.S. Gives Cedras a Lucrative Deal to Get Out of Haiti," *LA Times* (14 October 1994): A1. Freed's sources included Cédras and U.S. officials.

Chapter Ten   Peacekeeping (15 October 1994–31 March 1995)

1. The following overview of Aristide's return to Haiti is drawn from Radio Métropole, "Mayor Paul Views Cleanup, Presidential Candidacy," *FBIS* (13 October 1994), 8; Signal FM, "Preparations for Aristide Return Reported," *FBIS* (14 October 1994), 12; Kevin Fedarko, "Deliverance," *Time* (24 October 1994): 28; Casper, *Falcon Brigade*, 234–235; Christopher, *In the Stream of History*, 182–183; Stotzky, *Silencing the Guns*, 1–4.
2. Warren Christopher, "Resuming the Journey to Freedom and Reconstruction," *USDOS Disp.*, vol. 5, no. 43 (DC: USGPO, 24 October 1994), 717.
3. Quoted in Stotzky, *Silencing the Guns*, 2.
4. Ken Ringle, "When Reality Loses Its Grip," *WP* (25 October 1994): D1; Aristide and Laura Flynn, *Eyes of the Heart: Seeking a Path for the Poor in the Age of Globalization* (Monroe, ME: Common Courage Press, 2000), 75.
5. Télévision Nationale d'Haïti, "Aristide Addresses Nation Upon Return," *FBIS* (17 October 1994), 15.
6. Stotzky, *Silencing the Guns*, 213.
7. "Crowds Swart Aristide's First Trip Outside Palace," *AFP Wire* (17 October 1994), Kenneth Freed personal interview with the author (10 April 2002).
8. Clinton, "U.S. Interests in Haiti," *USDOS Disp.*, vol. 5, no. 38 (19 September 1994), 606. Clinton's vision conflicted with what Boutros-Ghali defined as the essential tasks of a peacekeeping mission: "disarming the previously warring parties and the restoration of

order, the custody and possible destruction of weapons, repatriating refugees, advisory and training support for security personnel, monitoring elections, advancing efforts to protect human rights, reforming or strengthening governmental institutions and promoting formal and informal processes of political participation." Boutros Boutros-Ghali, *An Agenda for Peace: Preventive Diplomacy, Peacemaking and Peace-Keeping* (NY: UN, 1992), 32.

9. UNSC, S/RES/940 (31 July 1994). Soldiers initially hoped that they would be back by Christmas, but the deadline for the transition to a UN force was finally set for March 1995. UNSC, S/RES/975 (30 January 1995).

10. The United States took over the sparsely populated northern reaches of Mexico after the war of 1848, but refused to annex Yucatán, the Dominican Republic, and Cuba when it had a chance to do so. At the height of U.S. interventionism in the Caribbean, the United States sent troops to Nicaragua (1910), Haiti (1915), and the Dominican Republic (1916), only to withdraw its forces a few years later. Whenever possible, the U.S. used surrogate forces to achieve its Cold War goals, as in Guatemala (1954), Cuba (1961), Brazil (1964), and Chile (1973). Schoultz, *Beneath the United States*, 41–43, 80–83, 139–140. On the U.S. preference for indirect influence, see Jerome Slater, "Is U.S. Foreign Policy 'Imperialist' or 'Imperial?'" *Political Science Quarterly*, vol. 91, no. 1 (Spring 1976), 63–87; James Petras et al., "The Monroe Doctrine and U.S. Hegemony in Latin America," in Petras, ed., *Latin America: From Dependence to Revolution* (NY: John Wiley, 1973).

11. Hans Schmidt, *The U.S. Occupation of Haiti, 1915–1934* (New Brunswick, NJ: Rutgers, 1971), 69–70, 82–84.

12. Schoultz, *Beneath the United States*, 258–260, 270–271.

13. "Règlements généraux des Forces Armées d'Haiti," *Le Moniteur* (13 July 1987).

14. Aristide eliminated the position of section chief in 1991, then again when he returned to power in 1994. For a description of the Haitian police's role and history, see Robert E. Maguire, *Demilitarizing Public Order in a Predatory State: The Case of Haiti, North-South Agenda Papers no. 17* (Coral Gables: North-South Center Press, 1995).

15. To further diminish reliance on U.S. personnel, the directive said, the United States should delegate training duties to police monitors drawn from third countries. U.S. State Dept. Office of International Information Programs, *White Paper, PDD 71, Strengthening Criminal Justice Systems in Support of Peace operations and Other Complex Contingencies* (24 February 2000), www.fas.org/irp/offdocs/pdd/index.html.

16. Larry Rohter, "Aristide Forces Retirement of Haiti's Top Military Officers," *NYT* (22 February 1995): A4.

17. Charles T. Williamson, *The U.S. Naval Mission to Haiti, 1959–1963* (Annapolis: Naval Institute Press, 1999), 83, 99.

18. "COL Michael L. Sullivan interview," in Hayden, *JTF-190 Oral History Interviews*, 353.

19. "COL Michael L. Sullivan interview," in Hayden, *JTF-190 Oral History Interviews*, 353.

20. The company, MVM Inc. provided 20 to 25 people for a minimum of $850,000 (depending on the duration of the mission). "US State Department Daily Press Briefing no. 147: Friday, 10/14/94," in State Dept. Bureau of Public Affairs, *US Foreign Affairs on CD-ROM, January 1990-May 1996*, vol. 4, no. 1 (DC: State Department, June 1996).

21. The Department of Justice's program was ICITAP (International Criminal Investigation Training Assistance Program), designed to help Latin American countries improve their judicial systems. Section 534(b)(3), *Foreign Assistance Act of 1961* (P.L. 87–195).

22. The following overview of the selection and role of the interim force is drawn from Human Rights Watch, *Security Compromised: Recycled Haitian Soldiers on the Police Front Line*, vol. 7, no. 3 (DC: HRW/Americas, 1995); *The Human Rights Record of the HNP*, vol. 9, no. 1 (DC: HRW/Americas, 1997).

23. William G. O'Neill, "Building a New Police Force and Justice System," *Crime and Justice International*, vol. 9, no. 3 (June-July 1996); Larry Rohter, "Haiti Resists Increasing Police Force," *NYT* (18 June 1995): section 1, 4; Douglas Farah, "Haiti Rests Hopes on New Police," *WP* (3 July 1995): A16.

24. The 24 December 1994 law creating the national police stated that policemen "are essentially apolitical," but the first cadres had to be chosen in priority among former soldiers and screened by political bodies such as the prime minister, the minister of justice, the minister of the interior, and the director of the police (himself a presidential appointee). Public outcry (clameur publique) could also disqualify policemen. *Le Moniteur* (28 December 1994): 714, 739.

25. Prosper Avril, *Vérités et révélations, II: L'armée d'Haïti, bourreau ou victime?* (PAP: Le Natal, 1997).

26. Michael Norton, "Firefight at Headquarters Underlines Danger Posed by Discharged Soldiers," *AP Wire* (27 December 1994).

27. Jonathan Dworken et al., *Haiti Demobilization and Reintegration Program: An Evaluation Prepared for the USAID* (Alexandria, VA.: Institute for Public Research, March 1997), 14, 1, 21. See also David Holiday and William Staley, "Beyond the Mountains, More Mountains: Demobilizing the Haitian Army," in Tommie Sue Montgomery, ed., *Peacemaking and Democratization in the Western Hemisphere* (Coral Gables, FL: North-South Center Press, 2000).

28. "MG David C. Meade Interview," in Hayden, *JTF-190 Oral History Interviews*, 10.

29. "Newsmaker Interview, Jean-Bertrand Aristide," *MacNeill-Lehrer News Hour* (12 October 1994).

30. Chris Torchia, "Former Costa Rican President Urges Haiti to Abolish Army," *AP Wire* (17 November 1994).

31. *Le Moniteur* (28 December 1994): 739.

32. Aristide and Flynn, *Eyes of the Heart*, 77.

33. Larry Rohter, "Aristide Forces Retirement of Haiti's Top Military Officers," *NYT* (22 February 1995): A4.

34. John Kifner, "To Cheers, U.S. Troops Clear Haitian Gunmen's Clubhouse," *NYT* (4 October 1991): A1.

35. Pierre-Yves Glass, "Ex-Soldiers Storm Army Headquarters," *AP Wire* (26 December 1994).

36. Michael McCabe, "Soldier from Cupertino Killed in Haiti," *San Francisco Chronicle* (14 January 1995): A17; "Wife of Slain Soldier Said He Did Feel Safe in Haiti," *Wilmington Star-News* (14 January 1995): 3B.

37. The following overview of the Mireille Durocher-Bertin case is drawn from documents declassified in three congressional hearings, *Haiti: Human Rights and Police Issues, Hearing before the CIR, HR, 4 January 1996* (DC: USGPO, 1996); *Administration Actions and Political Murders in Haiti, Hearing before the CIR, HR, 26 June 1996* (DC: USGPO, 1996); *Administration Actions and Political Murders in Haiti, Part II, Hearing before the CIR, HR, 27 September 1996* (DC: USGPO, 1996).

38. Michael Norton, "Haiti Coup Supporter Assassinated," *AP Wire* (28 March 1995); Dominique Levanti, "Murder of Aristide Opponent Unsettles UN Handover," *AFP Wire* (29 March 1995).

39. "Maj. General George A. Fisher to Honorable Jean Joseph Exumé, 22 March 1995," in *Haiti: Human Rights and Police Issues, Hearing before the CIR, HR, 4 January 1996* (DC: USGPO, 1996), 99–100.

40. "Jean Bertin to Senator Jesse Helms, 31 March 1995," in *Haiti: Human Rights and Police Issues, Hearing before the CIR, HR, 4 January 1996* (DC: USGPO, 1996), 101.

41. Eric Schmitt, "Pentagon lists 27 People who Face Threat of Death in Haiti," *NYT* (7 April 1995): A1.

42. "Edwin H. Boldt to Jean-Claude Nord, 13 July 1995," in *Haiti: Human Rights and Police Issues, Hearing before the CIR, HR, 4 January 1996* (DC: USGPO, 1996), 195–196.

43. "Ambassador William L. Swing to his Excellency Jean-Bertrand Aristide, 11 July 1995," "Swing to Aristide, 27 July 1995," in *Haiti: Human Rights and Police Issues, Hearing before the CIR, HR, 4 January 1996* (DC: USGPO, 1996), 95–98.

44. "Swing to Aristide, 11 July 1995," in *Haiti: Human Rights and Police Issues, Hearing before the CIR, HR, 4 January 1996* (DC: USGPO, 1996), 95–96.

45. "James McGuirk to Richard J. Giannotti, 10 July 1995," in *Haiti: Human Rights and Police Issues, Hearing before the CIR, HR, 4 January 1996* (DC: USGPO, 1996), 193–194.

46. "Paul E. Mallet to James McGuirk, 16 August 1995," in *Haiti: Human Rights and Police Issues, Hearing before the CIR, HR, 4 January 1996* (DC: USGPO, 1996), 247.

47. "Burton V. Wides to Richard A. Clarke, 23 August 1995," in *Haiti: Human Rights and Police Issues, Hearing before the CIR, HR, 4 January 1996* (DC: USGPO, 1996), 255–256.

48. "PAP 6276, 1 September 1995," in *Administration Actions and Political Murders in Haiti, Part II, Hearing before the CIR, HR, 27 September 1996* (DC: USGPO, 1996), 79.

49. *Human Rights and Police Issues, Hearing before the CIR, HR, 4 January 1996* (DC: USGPO, 1996), 19.

50. Classified documents reproduced in congressional hearings are too expurgated to confirm or contradict this assertion. *Administration Actions and Political Murders in Haiti, Hearing before the CIR, HR, 26 June 1996* (DC: USGPO, 1996), 7–9, 37–53.

51. "Burton V. Wides to Mark M. Richard, 2 May 1995," "Wides to Richard, 8 June 1995," in *Haiti: Human Rights and Police Issues, Hearing before the CIR, HR, 4 January 1996* (DC: USGPO, 1996), 154–161.

52. Radio Métropole, "Moise Brothers Denounce U.S. Republicans," *FBIS* (6 October 1995), 12.

53. "James F. Dobbins to the Deputy Secretary, 16 August 1996," in *Administration Actions and Political Murders in Haiti, Part II, Hearing before the CIR, HR, 27 September 1996* (DC: USGPO, 1996), 80.

54. *Administration Actions and Political Murders in Haiti, Hearing before the CIR, HR, 26 June 1996* (DC: USGPO, 1996), 18.

55. "Smarck Michel To Whom It May Concern, 19 May 1995" in *Haiti: Human Rights and Police Issues, Hearing before the CIR, HR, 4 January 1996* (DC: USGPO, 1996), 173.

56. "Burton V. Wides to Louis H. Freeh, 26 June 1995," in *Haiti: Human Rights and Police Issues, Hearing before the CIR, HR, 4 January 1996* (DC: USGPO, 1996), 169–172.

57. "Paul E. Mallett to James McGuirk, 26 July 1995," "McGuirk to Mallett, 27 July 1995," in *Haiti: Human Rights and Police Issues, Hearing before the CIR, HR, 4 January 1996* (DC: USGPO, 1996), 201–202.

58. Burton Wides, "Do as we Say, Not as we Do: The Real Record of Haiti's Cooperation with the FBI in the Durocher-Bertin Case," in *Haiti: Human Rights and Police Issues, Hearing before the CIR, HR, 4 January 1996* (DC: USGPO, 1996), 319–320; *CR* (21 September 1995), S14070–S14071.

Chapter Eleven   Nation Building: Great Expectations
(31 March 1995–June 1997)

1. UNSC, S/RES/975 (30 January 1995), 1. MNF Commander Meade had declared that such an environment existed as early as 4 January, 1995. White House Office of the Press Secretary, "Fact Sheet on Haiti," in Ballard, *Upholding Democracy*, 238.

2. UNSC, S/RES/975 (30 January 1995), 1, S/1995/46 (17 January 1995), par. 87.

3. *Public Papers: Clinton, vol.* 1 (1995), 438; Larry Rohter, "Clinton, in Haiti, Marks the Withdrawal of GIs," *NYT* (1 April 1995): section 1, 1.

4. Boutros-Ghali, *Unvanquished*, 219.

5. Boutros-Ghali, *Fiftieth Anniversary Annual Report on the Work of the Organization* (NY: UN, 1996), 235.

6. UNSC, S/RES/975 (30 January 1995), S/RES/1048 (29 February 1996), S/RES/1063 (28 June 1996).

7. *Public Papers: Clinton*, vol. 1 (1995), 437.

8. "Remarks by President Clinton, Boutros-Ghali, Aristide at UN Transition Ceremony March 31," *U.S. Newswire* (3 April 1995).

9. Richard E. Feinberg telephone interview with the author (10 December 2001). Feinberg was referring to Irwin P. Stotzky's *Silencing the Guns in Haiti: The Promise of Deliberative Democracy* (Chicago: U. of Chicago Press, 1997), which blamed Haiti's subsequent political and economic failure on a lack of U.S. commitment.

10. Anthony Lake interview with the author (18 May 2001).

11. PL 104–107 (HR 1868), section 583 (a), *CR* (21 September 1995), S14070–S14071, Thomas W. Lippman, "GOP Maneuvers Delay Money for Haiti Elections," *WP* (8 October 1995): A18. When the administration issued the required certification, Dole wrote Clinton accusing Aristide and Préval of having masterminded political murders. *Haiti: The Situation after the Departure of the US Contingent from UNMIH, Hearing before the SWHA, CIR, HR, 28 February 1996* (DC: USGPO, 1996), 63–64.

12. Michael Wines, "GOP Adds Hearings to its Election Arsenal," *NYT* (23 July 1996): A13; Frank Swoboda, "House Republicans Question Clinton Ties to 'Mob-Dominated' Labor Union," *WP* (26 July 1996): A28.

13. *Haiti: Human Rights and Police Issues, Hearing before the CIR, HR, 4 January 1996* (DC: USGPO, 1996), *Administration Actions and Political Murders in Haiti, Hearing before the CIR, HR, 26 June 1996* (DC: USGPO, 1996), *Administration Actions and Political Murders in Haiti, Part II, Hearing before the CIR, HR, 27 September 1996* (DC: USGPO, 1996).

14. Schmidt, *The U.S. Occupation of Haiti*, 99.

15. Quoted in Heinl, *Written in Blood*, 503.

16. "I will not be—and cannot be—a candidate," Aristide declared at the White House on 16 September 1994. "Meeting of the Multinational Force Coalition in Haiti," *USDOS Disp.*, vol. 5, no. 38 (19 September 1994), 609.

17. Larry Rohter, "The Suspense Isn't Over in Haiti," *NYT* (15 October 1995): section 4, 1; Michael Norton, "Haiti's Aristide: Will He Or Won't He Step Down?" *AP Wire* (18 October 1995).

18. Radio Galaxie, "Aristide Announces Upcoming Change of Government," *FBIS* (23 October 1995), 39–40.

19. "This Week with David Brinley," *ABC News* (26 November 1995). See also Clinton's interview in Wickham, *Clinton and Black America*, 199.

20. Michelle Faul, "New Leader Takes Power in Haiti," *AP Wire* (7 February 1996).

21. The following overview of Préval's life is drawn from Michael Norton, "Préval: From Middle-Class to Grass Roots to President," *AP Wire* (7 Februrary 1996).

22. Michelle Faul, "New Leader Takes Power in Haiti," *AP Wire* (7 February 1996).

23. Quoted in "Nul ou médiocre?" *L'Express*, no. 2321 (28 December 1995): 7.

24. MICIVIH, *Communiqué de presse CP/MOE/97/03* (8 April 1997); Amnesty International, *Haiti: Still Crying Out for Justice* (London: AI Publications, July 1998), 3–4; Michael Norton, "OAS Observers Question Legality of Discounting Blank Ballots," *AP Wire* (10 May 1997).

25. "Meeting of the Multinational Force Coalition in Haiti," *USDOS Disp.*, vol. 5, no. 38 (19 September 1994), 609. After the invasion, but before he came back to Haiti, Aristide's promises, made in a speech to the UN General Assembly, had shifted to the more ambiguous "Yes to reconciliation! No to violence! No to vengeance! *No to impunity*! Yes to justice!" [emphasis added.] Quoted in "Aristide's Talk: 'Yes to Reconciliation,'" *NYT* (5 October 1994): A17.

26. On 30 October 1994, 100 prisoners, including former police officers held on human rights charges, escaped from Haiti's National Penitentiary. Larry Rohter, "Over 100 Inmates Escape From Haiti's main prison," *NYT* (1 November 1994): A16.

27. "Rights Groups Say no Haitian Amnesty for Crimes against Humanity," *AFP Wire* (8 October 1994). Under ART. 147 of the 1987 Constitution, the president can only give political, not criminal, amnesty.

28. Human Rights Watch, *Thirst for Justice: A Decade of Impunity in Haiti*, vol. 8, no. 7B (NY: HRW, September 1996).

29. "An Interview with Father Adrien," *America* (18 February 1995): 15.
30. *Le Moniteur* (17 August 1998): 12158.
31. The following overview of the CNVJ's activities is drawn from CNVJ, *Si M Pa Rele*. The CNVJ was composed of Françoise Boucard (president), three Haitians (Ertha Elysée, Freud Jean, René Magloire), and three foreigners (Oliver Jackman from Barbados, replaced by Trinidad's Emmanuel Des Iles on 20 April 1995, Senegal's Wally Ndiaye, and Jamaica's Patrick Robinson).
32. *Le Moniteur* (30 March 1995): 353.
33. CNVJ, *Si m Pa Rele*, chapter 5, C2.
34. Amnesty International, *Haiti: Still Crying Out for Justice* (London: AI Publications, July 1998), 7–9, *Annual Report 1999* (London: AI Publications, 1999), 186–187.
35. State Department, *Country Reports on Human Rights Practices for 1998* (DC: USGPO, February 1999), *Le Moniteur* (17 August 1998): 1158.
36. Human Rights Watch, *World Report 1999* (NY: HRW, 1999), 130–131, *World Report 2000* (NY: HRW, 2000), 132.
37. "LTG Henry H. Shelton interview," in Hayden, *JTF-180 Oral History Interviews*, 65–66.
38. "Defendants' Memorandum in Support of Their Motion to Dismiss, Constant vs. Christopher and Reno, Civil Action no. WMN95–3814 (11 May 1996)," 3–4, personal collection (DOJ FOIA request).
39. "Defendants' Memorandum in Support of their Motion to Dismiss, Constant vs. Christopher and Reno, Civil Action no. WMN95–3814 (11 May 1996)," 4–5, personal collection (DOJ FOIA request).
40. "Janet Reno to Warren Christopher (20 April 1995)," 1, "Memorandum for the Attorney General (12 April 1995)," 1, personal collection (DOJ FOIA request), U.S. Immigration Court, Baltimore, "In the Matter of Emmanuel Constant, Respondent," (11 September 1998), 2–3, personal collection (INS FOIA request).
41. U.S. Immigration Court, Baltimore, "In the Matter of Emmanuel Constant, Respondent" (1 September 1995), 15, 18, personal collection (INS FOIA request); Matthew Purdy, "Hiding in Plain Sight: Search for a Haitian Exile," *NYT* (24 May 1995): section B, 1.
42. "Defendants' Memorandum in Support of their Motion to Dismiss, Constant vs. Christopher and Reno, Civil Action no. WMN95–3814 (11 May 1996)," 2–3, personal collection (DOJ FOIA request). Constant then dropped his financial claim and asked for declaratory relief only.
43. Ibid., 1–2, 18.
44. Ibid., 4–5, 10–16.
45. Quoted in William Branigin, "Foe of Aristide Now a 'Detainee' in Maryland Jail," *WP* (27 October 1995): A3.
46. Ed Bradley, "Toto Constant," *CBS 60 Minutes* (3 December 1995).
47. Human rights violators deemed particularly useful for national security could remain on the CIA payroll with a special authorization. The cleanup was motivated by the case of Col. Julio Roberto Alpirez, a Guatemalan CIA informer who tortured to death the husband of Boston lawyer Jennifer Harbury. R. Jeffrey Smith, "CIA Drops Over 1,000 Informants; Two-Year 'Scrub' Finds Poor Sources, Serious Criminals," *WP* (2 March 1997): A1.
48. U.S. Immigration Court, Baltimore, "In the Matter of Emmanuel Constant, Respondent" (11 September 1998), 13, personal collection (INS FOIA request).
49. Marie-Andre Auguste, "Coup Leader, Army Officers Given Life in Prison for 1994 Haitian Massacre," *AP Wire* (16 November 2000); Sarah Kershaw, "Renewed Outcry on Haitian Fugitive in Queens," *NYT* (12 August 2000): B2.
50. "Rep. Joseph P. Kennedy III to William J. Clinton (11 July 1996)," 1, personal collection (DOJ FOIA request). See also Larry Rohter, "A Haitian Set for Deportation is Instead Set Free by the US," *NYT* (22 June 1996): A5.

51. "Assistant Attorney General Andrew Fois to Rep. Joseph P. Kennedy III (30 August 1996)," personal collection (DOJ FOIA request).

52. "Defendants' Memorandum in Support of their Motion to Dismiss, Constant vs. Christopher and Reno, Civil Action no. WMN95–3814 (11 May 1996)," 6, 4–5, 37, personal collection (DOJ FOIA request).

53. U.S. Immigration Court, Baltimore, "In the Matter of Emmanuel Constant, Respondent" (11 September 1998), 5, personal collection (INS FOIA request); David Grann, "Giving 'The Devil' His Due," *Atlantic Monthly* (June 2001): 68.

54. "Mary Jane Candaux to Amy, Gerry and Seth [Waxman] (20 May 1996)," 1, "Jamie S. Gorelick Memorandum (24 May 1996)," 1, personal collection (DOJ FOIA request).

55. "Molly to Seth [Waxman] (22 May 1996)," 1, personal collection (DOJ FOIA request). The actual text of the embassy's cable is not declassified.

56. "CIA to Seth Waxman" (11 June 1996), personal collection (CIA FOIA request); David Grann, "Giving 'The Devil' His Due," *Atlantic Monthly* (June 2001): 68.

57. "Office of Immigration Litigation Bill Howard to Seth Waxman (14 June 1996)," 4, personal collection (DOJ FOIA request). See also Attorney General, "Memorandum for the Office of Cabinet Affairs, The White House" (20 June 1996), personal collection (DOJ FOIA request).

58. David Grann, "Giving 'The Devil' His Due," *Atlantic Monthly* (June 2001): 68.

59. IMF, *Haiti: Selected Issues* (DC: IMF, February 2002), 4, IMF; Mark Weisbrot et al., *The Emperor has no Growth: Declining Economic Rates in the Era of Globalization* (DC: Center for Economic and Policy Research, September 2000) 17; Robert G. King and Ross Levine, "Finance, Entrepreneurship, and Growth: Theory and Evidence," *Journal of Monetary Economics*, vol. 32, no. 3 (December 1993), 513–542.

60. World Bank, *World Development Indicators 2001* (DC: World Bank, 2001), 44, 194.

61. Coopers and Lybrand, *Haiti: Private Sector Assessment* (July 1997), iii, microenterprise collection, USAID Library, PAP.

62. Clinton, *Between Hope and History*, 163. "I keep telling everybody, whether it's in Haiti or the Middle East, we've got to prove that these poor people can get some benefits from peace," said Clinton in a November 1995 interview. Wickham, *Clinton and Black America*, 199.

63. Heinl, *Written in Blood*, 561.

64. Patrick J. Sloyan, "Army's Role in Rebuilding Haiti," *Newsday* (9 October 1994): A5.

65. Stan Goff, *Hideous Dream*, 119–120.

66. "LTC Edward J. Anderson Interview," in Hayden, *JTF-180 Oral History Interviews*, 308.

67. James L. Walker and Giovanni Caprio, *Haiti Macroeconomic Assessment, Staff Working Papers* no. 3 (February 1991), 2, financial assistance collection, USAID Library, PAP.

68. IBRD, *Consultative Group for Haiti, Paris, Jan. 30–31, 1995, Chairman's Report of Proceedings, For Official Use Only* (3 May 1995), financial assistance collection, USAID Library, PAP.

69. "U.S. Signs Agreement to Help Haiti Revitalize Its Economy," *NYT* (16 December 1994): A5.

70. World Bank Poverty Reduction and Economic Management Unit, *Report no. 17242–HA, Haiti: The Challenges of Poverty Reduction, Volume I* (DC: World Bank, August 1998), 20.

71. Coopers and Lybrand *Haiti: Private Sector Assessment* (July 1997), iv, microenterprise collection, USAID Library, PAP.

72. *U.S. Policy and Activities in Haiti, Hearing before the CIR, HR, 24 February 1995* (DC: USGPO, 1995), 14.

73. Coopers and Lybrand, *Haiti: Private Sector Assessment* (July 1997), International Development Association, *Haiti: Economic Policy Framework Paper for FY 1996–1997 to 1998–1999, For Official Use Only* (30 September 1996); Phillip W. Rourk, *Projection des éventuelles opportunités d'un commerce complémentaire entre Haïti et la République Dominicaine* (22 September 1995), *microenterprise collection;* Haiti consultative group,

Absorptive Capacities: Provisional Report (11–12 May 1995); Paul Moreno-López et al. [Inter-American Development Bank], *Haiti: Country Paper* (October 1996), financial assistance collection, USAID library, PAP.

74. U.S. State Department, *1998 Country Reports on Economic Policy and Trade Practices* (DC: USGPO, January 1999), 274, *2000 Country Reports* (DC: USGPO, 2001), 279.

75. Coopers and Lybrand, *Haiti: Private Sector Assessment* (July 1997), v, microenterprise collection, USAID library, PAP. See also Haiti consultative group, *Absorptive Capacities: Provisional Report* (11–12 May 1995), 1, financial assistance collection.

76. World Bank Poverty Reduction and Economic Management Unit, *Report no. 17242–HA, Haiti: The Challenges of Poverty Reduction, Volume I* (DC: World Bank, August 1998), 20.

77. World Bank, *Report no. 13849–HA, Road Maintenance and Rehabilitation Project* (DC: World Bank, 28 February 1995), 23, 31–32.

78. Paul Moreno-López et al. [Inter-American Development Bank], *Haiti: Country Paper* (October 1996), annex III, 15, financial assistance collection, USAID library, PAP.

79. Schmidt, *The U.S. Occupation of Haiti*, 96–97.

80. U.S. State Department, *FY 2000 Country Commercial Guide: Haiti* (DC: USGPO, 1999), 32.

81. U.S. State Department, *2000 Country Reports on Economic Policy and Trade Practices* (DC: USGPO, 2001), 276.

82. Al Gore, "Haiti: Celebrating One Year of the Return to Freedom and Democracy," *USDOS Disp.*, vol. 6, no. 44 (May 1995), 792–793.

83. *U.S. Policy and Activities in Haiti, Hearing before the CIR, HR, 24 February 1995* (DC: USGPO, 1995), 96–105; *Haiti: The Situation after the Departure of the U.S. Contingent from UNMIH, Hearing before the SWHA, CIR, HR, 28 February 1996* (DC: 1996), 25–27.

84. *Haiti: The Situation after the Departure of the US Contingent from UNMIH, Hearing before the SWHA, CIR, HR, 28 February 1996* (DC: USGPO, 1996), 7.

85. HR 2606 Sec 559 (a), 4–6. Clinton vetoed the bill because the amounts spent on foreign aid and other foreign activities were too small. *CR* (18 October 1999), H10, 142–10, 143

86. In addition to the 7–8 March 1995 mission led by Strobe Talbott, tours were held on 24–26 July 1995 (agribusiness), 8–10 August 1995 (handicrafts), 22–24 August 1995 (minority business), and 29–31 October 1995 (light manufacturing).

87. "US State Department Daily Press Briefing no. 29, 03/06/95," in State Dept Bureau of Public Affairs, *US Foreign Affairs on CD-ROM, January 1990–May 1996*, vol. 4, no. 1 (DC: State Dept., June 1996).

88. "Plan of Action," *USDOS Disp. Supplement*, vol. 6, no. 2 (May 1995), 16.

89. Public Law 106–200 (H.R. 434).

90. IMF, *IMF Staff Country Report, Haiti: Selected Issues* (DC: IMF, January 2001), 41.

91. Abbott, *The Duvaliers and Their Legacy*, 203, 276; Heinl, *Written in Blood*, 683.

92. Inspector General, USAID, *PL 480, Title II Food Program: Three PVOs: CARE, CWS, SAWS USAID/Haiti, Audit Report no. 1–521–83–9* (29 April 1983); Inspector General, USAID, *PL 480, Title II Food Program: Catholic Relief Services, USAID/Haiti, Audit Report no. 1–521–83–10* (29 April 1983), NSA. See also Inspector General, USAID, *Audit of Rural Health Delivery Systems, USAID/Haiti project no. 521–0091, Audit Report no. 1–521–86–03* (26 November 1985), NSA.

93. International Development Association, *Haiti: Economic Policy Framework Paper for FY 1996–1997 to 1998–1999, For Official Use Only* (30 September 1996), 27–38, microenterprise collection, USAID Library, PAP.

94. IBRD, *Consultative Group for Haiti, Paris, Jan. 30–31, 1995, Chairman's Report of Proceedings, For Official Use Only* (3 May 1995); Paul Moreno-López et al. [Inter-American Development Bank], *Haiti: Country Paper* (October 1996), annex IX, financial assistance collection, USAID Library, PAP. The small U.S. share in the overall aid package apparently resulted from congressional opposition, not from the Clinton administration's skimpiness. Wickham, *Clinton and Black America*, 199–200.

95. Paul Moreno-López et al. [Inter-American Development Bank], *Haiti: Country Paper* (October 1996), v, annex VIII, 1, financial assistance collection, USAID Library, PAP.
96. State Dept., 1998 *Country Reports on Economic Policy and Trade Practices* (DC: USGPO, January 1999), 270–274.
97. *Rapport du Secrétaire Général sur les Missions des Nations Unies en Haïti* (14 February 1996), UN/S/1996/112.
98. Axel van Trotsenburg and Alan MacArthur, *The HIPC Initiative: Delivering Debt Relied to Poor Countries* (DC: IMF, February 1999), www.worldbank.org/hipc/related-papers/related-papers.html, State Department., *1998 Country Reports on Economic Policy and Trade Practices* (DC: USGPO, January 1999), 270–274; IMF, *Heavily Indebted Poor Countries* (HIPC) *Initiative—Perspectives on the Current Framework and Options for Change* (DC: IMF, April 1999).
99. "Carrying Privatization Football, Aristide Feints Left, Cuts Right," *Haïti Progrès* (13 September 1995): 1; Michael Norton, "Haitians Protest Presence of Foreign Troops, Privatization Plans," *AP Wire* (19 September 1995).
100. "Tipper Gore's Staff Scared, but Unhurt in Stone-Throwing Incident," *AP Wire* (15 October 1995).
101. Michael Norton, "Former Dictator Flees to Embassy after Police Arrest Daughter," *AP Wire* (8 November 1995).
102. Quoted in Douglas Farah, "Haiti's Nascent Prospects Turn Suddenly Bleak," *WP* (26 November 1995): A1.
103. Prosper Avril, *Vérités et révélations, II: L'armée d'Haïti, bourreau ou victime?* (PAP: Le Natal,1997), 465–467; Douglas Farah, "U.S.-Haitian Relations Deteriorate; Disarmament Dispute, Contact with Ex-Ruler Infuriate Aristide," *WP* (29 November 1995): A1. In May 2001, Haitian policemen finally arrested Avril and sent him to prison. "Prosper Avril restera-t-il sous les verrous?" *Haïti Progrès* (30 May 2001): 1.
104. Télévision Nationale d'Haïti, "Aristide Speaks at Funeral Ceremony, Urges Disarmament," *FBIS* (14 November 1995), 3–6. See also Mouterde and Wargny, *Apre bal, tanbou lou*, 206–207.
105. Douglas Farah, "Haiti's Nascent Prospects Turn Suddenly Bleak," *WP* (26 November 1995): A1.

Chapter Twelve   Nation Building: Hard Times
(9 June 1997–7 February 2001)

1. Micivih, *Communiqué de presse CP/MOE/97/03* (8 April 1997), *Communiqué de presse CP/MOE/97/04* (27 May 1997), www.un.org/rights/micivih/elecen.htm, Amnesty International, *Haiti: Still Crying Out for Justice* (London: AI Publications, July 1998), 3–4; Michael Norton, "OAS Observers Question Legality of Discounting Blank Ballots," *AP Wire* (10 May 1997).
2. "Haitian Premier Resigns Amid Election Fraud Crisis," *AP Wire* (9 June 1997).
3. Michael Norton, "Gunshots Fired at Haiti's National Palace," *AP Wire* (19 August 1996); Dominique Levanti, "Police Quell Attempted Coup at Haiti's Presidential Palace," *AFP Wire* (17 December 2001).
4. Under the 1987 Constitution, the government must be confirmed by both chambers of Parliament (ART. 158).
5. World Bank, *Haiti: External Financing* (December 1997), 1, microenterprise collection, USAID Library, PAP.
6. "Haiti Leader to Rule by Decree; An Attack Follows," *NYT* (13 January 1999): A8.
7. Amnesty International, *Haiti: Unfinished Business, Justice and Liberties at Risk* (NY: AI USA Publications, 2000), 2; Larry Rohter, "Political Feuds Rock Haiti: So Much for Its High Hopes," *NYT* (19 October 1998): A6.

8. Amnesty International, *Haiti: Unfinished Business, Justice and Liberties at Risk* (NY: AI USA Publications, 2000), 14. See also Human Rights Watch, *The Human Rights Record of the HNP*, vol. 9, no. 1 (DC: HRW/Americas, 1997), 17–25. One must point out that the previous police force, even more violent and corrupt, encouraged, rather than fired, bad apples.

9. Human Rights Watch, *The Human Rights Record of the HNP*, vol. 9, no. 1 (DC: HRW/Americas, 1997), 7. See also *Security Compromised: Recycled Haitian Soldiers on the Police Front Line*, vol. 7, no. 3 (DC: HRW/Americas, 1995).

10. Amnesty International, *Haiti: Unfinished Business, Justice and Liberties at Risk* (NY: AI USA Publications, 2000), 9–10.

11. Tammerlin Drummond, "A Constabulary of Thugs," *Time* (17 February 1997): 62.

12. Larry Rohter, "UN Troops to Leave Haiti as Feeble as they Found It," *NYT* (4 December 1997): A1; "Haitian Dissident is Freed," *NYT* (12 December 1997): A15.

13. Mark Fineman, "Despite US Intervention, Strife Still Plagues Haiti," *LA Times* (15 November 1999): A1; David Gonzalez, "Civilian Police Force Brings New Problems in Haiti," *NYT* (26 November 1999): A26.

14. Human Rights Watch, *World Report 2001* (NY: HRW, 2001), 133.

15. The army prevented families of victims from retrieving bodies, so the exact number of victims remains uncertain. Marie-Andre Auguste, "Coup Leader, Army Officers Given Life in Prison for 1994 Haitian Massacre," *AP Wire* (16 November 2000).

16. Antoine responded favorably. "François Séverin à Pierre Max Antoine, 7 janvier 1999," "François Séverin à Pierre Max Antoine, 29 décembre 1999," folder 3, Correspondance du cabinet présidentiel, 1998, Haitian Ministry of Justice archives.

17. Amnesty International, *Haiti: Unfinished Business, Justice and Liberties at Risk* (NY: AI USA Publications, 2000), 16–20; Peter Bosch and Yves Colon, "Haiti's Prisons: Inside the Gates of Hell," *Miami Herald* (25 March 2001): 1L.

18. Quoted in Jean-Michel Caroit, "En toute impunité, les 'chimères' font régner la terreur en Haïti," *Le Monde* (11 April 2000): 4. See also "Ceux qui ont assassiné Jean Dominique . . . ," *Haïti Progrès* (5 April 2000): 1, "Dignes et émouvantes funérailles pour Jean Dominique," *Haïti Progrès* (12 April 2000): 1.

19. Human Rights Watch, *World Report 2001*, 130–131.

20. In June 2001, the judge investigating the case temporarily left Haiti, fearing for his life. "Qu'est-ce qui fait encore 'hurler' Dany Toussaint?" *Haïti Progrès* (6 June 2001): 1, "Le juge Gassant pourra-t-il reprendre le dossier?" *Haïti Progrès* (27 June 2001): 1.

21. David Gonzalez, "Dumped Ballots Raise Worries in Haiti Vote," *NYT* (23 May 2000): A3.

22. "Haiti's Top Election Official Flees Nation for US," *NYT* (19 June 2000): A10.

23. "Haiti Opposition Reports Post-Election Arrests," *NYT* (26 May 2000): A9.

24. Human Rights Watch, *World Report 2001*, 131–132.

25. "L'Axe: Convergence-IRI-Union Européenne, un cheval de Troie nommé la France," *Haïti en Marche* (10 February 2001): 1.

26. "Détournement de fonds publics!" *Haïti Progrès* (21 March 2001): 1.

27. Broadcast on *Radio Métropole* (21 June 2001). Art. 20 of the 1987 Constitution prohibits the death penalty.

28. Eric Schmitt, "A Quick Landing to Cheers of 'Merci, Merci!'" *NYT* (21 September 1994): A14.

29. Pierre-Raymond Dumas, "Problèmes en perspectives," *Le Nouvelliste* (26 September 1994): 5, "Le 'nasyonalis' tounen kolabo," *Libete* no. 105 (7–27 September 1994): 1.

30. Quoted in Douglas Farah, "U.S.-Haitian Relations Deteriorate; Disarmament Dispute, Contact with Ex-Ruler Infuriate Aristide," *WP* (29 November 1995): A1.

31. Aristide et al., "Pour la concorde nationale: déclaration de Floride" (26–29 June 1992), 6, folder "Accord de Governors' Island, 1993," box 320.04 SIT, Collège St. Martial library.

32. IBRD, *Consultative Group for Haiti, Paris, Jan. 30–31, 1995, Chairman's Report of Proceedings, For Official Use Only* (3 May 1995), 4, 6, annex 3, 1–3, financial assistance collection, USAID Library, PAP.

33. Aristide and Flynn, *Eyes of the Heart*, 30–31.
34. Signal FM, "Aristide Speaks out on Privatization," *FBIS* (4 October 1995), 8. See also Aristide, *Eyes of the Heart*, 32. Aristide also called for land reform, not privatization. "We will continue to work together so we can manage to assure that Haiti does not remain in the hands of a few people without being able to produce" enough food for everyone. Signal FM, "President Highlights Land Reform at Commemorative Mass," *FBIS* (19 October 1995), 30.
35. Radio Métropole, "Prime Minister Discusses Privatization," *FBIS* (2 October 1995), 10; Rosny Smarth et al., *Haïti: possibilités économiques et privatisation* (PAP: La Ruche, 1996), 12; "Haitian Premier Resigns Amid Election Fraud Crisis," *AP Wire* (9 June 1997).
36. State Department, *2000 Country Reports on Economic Policy and Trade Practices* (DC: USGPO, 2001), 276.
37. Aristide and Flynn, *Eyes of the Heart*, 9–17.
38. "President of the Republic of Haiti to the Secretary General" (23 June 1995), UN A/49/926, 8.
39. "Louis Harold Joseph à Fritz Longchamp, 15 mars 1999," folder 3, Correspondance du cabinet présidentiel, 1998, Haitian Ministry of Justice archives.
40. The UN secretary general did not even bother to transmit the request to the UN Security Council. UNSC S/2001/328 through /500, "Pourquoi Fanmi Lavalas veut-il une nouvelle mission de l'ONU?" *Haïti Progrès* (18 April 2001): 1.
41. Garry Pierre-Pierre, "Haitians Expect Thousands to March Against Brutality," *NYT* (28 August 1997): B4; Robert D. McFadden and Tina Kelley, "Angry Mourners and Police Clash at Funeral of Man Shot by Officer," *NYT* (26 March 2000): section 1, 1. Most officers involved in the Louima case were later acquitted. William Glaberson, "A Ruling on Legal Basics," *NYT* (1 March 2002): A1.
42. Quoted in Michael Norton, "Back on Center Stage, Haiti's Aristide is Frustrating Washington-Again," *AP Wire* (13 June 1997).
43. Quoted in *Report of the Secretary General on the UN Transition Mission to Haiti* (31 October 1997), S/1997/832, *Le Moniteur* (17 August 1998), 1159.
44. The following overview of the Navassa controversy is drawn from Roy F. Nichols, "Navassa: A Forgotten Acquisition," *American Historical Review*, vol. 38 no. 3 (April 1933), 505–510, U.S. Code, Title 48, Chapter 8, Sections 1411–1419, Secretary's Order 3210 (3 December 1999), Geoffrey Mohan and Mark Fineman, "U.S., Haiti Dispute Guano Island's Fate," *Newsday* (22 November 1998); Larry Rohter, "Whose Rock is It? And, Yes, the Haitians Care," *NYT* (19 October 1998): A4, A20.
45. "SS (31 August 1996)," 14, 21, folder "Hogan and Hartson (#2244)," FARA.
46. Ibid., 18.
47. Wides' monthly retainer further dropped to $6,500 in 2000. "SS (1 August 1995)," 15; "RS (1 October 1998)," exhibit A; "SS (31 October 1999)," 11–17; "SS (31 October 2000)," 5, folder "Arent Fox (#2661)," FARA.
48. "SS (31 August 1995)," 5; "SS (28 February 1996)," 5; "SS (31 August 1996)," 5; "SS (28 February 1997)," 5; "SS (1 August 1997)," 5; "SS (28 February 1998)," 5; "SS (28 August 1998)," 5; "SS (28 February 1999)," 5; "SS (29 February 2000)," 5; folder "Hazel Ross-Robinson (#4992), FARA.
49. "SS (30 June 1995)," 11–16; "SS (31 December 1995)," 12–18; "SS (28 June 1996)," 11–16, "SS (31 December 1996)," 11–15, folder "Kurzban and Kurzban (#4604)," FARA.
50. U.S. Attorney General, *Report of the Attorney General to the Congress of the U.S. on the Administration of the Foreign Agents Registration Act of 1938, As Amended* (DC: USGPO, 1995), 300–305, ibid. (1996), 187–190.
51. Al Gore, "Haiti: Celebrating One Year of the Return to Freedom and Democracy," *USDOS Disp.*, vol. 6, no. 44 (May 1995), 792.
52. *Policy toward Haiti Following the Withdrawal of UN Forces, Hearing before the CIR, HR, 9 December 1997* (DC: USGPO, 1997), 13.

53. U.S. Department of State, *Focus on the Issues: The Americas, Excerpts of Testimony, Speeches and Remarks by Madeleine K. Albright on Colombia, Economic Issues, Panama, Mexico, Cuba, Caribbean Ministerial, and Haiti* (DC: State Dept. Department), 2000, 45.

54. Douglas Farah, "General Calls for Pullout from Haiti," *WP* (13 March 1999): A13.

55. *Haiti: Prospects for Free and Fair Elections, Hearing before the CIR, HR, 5 April 2000* (DC: USGPO, 2000), 5–6.

56. The cover read "Failing Haiti: American Illusions Meet Caribbean Reality." Charles Lane, "Haiti's Deteriorating Democracy: Island of Disenchantment," *New Republic* (29 September 1997): 17–24.

57. Johanna McGeary, "Did the America Mission Matter?" *Time* (19 February 1996): 36; Jean-Michel Caroit, "Haïti, la grande désespérance," *Le Monde* (2 July 1999): 14.

58. UNSC, S/RES/1212 (25 November 1998).

59. Human Development Sector Management Unit, Latin America and the Caribbean Region, *HIV/AIDS in the Caribbean: Issues and Options: A Background Report, Report no. 20491-LAC* (DC: World Bank, June 2000), 11.

60. By 1999, only two of Haiti's nine public companies, the flour and cement factories, had been privatized. Others (including two banks, the port and airport authorities, and the telephone company) remained publicly owned. State Dept *2000 Country Reports on Economic Policy and Trade Practices* (DC: USGPO, 2001), 276.

61. Michel Camdessus, *Press Conference* (DC: 24 April 1997), www.imf.org/external/np/tr/1997/tr970424.htm. In September 2000, the United States finally decided that further aid to Haiti would be funneled through private channels. David Gonzalez, "US to Withhold Money for Haiti's Presidential Elections," *NYT* (6 September 2000): A10.

62. Aristide and Flynn, *Eyes of the Heart*, 11–12.

63. Ibid., 79.

64. "Fanmi Lavalas: un choix sans retour," *Haïti Progrès* (11 April 2001): 1.

65. Personal experience.

66. République d'Haïti, *Plan d'action gouvernemental* (May 1999), 65, microenterprise collection, USAID Library, PAP.

67. IMF, *IMF Staff Country Report, Haiti: Selected Issues* (DC: IMF, January 2001), 9, IMF, *World Economic Outlook* (DC: IMF, 26 April 2001), 174.

68. Coopers and Lybrand, *Haiti: Private Sector Assessment* (July 1997), iii, microenterprise collection, USAID Library, PAP.

69. Eric Verhoogen et al., *The U.S. in Haiti: How to Get Rich on 11 Cents an Hour* (NY: National Labor Committee, January 1996).

70. Jamil Salmi, *Equity and Quality in Private Education: The Haitian Paradox, LCSHD Paper Series no. 18* (DC: World Bank, May 1998), 16.

71. International Narcotics Control Strategy Reports are available on the State Department's website at www.state.gov/www/global/narcotics_law/narc_reports_mainhp.html.

72. Bureau for International Narcotics and Law, *1996 International Narcotics Control Strategy Report* (DC: U.S. Department of State, 1997), www.state.gov/www/global/narcotics_law/1996_narc_report_carib96.html.

73. Ibid., *1997 Report*, www.state.gov/www/global/narcotics_law/1997_narc_report_carib97.html.

74. Ibid., *1998 Report*, www.state.gov/www/global/narcotics_law/1998_narc_report_carib98_part2.html.

75. Ibid.

76. Tim Weiner, "A Leader of Former Haitian Junta is Charged with Smuggling Tons of Drugs to US," *NYT* (8 March 1997): A6; William Branigin, "INS Inspector Charged in Drug Scheme; Indictment Says Smuggling Ring Headed by Haitian Fugitive Exploited Ethnic Ties," *WP* (2 May 1998): A2.

77. Bureau for International Narcotics and Law, *1996 report, 1997 report, 1998 report, 1999 report*. See also Committee on Government Reform and Oversight, *National Drug Policy: A Review of the Status of the Drug War* (DC: USGPO, 1996).

78. Bureau for International Narcotics and Law, *1999 Report*, www.state.gov/www/global/narcotics_law/1999_narc_report_carib99_part3a.html.
79. Ibid., *2000 Report*, www.state.gov/www/g/inl/rls/nrcrpt/2000/889.htm.
80. A country is subject to certification when it presents a significant drug problem. It is certified if it collaborates with the U.S. government in the antidrug war. If it does not, a country can nevertheless be certified for national security reasons. Otherwise, a country loses its certification, which translates into a U.S. refusal to send foreign aid or to vote for foreign aid in international institutions such as the IMF. In 2001, out of 24 countries subject to certification, 20 received a full certification, 2 (including Haiti) were certified on national security grounds, and two were denied certification entirely. Bureau for International Narcotics and Law, *2000 Report*. In 2002, the numbers were 23, 2 (Haiti and Afghanistan), and 1 (Burma), respectively; in 2003, 23, 2 (Haiti and Guatemala), and 1 (Burma). Bureau for International Narcotics and Law, *2001 Report*, www.state.gov/www/g/inl/rls/nrcrpt/2001/rpt/8479.htm, Bureau for International Narcotics and Law, *2002 Report*, www.state.gov/g/inl/rls/nrcrpt/2002/html.
81. *CR* (2000), H5977.
82. *CR* (2000), H5975–5977, PL 106–429 (HR 4811), Sec 558 (a).
83. "More than 400 Haitian Boat People Repatriated," *AP Wire* (24 November 1997).
84. "Cuba, Haiti," *Migration News,* vol. 6, no. 3 (March 1999).
85. Michael Norton, untitled [international news], *AP Wire* (30 November 1995).
86. Michael Finkel, "Desperate Passage," *NYT* (18 June 2000): Section 6, 50, is the exception.
87. Public Law 105–100 (HR 2607), 19 November 1997.
88. Public Law 105–277 (HR 4328), 21 October 1998.
89. *Public Papers: Clinton*, vol. 1 (1996), 476–477.
90. The following overview of the departure of U.S. troops is drawn from Michael Norton, untitled, *AP Wire* (18 January 2000); Dan Perry, "Last U.S. Military Plane Leaves Haiti, Marking End of Permanent Mission," *AP Wire* (20 January 2000); "U.S. Military Support Group in Haiti Pulling Out January 21," *AFP Wire* (20 January 2000); Rita Braver, "Mission Accomplished?" *CBS Sunday Morning* (30 January 2000); "Relocalisation de bases US en Haïti?" *Haïti Progrès* (19 January 2000), "Une nouvelle stratégie électorale des USA?" *Haïti Progrès* (26 January 2000): 1.
91. Shown on Rita Braver, "Mission Accomplished?," *CBS Sunday Morning* (30 January 2000).
92. Quoted in Dan Perry, "Last U.S. Military Plane Leaves Haiti, Marking End of Permanent Mission," *AP Wire* (20 January 2000).
93. On 31 January, a four-man rear group led by Army Lt. Col. Ray Duncan, who had stayed behind to shut the camp and turn off the lights, left Haiti on a civilian flight. Temporary U.S. missions of 150–200 soldiers later visited Cap Haïtien (January–March 2000), then Jacmel (May–October 2000).
94. The following overview of the departure of UN troops is drawn from Paisley Dodds, "UN Mission Ends on Melancholy Note on Eve of Aristide Inauguration," *AP Wire* (3 February 2001); Paisley Dodds, "U.S. Says it Won't Send Official Delegation for Aristide Inauguration," *AP Wire* (6 February 2001); "UN Mission in Haiti Winds Up," *AP Wire* (6 February 2001).
95. *Report of the Secretary General on the UN International Civilian Support Mission in Haiti* (9 November 2000), UN A/55/618.

Chapter Thirteen   Conclusion

1. Richard E. Feinberg telephone interview with the author (10 December 2001).
2. Clinton's approval rate only dipped to 50% in 1993, when he withdrew his support for a prominent affirmative action supporter's nomination. DeWayne Wickham, *Bill Clinton and Black America* (NY: Ballantine Books, 2002), 47, 120–121.

3. Aristide and Flynn, *Eyes of the Heart*, 16. See also Stotzky, *Silencing the Guns*, 43–61, "L'Axe: Convergence-IRI-Union Européenne, un cheval de Troie nommé la France," *Haïti en Marche* (10 February 2001): 1.
4. Kenneth Freed personal interview with the author (10 April 2002).
5. Richard E. Feinberg telephone interview with the author (10 December 2001).
6. Hugh Schofield, "Haiti Seeks Reparations for Colonial Rule—Right Down to the Last Cent," *AFP Wire* (8 October 2003).

Appendices

1. U.S. Bureau of the Census' website at www.census.gov/foreign-trade.
2. Source: Center for Responsive Politics, www.opensecrets.org, based on numbers from the Federal Electrol Commision.
3 Department of Justice (INS), *1994 Statistical Yearbook of the Immigration and Naturalization Service* (DC: USGPO, 1996), 31, 45, 179, INS, *1995 Yearbook*, 183.
4. Paul Moreno-López et al., *Haiti: Country Paper* (October 1996), annex IX, financial assistance coll., USAID library.
5. World Bank, *Haiti: External Financing* (December 1997), 1, microenterprise collection, USAID library.
6. State Dept., *1998 Country Reports on Economic Policy and Trade Practices* (DC: USGPO, 1999), 270, *2000 Country Reports*, 275.
7. www.un.org/documents/scres.htm.
8. Reproduced in "Scandale financier," *Haiti Observateur* (24 November 1993): 7.
9. *Report of the Attorney General to the Congress of the U.S. on the Administration of the Foreign Agents Registration Act of 1938, As Amended* (DC: USGPO, 1995), 300–305, ibid. (1996), 187–190.

BIBLIOGRAPHY

I. Primary Sources

A. Archives

Collège St. Martial Library (Port-au-Prince, Haiti)
Box 320.01 COM "Commission présidentielle, 1993"
    folder "commission présidentielle"
    folder "manuscrits commission présidentielle"
    folder "documents CP (interne)"
    folder "correspondance reçue"
Box 320.04 SIT, "Situation politique en Haïti, 1993–94"
    folder "accord de Governor's Island, 1993"
    folder "situation politique en Haïti 1994"
    blue folder
Video collection
    #725 "Haïti: événements 1991–93"
    #707 "événements sept-oct 1993"

Ministry of Foreign Affairs archives (Port-au-Prince, Haiti)
Government in exile collection [access denied]

Ministry of Justice archives (Port-au-Prince, Haiti)
Haitian legal documents
Commission Nationale de Vérité et de Justice documents
Correspondance du cabinet présidentiel

USAID Library (Port-au-Prince, Haiti)
Microenterprise collection
Financial assistance collection

Central Intelligence Agency (Langley, Virginia)
File "Emmanuel Constant" [obtained under the Freedom of Information Act]

Department of Justice (Washington, D.C.)
Foreign Agents Registration Unit
    folder "Arent, Fox (registration #2661)"
    folder "Hazel Ross-Robinson (registration #4992)"
    folder "Hogan and Hartson (registration #2244)"

folder "Kurzban and Kurzban (registration #4604)"
folder "McKinney and McDowell associates (registration #5139)"
folder "Mildred Trouillot (registration #4763)"
Immigration and Naturalization Service
    File "Emmanuel Constant" [obtained under the Freedom of Information Act]

International Monetary Fund (www.imf.org)
Camdessus, Michel. Press Conference. D.C.: IMF, 24 April 1997.
Government of Haiti to IMF. Lettre d'intention. 19 November 1998.
Government of Haiti to IMF. Letter of Intent and Memorandum of Economic and Financial
    Policies for FY 2000–2001. 7 November 2000.
IMF. Haiti—Recent Economic Development Series: IMF Staff Country Report #95/34.
    D.C.: IMF, 10 May 1995.
IMF. IMF Staff Country Report, Haiti: Selected Issues. D.C.: IMF, January 2001.

Library of Congress (Washington, D.C.)
Le Nouvelliste
El Universal

National Archives (Washington, D.C.)
Congressional hearings
Congressional Quarterly
Congressional Record
Federal Register

National Security Archives (Washington, D.C.)
Kwitny Jonathan Collection
    Box 4, folder Haiti
Human Rights Collection
    Box 2, folder Haiti
    Box 4, folder Haiti
Congressional Hearings on Drugs
    Boxes 1–3
Electronic Briefing Books
    Lessons learned from humanitarian interventions abroad
Microfiche Collections
    U.S. espionage and intelligence
Presidential directives on national security from Truman to Clinton

OAS Columbus Library (Washington, D.C.)
General Assembly debates
MICIVIH reports
Private correspondence (Jean-Bertrand Aristide, Joao Clemente Baena Soares, Dante Caputo,
    Boutros Boutros-Ghali)
Resolutions

United Nations depository collection (Cleveland Public Library and www.un.gov)
Security Council Documents

General Assembly Documents
Secretariat General Documents

World Bank (www.worldbank.org and USAID Library, Port-au-Prince)

Bank Mondyal. *Ayiti: defi nan batay kont lamizè, Rapó #17242-HA*. 2 vols. PAP: World Bank, Aug. 1998.

Dayton, Julia. *WDP # 389, World Bank HIV/AIDS Intervention, Ex-Ante and Ex-Post Evaluation*. D.C.: World Bank, June 1998.

Department 11, World Bank. *Staff Appraisal Report, Haiti: Road Maintenance and Rehabilitation Project*. D.C.: World Bank, 28 February 1995.

Natural Resources and Rural Poverty Operations Division, World Bank. *Staff Appraisal Report # 14510-HA: Haiti: Employment Generation Project*. D.C.: World Bank, 16 June 1995.

Salmi, Jamil. *LCSHD Paper Series #18, Equity and Quality in Private Education: The Haitian Paradox*. D.C.: World Bank, May 1998.

World Bank. *Report # T6715-HA, Technical Annex to the Memorandum on a Proposed Credit to the Government of Haiti for a Second Technical Assistance Project*. D.C.: World Bank, 14 August 1996.

World Bank. *Report # T6948-HA, Technical Annex to the Memorandum on a Proposed Credit to the Government of Haiti for a Forest and Parks Technical Assistance Project*. D.C.: World Bank, 19 August 1996.

World Bank. *Report # PID 1271, Emergency Economic Recovery Credit* D.C.: World Bank, 5 September 1997.

World Bank. *Report # PID 4821, Haiti—Basic Education*. D.C.: World Bank, 5 September 1997.

World Bank. *Report # PID 5894, Haiti-Second Economic and Social Fund (FAES II)*. D.C.: World Bank, 1 October 1997.

World Bank. *Report # PID 6722, Haiti—Sustainable Intensification of Agriculture*. D.C.: World Bank, 12 August 1998.

World Bank. *Report # 13849-HA, Road Maintenance and Rehabilitation Project*. D.C.: World Bank, 28 February 1995.

World Bank Poverty Reduction and Economic Management Unit. *Report #17242-HA, Haiti: The Challenges of Poverty Reduction*. 2 vols. D.C.: World Bank, 1 August 1998.

World Bank. *World Development Indicators*. D.C.: World Bank, 1997, 1999–2001.

B. Published Documents

Amnesty International. *Amnesty International Report*. London: AI, 1990–1991, 1995, 1998–2001.

———. *The Amnesty International Report on Human Rights Around the World*. London: AI, 1993–1994.

———. *Haiti: A Question of Justice*. London: AI, 1996.

———. *Haiti: Still Crying Out for Justice*. London: AI, 1998.

———. *Haiti: Unfinished Business: Justice and Liberties at Risk*. London: AI, 2000.

Bonnardot, Martin-Luc, and Gilles Danroc. *La chute de la maison Duvalier: textes pour l'histoire*. Paris: Karthala, 1989.

Boutros-Ghali, Boutros. *An Agenda for Peace: Preventive Diplomacy, Peacemaking and Peace-keeping*. NY: United Nations, 1992.

———. *An Agenda for Development*. NY: United Nations, 1994.

———. *An Agenda for Democratization*. NY: United Nations, 1996.

———. *Fiftieth Anniversary Annual Report on the Work of the Organization*. NY: United Nations, 1996.

Bureau of Public Affairs. *US Foreign Affairs on CD-ROM, January 1990-May 1996*. Vol. 4, #1. D.C.: State Department, June 1996.

Carter Center. *Mission to Haiti #2, February 23–26, 1995*. Emory University: Carter Center Working Paper Series, 1995.

Center for Defense Information. *Confronting the Crisis in Haiti*. D.C.: Center for Defense Information, 1994. 29 min.

Commission Nationale de Vérité et de Justice. *Si M Pa Rele*. 1996. Reprint. PAP: Ministry of Justice: 1997.

Discours du Président de la République SEM René Préval. PAP: Cabinet particulier de R. Préval, March 1999.

Foreign Broadcast Information Service. *FBIS Daily Report* [translations of speeches broadcast in Haiti.]

Gallup, George Jr. *The Gallup Poll: Public Opinion, 1994*. Wilmington: Scholarly Resources, 1995.

Headquarters, Department of the Army. *Field Manuel 41–10, 11 January 1993*. D.C.: USGPO, 1994.

Human Rights Watch. *World Report*. NY: HRW, 1990–2001.

———. *Haiti: Human Rights after Aristide's Return*. NY: HRW, 1995.

———. *The Human Rights Record of the Haitian National Police*. NY: HRW, 1997.

Kernaghan, Charles et al. *Haiti after the Coup*. NY: National Labor Committee, 1993.

Lawyers Committee for Human Rights. *Paper Laws, Steel Bayonets: Breakdown of the Rule of Law in Haiti*. NY: Lawyers Committee on Human Rights, November 1990.

———. *Haiti: Learning the Hard Way, The UN/OAS Human Rights Monitoring Operation in Haiti, 1993–1994*. NY: Lawyers Committee on Human Rights, 1995.

Menidburu, Marcos and Sarah Meek. *Managing Arms in Peace Processes: Haiti*. NY: United Nations, 1996.

Ministère de l'éducation nationale, de la jeunesse et des sports. *L'éducation haïtienne dans la crise politique actuelle: résultats d'un sondage*. PAP: CERCSE, March 1992.

Le Moniteur [Haitian laws.]

Pierre, Yves-François. *Un état des lieux sur la jeunesse haïtienne*. PAP: SEJSSC and PNUD, July 1997.

Public Papers of the Presidents of the United States: Richard Nixon. D.C.: USGPO, 1969–1974.

Public Papers of the Presidents of the United States: George Bush. D.C.: USGPO, 1989–1993.

Public Papers of the Presidents of the United States: William J. Clinton. D.C.: USPO, 1993–2001.

Pwojè administrasyon jidisyè. *Konesans lalwa*. PAP: Checchi and Ministry of Justice, February 1999.

Report of the Attorney General to the Congress of the U.S. on the Administration of the Foreign Agents Registration Act of 1938, As Amended. D.C.: USGPO, 1980–1991, 1994–1997.

Rubinstein, Alvin, Albina Shayevich, and Boris Zlotnikov, eds. *The Clinton Foreign Policy Reader: Presidential Speeches with Commentary*. London: M.E. Sharpe, 2000.

Secrétariat d'Etat à la jeunesse, aux sports et au service civique and PNUD. *Forum national de la jeunesse: les actes du forum*. SEJSSC and PNUD: January 1997.

Semur, François. *Regards sur les constitutions haïtiennes, 1805–1987*. PAP: Mission française de coopération, 1997.

State Department briefings and press statements. http://secretary.state.gov/www/briefings/-index.html, http://secretary.state.gov/www/briefings/ statements/index.html.

U.S. State Department Dispatch.

Verhoogen, Eric et al. *The US in Haiti: How to Get Rich on 11 Cents an Hour*. NY: National Labor Committee, 1996.

Wells, Sherrill Brown, ed. *American Foreign Policy Current Documents, 1990*. D.C.: Department of State, 1991.

White Paper, PDD 25, Reforming Multilateral Peace Operations. 3 May 1994. www.fas.org/irp/offdocs/pdd/index.html

White Paper, PDD 56, Managing Complex Contingency Operations. May 1997. www.fas.org/irp/offdocs/pdd/index.html.

White Paper, PDD 71, Strengthening Criminal Justice Systems in Support of Peace operations and Other Complex Contingencies. 24 February 2000. www.fas.org/irp/offdocs/pdd/ index.html

C. Newspapers, Journals, Magazines, Television, and Radio

British Media
London Independent
London Times

Canadian Media
Toronto Star

French Media
Agence France Presse
L'Express
Faim Développement Magazine
Le Figaro
Libération
Le Monde
Le Monde Diplomatique
Le Point

Haitian Media
Haïti Observateur
Haïti Progrès
Haïti en Marche
Le Nouvelliste
Libete
Radio Galaxie
Radio Haïti-Inter
Radio Métropole
Radio Nationale
Télévision Nationale d'Haïti

U.S. Media
ABC News
America
American Spectator
Associated Press
CBS *News, 60 Minutes*
Christian Century
Crime and Justice International
Current History
Federal News Service
Foreign Affairs
Journal of Caribbean History
Journal of Haitian Studies
Journal of Monetary Economics
Los Angeles Times
Miami Herald
Military Review

Nation
National Review
NBC Meet the Press
New Jersey Law Journal
New Leader
New Republic
Newsday
Newsweek
New Yorker
New York Law Journal
New York Times
New York Times Review of Books
New York Times Magazine
NPR *All Things Considered, Weekend Edition*
PBS *McNeill-Lehrer Newshour, Charlie Rose, Frontline*
Progressive
Time
UN Chronicle
United Press
U.S. News and World Report
Vanity Fair
Wall Street Journal
Washington Post
Washington Times

Venezuelan Media
El Universal

D. *Memoirs, Works by Participants*
Albright, Madeleine. *Madam Secretary: A Memoir.* NY: Miramax, 2003.
Aristide, Jean-Bertrand. *La vérité en vérité.* Port-au-Prince: Le Natal, 1989.
———. *In the Parish of the Poor.* 1990. Reprint. NY: Orbis Books, 1993.
———. *Théologie et Politique.* Montréal: Centre international de documentation et d'information haïtienne, caraïbéenne et afro-canadienne, 1992.
———. *Haïti, un an après le coup d'état.* Montréal: CIDIHCA, 1992.
———, and Christophe Wargny. *Tou moun se moun: tout homme est un homme.* Paris: Seuil, 1992. Translated by Linda M. Maloney, under the title *Aristide: An Autobiography.* NY: Orbis Books, 1993.
———. *Névrose vétéro-testamentaire.* Montréal: CIDIHCA, 1994.
———. *Strategy of Aristide government for Social and Economic Reconstruction.* Lawrence, Kans.: Institute of Haitian Studies, U. of Kansas, 1994.
———. and Mireille Nicolas. *Jistis: murs peints d'Haïti, décembre 1990-février 1991.* Montréal: CIDIHCA, 1994.
———. *Peace, Justice, and Power: my Return to Haiti, the United States, and the New World Order.* Washington, D.C.: National Press Books, 1995.
———. *Dignité.* Paris: Le Seuil, 1994. Translated by Carrol F. Coates, under the title *Dignity.* Charlottesville: U. Press of Virginia, 1996.
———. et al. *Haiti: Harvest of Hope.* Hyatsville, Md.: Haiti Reborn/Quixote Center, 1998. 56 min.
———. et al. *Media's Dark Age: The Rise and Fall of Western Journalism.* NY: International Action Center, 1999.

Aristide, and Laura Flynn. *Eyes of the Heart: Seeking a Path for the Poor in the Age of Globalization*. Monroe, Me.: Common Courage Press, 2000.

———. and Lenora Foerstel. *War, Lies, and Videotape: How Media Monopoly Stifles Truth*. NY: International Action Center, 2000.

Avril, Prosper. *Vérités et révélations*. 3 vols. PAP: Le Natal, 1997.

Baker, James. *The Politics of Diplomacy*. NY: Putnam's Sons, 1995.

Boutros-Ghali, Boutros. *Unvanquished: A US-UN Saga*. NY: Random House, 1999.

Carter, James E. *Talking Peace: A Vision for the Next Generation*. NY: Dutton Children's Books, 1993.

Cervetti, Marie and Emmanuelle Ott. *Des bleus sans casque: chronique d'une mission civile de l'ONU en Haïti*. Paris: Austral, 1994.

Christopher, Warren. *In the Stream of History: Shaping Foreign Policy for a New Era*. Stanford: U. of California Press, 1998.

———. *Chances of A Lifetime*. NY: Scribner, 2001.

Clinton, Bill. *Putting People First: How We Can All Change America*. NY: Times Books, 1992.

———. *Between Hope and History: Meeting America's Challenges for the Twenty-First Century*. NY: Times Books, 1996.

———. *My Life*. NY: Knopf, 2004.

Clinton, Hillary. *Living History*. NY: Simon and Schuster, 2003.

Dole, Bob, Elizabeth Dole, Richard N. Smith, and Kerry Tymchuk. *Unlimited Partners: Our American Story*. NY: Simon and Schuster, 1996.

Garrison, Lynn. *Voodoo Politics: The Clinton-Gore Destruction of Haiti*. Los Angeles: Leprechaun Publishing, 2000.

Gergen, David. *Eyewitness to Power: The Essence of Leadership, Nixon to Clinton*. NY: Simon and Schuster, 2000.

Goff, Stan. *Hideous Dream: A Soldier's Memoir of the US Invasion of Haiti*. NY: Soft Skull Press, 2000.

Granderson, Colin. "Military-Humanitarian Ambiguities in Haiti." In *Hard Choices: Moral Dilemmas in Humanitarian Intervention*, edited by Jonathan Moore. NY: Rowman and Littlefield, 1998.

Holbrooke, Richard. "Presidents, Bureaucrats, and Something In-Between." In *The Vietnam Legacy: The War, American Society and the Future of American Foreign Policy*, edited by Anthony Lake. NY: NY U. Press, 1976, 142–165.

Lake, Anthony, ed. *The Vietnam Legacy: The War, American Society and the Future of American Foreign Policy*. NY: NY U. Press, 1976.

———. et al. *Our Worst Enemy: The Unmaking of American Foreign Policy*. NY: Simon and Schuster, 1984.

———. "Confronting Backlash States." *Foreign Affairs* vol. 73, #2 (March–April 1994): 45.

———. *Six Nightmares: Real Threats in a Dangerous World and How America Can Meet Them*. NY: Little Brown, 2000.

Malval, Robert. *L'année de toutes les duperies*. PAP: Editions Regain, 1996.

Meade, David. *Emerald Express '97, Multinational Force Operations in Haiti*. Camp Pendleton, Ca.: Training Audiovisual Support Center, 1997. 53 min.

Morris, Dick. *Behind the Oval Office: Getting Reelected against all Odds*. 1997. Reprint. LA: Renaissance Books, 1999.

———. *The New Prince: Machiavelli Updated for the Twenty-First Century*. LA: Renaissance Books, 1999.

Pastor, Robert A. *Mission to Haiti #3, June 23–26, 1995*. Atlanta: Carter Center, 17 July 1995.

Powell, Colin L. *My American Journey*. NY: Random House, 1995.

Shultz, George. *Turmoil and Triumph: My Years as Secretary of State*. NY: Scribners, 1993.

Stephanopoulos, George. *All Too Human: A Political Education*. NY: Little Brown, 1999.

Ulysse, Robert. *Plan de libération économique et sociale d'Haïti*. PAP: Parti Démocrate Chrétien Haitien, 1999.

E. Interviews

Interviews by the Author

Chenet, Jean-Baptiste. Human Rights activist. 3 July 2001, Port-au-Prince.
Christophe. Economics teacher, *Lycée français*. 30 June 2001, Séguin, Haïti.
Elie, Patrick. Personal friend of Aristide. 11 July 2001, Port-au-Prince.
Feinberg, Richard E. Latin America specialist, NSC. 10 December 2001, University of California, San Diego.
Freed, Kenneth. *LA Times* Caribbean bureau chief, 1991–1996. 10 April 2002, Athens, OH.
Gaillard, Micha. Former member of the *commission présidentielle*, member of Convergence Démocratique. 9 July 2001, Port-au-Prince.
Garrison, Lynn. Haitian honorary consul, adviser to Cédras. 10 May 2001, Ft. Lauderdale.
Lake, Anthony. NSA, 1993–1997. 18 May 2001, Washington, D.C.
D'Orsinville, Félix. History teacher, *Lycée français*. 4 July 2001, Port-au-Prince.
Pastor, Robert. Carter adviser. 10 December 2001, Emory University.
Pierre-Louis, Ronald. Human rights activist, CEHDHABEL. 4 July 2001, Port-au-Prince.
Rockwood, Lawrence P. Intelligence officer, JTF-190. 26 February 2001, University of California, San Marcos.
Wilber, Doug, Sarah Phelps, Gustavo Setrini, Melvin Butler. Episcopalian Church volunteers. 27 June 2001, Port-au-Prince.

Other Interviews

Albright, Madeleine
    "Newsmaker Interview, Madeleine Albright." *MacNeill-Lehrer News Hour* (10 June 1994).
Aristide, Jean-Bertrand
    Folder Haiti, Box 4, Kwitny Jonathan Collection, National Security Archives.
    "Aristide Interview on Economy, Foreign Relations." *FBIS* (21 March 1991): 20.
    "Newsmaker Interview, Jean-Bertrand Aristide." *MacNeill-Lehrer News Hour* (4 October 1991).
    "Interview with Père Aristide." *America* (12 October 1991): 236
    "I am President of Haiti." *Time* (14 October 1991): 36
    "Newsmaker Interview, Jean-Bertrand Aristide." *MacNeill-Lehrer News Hour* (4 June 1992).
    "Newsmaker Interview, Jean-Bertrand Aristide." *MacNeill-Lehrer News Hour* (22 October 1993).
    "It's not if I Go Back, but When." *Time* (1 November 1993): 28
    "President Aristide Says Haiti Needs Reconciliation." *NPR Weekend Edition* (25 June 1994).
    "Le Père Aristide: 'Oui à la réconciliation.'" *Le Monde* (9 September 1994): 1, 4.
    "Newsmaker Interview, Jean-Bertrand Aristide." *MacNeill-Lehrer News Hour* (12 October 1994).
    "Remembrance, not Vengeance." *Time* (17 October 1994): 32.
"Rebuilding Haiti." *America* (15 February 1997): 12–16.
Boutros-Ghali, Boutros
    "Les Nations Unies 'ne peuvent pas imposer la paix.'" *Le Monde* (19 October 1993): 4.
Cédras, Raoul
    "A Place Called Fear." *Vanity Fair* (February 1994): 72.
    "Charting the Course, Raoul Cédras Interview." *MacNeill-Lehrer News Hour* (18 October 1993).
    "Interview de Cédras." *Haïti Observateur* (20 October 1993): 6.
    "Eye to Eye with Connie Chung." *CBS News* (15 September 1994).
Christopher, Warren
    "Meet the Press." *NBC* (11 September 1994).
Constant, Emmanuel
    Bradley, Ed. "Toto Constant." *CBS 60 Minutes* (3 December 1995).

Grann, David. "Giving 'The Devil' His Due." *Atlantic Monthly* (June 2001): 54–75.
Gray III, William
    "Newsmaker Interview, William Gray." *MacNeill-Lehrer News Hour* (23 May 1994).
Perry, William
    "Newsmaker Interview, William Perry." *MacNeill-Lehrer News Hour* (5 October 1994).
Pezzullo, Lawrence
    "Newsmaker Interview, Lawrence Pezzullo." *MacNeill-Lehrer News Hour* (13 October 1993).
Multiple Interviews
    Morse, Richard M., ed. *Haiti's Future: Views of Twelve Haitian Leaders.* Washington: Wilson
        Center Press, 1988.
    Frontline. *Showdown in Haiti* (9 November 1993).
    Frontline. *Frontline Special: The Clinton Years.* PBS: 16 January 2001.
    Hayden, Cynthia L. *JTF-180 Operation Uphold Democracy: Oral History Interviews.* Fort
        Bragg, NC: XVIII Airborne Corps, 1995.
    ———. *JTF-190 Operation Uphold Democracy: Oral History Interviews.* Fort Bragg, N.C.:
        XVIII Airborne Corps, 1995.
    Wickham, DeWayne. *Bill Clinton and Black America.* NY: Ballantine Books, 2002.

II. Secondary Literature

10th Mountain Division. *Operation Uphold Democracy: Operations in Haiti: Planning,
    Preparation, Execution, August 1994 thru January 1995.* Carlisle, Pa.: US Army War
    College, 1995.
Abbott, Elizabeth. *Haiti: The Duvaliers and Their Legacy.* 1988. Reprint. NY: Simon and
    Schuster, 1991.
Abrams, Elliot. *Security and Sacrifice: Isolation, Intervention, and American Foreign Policy.*
    Indianapolis: Hudson Institute, 1995.
Abric, Isabelle et al. *A Work in Progress: Human Rights in Haiti.* NY: Filmakers Library, 1999.
    56 min.
Adams, Thomas K. "Intervention in Haiti: Lessons Relearned." *Military Review*
    (September–October 1996): 45–56.
Agence Haïtienne de Presse. *La presse sous la mitraille.* Montréal: CIDIHCA, 1992.
Almond, Gabriel. *The American People and Foreign Policy.* 1950. Reprint. NY: Praeger, 1960.
Barber, Benjamin R. *Jihad vs. McWorld: How the World is Falling Apart and Coming Together—
    And What this Means for Democracy.* NY: Times Books, 1995.
Ballard, John R. *Upholding Democracy: The U.S. Military Campaign in Haiti, 1994–1997.*
    Westport, Conn: Praeger, 1998.
Barros, Jacques. *Haïti de 1804 à nos jours.* 2 vols. Paris: L'Harmattan, 1984.
Berman, William C. *From the Center to the Edge : The Politics and Policies of the Clinton
    Presidency.* NY : Rowman and Littlefield, 2001.
Bernardin, Ernst A. *Histoire économique et sociale d'Haïti de 1804 à nos jours: l'Etat complice
    et la faillite d'un système.* PAP: INAGHEI, 1999.
Brune, Lester H. *The U.S. and Post-Cold-War Interventions: Bush and Clinton in Somalia,
    Haiti and Bosnia, 1992–1998.* Claremont, Calif.: Penguin Books, 1999.
Brutus, Fred. *L'intervention en paroles et en images.* PAP: Toumedia, 1995.
Cajou, Henri Robert. *Le pouvoir Lavalas: du mythe à la mystification, essai politique.* PAP:
    Editions Choucoune, 1997.
Callahan, David. *Unwinnable Wars: American Power and Ethnic Conflict.* NY: Hill and Wang,
    1997.
Campbell, Colin, and Bert Rockman, eds. *The Clinton Legacy.* NY: Chatham House
    Publishers, 2000.
Carpozi, George Jr. *Clinton Confidential: The Climb to Power, the Unauthorized Biography of
    Bill and Hillary Clinton.* Del Mar, Calif.: Emery Dalton Books, 1995.

Carr, Damian P. "U.S. Army Public Affairs during Operation Uphold Democracy." Master's thesis, U.S. Army Command and General Staff College, 1996.

Casper, Lawrence E. *Falcon Brigade: Combat and Command in Somalia and Haiti.* Boulder, Co.: Lynne Rienner, 2001.

Castor, Suzy. *La ocupacion norteamericana de Hayti y sus consecuencias, 1915–1934.* Havana: Casa de las Americas, 1978.

Center for Army Lessons Learned. Haiti: *The US Army and United Nations Peacekeeping.* Fort Leavenworth, Kans.: US Army Training and Doctrine Command, 1995.

———. *Haiti: Operations other than War.* 2 vols. Fort Leavenworth, Kans.: US Army Training and Doctrine Command, 1994–1995.

Center for Law and Military Operations. *Law and Military Operations in Haiti, 1994–1995: Lessons learned for Judge Advocates.* Charlottesville, Va.: Judge Advocate General's School, 1995.

Charles, Etzer. *Le pouvoir politique en Haiti de 1957 à nos jours.* Paris: Karthala, 1994.

Chen, L. et al. *Sanctions in Haiti: Crisis in Humanitarian Action, Working Paper No. 93.07.* Harvard University Center for Population and Development Studies: November 1993.

Chenet, Jean-Baptiste. "Haïti: intervention militaire américaine (1994) et droits de l'homme." Master's thesis, Paris III Sorbonne, 2000.

Clancy, Tom and John Grisham. *Special Forces: A Guided Tour of US. Army Special Forces.* NY: Berkley Publishing Group, 2000.

Colomé, Anne-Marie. *Haïti chérie ou le rêve confisqué.* Paris: L'Harmattan, 1994.

Dabel, Verly. *La crise haïtienne: quelle(s) issue(s).* PAP: Arnegraph, 1993.

———. *Haïti: le prix d'un coup d'état.* Montréal: Eurographix, 1995.

Danroc, Gilles and Daniel Roussière. *La répression au quotidien en Haiti, 1991–1994.* PAP: HIS, 1995.

Daudet, Yves, ed. *La crise d'Haïti, 1991–1996.* Paris: Monchrestien, 1996.

Dejean, Paul. *Haïti, l'inéluctable retour.* Montréal: CIDIHCA, 1994.

Delince, Kern. *Les forces politiques en Haïti.* Paris: Karthala, 1993.

———. *Quelle armée pour Haïti? Militarisme et démocratie.* PAP: Karthala, 1994.

Denton, Robert E. Jr. and Rachel L. Holloway, eds. *The Clinton Presidency: Images, Issues and Communication Strategies.* Westport: Praeger, 1996.

Diederich, Bernard and Al Burt. *Papa Doc: Haiti and Its Dictator.* 1969. Reprint. Maplewood, N.J.: Waterfront Press, 1991.

Dorléans, Henri M. *La communauté internationale et les droits de l'homme dans les petits pays: l'expérience de la Mission Civile Internationale OEA-ONU en Haïti (MICIVIH).* PAP: Centre Toussaint L'Ouverture pour les droits de l'homme, la démocratie et le développement, 1999.

Drew, Elizabeth. *On the Edge: The Clinton Presidency.* NY: Simon and Schuster, 1994.

———. *Showdown: The Struggle between the Gingrich Congress and the Clinton White House.* NY: Simon and Schuster, 1997.

Dumas, Pierre-Raymond. *Fin du militarisme haïtien?* PAP : L'Imprimeur II, 1996.

———. *La transition d'Haïti vers la démocratie: essai sur la dérive despotico-libérale.* PAP: L'Imprimeur II, 1997.

Dupuy, Alex. *Haiti in the World Economy: Class, Race and Underdevelopment since 1700.* Boulder: Westview Press, 1989.

———. *Haiti in the New World Order: The Limits of the Democratic Revolution.* Boulder, Co.: Westview Press, 1997.

Etienne, Sauveur-Pierre. *Haïti: misère de la démocratie.* Paris: L'Harmattan, 1999.

Fanning, David. *Showdown in Haiti.* Alexandria, Va.: PBS video, 1994. 59 min.

Farmer, Paul. *The Uses of Haiti.* Monroe, Me.: Common Courage Press, 1994.

Fass, Simon. *Political Economy in Haiti: The Drama of Survival.* New Brunswick, N.J.: Transaction, 1990.

Fauriol, Georges A., ed. *Haitian Frustrations: Dilemmas for U.S. Policy*. Washington: Center for Strategic and International Studies, 1995.

———. *The Haitian Challenge: U.S. Policy Considerations*. Washington: Center for Strategic and International Studies, 1993.

Fischer, Joseph R. et al. *Operation Uphold/Restore/Maintain Democracy: The Role of Army Special Operations, November 1991–June 1995*. Fort Bragg, N.C.: USASOC Directorate of History, 1997.

Fujii, Lee Ann. "Finding the Middle: An Analysis of Johnson's 1965 Decision to Escalate the War in Vietnam." *International Relations Journal* (Winter–Spring 2000–2001): 72.

Fukuyama, Francis. "The End of History?" *National Interest* (Summer 1989): 3.

———. *The End of History and the Last Man*. NY: Free Press, 1992.

Fuller, Anne et al. *Return to the Darkest Days: Human Rights in Haiti since the Coup*. NY: Americas Watch, 1991.

Gallen, David. *Bill Clinton as They Know Him: An Oral Biography*. NY: Gallen Publishing Group, 1994.

Gertz, Bill. *Betrayal: How the Clinton Administration Undermined American Security*. D.C.: Regnery Publishing.

Gibbons, Elizabeth D. *Sanctions in Haiti: Human Rights and Democracy under Assault*. Westport, Conn.: Praeger, 1999.

Girard, Philippe. "Operation Restore Democracy?" *Journal of Haitian Studies* 8:2 (Fall 2002): 70–85.

———. "Credibility, Domestic Politics, and Decision-Making: William J. Clinton and Haiti, 1994–2000." *Journal of Caribbean History* 36:1 (2002): 127–155.

Gold, Herbert. *Best Nightmare on Earth: A Life in Haiti*. NY: Simon and Schuster, 1991.

Griffith, Leslie. *The Aristide Factor*. Oxford: Lion, 1997.

Grotzky, Craig L. *The Impact of the Standing Rules of Engagement (SROE) on Peace Enforcement Operations*. Newport, R.I.: Naval War College, 1996.

Haass, Richard N. *Intervention: The Use of American Military Force in the Post-Cold War World*. 1994. Reprint. Washington: Brookings Institution Press, 1999.

Hackworth, David H. and Tom Mathews. *Hazardous Duty: America's Most Decorated Living Soldier Reports from the Front and Tells it the Way it is*. NY: William Morrow, 1996.

Haïti: votre cri ne sera pas étouffé. Genève: CHRD, COTMEC, Haïti-Info, 1993.

Halberstam, David. *War in a Time of Peace: Bush, Clinton, and the Generals*. NY: Scribner, 2001.

Hall, Warren D. *The Obligation to Protect Human Rights: A New Legal Requirement for Commanders?* Carlisle Barracks, Pa.: US Army War College, 1996.

Hardy-Jackson, Patricia. "Haitian Crisis 1991–1994: An Opportunity for a Shift in U.S. 21st Century Foreign Policy." Ph.D. diss., Salve Regina U. 1997.

Harrison, Lawrence E. *Underdevelopment is a State of Mind: The Latin American Case*. Cambridge, Mass.: Harvard university Press, 1985.

Hassner, Pierre. "From War and Peace to Violence and Intervention: Permanent Moral Dilemmas under Changing Political and Technological Conditions." In *Hard Choices: Moral Dilemmas in Humanitarian Intervention*, edited by Jonathan Moore. NY: Rowman and Littlefield, 1998.

Hayes, Margaret Daly and Gary W. Wheatley. *Interagency and Political-Military Dimensions of Peace Operations: Haiti, a Case Study*. D.C.: National Defense University, 1996.

Haynes, John T. "A Comparative Study of Civil-Military Operations Perspectives as They Apply to Peace Support Operations." Master's thesis, Naval Postgraduate School, 1996.

Hector, Cary and Hérard Jadotte, eds. *Haïti et l'après-Duvalier, continuités et ruptures*. PAP: Henri Deschamps, 1991.

Heinl, Robert D., Nancy G. and Michael. *Written in Blood: The Story of the Haitian People, 1492–1995*. NY: U. Press of America, 1996.

Hendrickson, David C. "The Recovery of Internationalism." *Foreign Affairs* vol. 73, #5 (September–October 1994): 26.

Henriksen, Thomas H. *Clinton's Foreign Policy in Somalia, Bosnia, Haiti and North Korea.* Stanford University: Hoover Institution, 1996.

Herskovits, Melville J. *Life in a Haitian Valley.* 1937. Reprint. NY: Doubleday, 1971.

Hohenberg, John. *The Bill Clinton Story: Winning the Presidency.* Syracuse: Syracuse U. Press, 1994.

Holiday, David, and William Staley. "Beyond the Mountains, More Mountains: Demobilizing the Haitian Army." *In Peacemaking and Democratization in the Western Hemisphere,* edited by Tommie Sue Montgomery. Coral Gables, Fla.: North-South Center Press, 2000.

Hunt, Michael. *Ideology and U.S. Foreign Policy.* New Haven: Yale U. Press, 1987.

Hurbon, Laënnec, ed. *Les transitions démocratiques.* Paris: Syros, 1996.

Hyacinthe, Wilbert. *Haïti: alternative à Aristide.* PAP: Editions des Antilles, March 1993.

Hyland, William G. *Clinton's World: Remaking American Foreign Policy.* Westport: Praeger, 1999.

Ignatieff, Michael. *The Warrior's Honor: Ethnic War and the Modern Conscience.* NY: Metropolitan Books, 1998.

Institute for European-Latin American Relations. *Haiti: An Impossible Democracy.* Madrid: IRELA, May 1992.

Jackson, Deborah. *The Coup Continues: Haiti under Occupation.* Haiti Films, 1995. 23 min.

Jallot, Nicolas and Laurent Lesage. *Haïti: dix ans d'histoire secrète.* Paris: Editions du Félin, 1995.

James, C. L. R. *The Black Jacobins: Toussaint L'Ouverture and the San Domingo Revolution.* 1938. Reprint. NY: Vintage Books, 1963.

Jean, Jean-Claude and Marc Maesschalck. *Transition politique en Haïti: radiographie du pouvoir Lavalas.* Paris: L'Harmattan, 1999.

Jean-François, Hérold. *Le coup de Cédras.* PAP: L'Imprimeur II, 1995.

Kean, Katharine. *Haïti, coup de grace?* Crowing Rooster Arts, 1995. 59 min.

Koh, Harold Hongju. "Closed-Door Policy for Refugees." *New Jersey Law Journal* (23 August 1993): 26.

Kretchik, Walter E. *Rhythm of the Streets.* Fort Leavenworth, Kans.: Combat Studies Institute, 1998. 70 min.

―――. Robert F. Baumann, and John T. Fishel. *Invasion, Intervention, "Intervasion."* Fort Leavenworth, Kans.: US Command and General Staff College Press, 1998.

Kumar, Chetan. *Building Peace in Haiti.* Boulder: Lynne Rienner Publishers, 1998.

Lafontant Gerdes, Raymond. *Fuerte Allen: la diáspora haitiana.* Río Pedras, Puerto Rico: Editorial Plaza Mayor, 1996.

Laguerre, Michel S. *American Odyssey: Haitians in NY City.* NY: Cornell U. Press, 1984.

―――. *Diasporic Citizenship: Haitian Americans in Transnational America.* NY: St. Martin's Press, 1998.

―――. *The Complete Haitiana: A Bibliographic Guide to the Scholarly Literature, 1900–1980.* 2 vols. Millwood, N.Y.: Kraus International Publications, 1982.

―――. *The Military and Society in Haiti.* Knoxville, Tenn.: U. of Tennessee Press, 1993.

Larose, Vernet. *Jean-Bertrand Aristide: l'irresponsabilité du démocrate materné.* PAP: [unspecified publishing house], May 1994.

Lawless, Robert. *Haiti: A Research Handbook.* NY: Garland Publishing., 1990.

Lemoine, Maurice. *Bitter Sugar: Slaves Today in the Caribbean.* Chicago: Banner Press, 1985.

Lettre de Lucia: radioscopie du coup d'état militaire. PAP: Le Natal, 1993.

Lionel, Bonny P. *Le Président Aristide reconquerra-t-il le pouvoir? Le gouvernement Lavalas face à la problématique de la démocratie en Haïti.* Brooklyn, NY: Courrier Publications, 1993.

Lionet, Christian. *Haïti: l'année Aristide.* Paris: L'Harmattan, 1992.

Maguire, Robert E. *Demilitarizing Public Order in a Predatory State: The Case of Haiti, North-South Agenda Papers #17.* Coral Gables: North-South Center Press, 1995.

———., ed. *Haïti prise en otage: les réponses internationales à la recherche d'une identité nationale de 1986 à 1996.* Providence, R.I.: Watson Institute for International Studies, 1997.

———. "Democracy and Human Rights in Haiti." *In Democracy and Human Rights in the Caribbean,* edited by Ivlelaw L. Griffith and Betty N. Sedoc-Dahlberg. Boulder: Westview Press, 1997.

Malone, David. *Decision-Making in the UN Security Council: The Case of Haiti, 1990–1997.* Oxford: Clarendon Press, 1998.

Manheim, Jarol B. *Strategic Public Diplomacy and American Foreign Policy: The Evolution of Influence.* NY: Oxford U. Press, 1994.

Manwaring, Max G., ed. *Security and Civil-Military Relations in the New World Disorder: The Use of Armed Forces in the Americas.* Carlisle, Pa.: Strategic Studies Institute, 1999.

Maraniss, David. *First in His Class: A Biography of Bill Clinton.* NY: Simon and Schuster, 1995.

Marotte, Cécile and Hervé Rakoto Razafimbakiny. *Mémoire oubliée: Haïti 1991–1995.* Montréal: CIDIHCA, 1997.

May, Ernest R. "An American Tradition in Foreign Policy: The Role of Public Opinion." *In Theory and Practice in American Politics,* edited by William H. Nelson and Francis L. Lowenheim. 1964. Reprint. Chicago: U. of Chicago Press, 1967.

McFadyen, Deirdre and Pierre LaRamée, eds. *Haiti: Dangerous Crossroads.* Boston: South End Press, 1995.

McMahon, Robert J. "Credibility and World Power: Exploring the Psychological Dimension in Postwar American Diplomacy." *Diplomatic History* (Fall 1991): 455.

McRae, Robert and Don Hubert. *Human Security and the New Diplomacy: Protecting People, Promoting Peace.* Montreal: McGill-Queen's University Press.

Miller, Scott. "Consumed by Credibility." Master's thesis, Ohio University, 1995.

Mintz, Sidney W. "Can Haiti Change?" *Foreign Affairs 74* (January–February 1995): 73–86.

Moïse, Claude. *Une constitution dans la tourmente: le nouveau régime politique haïtien et la crise nationale, 1987–1993.* Montréal: Images, 1994.

Moore, Jim. Clinton: *Young Man in a Hurry.* Fort Worth, Tex.: Summit Group, 1992.

Moral, Paul. *Le paysan haïtien: étude sur la vie rurale en Haïti.* 1961. Reprint. PAP: Editions Fardin, 1978.

Morley, Morris and Chris McGillion. "Disobedient Generals and the Politics of Redemocratization: The Clinton Administration and Haiti." *The New American Interventionism: Lessons from Successes and Failures,* edited by Demetrios J. Caraley. NY: Columbia U. Press, 1999.

Morquette, Marc-Ferl. *Les nouveaux marrons: essai sur un aspect de la crise politique, 1989–1998.* PAP: L'imprimeur II, 1999.

Morris, Roger. *Partners in Power: The Clintons and Their America.* NY: Henry Holt, 1996.

Myers, Graves T. *The Development of the Civil Police in Haiti, September 1994 to August 1996.* Carlisle Barracks, Pa.: US Army War College, 1997.

Ninkovich, Frank. *The Wilsonian Century: U.S. Foreign Policy since 1900.* Chicago: U. of Chicago Press, 1999.

[Le Nouvelliste.] *L'actualité en question: Haïti 1993.* PAP: Le Centenaire, 1994.

O'Neill, William G. "Building a New Police Force and Justice System." *Crime and Justice International* vol. 9, #3 (June–July 1996).

Pastor, Robert A. *Whirlpool: U.S. Foreign Policy Toward Latin America and the Caribbean.* Princeton, N.J.: Princeton U. Press, 1992.

Pastor et al., eds. *Democracy in the Caribbean: Political, Economic, and Social Perspectives.* Baltimore: Johns Hopkins U. Press, 1993.

Pastor et al., *Collective Responses to Regional Problems: The Case of Latin America and the Caribbean.* Cambridge, Mass.: Committee on International Security Studies, 1994.

Perlmutter, Amos. *Making the World Safe for Democracy: A Century of Wilsonianism and its Totalitarian Challengers.* Chapel Hill: U. of North Carolina Press, 1997.

Perusse, Roland I. *Historical Dictionary of Haiti.* Metuchen, N.J.: Scarecrow Press, 1977.

———. *Haitian Democracy Restored, 1991–1995.* NY: U. Press of America, 1995.

Petras, James F., et al. "The Monroe Doctrine and U.S. Hegemony in Latin America." *In Latin America: From Dependence to Revolution,* edited by Petras. NY: John Wiley, 1973.

Pierre-Etienne, Sauveur. *Haïti: l'invasion des ONG.* Montréal: CIDIHCA, 1997.

Plummer, Brenda Gayle. *Haiti and the Great Powers, 1902–1915.* Baton Rouge: Louisiana State University, 1988.

———. *Haiti and the U.S.: The Psychological Moment.* Athens: University of Georgia Press, 1992.

Renda, Mary A. *Taking Haiti: Military Occupation and the Culture of U.S. Imperialism, 1915–1940.* Chapel Hill: University of North Caroline Press, 2001.

Ridgeway, James, ed. *The Haiti Files: Decoding the Crisis.* DC: Essential Books, 1994.

Riehm, Peter J.A. "The U.S.S. *Harlan County Affair.*" *Military Review* (July August 1997): 31–36.

Rosenau, James N. *Public Opinion and Foreign Policy: An Operational Formulation.* 1961. Reprint. NY: Random House, 1967.

———., ed. *Domestic Sources of Foreign Policy.* NY: The Free Press, 1967.

Rotberg, Robert I., ed. *Haiti Renewed: Political and Economic Prospects.* Washington, D.C.: Brookings Institution Press, 1997.

Rudel, Christian. *Haïti, les chaînes d'Aristide.* Paris: Editions de l'Atelier, 1994.

Schmidt, Hans. *The United States Occupation of Haiti, 1915–1934.* New Brunswick, N.J.: Rutgers, 1971.

Schoultz, Lars. *Beneath the United States: A History of U.S. Policy toward Latin America.* Cambridge: Harvard U. Press, 1998.

———. *National Security and United States Policy toward Latin America.* Princeton: Princeton University Press, 1987.

Schulz, Donald E., and Gabriel Marcella. *Reconciling the Irreconcilable: The Troubled Outlook for U.S. Policy toward Haiti.* Carlisle Barracks, Pa.: Strategic Studies Institute, U.S. Army War College, 10 March 1994.

———. "The Challenge of Haiti's Future." *In Toward Responsibility in the New World Disorder: Challenges and Lessons of Peace Operations,* edited by Max G. Manwaring and John T. Fishel. London: Frank Cass, 1998.

Scully, Michael A. *The Media: An Influence on US Foreign and Military Policy by any other Means.* Fort Leavenworth, kans.: School of Advanced Military Studies, 1998.

Sella, Orlando Enrique. *La caída de Aristide: crónica de una frustración popular.* Heredia, Costa Rica: Escuela de relaciones internacionales, Universidad Nacional, 1996.

Shacochis, Bob. *The Immaculate Invasion.* 2000. Reprint. NY: Viking, 1999.

Shaw, Robert C. *An Assessment of Conventional and Special Operations Forces Integration in Haiti.* Fort Leavenworth, Kans.: School of Advanced Military Studies, 1996.

Skulrak, Robin Suzanne. *United States Humanitarian Intervention in the Post-Cold War Era: Haiti and Bosnia: A Study of When and Why Washington Intervenes.* Millersville University, Pa.: unpublished honors thesis, 1999.

Slater, Jerome. "Is U.S. Foreign Policy 'Imperialist' or 'Imperial?'" *Political Science Quarterly* vol. 91, no. 1 (Spring 1976): 63–87.

Stepick, Alex. "The Roots of Haitian Migration." *In Haiti—Today and Tomorrow: An Interdisciplinary Study,* edited by Charles R. Foster and Albert Valdman. Lanham, Md.: U. Press of America, 1984.

———. "Flight into Despair." *International Migration Review* 21 (1986): 329–350.

Stern, Rudi. *Haiti: Killing the Dream.* Crowing Rooster Productions, 1992.

Stotzky, Irwin P. *Silencing the Guns in Haiti: The Promise of Deliberative Democracy.* Chicago: U. of Chicago Press, 1997.

Thompson, Andrew S. "The Politics of Intervention: Haiti, Human Rights, and the Influence of the International Community, 1957–1994." Master's thesis, University of Western Ontario, 1999.

Thompson, Hunter S. *Better Than Sex : Confessions of a Political Junkie*. NY: Random House, 1994.

Wargny, Christophe and Pierre Mouterde. *Apre bal, tanbou lou: cinq ans de duplicité américaine en Haïti, 1991–1996*. Paris: Editions Austral, 1996.

Weinstein, Brian and Aaron Segal. *Haiti: The Failure of Politics*. NY: Praeger, 1992.

Weiss, Thomas G. *Military-Civilian Interactions: Intervening in Humanitarian Crises*. NY: Rowman and Littlefield, 1999.

Wiarda, Howard J., ed. *U.S. Foreign Policy and Strategic Policy in the Post-Cold War Era: A Geopolitical Perspective*. Westport, Conn.: Greenwood Press, 1996.

Wickham, DeWayne. *Bill Clinton and Black America*. NY: Ballantine Books, 2002.

Wilentz, Amy. *The Rainy Season: Haiti since Duvalier*. NY: Simon and Schuster, 1989).

Williamson, Charles T. *The U.S. Naval Mission to Haiti, 1959–1963*. Annapolis: Naval Institute Press, 1999.

Woodward, Bob. *The Agenda: Inside the Clinton White House*. NY: Simon and Schuster, 1994.

——. *The Choice: How Clinton Won*. NY: Touchstone, 1996.

Wucker, Michèle. *Why the Cocks Fight: Dominicans, Haitians, and the Struggle for Hispaniola*. NY: Hill and Wang, 1999.

Index